"Bennett and Strange have assembled an original, wide-ranging interrogation of 'independence' as it is mobilized across media industries and national contexts. Together, the essays in this book breathe new life into this often-abused and misused term, making an impassioned case for protecting true independent vision and values in our media culture."

—*Jennifer Holt, Associate Professor of Film and Media Studies, University of California, Santa Barbara, USA*

"Bennett and Strange's collection impressively maps the varied sociopolitical, aesthetic, industrial and rhetorical meanings of 'media independence' even as it grounds the concept in rich case studies covering film, television, gaming, music, the Internet and more. *Media Independence* is an invaluable resource for thinking through the complex dynamics of creativity, work and industry across a range of contemporary national contexts. A must read."

—*Alisa Perren, Associate Professor in the Department of Radio-TV-Film, University of Texas at Austin, USA*

Media Independence

Media independence is central to the organization, make-up, working practices and output of media systems across the globe. Often stemming from Western notions of individual and political freedoms, independence has informed the development of media across a range of platforms: from the freedom of the press as the "fourth estate" and the rise of Hollywood's independent studios and independent television in Britain, through to the importance of "Indy" labels in music and gaming and the increasing importance of independence of voice in citizen journalism. Media independence for many, therefore, has come to mean working with freedom: from state control or interference, from monopoly, from market forces, as well as freedom to report, comment, create and document without fear of persecution. However, far from a stable concept that informs all media systems, the notion of media independence has long been contested, forming a crucial tension point in the regulation, shape, size and role of the media around the globe.

Contributors including David Hesmondhalgh, Gholam Khiabany, José van Dijck, Hector Postigo, Anthony Fung and Stuart Allan demonstrate how the notion of independence has remained paramount, but contested, in ideals of what the media is for, how it should be regulated, what it should produce and what working within it should be like. They address questions of economics, labor relations, production cultures, ideologies and social functions.

James Bennett is the head of the Media Arts Department and a reader in television and digital culture at Royal Holloway, University of London, UK.

Niki Strange is a research fellow at University of Sussex, UK and runs her own digital media consultancy, Strange Digital, where she provides research, business development and strategy consulting for creative businesses and organizations.

Routledge Research in Cultural and Media Studies

For a full list of titles in this series, please visit www.routledge.com

Media Independence

Working with Freedom or
Working for Free?

**Edited by James Bennett
and Niki Strange**

Routledge
Taylor & Francis Group

NEW YORK AND LONDON

First published 2015
by Routledge
711 Third Avenue, New York, NY 10017

and by Routledge
2 Park Square, Milton Park, Abingdon, Oxon OX14 4RN

Routledge is an imprint of the Taylor & Francis Group, an informa business.

Library of Congress Cataloging-in-Publication Data
Media independence : working with freedom or working for free? /
    edited by James Bennett and Niki Strange.
        pages cm. — (Routledge research in cultural and media studies ; 69)
    Includes bibliographical references and index.
    1. Mass media—Political aspects.   2. Social media—Political aspects.
3. Citizen journalism—Political aspects.   4. Freedom of the press.
5. Censorship.   6. Government and the press.   I. Bennett, James,
1978– editor.   II. Strange, Niki, 1979– editor.
    P95.8.M3932 2014
    323.44'5—dc23
    2014030737

ISBN: 978-1-138-02348-2 (hbk)
ISBN: 978-1-315-77639-2 (ebk)

Typeset in Sabon
by Apex CoVantage, LLC

Printed and bound in Great Britain by
TJ International Ltd, Padstow, Cornwall

For Noah:
You may not know it yet, but you're an inspiration to us both.

Contents

SECTION II
Working with Freedom or Working for Free

SECTION III
Independence in a Cold Political Climate

Acknowledgments

The impetus for this work arose out of an Arts and Humanities Research Council (AHRC) grant to explore multiplatform public service broadcast production in the United Kingdom's independent sector (AH-H018522–2). We are grateful to the AHRC for that grant and the stimulus it provided for this collection. This wouldn't have been possible without a great research team, and our thanks go to Paul Kerr and Andrea Medrado for their input into the project and the ideas for this volume.

Our contributors have been a joy to work with. As we have pushed them to explore and explain what independence has meant in each context, they have responded willingly and generously to our comments making connections between chapters. We hope this has been as enjoyable an experience for them as it has for us. It has certainly produced a collection that we feel is stronger as a result.

Thanks must also go to the team at Routledge, especially Felisa Salvago-Keyes. We also benefited greatly from the reviewers of the original proposal, who pushed our thinking and ambitions for the collection.

Finally, our greatest thanks go to each other—having produced one previous collection together (*Television as Digital Media*), it has been great to know our marriage could stand the test of another coedited book. To love at first cite.

Introduction

The Utopia of Independent Media: Independence, Working with Freedom and Working for Free

James Bennett

Independence: The condition or quality of being independent; the fact of not depending on another; exemption from external control or support; freedom from subjection, or from the influence of others; individual liberty of thought or action. Rarely in bad sense: Want of subjection to rightful authority, insubordination.

Independent: Not depending upon the authority of another, not in a position of subordination or subjection; not subject to external control or rule; self-governing, autonomous, free.

—*Oxford English Dictionary*

Media independence is central to the organization, make-up, working practices and output of media systems across the globe. This collection addresses the notion of independence as a sociopolitical, aesthetic, industrial and rhetorical ideal that has defined how the media operate in a range of national and international contexts. As the *Oxford English Dictionary* suggests, independence is rarely perceived in a "bad sense," stemming from Western notions of individual and political freedoms that have informed the development of media across a range of platforms: from the freedom of the press as the "fourth estate," through to the introduction of competitors to break up the monopolies of state broadcasters and Hollywood studios, and more recently its influence on the development of digital culture via such foundational polemics as John Perry Barlow's *Declaration of the Independence of Cyberspace*. For many media independence has come to mean working with freedom: from state control or interference, from monopoly, from market forces, as well as freedom to report, comment, create and document without fear of persecution. As this chapter argues, it is this rhetorical ideal that offers a utopian vision for a variety of independent media formations: impractical, unrealistic, impossible and yet, nonetheless, hopeful.

Just as there are many competing and often contradictory visions of utopia, independent media are envisioned and take shape in a variety of ways in a range of different sociopolitical contexts. Far from a stable concept that informs all media systems, the notion of media independence has long been contested, forming a crucial tension point in the regulation, shape, size and role of the media around the globe. In the United Kingdom, where freedom of the press has long been established, such liberties have been called into question since 2011 when the phone-hacking scandal at the *News of the World* demonstrated that independence from regulation could push ethical, moral and legal boundaries to the breaking point (discussed by Stephen Jukes and Stuart Allan in this volume). Elsewhere, the meaning and value of independence is still being established. In the emergence of independent media during the Arab Spring, discussed by Gholam Khiabany in Chapter 12, the rush to proclaim the importance of citizen journalism by many inside and outside Iran, Tunisia and Egypt also led mainstream media to fail to verify these independent accounts, creating a tension with the fourth estate that was dramatically exposed by the *Gay Girl in Damascus* blog.[1] In China the establishment of "independent," yet state-owned, television and news outlets discussed by Anthony Fung, Xiaoxiao Zhang and Luzhou Li in Chapter 11 demonstrates that whilst media independence might be a universal rhetorical goal, its meaning is capable of significant shifts. The dynamic and mutable nature of media independence is, perhaps, most apparent in the way the "New Economy" of the creative industries has increasingly embraced different notions of independence in the move toward outsourcing, freelance and precarious labor. Here, to be independent within the media is to derive autonomy, creative freedom and choice in one's work in exchange for risk, flexibility and self-exploitation. As suggested by this book's title, the notion of independence has therefore become a central paradox in global media systems: at once promising and proclaiming the importance of media freedoms whilst simultaneously exposing those who work within them to conditions of free labor.

In this chapter I argue that media independence must be understood as a utopian ideal, constructed across four sites—the sociopolitical, the industrial, the formal and the rhetorical or discursive. It is the final, rhetorical function of media independence that is the most crucial to the formation and role of independent media in the variety of contexts that are studied in this collection and that is the focus of my attention in the following section of this chapter. I argue that media independence functions as a utopian vision of the media's role in society for those who regulate it, own it, work within it and even study it. This chapter then outlines how the terms "independent media" and "media independence" act as relational qualities before turning to each of the remaining three sites of concern: the sociopolitical, the industrial and the formal. The conclusion looks toward how the utopian promise of media independence might continue to structure our media experiences, and study, in the future.

Before turning to the question of how media independence functions as a utopian ideal, it is worth briefly outlining what we mean by the terms "media independence" and "independent media," along with how they can be considered at four interconnected sites: the industrial, the formal, the sociopolitical and the rhetorical.

Whilst, as the definitions from the *OED* at the head of this chapter suggest, the terms "independence" and "independent" have a necessary overlap, we can make some important distinctions in relation to media to clear the conceptual ground for this collection. The term "independent media" therefore refers to the specific, often industrial, media formation: for example, independent cinema, independent television, independent newspaper, independent games, independent music and so on. The term "Indie" is often used in this context to designate a particular set of companies, publications, bands, studios or presses as independent media (King 2013), as well as to demarcate a particular aesthetic style. But the term "independent media" is always a loaded one. We must ask by whom, and for what purpose, is it being mobilized? In turn, "media independence" speaks to the wider role that an independent media might play within society, particularly the functioning of a better, more democratic, diverse, just and open society. "Media independence" operates as a term in conjunction with independent media, functioning primarily in a rhetorical fashion to suggest the kinds of cultural goods that should be produced and the working conditions available to individuals. Here David Hesmondhalgh and Sarah Baker's notion of "good work" is illuminating for its ability to speak to the kinds of conditions that might be enjoyed by those in the media and creative industries, where working with freedom, dignity and autonomy is aligned with the potential to create cultural products of quality "and their potential contribution to the well-being of others, including (potentially) the common good" (Hesmondhalgh and Baker 2011: 17). In this, its rhetorical and discursive function, media independence often operates as a utopian vision at both a macro and a micro level—tying together the industrial, sociopolitical and formal sites and contradictions at which it operates.

Independence may be present, or contested, at one or all of these sites:

- *The sociopolitical*: independent media are often taken as axiomatic of liberal democracies. In particular, a free press is seen as fundamental to the functioning of democratic societies, acting as a watchdog on the government of the day (discussed by Jukes and Allan). But independent media are further politicized in the way they often provide space for left-leaning critiques of capitalism and the market or issues related to identity politics, such as feminism. However, because independent media are not entirely free from the market they are not *always* radically political in the same sense, unlike alternative media;
- *The industrial*: most crucially such independence operates in terms of economic and regulatory arrangements. In this context independent media are those that operate with "freedom," from (excessive) state

regulation or commercial imperatives. But independent media are also understood to operate in the creative spaces free from (in reality or rhetorically) the mainstream. This meaning of media independence is intimately connected to the freedoms offered to workers within the media and creative industries, whereby job security and roles within large organizations are exchanged for autonomy, choice and individual independence (Leadbetter and Oakley 1999). Here, working with freedom often merges into working for free;

- *The formal*: whereby independent media produce and mobilize an ensemble of particular aesthetic and taste codes. In this context, heavy emphasis is placed on the "authenticity" of the cultural goods produced (du Gay and Hall 1996). A prerequisite for understanding and appreciating such "authentic" media art forms, therefore, is cultural capital—with independent media often dealing in aesthetic forms that are challenging, innovative, radical and so forth. This cultural capital mobilizes the audiences and producers of independent media, in terms of not only what gets made but under what (industrial) conditions—with the emphasis often placed on creative freedom over and above monetary reward. Paradoxically, as Aymar Jean Christian's work here and elsewhere suggests (2011), the catering to niche and often elite tastes can prove a profitable business strategy;
- *The rhetorical or discursive*: this register operates across the other three sites and is mobilized by producers, audiences, regulators, businesses and a range of vested interests in declaring this or that formation to be "independent media." It is here we find media independence most often expressed as a utopian ideal within which a particular "independent media" might operate—for example, the free press, or "Indie" music or film. This ideal is often tinged with a moral or ethical dimension that, as Niki Strange, Andrea Medrado and myself suggest in Chapter 6, guides the business and working practices of companies and individuals within independent media.

These sites overlap and reinforce one another. Thus, David Hesmondhalgh has noted how the emergence of the term "independent" to designate a genre of music in the 1990s was highly significant. It was the first music genre to take its "name from the form of industrial organization behind it," which at once underpinned its proponents' claims that its aesthetics were "superior to other genres not only because it was more relevant or authentic to the youth who produced and consumed . . . because it was based on new relationships between creativity and commerce" (1999: 35). In turn, the genre drew on the historical associations of independence with punk activists who had "politicized [the concept] more radically," with post-punk companies seeing "independents as a means of reconciling the commercial nature of pop with the goal of artistic autonomy for musicians" (ibid.).

As Hesmondhalgh and Leslie Meier contend in this volume, this complex aesthetic, sociopolitical, industrial and rhetorical history of independence within the music industry has made "independent music" perhaps the most important site of independence in the media.

Analyzing independence across these four sites in relation to any media system, however, produces a complex, and at times contradictory, understanding of the concept that demonstrates how different actors within a given media system enlist independence rhetorically and discursively to meet particular ideals. It is not, however, helpful to speak of an "independent audience" or "audience independence." Thus whilst each chapter in this volume, to greater or lesser extents, shows a concern with the question of who the audience of independent media is, how it interacts with their producers and in what ways it shapes the meaning, value and potential of their independence, this book is not organized around a traditional media studies producer-text-audience triumvirate.

Independent media must, of necessity, have an audience. Moreover, and crucially, independent media must find the right kind of audience—one that is committed to the industrial, aesthetic, ethical and sociopolitical ideals of that media and that is enlisted in the discursive struggle over its meaning and value. This often links independent media to particular subcultures, such as gaming, discussed by Hector Postigo in Chapter 9, which demonstrates how independence is often elided with "alternative" media and audiences (discussed further later). Even though producers and audiences alike may cultivate an "indie sensibility" connected to particular forms of cultural and economic capital and away from the mainstream, this does not, of necessity, mean that the audience for independent media is always or only niche or marginal.

Indeed, discussions of "Indie" music have focused on its status as "opposition 'within' popular culture" (Hesmondhalgh 1999: 35). In the case of a free and independent press, the audience must of necessity be the mainstream in order for the sociopolitical role of journalism to speak to the collective and widespread citizenry in order to perform its role in democratic society. At the same time, and as a necessary consequence, however, the independence of the press generally does not extend to its industrial formation: with a free press still dependent on major media conglomerates that can call into question the editorial independence of any particular newspaper. Moreover at the formal level, even as a watchdog, the free press remain dependent on the very sources they promise to watch over for their content—government, big business, political and cultural elites and so on (Couldry and Curran 2003)—in order to bring audiences the stories that help attract them in large enough numbers to sustain newspapers' business models. Fundamentally, media independence operates relationally—there is always the question of what any individual media formation is proclaiming to be independent of—and as an ideal that discursively shapes media systems around the globe.

OF INDEPENDENTS, INDEPENDENCE AND UTOPIAS

> Utopia means *nowhere* or *no-place*. . . . But it is not every nowhere that
> can call itself a utopia. . . . To count as a utopia, an imaginary place
> must be an expression of desire.
>
> (Carey 1999: xi)

If this brief discussion outlines the distinction between media independence
and independent media as well as our approach to these terms in this volume, we need to also understand how the former functions as a utopian ideal
that the latter attempts to realize. Ruth Levitas, the utopian scholar, posits
that utopias are "not just a dream to be enjoyed, but a vision to be pursued"
(Levitas 2010: 1). In such visions, utopias become an "expression for a better way of living" (Levitas 2003: 4). More particularly, as Avery Gordon sets
out in her survey of the term, the drive of utopianism can be understood as a
desire to "create a better and good society . . . Based on a critical diagnosis
of existing political and social arrangements and the values which underlie
them, utopians always offer alternative ideals and claim these are realizable,
often describing new institutional arrangements for doing so" (2005: 363).
For those who champion the cause of independent media, these new institutional arrangements must include a media system that is more just, open,
democratic and diverse: free from government interference and, at the same
time, commercial pressures. Regardless of whether such transformations are
achieved, media independence *matters*: as a utopian ideal it motivates and
mobilizes people in a belief that, as Richard Dyer has put it, "things could
be better" (1985: 222).

In articulating a vision of such absolute freedoms, the utopian—and
impossible—nature of media independence becomes clear. As King concludes in this volume, "ultimately, of course, there is no such thing as *absolutely* true independence, in the sense of any form of cultural production that
is one-hundred percent lacking in dependence on anything of any sort."
Indeed, independence is often at the heart of utopian ideals and their criti-
cisms: Marx and Engels labeled the utopian socialists as naïve, remaining
"suspicious of an individual's or group's ability to think and act *independently* of, and ultimately to transcend, the law-like dictates of the capitalist
system" (Gordon 2005: 363, emphasis mine). Such a transcendental system
was at the heart of John Perry Barlow's vision for the future of cyberspace
discussed by Daniel Kreiss in this volume, leading Kreiss to term it the "myth
of independence." Barlow's *Declaration of Independence of Cyberspace*
promised the new digital citizens of the online world a commonweal outside
the terrestrial, outmoded structures of state, capitalism and "old media."
Indeed, utopian visions often invoke the notion of community. Drawing
on Ernest Bloch's work on utopias as expressions of what is missing,
Levitas suggests that the notion of community appealed to is always
ambiguous—sometimes oppositional, alternative or defensive. But "in general,

the language of communitarianism involves a suppression of power relations within so-called communities" (2000: 190–193).

Issues of power, and their ideological and economic underpinnings, are therefore often at stake in the utopian visions of community set out for new forms of independent media. Thus, in this volume, Aymar Jean Christian's chapter points to the way the emergence and celebration of an online, DIY community of independent TV producers operating outside of the mainstream disguises the imbalance of power between creatives within this community, including the exploitation of free labor in the service of fulfilling community ideals of independence. Thomas Poell and José van Dijck's examination of the rise of social news, premised on "open development" and "communal evaluation," highlights how such rhetoric serves to suppress the power of algorithms—and the corporations who own them—that increasingly shape journalistic values and processes. Equally, in Chapter 12 Gholam Khiabany sets out how the ideal of a social media revolution in Iran was one perpetuated by Western media in a spirit of global community and validation of the community of citizen-journalists represented by Iranian bloggers through so-called technologies of freedom (Sola Pool 1983). But the slogan "You are the media" was one that downplayed questions of "who gets noticed, who gets to speak, and who is allowed to 'represent' the public." Finally, Hector Postigo's contribution notes how not all users within an online community are equal, with leading video game "directors" having the power to shape the aesthetic norms—and economic rewards that follow—of the community. The utopias called forth in relation to particular instances of independent media, therefore, are always an ideal that expresses particular ideological, economic, cultural and aesthetic interests whilst concealing others.

Understanding media independence as a utopian vision remains helpful because it produces real-world consequences, shaping media systems and the lives of those working within them. For example, in his essay for this volume James Rodgers explores the way Russia's political independence during the 1990s shaped and reshaped not only the economic arrangements for independent newspapers and broadcast outlets, but also a generation of journalists' approach to news reportage and their work in Russian media. At the time of writing, the ongoing conflict between the Ukraine and Russia over Chechnyian independence—told through the claims to independence of both countries' newspapers as well as wider Western media—demonstrates why such utopian visions of independence matter. As the emerging crisis in Ukraine vividly demonstrates, independence can prove a concept equally unstable and changeable in both political and media spheres.

In this sense the utopia of media independence is often premised on what Marxist utopian philosopher Ernst Bloch argued was the ability of such visions to fill in "what is perceived to be missing" (Bloch 1986). In such visions, Bloch argues, utopias function as a form of hope that mobilizes action. Here the sociopolitical function of independent media is to the fore, such as in the range of independent voices harnessed by Barack Obama's social media campaign in 2008 (Kreiss 2012), or in the IndyMedia Collective's (discussed further later) attempt to bring about direct change on a range of political issues from climate change to the financial crisis. In turn, therefore, Bloch's description of utopia as a vision that promises to fulfill that which is perceived to be missing helps understand the way media independence often functions as an argument and a call to action, to create space for new, diverse and divergent voices within a given media system. Thus in Chapter 3, I explore how the call for—and rise of—independent television in Britain can be understood as a direct response to a perceived need for more varied voices that reflect an increasingly multicultural Britain populated by minorities of race, ethnicity and sexuality that require on- and off-screen representation by and in the UK television industry.

More widely the growing ubiquity of digital media in terms of platforms and tools has led to a rise of new voices within the media stream, which has often been understood as offering new forms of independent media (discussed by Khiabany, Christian, Postigo, Poell and van Dijck in this volume). Recognizing the role hope plays in shaping media systems, therefore, is a challenge we need to take up in understanding how media independence functions at both a micro and macro level. Hope, as Helen Kennedy concludes in her study of ethics and values in Web design, is "a strategic as well as an empirical necessity, because it suggests the possibility of agency, and of action which is not in the service of capital" (2012: 216). Thus, as Fung, Zhang and Li hope in their entry to this volume, the "passionate and educated media personnel" working in Chinese television who believe in "a greater degree of media freedom . . . might not be influential now. But they will be in times to come."

Indeed, the utopian visions of media independence are far from settled. Utopia is, after all, a flexible concept that is "conceptually as well as substantively contested" (Levitas 2000: 5). Independent media themselves act as sites of conflict over different values and levels of independence: industrially, politically, formally or rhetorically. Thus within any given media platform there may be a range of different movements, studios, labels, companies or individual actors laying claim to be "independent media" or, as discussed later, exhibiting different levels of independence.

However, as a utopian vision that promises artistic freedom and independence from commercial pressures, media independence is almost always in crises or compromise. This may be part of wider social shifts marked by neoliberalism and a turn away from a concern with collective well-being, replaced with a focus on individualism. Thus Zygmant Bauman has applied his (overused) notion of liquid modernity to analyze utopian aspirations in the age of neoliberalism to suggest they have become "imagination privatized," in which "happiness has become a *private affair*; and a matter for *here and now*. The happiness of others is no more . . . a condition of one's own felicity" (Bauman 2003: 12–14). But the crisis of media independence may also be because of some of the inherent contradictions found in aesthetic notions of independent media as expressions of "authentic" culture. Thus Kurt Cobain's suicide note

> began by discussing his inability to square Nirvana's vast commercial success with what he called the "ethics involved with independence" . . . it was impossible for an "alternative" rock band to become as successful as Nirvana had without losing something important in the process.
> (Petridis 2014)

Cobain's suicide was, to an extent, indicative of the wider problematic: funding truly independent media away from either the market or the state makes independent media an inherently precarious enterprise, particularly if a large audience is sought. Moreover, as independent artists or movements achieve recognition and a larger audience, their perceived independence—from the mainstream—is often compromised. Here the label "sellout" functions to deride and devalue those who fail to reach or maintain the utopian ideal of media independence (see Hesmondhalgh and Meier's contribution to this volume). But media rarely operate, or should be understood, in such black and white terms.

The challenge, for both makers of independent media and scholars, is to reconcile this process of crises and compromise with the utopian visions of media independence. Here we can often see that independent media exist—and produce—new hybrid arrangements that offer genuine—if not absolute—alternatives to the mainstream. Thus independent media can often be understood in terms of hybridity across their industrial, sociopolitical and formal structures. For example, Fung, Zhang and Li's chapter discusses Chinese independent television in terms of new economic and regulatory arrangements between the state and the market, whilst Hector Postigo demonstrates how independence can be negotiated between individual and platform owner; or as Strange, myself and Medrado explore, between profit and public service. Whilst it is easy to see these hybrid arrangements as irrevocable compromises in the pursuit of media independence—as Cobain arguably did—these hybrid arrangements can also be understood to help independent media balance the financial and regulatory pressures pragmatically with the individual and creative freedoms sought.

Perhaps, then, more than anything else media independence should be understood in the utopian terms as originally proposed by Thomas More: "a good, but non-existent and therefore impossible society" (quoted in Levitas 2010: 2). As a utopian ideal, media independence must remain either permanently out of reach or ultimately compromised. This collection, however, suggests that not only can these compromises be productive of new hybrid arrangements that do produce "good work," aimed at creating a better society, but also that an approach to utopia that recognizes it as "the expression of desire for a better way of being" is itself productive (ibid.: 9). Thus whilst how media independence functions and what independent media are is subject to significant variation and contestation in the chapters that follow, I suggest that the utopian ideal remains present throughout as a motivating factor and discursive structure that influences media systems, and the individuals who work within them, around the globe. As Levitas explains: "whatever we think of particular utopias, we learn a lot about the experience of living under any set of conditions by reflecting upon the desire which those conditions generate and yet leave unfulfilled" (ibid.).

A RELATIONAL QUALITY: INDEPENDENT OF . . .

As King argues in this volume, "'independent' is always a relational term—implying independent *of* something, more or less specific—it is also often a *relative* quality rather than one that entails absolute or clear-cut distinctions between one thing and another." This collection seeks to understand independent media in these relative terms—with authors offering a range of perspective on the way independent media function in particular industrial, sociopolitical, aesthetic and rhetorical spaces. The primary relation against which independent media are set is "the mainstream." The notion of independence is, in turn, often constructed in terms of binaries, most obviously to not be dependent (OED). But a series of further oppositions are also in play, as set out in Table 1:

Table 1

Independent	Dependent
Niche	Mainstream
Authentic	Fake/Commercial
High culture	Mass culture
Radical	Popular
Libertarian	Regulated
Free market	Monopoly
Nonprofit	Free market
Free	Controlled
Left wing	Conservative
Neoliberal	State
Small scale	Media conglomerate
Craft	Industrial
Ethical	Exploitative
Low budget	High budget
Credible	"Sellout"
Innovative/Experimental	Formatted/Predictable
Subculture	Dominant

Whilst media may rarely operate in such black and white terms, these binaries often shape the utopian ideals of media independence. Some of these oppositions coalesce to create powerful ideological rhetorical arguments for the need, role and scope for independent media. An independent press is, perhaps, the most famous and widely understood example of independent media—being necessary to act as a watchdog on the government of the day (see Jukes and Allan in this volume). It is premised on mobilizing notions of freedom, the free market, libertarianism and authenticity (the journalistic truth) against control, monopoly, regulation, the state and the inauthentic (propaganda).

However, not all these oppositions are mobilized in each particular context and, indeed, some of these binaries are not only contradictory, but also oscillate according to what kinds of independence are being declared. Thus whilst many independent media formations and movements are radical *and* left wing, this is not a necessary consequence of independence: independent press can be of left- or right-wing persuasion; independent and niche film movements circulate around fundamentalist religious ideals as much as they do around progressive sensibilities. Equally, Daniel Kreiss demonstrates in this volume that the "New Communalists" of early "cyberspace" collected around a vision of the Internet as a space free and independent from government control, but perfectly in hock with a neo-right, neoliberal agenda. Moreover, independence might differ in degree and kind across the four sites discussed earlier. Thus, whilst a strong rhetoric of independence can be found in American cinema, there is much lower formal and industrial independence found in those films generally termed "Indie" (King 2014). As Janet Staiger astutely concludes in her analysis of the term "independent cinema," practices independent to the mainstream are not "*in themselves* [a] guarantee that alternative is better," and can often reinforce dominant ideologies and hegemony (2013: 25). These oscillating binaries, therefore, have much to do with not only by whom the notion of media independence is mobilized, but also the fact that is not just the mainstream against which independent media are defined. Here we need to understand that a third term is in play in the way independent media are defined in relation to: "alternative media."

We might conceive independent media as existing on a continuum between mainstream and alternative, operating on a sliding scale between dependence and independence, freedom and control, nonprofit and free market, center and margin: often invoking hybrid arrangements in order to continue to operate in the space between these other media sources.

Alternative Media ———— Independent Media ———— Mainstream

The literature on alternative media tends to concentrate on the industrial and sociopolitical. But as discussed earlier, these overlap with issues of rhetorical and aesthetic independence. This is perhaps most evident in the case of music and film, where "alternative" and "independent" are sometimes used interchangeably (Newman 2009) to designate a particular aesthetic style that is closely connected to a specific industrial organization of companies operating outside of the mainstream. Here the status of alternative media as a challenge to the mainstream by producing counter-hegemonic works is especially important for the way such media speak to individual subcultures. For the sake of clarity of argument, this notion of alternative and the link to subcultures is discussed in relation to aesthetics further later. For now, I want to concentrate on issues of power and the rhetorical goals and ideals of alternative media wrapped in questions of sociopolitical and industrial independence.

Nick Couldry and James Curran define alternative media as "media production that challenges, at least implicitly, actual concentrations of media power, whatever form those concentrations may take in different locations" (2003: 7). In contrast to independent media, alternative media tend to be leftist, if not socialist, in orientation and predominantly take the form of initiatives in journalism or informing and mobilizing a political public: they are inherently participatory, grassroots, counter-hegemonic, nonhierarchical, one-to-one, small scale and on the margins. Particularly through digital tools and technologies, alternative media—in their utopian visions—promise to provide marginalized and disenfranchised groups with a platform and a voice. Here there is a close link between independence and diversity, discussed further in Chapter 3. In this sense, whilst alternative media promise participation *through* the media, independent media are still more likely to conform to promoting participation *in* the media (Bailey, Cammaerts and Carpentier 2007: 11). That is, independent media tend to be professional—although perhaps not exclusively so—and dictate the terms on which non-professionals have access to the platform. This can mean that independent media operate with less flexible industrial and formal structures—for example, privileging particular sources within a news bulletin—which, to many, can compromise (in a negative sense) the sociopolitical power of independent media. However, it can also mean that alternative media are reliant on free labor to an even greater extent than the fragile economies of independent media (Hesmondhalgh 1999). As Nick Couldry notes, production must happen in people's spare time—restricting access to those with the resources available to give up time in this way (2003: 47). This is an issue that shall be returned to later.

From a social-reforming, liberal or social democratic point of view, alternative media are necessary because, as Richard Johnson has argued in his history of the term "alternative," "it is not enough . . . to criticise or to protest; we must develop alternatives . . . the failure to do so is the characteristic flaw of the 'impossible' left and its intellectuals" (2005: 4). In such a view, the compromises independent media make in their utopian visions of transforming society into a more just and open system in order to secure audiences, funding and revenue, therefore, are failures to think outside that system: a "sellout," if not a cop out. In turn, the way independent media function within capitalism and current political arrangements—even if in hybrid form—means they operate more within hegemony rather than against it. For avowed supporters of alternative media, the compromises of independent media are indicative of the mantra "There Is No Alternative (TINA)," which came to the fore in the neoliberal economics of the 1980s in the United States and Europe. Thus, as Johnson demonstrates, "alternative" marks the need for a political extension beyond the ruling elite, usually referring to better public policies (ibid.). In the context of the media, Couldry and Curran argue it is insufficient for the (independent) media to be there solely "to guard us against the overweening influence of other forms of power (especially government)." Rather, "media power is itself part of what power watchers need to watch" (2003: 4). In turn, such a view necessitates that another form of media must exist to keep a check on the (mainstream) media itself: alternative media.

To better understand the relationship between independent and alternative media it is worth briefly exploring one of the most frequently cited examples of alternative media: the IndyMedia collective (IMC) (Couldry 2003; Milioni 2009; Platon and Deuze 2003). Emerging in 1999–2000 out of coverage of protest movements in Seattle against the World Trade Organization and in Washington against the World Bank and International Monetary Funds, the IMC has avowedly socialist and anarchist beginnings. Indeed, citing Atton's work, Christian Fuchs has noted that "alternative media studies are strongly connected to Anarchist perspectives" (2010: 174). Milioni (2009) argues there are three functional differences between the IndyMedia model and mainstream journalism. First, the exemplary function, which concerns the structural, ethical and normative characteristics of IndyMedia production—such as its explicitly political character, its editorial independence from state or commerce, its nonhierarchical, nonprofessional news gathering structure and the consequential promotion of diverse voices. Second, a competitive function, which might include using and commenting on mainstream news. Third, a supplementary function, "which allows users to reframe news stories and check on the authenticity and objectivity of the media, thus limiting their [mainstream media's] power over the construction of reality" (2009: 419–420). The IMC thus describes itself as a nonhierarchical collection of organizations and journalists "offering grassroots, non-corporate coverage . . . [as] a democratic media outlet for the creation of radical, accurate, and passionate tellings of truth" (IMC n.d.).

Such a radical critique of not just the mainstream media, but also independent media, however, risks a precarious position: one in which it is possible for media to work with freedom of expression in terms of state regulation, as well as freedom from the demands of profit, but at the expense of not being heard or paid. The position of alternative media is, therefore, perhaps an even more utopian and impossible vision than that of independent media. Thus the FAQ page for the IndyMedia collective espouses an ideal form of independence in response to the question "of what are you 'independent?'"

> No corporation owns Indymedia, no government manages the organization, no single donor finances the project. Indymedia is not the mouthpiece of any political party or organization. . . . Anyone may participate in Indymedia organizing and anyone may post to the Indymedia newswires.

To return to the notion of hope within such utopias, it is instructive to note the way alternative has been enlisted by a range of sociopolitical movements to promote a way of "'Living differently'—more co-operatively, less competitively or hierarchically for example—[which] has been seen as expressing hope for the future, but also as a kind of direct action" (Johnson 2005: 5). Alternative media often operate with such direct causes, such as the IndyMedia collective, seeking to effect sociopolitical change from a radical, alternative, often Socialist perspective (Hesmondhalgh 1997).

However, taken to the extreme of their own logic of independence, such political projects demonstrate the ultimate futility of the utopian vision of alternative media. Sara Platon and Mark Deuze have argued that whilst IMC's independence from commercial, corporate and government interests is to the fore, "they are not independent in the strictest sense of the word. Often the code and content of the news are made and regulated by people that are, in one way or another, affiliated with many movements providing their own content" (2003: 338). Even in such avowedly radical and anti-mainstream practices such as IndyMedia, therefore, independence might remain a myth.

As Christian Fuchs has admitted, "alternative media studies . . . tend to idealize small-scale production and tend to neglect orientation towards the political public" (2010: 174). Similarly Bailey, Cammaerts, Carpentier suggest that "fighting a war of position on numerous fronts has left the alternative media movement in a rather problematic, vulnerable and isolated position" (2007: 31). By privileging small-scale, local organization, alternative media are often trapped in an economic dilemma that can force the "the adoption of commercial media formats in their efforts to survive" (2007: 15): a compromise frequently equated with failure, or a loss of the radical, alternative voice once promised. That is, the "sellout."

The problem for alternative media is to always be on the margins—and thus not be heard. As Tanja Dreher argues, media power involves not only the power to speak, but also to listen—and ignore:

> we might also analyze the refusal to listen on the part of the dominant as active, as a refusal to quiet the inner voice or to open up a possibility of active engagement with the other . . . Media power might entail the privilege of choosing to listen or not, the power to enter into dialogue or not, to seek to comprehend the other or not.
>
> (Dreher 2010: 100–101)

Consequently, alternative media's reliance on community volunteerism, donations and gifts ensures they remain relatively small, operating at the margins of the global media ecology and society more generally. In contrast, independent media achieve greater reach and impact through compromise and the development of hybrid arrangements to ensure larger audiences and relative economic stability—although, as discussed later, this does not prevent them from existing in a state of near perpetual (financial) crisis. This is not to suggest that independent media are necessarily any less of a utopian ideal than that of alternative media, but rather to stress the way compromise, challenge and change are met is different in each of these sectors and their study. In the following section, I turn to the sociopolitical terrain of independent media to set out why independence matters—even if the utopian vision is invariably compromised.

WHY INDEPENDENCE MATTERS: THE SOCIO-POLITICS OF INDEPENDENT MEDIA

If, as I suggested earlier, the utopian function of media independence posits it as an unrealizable idyll, this has not prevented it from having real impact on the way media operate in societies around the world. The term "independence" calls up an imaginarie of ideals, particularly sociopolitical ones, which have shaped media systems around the world: most obviously, and famously, the American *Declaration of Independence*, where the first amendment has been taken to enshrine a free and independent press (Schudson 2002). More widely, and more recently, independent media—or at least the call for such media—has been part of the processes of decolonization of many former "subject nations" in Africa and Asia, as well as the movement away from autocracies and totalitarian regimes, in South America, Asia and Eastern Europe.

The utopian notion of media independence is nonetheless a vision that inspires action. In this light, the rhetorical and discursive level of media independence can be seen as intimately connected to the sociopolitical: independent media have been seen as crucial to these political movements. Francis Kasoma has argued, writing amidst the turbulence of African countries' emerging independence from their colonial masters during the 1990s, "there is a causal linkage between a free press and democracy" (Kasoma 1995: 539). Thus, any search for "media independence" in global newswires finds a continuing concern with the state of the free press in emerging democracies: for example, in June 2013 an international delegation from the World Association of Newspapers and News Publishers and the Ethical Journalism Network went to Myanmar to call for greater reform to enable media independence (*States News Service*, June 7, 2013). In 2012–2013 alone, *BBC Monitoring International Reports* detailed calls for or concerns over independent media in Uganda, Kenya, Tanzania, Tunisia, Bulgaria, Turkey,

Macedonia, South Korea, Thailand, Pakistan, Syria and Iran. The previous year, 2011, Reporters Without Borders named "Crackdown" as the word of the year, declaring, "Never have acts of censorship and physical attacks on journalists seemed so numerous. The equation is simple: the absence or suppression of civil liberties leads necessarily to the suppression of media freedom" (BBC 2012).

In 2013 Freedom House's *Freedom of the Press Report*, which measures press freedom in terms of legal, political and economic environment, posited that just 32 percent of nations had a "free press" (Deutsch-Karlekar and Dunham 2013). Whilst all of Western Europe and North America's press were included in this figure, their report surmised that in population terms this meant that just 13 percent of the world's population experienced a free press, with 45 percent found to be living under conditions defined as "not free." In those countries deemed "the worst of the worst," including North Korea, Belarus, Turkmenistan, Cuba, Equatorial Guinea, Eritrea and Iran, "independent media are either nonexistent or barely able to operate, the press acts as a mouthpiece for the regime, citizens' access to unbiased information is severely limited, and dissent is crushed through imprisonment, torture, and other forms of repression" (ibid.: 4). Yet the relationship between independent media and democracy is not always so straightforward or one way. James Rodgers's chapter in this volume demonstrates that independent media as a replacement for state-run monopolies is no guarantee of politically unbiased reporting—with mutually advantageous relationships emerging in post-Soviet Russia that benefited both journalists and the reigning government as preferable to a return to communism.

More widely than the freedom of the press that is at stake in the earlier discussion, and to return to the theme of utopia, media independence might matter in terms of the kind of society we (want to) live in. Charles Leadbetter and Kate Oakley's survey of the emergence of the "new independents" in Britain's creative economy concludes that there is a mutually reinforcing relationship between democracy and an independent creative sector that benefits both:

> Creative industries thrive in an environment that promotes openness, free speech, diversity and expression. Our [Britain's] capacity to breed businesses based on creative independent thought is intimately linked, in the long run, to the strength of our democratic traditions of self-governance and freedom of speech. That is why these industries are vital not just for jobs and growth but to the quality of our lives as citizens as well.
>
> (1999: 49)

However, whilst Leadbetter and Oakley may trace an indelible link between independent media and democracy, the story of liberalizing authoritarian states' control of the media in favor of a more free press has not always resulted in a more democratic or broad-based public sphere. Thus whilst Kasoma's account in the mid-1990s may have welcomed commercial media as an independent voice compared to the mouthpieces of state-controlled radio, television and press, Chin-Chuan Lee's work on Taiwan (2003) has shown that liberalizing the communications and media market may diminish the prospects for democratic change. Here, global media corporations—particularly Rupert Murdoch's Star TV—can dominate the market, offering little space for counter-hegemonic voices that are splintered into increasingly marginal spaces.

Thus far I have been concerned to discuss the role of media independence at the macro level. However, beyond the hope for a better society that might be created through an independent media, the notion of freedom promised by media independence has been held up as an idyll for the individual in relationship to their working lives, particularly in creative industries. As Angela McRobbie has argued:

> In fields like film-making or fashion design there is a euphoric sense among practitioners of by-passing tradition, pre-empting conscription into the dullness of 9–5 and evading the constraints of institutional processes. There is a utopian thread embedded in this wholehearted attempt to make-over the world of work into something closer to a life of enthusiasm and enjoyment.
>
> (2002: 521)

However, in this new utopia, McRobbie suggests, there has actually been a move away from what she terms "independent work." Tracing the decline of the independent fashion scene—replaced by the high street behemoths and the neoliberal drift away from support for the arts and crafts—there has been a "shift from there being 'independent work'" to freelance work, accompanied by a "shift in the balance of power from a social 'milieu of innovation' to a world of individual 'projects'" (2002: 524). Although "independent work" has not been a concept widely taken up by media and cultural studies (although there is a burgeoning literature on the subject in education), the shift that McRobbie points to has been explored through work on precarious, self-exploitation and freelance labor in what Andrew Ross has termed "the new economy," of which the creative industries have been emblematic (2004). Here the role of work is intimately linked to autonomy and personal freedom.

For its celebrants, the new economy's freedoms are easily aligned with the perceived benefits and utopias of independence. As Mark Deuze argues:

> The worker of today must become an enterprise of her own: perfectly adept at managing herself, unlearning old skills whilst reflexively adapting to new demands, preferring individual independence and autonomy over the relative stability of a life-long work style.
>
> (Deuze, quoted in Kennedy 2012: 6)

Autonomy bleeds seamlessly into the ideal of independence at a micro level. This "creative class," as Richard Florida terms them (2003), are flexible, self-enterprising citizens on whom the future of creative industries and national economies relies (Hartley 2005).

But such autonomy is not without risk. As Leadbetter and Oakley admit:

> Life as an Independent is not nirvana, nor even necessarily a recipe for making money. It can provide choice, autonomy and satisfaction but it also involves constant uncertainty, insecurity and change.
>
> (1999: 15)

For other scholars, therefore, the promise of working with freedom is too easily elided with the need to work for free. Andrew Ross's classic formulation of the dilemma posits that with the freedoms of the new economy comes the drive for "employees' free-est thoughts and impulses in the service of salaried time" (Ross 2004: 17–19). In such a neoliberal economy the distinction between work and leisure, office and home is elided so that, as Nikolas Rose argues, work has been redefined as "a capacity for self-realisation which can be obtained only through individual activity" (1999: 145).

More recently, work by scholars such as David Hesmondhalgh and Sarah Baker (2011), David Lee (2012), Mark Banks (2006) and others has provided a more nuanced account of work within the creative industries that attempts to balance the positive aspects of freedom and autonomy found in such work with the way it can be exploited as a pool of free labor. As Gholam Khiabany argues in this volume, the post-Foucauldian and autonomist-Marxist critiques of the cultural industries' celebrants focus too overwhelmingly on the question of "working for free." In so doing, they ignore "the varying composition of work, production, and control" experienced by those within the media industries—independent and otherwise. Moreover, as my own chapter with Niki Strange and Andrea Medrado demonstrates, paying attention to the operation of a "moral economy" can help us understand how those within independent media negotiate the risks of working with freedom against the pressure to work for free by focusing on how the drive for independence can manifest itself in the production and experience of "good work."

But what remains evident from these debates is that independent media—and work within them—are inherently precarious: they attempt to balance the ethical, aesthetic, sociopolitical drives of independence with the economic realities of media production. Thus there is an important limit to the rhetorical and discursive calls for freedom in understandings of media independence to bear in mind: a free press, or creative freedom, does not equate to free media—as in free beer. The economics and industrial structures of independent media mean companies and individuals operating within the sector must turn a profit—and this can bring with it crises and compromises in ethics, aesthetics and economics.

INDEPENDENT MEDIA INDUSTRIES: CRISIS, COMPROMISE AND HYBRIDITY

Ostensibly "independent media" would have no ties with media conglomerates, the state or other mainstream sources of funding. As Michael Newman argues, extrapolating from independent cinema,

> indie culture . . . derives its identity from challenging the mainstream. This challenge is figured first of all from an economic distinction between modes of production. "Indie" connotes small-scale, personal, artistic, and creative; "mainstream" implies a large-scale commercial media industry that values money more than art.
>
> (2009: 16)

As Newman goes on, however, the term "indie" has come to "far exceed the literal designation of media product that are made independent of major firms" (ibid.). I hoped to have demonstrated, however, such a position remains a utopian goal rather than a reality, and to exclude all those companies and individuals who have any such economic or industrial ties would risk too marginalizing an approach to "independent media." Indeed, this is the problem of alternative media formations I outlined earlier. For example, Jennifer Waits's study of U.S. college radio in the late 1990s demonstrated how a policy to bar music from any artist who had any connect with major label distribution meant that resident DJs tied themselves in knots over their playlists. In particular, as "alternative" bands like Nirvana became increasingly mainstream, what was permissible as "Indie" became an ever-decreasing selection of music (2007).

Another way to understand the utopian visions of media independence, then, is to recognize that—almost as a necessary consequence of their refusal to occupy the margins of radically alternative media—independent media are in a nearly perpetual state of crises. Such crises may be economic—in terms of lack of funding as well as ethical or sociopolitical judgments over sources of funding—or formal—in terms of the kinds of cultural goods produced and their appeal to an (economically viable) audience. As Geoff King has argued elsewhere, independent cinema—as with other media—can often be considered as simultaneously in crisis and renewal. However, "the two positions are mutually implicated rather than simply opposed," so that whilst such cinema might appear "in a state of close-to-permanent crises of one kind or another," it also retains "some potential either to continue to thrive . . . or to undergo a revival at some point in the future" (2013: 45).

Tim Wu suggests this movement between crisis and renewal is characterized by a shift from "open to closed" media systems. Terming this process "the cycle," Wu argues that the development of almost all media can be understood as a shift from state-owned monopoly, to competition, to oligopoly or commercial monopoly. Whilst Wu's argument is perhaps too totalizing an account of how media systems develop and undergo transformation, it usefully returns our attention to the utopian role media independence has in shaping the industrial organization of media. Without directly invoking the notion of utopia, Wu's argument is suggestive of the role that hope plays in media histories: "each new communications technology inspires dreams of a better society, new forms of expression, alternative types of journalism. Yet each . . . eventually reveals its flaws, kinks and limitations" to consumers, industry and regulators alike (2010).

Whilst the utopian phase often promises independent media, via a process of deregulation and the promotion of the free market in opposition to state-run media, Wu suggests, at a later point a new monopoly or oligopoly will be permitted in the name of creating a more "orderly and efficient regime for the betterment of all users" (ibid.). He uses the story of the American telephone industry to exemplify this. During the early 1900s hundreds of independent firms had blossomed after the expiration of the monopoly based on Bell's patent in 1894. However, competition did not bring a better system as variable line services and disconnected local networks proved unprofitable for businesses and unreliable for customers. In turn, a new state-sanctioned commercial monopoly emerged that enabled the Bell Company to return to a position of total market dominance in exchange for undertaking a duty to carry all competitors' services on its networks. As Wu explains, CEO of the Bell Company Henry Vail sacrificed greater profits for economic security in the moral belief that competition meant "strife, industrial warfare [and] contention, [which were] giving American business a bad name." Such decisions are arguably at the heart of how individuals and companies navigate the compromises necessary to turn a profit whilst simultaneously pursuing the utopian desire for independence (see Chapter 6 in this volume).

Wu's story of the U.S. telecommunications network exemplifies how the ideal of independent media can structure an industry, often producing a process whereby companies, and individuals within them, experience crisis, compromise and renewal—often via the creation of new hybrid arrangements. Thus if the Bell Company's state-sanctioned monopoly seemed unique at the time, it is no longer alone in the kinds of arrangements that typify different forms of independent media. In the United Kingdom, the development of television has been shaped by the ideal of independence, including the original monopoly granted to the BBC in the name of freedom from government interference. As I explore in Chapter 3, the founding role of independence in British broadcasting has brought both new hybrid arrangements—whereby public service and profit are no longer antithetical to one another—as well as a more problematic elision between independence and independents. In China, independent television has another meaning again—producing a system in which privately operated but state-owned companies and networks balance the demands of the political regime with the desire for more oppositional programming. As Anthony Fung, Xiaoxiao Zhang and Luzhou Li explore in this volume, independent television in China must perform a delicate balancing act between the performance of subservience, editorial freedom and economic returns. Understanding independence as a relational term, therefore, must include acknowledging the hybrid arrangements and compromises that allow independent media to continue to function as businesses—for, as the chapters in Part II of this collection suggest, the economic and creative livelihood and freedoms of those working in independent media remain at stake.

FORMAL INDEPENDENCE: AUTHENTIC AESTHETICS, TASTE AND CULTURAL CAPITAL

As King is careful to point out, this process of crisis and renewal is not simply a matter of economic or industrial independence, but relates to the formal as well (2013). Here independent media's claims to "authenticity" are understood in equally utopian terms as opposition to the mainstream, mass and commercial: grassroots media with a "do-it-yourself aesthetic at the lower-budget end of the scale . . . [coupled with] a strong tendency to distrust of anything that achieves wider popularity . . . that this must be the result of 'selling out' or diluting the basic principles of the indie aesthetic in some way" (ibid.: 48). For many the line between independence and dependence is a thin one—with many "independent" companies reliant on relationships with the mainstream that compromise their "indie" credentials. As McRobbie noted of the UK fashion industry, "by the end of the 1990s the only way to be 'independent' was to be 'dependent' on Kookai, Debenhams, Top Shop. Indeed the only way fashion design could survive was to sign up with a bigger company and more or less relinquish 'creative independence'" (2002: 521). McRobbie's analysis equates the mainstream and commercial with "tainting" the independent aesthetic that, as discussed later, is closely associated with authenticity, thus reducing the kinds of innovation and creativity she found in her study. For McRobbie, as with others, such compromises and hybrid arrangements undermine the role of independents in creating alternative visions.

But this simply raises the utopian specter again that such a vision is never achievable. In previous work on "Indie" music, David Hesmondhalgh has demonstrated how a "pure" aesthetic, let alone economic, ethos of such music was a fallacy (1997; 1999). As he suggests, "there is now a huge amount of cultural production taking place on the boundaries between subfields of mass and restricted production" (2006: 222). Aesthetics are therefore closely linked to the industrial formation discussed earlier, especially in terms of the autonomy of individuals to "work with freedom": "creative autonomy from commercial restraint is a theme which has often been used to mystify artistic production by making the isolated genius the hero of cultural myth" (Hesmondhalgh 1999: 35). As Michael Newman explains, in "independent music and movies, the ideal of separation is most often figured as autonomy, as the power artists retain to control their creative process. Autonomy, in turn, is seen as a guarantee of authenticity" (2009: 19). Authenticity, in turn, functions as a guarantor of the value of independent media's outputs for audiences in opposition to the mainstream. Thus, to return to the binaries set out earlier in this chapter, Michelle Wallace "traces how the definition of authenticity relies upon being over-layered by other binaries of value: serious/trivial, authentic/commodified, natural/artificial" (paraphrased in Skeggs 2004: 105).

At a formal level, the result of such binaries is that independent cultural products have often been associated with a low-budget aesthetic. As Hesmondhalgh notes, authenticity in independent music has been closely associated with working-class culture and a punk, do-it-yourself attitude (1997; 1999). The emphasis on self-representation and DIY cultures in independent media brings independent media in close proximity to their audiences. Here the opposition to the mainstream of such independent media is particularly apparent in the way—discursively—they are enlisted by and for subcultures as means of challenging the dominant aesthetics and socio-politics of the center. In turn, we can understand a further bleeding of the goals of independence with those of alternative media—whereby both share a "rejection of the production values of the 'professional' working in mainstream media," in the hope that a space will be created for greater "diversity of formats and genres and . . . experimentation with content and form" (Bailey et al. 2007: 20). Diversity of producers in independent media—as I explore in Chapter 3 on British television—often becomes synonymous with the goal of experimentation in diversity of form, with such media often seen as a "breeding ground for innovation," defined not only in opposition to the mainstream, but also constantly under threat of co-option by it (ibid.).

If financial bankruptcy is always a risk of the creative freedoms of independent media, then co-option by the mainstream represents its polar (financial) opposite: gaining financial stability but losing the artistic credibility of authenticity—that is, "selling out." But authenticity can be understood as a paradoxical position here, particularly as it is related to the taste cultures of independent media. On the one hand, authenticity can signify artistic value—often associated with cultural elites (discussed further later)—and on the other, it can connote a connection to working-class cultures that are simultaneously devalued as sites of popular, mass entertainment consumption, at the same time as they are venerated as embodiments of preindustrial folk culture. As Beverley Skeggs suggests, the association of authenticity with working-class cultures can easily be treated as "exchange value to others who want to attach authenticity to themselves and to those who require boundary markers to signify their own propriety": that is, the middle classes (2004: 107). As Skeggs explains, working-class culture becomes:

> fixed, but plundered . . . the middle classes appropriate parts of working-class culture as a resource [but] they only take the bits that are useful,

such as the criminal associations, the sexuality, the immoral bits, essentializing qualities with the working-classes . . . the plundered attributes have to remain associated with the "originary" group in order to guarantee the attribution of "the real" and authentic.

(ibid.: 187)

As a result, middle-class mobility can only be understood as "progression and progressiveness predicated on holding in place—fixing—that which must signify stagnation and immobility": the working class (ibid.). Understood in relation to questions of taste, therefore, the "authenticity" of independent media can be highly problematic.

As Michael Newman has argued, "the discourse of alternativeness remains central to crafting indie's appeal to a market ripe for exploitation" so that whilst it claims on the one hand to "counter and implicitly criticizes hegemonic mass culture, desiring to be an authentic alternative to it," it simultaneously "serves as a taste culture perpetuating the privilege of a social elite of upscale consumers" (2009: 17). As Newman goes on to suggest, "the oppositional stance that defines indie culture is one key to its status as a source of distinction, a means by which its audience asserts its superior taste" (ibid.: 22).

Consumers and marketers of independent media turn the oppositions set out earlier in this chapter into taste distinctions of aesthetics that enable them to separate their own—elite—tastes from mass culture. Drawing on Pierre Bourdieu's work, Tony Bennett and the Center for Research on Socio-Cultural Change's project on culture, class and distinction in Britain found that class was an important factor in preferences for "art house" films aligned with independence, which "young professionals working in the cultural sector . . . interpreted as a more cerebral or authentic form of participation than the mainstream films associated with multiplex cinema" (Bennett et al. 2009: 140–141). Here the low-budget, experimental, small-scale and diverse modes of production mix with aesthetic markers of authenticity and credibility in opposition to the high-budget, formatted, industrial-scale production of the mainstream's more "predictable" fare. But this leaves independent media and their audiences in a paradoxical position in terms of their claims to be counter to the mainstream. As Newman summarizes, "indie is at once oppositional and privileged; it asserts its privilege by opposing itself to the mainstream" (2009: 24).

However, it is important to recall that whilst independent media may share some of the same aesthetic registers and sociopolitical goals of alternative media, we cannot simply equate the one with the other or elide the terms. We must understand compromise as a productive and necessary consequence of independence. Thus, as both Hesmondhalgh and Newman have argued, it is possible for independent artists to experience mainstream success without "selling out," by reaching a compromise with their fans and an aesthetic form that enables both artist and consumer to understand wider popularity as a form of "infiltration of the establishment [that] recuperates the credibility of the indie artist" (Newman 2009: 22). Or, as Hesmondhalgh puts it, the drive toward professionalization and partnerships with major labels can be understood as a form of opposition "within" the mainstream (1999). It is unhelpful to simply buy into the rhetorical ideals of independence as a somehow more "authentic" or "autonomous" culture separate from the mainstream, which perceives any compromise as a sellout or co-option of "indie" culture. To do so would, to return to Skeggs's point about class, maintain the "already privileged [independent culture's] authority to define not only itself, but also its Other," recognizing its "own agency while configuring the dominant culture's consumers as passive victims of corporate-consumerist ideology" (Newman 2009: 33). Independence, then, at the formal level is more complex, hybrid and liable to compromise than such absolute distinctions can account for. We must pay attention to not only what "independent media" look or sound like, but also who mobilizes the rhetoric of independence, in the service of what kinds of cultural goods and sectors and for what sociopolitical purposes.

CONCLUSION: THE HOPEFUL STUDY OF INDEPENDENT MEDIA

> *Hope*: Expectation of something desired; desire combined with expectation.
>
> —*Oxford English Dictionary*

At the outset of this chapter I suggested that media independence was best understood as a utopia: a desire for a better way of being, which might be achieved through media. I want to conclude this introductory chapter by returning to this notion of utopian desire as "hope" in terms of both the future for independent media and its study.

For Ernest Bloch—drawing on his experiences as a radical German intellectual of Jewish origin who, like Theodor Adorno, had spent the 1930s exiled in the United States—recuperating the concept of utopia within Marxism, at a point when the meaning of communism was being established in the new Soviet Union, meant recognizing that "hope was a practical as well as a theoretical matter" (Levitas 2010: 98). How the utopian desire was discursively shaped *mattered*, which was a creative act called forth from the "Not-Yet-Conscious" part of the human psyche—which is "expressed *par excellence* in the creative arts and is intensely present in times of change, particularly revolutionary change" (ibid.: 101). As the current age seems beset by revolutions of one kind or another, often apparently built on the new creative foundations of digital media, it is worth addressing this question of hope in terms of the digital transitions being experienced across global media systems. Indeed, new media studies have often been at the forefront of either proclaiming these revolutions or heralding their coming. This can become tiresome, as we are promised yet another radical break with the past and a utopian future soon to open forth.

However, as Helen Kennedy has astutely suggested, the tendency for new media studies to "focus on *what could be*" can be productive. Drawing on Pierre Levy's discussion of why the virtual is not opposed to the real, Kennedy argues that such visions remain a driving force in how and why companies and individuals work in digital media, "and why, despite the proliferation of empirical studies of what is, the rhetoric of what might be survives" (2012: 10). Read in conjunction with my call to understand independent media as invariably hybrid, and often productively compromised, the hope of what independent media might emerge and what forms they may take must be an urgent area of media and cultural studies scholarship. Fostering the conditions—regulatory, economically, aesthetically, sociopolitically and pedagogically—that might promote independent media is an important task for any media or cultural scholar concerned with how and why media matter to the creation of a "better way of being," creating a more open, just and democratic society.

This does not mean we should be blind or overly optimistic. New platforms and voices do not necessarily give rise to greater freedoms or democracy. As the Freedom House report on press freedom makes clear, there has been a paradoxical overall decline in world press freedom in the past decade despite the "increasingly diverse news sources and ever-expanding means of political communication" made available through online services. Indeed, the growth of such digital services has also

> triggered a repressive backlash by authoritarian regimes that have carefully controlled television and other mass media and are now alert to the dangers of unfettered political commentary online.
>
> (Deutsch-Karlekar and Dunham 2013: 1)

These are trends picked up in chapters from James Rodgers and Gholam Khiabany here and which, as the example of Turkey's recent "banning" of Twitter demonstrates, continue to have a profound impact on the shape of media systems around the world and the importance of independence to them.

But it is not just authoritarian regimes that have the power to delimit independence as a form of freedom, diversity and challenge in the media. Independence within the new digital economy is equally fragile. As Thomas Poell and José van Dijck's essay in this volume demonstrates, the promise of more democratic news through social media has so far proved illusory. Rather than creating new freedoms, the architectures of participation (Bennett 2011) of social media platforms actually produce new forms of dependence that insert further commercial constraints and imperatives on independent journalism. As Tim Wu argues, the celebration of new communications technologies as more open, free and democratic is just "a phase of revolutionary novelty and youthful utopianism" that becomes closed down by a "highly centralized and integrated new industry . . . strictly controlled for reasons of commerce" (2010). Thus whilst new entrants onto the tech scene are often celebrated for diversity, innovation and difference, they are also often the subject of co-option through corporate takeovers from the mainstream conglomerates—such as Google's purchase of YouTube, Facebook's incorporation of Instagram and so forth. Where companies resist, such as Snapchat's decision to turn down a reported £3bn offer from Facebook, they often find themselves powerless in the face of corporate power's ability to utilize the very freedoms—as in the malleability and openness of computer code—that underpin digital work cultures: thus Facebook and Twitter quickly built Snapchat-like features into their platforms once their offers had been turned down.

And yet, as all these examples also suggest, hope must live on because the utopian desire of media independence is something that cannot be regulated, purchased or otherwise bullied and co-opted out of existence. The desire to create a better way of living through the media is one that motivates many who work in, regulate, finance and study the media. As a utopian promise it remains a vision to be pursued. We hope that this collection helps those interested in studying and making media pursue that vision and that it stimulates further work and debate on this critical area of inquiry. Media independence, after all, matters.

NOTE

1. The *Gay Girl in Damascus* blog was purportedly written by a twenty-five-year-old half-Syrian, half-American woman living in Damascus during early 2011 at the outset of the Syrian uprising. The views, and interviews, of the blogger were widely circulated by the Western media, especially after guards of President Bashar al-Assad apparently captured the blogger. However, when pictures of the blogger were circulated it was revealed the site was a hoax, written by an American man studying in Scotland.

REFERENCES

Anon (2013) "Press freedom mission to Myanmar calls for media independence," *States News Service*, June 7, 2013.

Bailey, O. G., Cammaerts, B. and Carpentier, N. (2007) *Understanding Alternative Media*. London: Open University Press/McGraw Hill.

Banks, M. (2006) "Moral economy and cultural work," *Sociology* 40, 3: 455–472.

Bauman, Z. (2003) "Utopia with no topos," *History of the Human Sciences* 16, 1: 11–25.

BBC. (2012) "Crackdown 'word of the year' for media freedom in 2011—RSF," *BBC BBC Monitoring World Media*, January 25, 2012.

Bennett, J. (2011) "Architectures of participation: Fame, television and web2.0," in J. Bennett and N. Strange (eds.), *Television as Digital Media*, 332–357. Durham, NC: Duke University Press.

Bennett, T. M., Savage, E., Bortolaia, S., Warde, A., Gayo-Cal, M. and Wright, D. (2009) *Culture, Class, Distinction*. London and New York: Routledge.

Bloch, E. (1986) *The Principles of Hope*, Volume 1. MA: MIT Press.

Carey, J. (ed.), (1999) *The Faber Book of Utopias*. London: Faber and Faber Limited.

Christian, A. J. (2011) "Fandom as industrial response: Producing identity in an independent web series," *Transformative Works and Cultures* 8, 2011. Available http: http://journal.transformativeworks.org/index.php/twc/article/view/250/237.

Couldry, N. (2003) "Beyond the hall of mirrors? Some theoretical reflections on the global contestation of media power," in N. Couldry and J. Curran, (eds.), *Contesting Media Power: Alternative Media in a Networked World*, 39–56. MD: Rowman & Littlefield Publishers.

Couldry, N. and Curran, J. (2003) *Contesting Media Power: Alternative Media in a Networked World*. MD: Rowman & Littlefield Publishers.

de Sola Pool, I. (1983) *Technologies of Freedom*. Cambridge, MA: Belknap Press.

Deutsch-Karlekar, K. and Dunham, J. (2013) *Freedom of the Press Report*. Washington, DC and New York: Freedom House.

Dreher, T. (2010) "Speaking up or being heard? Community media interventions and the politics of listening," *Media, Culture & Society* 32, 1: 85–103.

du Gay, P. and Hall, S. (1996) *Questions of Cultural Identity*. London: Sage Publications.

Dyer, R. (1985) *Only Entertainment*. 1st edition. London: Routledge.

Florida, R. (2003) *The Rise of the Creative Class: And How It's Transforming Work, Leisure, Community & Everyday Life*. New York: Basic Books.

Fuchs, C. (2010) "Alternative media as critical media," *European Journal of Social Theory* 13, 2: 173–192.

Gordon, A. (2005) "Utopia," in T. Bennett, J. Frow and M. Morris (eds.), *New Keywords: A Revised Vocabulary of Culture and Society*, 362–364. London: Wiley Blackwell.

Hartley, J. (2005) "Creative industries," in J. Hartley (ed.), *Creative Industries*, 1–40. Oxford: Blackwell Publishing.

Hesmondhalgh, D. (1997) "Post-punk's attempt to democratise the music industry: The success and failure of rough trade," *Popular Music* 16, 3: 255–274.

Hesmondhalgh, D. (1999) "Indie: The institutional politics and aesthetics of a popular music genre," *Cultural Studies* 13, 1: 34–61.

Hesmondhalgh, D. (2006) "Bourdieu, the media and cultural production," *Media, Culture & Society* 28, 2: 211–231.

Hesmondhalgh, D. and Baker, S. (2011) *Creative Labour: Media Work in Three Cultural Industries*. London: Routledge.

IMC (no date) "FAQ," *Indymedia Collective*, Available http: http://docs.indymedia.org/view/Global/FrequentlyAskedQuestions.

Johnson, R. (2005) "Alternative," in T. Bennett, J. Frow and M. Morris (eds.), *New Keywords: A Revised Vocabulary of Culture and Society*, 3–5. London: Wiley Blackwell.

Kasoma, F. P. (1995) "The role of the independent media in Africa's change to democracy," *Media, Culture & Society* 17, 4: 537–555.

Kennedy, H. (2012) *Net Work: Ethics and Values in Web Design*. Basingstoke: Palgrave MacMillan.

King, G. (2013) "Thriving or in permanent crisis? Discourses on the state of indie cinema," in G. King, C. Molloy and Y. Tzioumakis,. (eds.), *American Independent Cinema: Indie, Indiewood and Beyond*, 41–52. London: Routledge.

King, G. (2014) *Indie 2.0: Change and Continuity in Contemporary Indie Film*. London: I. B. Tauris.

Kreiss, D. (2012) *Taking our Country Back: The Crafting of Networked Politics from Howard Dean to Barack Obama*. London and New York: Oxford University Press.

Leadbetter, C and Oakley, K. (1999) *The Independents: Britain's New Cultural Entrepreneur*. London: Demos.

Lee, C. (2003) "Liberalization without full democracy: Guerrilla media and political movements in Taiwan," in N. Couldry and J. Curran (eds.), *Contesting Media Power: Alternative Media in a Networked World*, 163–176. MD: Rowman & Littlefield Publishers.

Lee, D. (2012) "The ethics of insecurity: Risk, individualization and value in British independent television production," *Television & New Media* 13, 6: 480–497.

Levitas, R. (2000) "Community, utopia and new Labour," *Local Economy* 15, 3: 188–197.

Levitas, R. (2003) "The elusive idea of utopia," *History of the Human Sciences* 16, 1: 1–10.

Levitas, R. (2010) *The Concept of Utopia*. London: Peter Lang Press.

Milioni, D. L. (2009) "Probing the online counterpublic sphere: The Case of Indymedia Athens," *Media, Culture & Society* 31, 3: 409–431.

McRobbie, A. (2002) "Clubs to companies: Notes on the decline of political culture in speeded up creative worlds," *Cultural Studies* 16, 4: 516–531.

Newman, M. (2009) "Indie culture: In pursuit of the authentic, autonomous alternative," *Cinema Journal* 48, 3: 16–34.

Petridis, A. (2014) "Britpop and Kurt Cobain 20 years on: Don't look back in anger," *The Guardian* April 3, 2014. Available http: www.theguardian.com/music/2014/apr/03/britpop-kurt-cobain-20-years-nirvana.

Platon, S. and Deuze, M. (2003) "Indymedia journalism: A radical way of making, selecting and sharing news?," *Journalism* 4, 3: 336–355.

Rose, N. (1999) *Powers of Freedom: Reframing Political Thought*. Cambridge: Cambridge University Press.

Ross, A. (2004). *No Collar: The Humane Workplace and Its Hidden Costs*. Philadelphia, PA: Temple University Press.

Schudson, M. (2002) "The news media as political institutions," *Annual Review of Political Science* 5, June: 249–269.

Skeggs, B. (2004) *Class, Self, Culture*. London and New York: Routledge.

Staiger, J. (2013). "Independent of what? Sorting out differences from Hollywood," in G. King, C. Molloy and Y. Tzioumakis (eds.), *American Independent Cinema: Indie, Indiewood and Beyond*, 15–27. London: Routledge.

Waits, J. C. (2007) "Does 'indie' mean independence? Freedom and restraint in a late 1990s US college radio community," *The Radio Journal—International Studies in Broadcast and Audio Media* 5, 2/3: 83–96.

Wu, T. (2010) *The Master Switch: The Rise and Fall of Information Empires*. New York: Alfred A. Knopf.

Section I
Indies, Independents and Independence

1   Guarding the Guardians
The Leveson Inquiry and the Future of Independent Journalism

Stephen Jukes and Stuart Allan

There have been too many times when, chasing the story, parts of the press have acted as if its own code, which it wrote, simply did not exist. This has caused real hardship and, on occasion, wreaked havoc with the lives of innocent people. . . .

—*Introduction to the Leveson Inquiry into the Culture, Practices and Ethics of the Press*

A judicial farce and a dark day for freedom.

—*Daily Mail*

INTRODUCTION: DRINKING IN THE LAST CHANCE SALOON

With the flick of a pen on a royal charter, Queen Elizabeth II signed away 300 years of British press freedom. Or so, at least, maintained a good number of the nation's newspapers the day after it happened in October 2013. The truth is probably somewhat less black and white but one thing is certain: the saga of press regulation will, to cite a newspaper cliché, run and run.

In Britain, impassioned appeals to freedom of the press have resounded throughout the centuries, but in recent years journalists have by common consent been "drinking in the last chance saloon."[1] Revelations in 2011 that reporters on the tabloid Sunday newspaper *News of the World* had hacked into the mobile phone of murdered schoolgirl Milly Dowler sparked public revulsion and prompted Prime Minister David Cameron to set up a judicial public inquiry into the "Culture, Practices and Ethics of the Press" chaired by Lord Justice Leveson. It was the seventh time in seventy years that a British government had launched a commission to investigate newspapers, but this time it was to be different. While previous inquiries were successfully fended off by newspaper owners seeking to defend their freedoms, the findings of the Leveson Inquiry, supported by a highly organized campaign calling for greater protection for the "victims" of press intrusion,[2] have led to the specter of regulation.

It is a telling feature of public life in most Western countries that newspapers are accorded a central role to uphold democratic governance—a concept widely held to be consistent with notions of an independent fourth estate—and yet, at the same time, no public interest obligations tend to be imposed upon them. The Leveson Inquiry's highly critical findings, prompting the signing of a royal charter to create a watchdog to oversee a new regulator, come at a time when the British press is mired in what has been described as the most serious crisis for journalism in modern times (Hewlett 2011: 23). The newspapers' freedom of expression and individuals' right to privacy have always been pitted against each other, with great care taken by parliamentarians and the courts alike not to tip the balance decisively in one direction. But the Leveson Inquiry, and the subsequent (at times sensational) phone-hacking trial of *News of the World* journalists, saw simmering tensions come to a boil. *The Times* dismissed the royal charter as a "medieval instrument." *The Sun* (another newspaper in the Rupert Murdoch stable) labeled the inquiry "discredited," contending that the process had "more in common with tyranny than a nation that founded parliamentary government." The *Daily Mirror* lamented "the death warrant for press freedom." In contrast the Hacked Off campaigners—who, fronted by Hugh Grant, called for tighter regulation—termed the press culture "cowardly, bullying and shocking."[3]

This chapter's discussion begins by tracing the emergence and eventual rhetorical purchase of the fourth estate ideal in order to place current debates over press independence in historical context. Against this backdrop, we proceed to discuss the key findings of the Leveson Inquiry, on the face of it a pivotal moment that could redefine the guiding principles of journalistic integrity in the United Kingdom. The ensuing discussion delves beneath the surface of the rhetoric of journalistic independence to examine just how newspapers came to adopt practices that have led them to be reviled by large sections of the British population. The list is long: how technological change has combined with economics to bring journalistic values into conflict with commercial pressures; how new business models have left journalists doing little more than repurposing "content" into multimedia formats under intense time pressure; how opportunities to produce original, investigative news holding authority to account are undermined as the boundaries between news and entertainment blur; and critically, how efforts to bolster sagging circulations have tempted some newspapers to cross the fine line between the public's right to know and an individual's right to privacy, even if it means breaking the law. In offering an evaluation of these findings, this chapter explores the ethical issues at stake for the regulation of a free and independent press in the light of calls to rethink journalism's public interest responsibilities. We will consider several of the perceived advantages as well as the possible dangers of implementing the Leveson Inquiry recommendations, paying particular attention to how the implications for competing ideals about newspaper independence were framed in rhetorical terms. In so doing, our aim is to question whether the soul searching unleashed by the hacking scandal will lead to lasting, progressive change or whether the independence long associated with the fourth estate role has effectively come to an end.

THE PRESS AS THE FOURTH ESTATE

Efforts to trace the history of journalism's investment in its perceived status as a fourth estate continue to attract lively debate, not least to the extent they invite differing perspectives about why such a normative ideal mattered in the first place. At the outset, it is useful to provide a brief history with a view to identifying tensions of continuing relevance to current discourses of newspaper independence in the United Kingdom.[4]

When seeking to unravel the rhetorical complexities of normative ideals, words matter. The term "fourth estate" has disputed origins, but many locate it in the work of Scottish philosopher Thomas Carlyle and his lecture "The Hero as Man of Letters: Johnson, Rousseau, Burns," published on May 19, 1840. Declaring the art of writing "the most miraculous of all things man has devised," Carlyle argued it had transformed "all modes of important work." Positioning printing as a "simple, inevitable and comparatively insignificant corollary" (1840: 160), Carlyle turned to consider the attendant implications for "the Government of men" in this regard. In impassioned prose, he contended that the status of Parliament as the preeminent place where the affairs of the nation may be deliberated and decided was proving increasingly open to question. "But does not, though the name Parliament subsists, the parliamentary debate go on now, everywhere and at all times, in a far more comprehensive way, *out* of Parliament altogether?" he asked (ibid.: 164). Just as "the writers of Newspapers, Pamphlets, Poems, Books" were decisively altering the nation's educational and religious institutions, it seemed apparent to him that they were similarly recasting the "great thing" of Parliament itself.

In what has since become the most noteworthy passage of the lecture, Carlyle invoked Edmund Burke's conception of Parliament's multiple estates, evidently highlighted by the Anglo-Irish statesman in a parliamentary debate concerned with press reporting of the House of Commons in 1787. In addition to the idea of "Three Estates in Parliament"—namely, it is presumed, the Lords Spiritual (bishops of the Church of England serving in the House of Lords), the Lords Temporal (secular members of the House of Lords) and the Commons—Burke is also credited by Carlyle with discerning a fourth: "in the Reporters' Gallery yonder, there sat a *Fourth Estate* more important far than they all" (ibid.: 164). The significance of such a realm, Carlyle proceeded to add, was of growing resonance decades later:

> It is not a figure of speech, or a witty saying; it is a literal fact—very momentous to us in these times. Literature is our Parliament too.

Printing, which comes necessarily out of Writing, I say often, is equivalent to Democracy: invent Writing, Democracy is inevitable. Writing brings Printing; brings universal every-day extempore Printing, as we see at present. Whoever can speak, speaking now to the whole nation, becomes a power, a branch of government, with inalienable weight in law-making, in all acts of authority.

(ibid.: 164)

Those actively participating in the realm of the fourth estate engendered by writing ("Those poor bits of rag-paper with black ink on them—from the Daily Newspaper to the sacred Hebrew book") were of supreme importance, in Carlyle's estimation. Far from performing an ancillary role, the Man of Letters was at the heart of democratic governance.

It matters not what rank he has, what revenues or garnitures: the requisite thing is, that he have a tongue which others will listen to; this and nothing more is requisite. The nation is governed by all that has tongue in the nation: Democracy is virtually *there*.

(ibid.)

The very nobility of the published thoughts expressed by the Man of Letters, it followed, would ensure the press was afforded its due recognition "with a sort of sentimental triumph and wonderment" for it is "to such a degree superseding the Pulpit, the Senate, the Senatus Academicus and much else."

Over the years, the conception of the fourth estate attributed to Carlyle's response to Burke has claimed a firm footing, although alternative histories have challenged its evidential basis. Some credit English essayist William Hazlitt for coining the term in an article about pamphleteer William Cobbett, published in "Table Talk" in 1821, whilst others privilege Thomas Macaulay's review of Henry Hallam's *Constitutional History of England*, which appeared in *The Edinburgh Review* in 1828. "The gallery in which the reporters sit has become a fourth estate of the realm," he observed. "The publication of the debates, a practice which seemed to the most liberal statesman of the old school full of danger to the great safeguards of public liberty," he continued, "is now regarded by many persons as a safeguard, tantamount, and more than tantamount, to all the rest together" (Macaulay 1828: 165). In the next sentence he turns to consider Burke's views on parliamentary reform, inviting speculation amongst some historians that perhaps Carlyle made an error—"a slip of the pen"—by awarding credit to Burke after reading Macaulay.

Contrary views about its precise origins notwithstanding, by the mid-nineteenth century the term was familiar enough in public debate to be employed in a book title, namely F. Knight Hunt's (1850) two-volume *The Fourth Estate: Contributions towards a history of newspapers, and the liberty of the press.* Its opening paragraph, which provides a flavor of its triumphant tenor, declared:

> ALL men, now-a-days, who read at all, read Newspapers. . . . What wonder, then, that Newspapers have grown upon us until they have become a positive necessity of civilized existence—a portion, indeed, of modern civilization.
>
> (Hunt 1850: 1)

This alignment of the newspaper with civilization—such that it "wields the power of a Fourth Estate" (ibid.: 8)—spoke to the perceived "value and fidelity" of the various services it offered members of the public, albeit vis-à-vis a sphere largely restricted to propertied, educated white males of the time (see also Fraser 1990; Habermas 1989). It is, however, a close reading of Hunt's book published five years later in the *Edinburgh Review* that affords a more nuanced evaluation of the fourth estate as a concept in its own right. The author—believed to be the *Review*'s editor, Henry Reeve (1855), formerly of *The Times*—found in Hunt's treatment a basis to elaborate his standpoint. "The Fourth Estate," he surmised, despite being "[o]f far more modern date than the other estates of the realm," had "overshadowed and surpassed them all" (1855: 470). More than the preeminent supplier of information on public topics, the newspaper press furnished interpretations—"notions and opinions"—regarding its relative merits: "It inquires, reflects, decides for us," effectively performing "all the thinking of the nation" (ibid.: 477).

A further, vital function of the daily press, Reeve continued, was "the opening it affords for the exposition of individual grievances and wrongs." To clarify, he compared the newspapers to the inaccessibility of the "courts of justice, which are tedious and costly; thousands can neither 'wait the law's delay' nor resist 'the oppressor's wrong,'" declaring that the press functioned as a "tribunal which is always open, which is open gratuitously, which is open to every complainant" (ibid.: 480). In the newspaper, it followed, every member of the public possessed a protector of their interests, a "guardian" that "no power can silence, no money can corrupt, and no flattery can lull to sleep" (ibid.: 480). In so doing, it assumed a representative role, one envisaged by Reeves as being situated between the government and "the People." "It supplies the latter with a safe channel for the expression of those feelings which might else find a vent in overt acts of discontent and insubordination," he maintained. At the same time, "it keeps the former cognisant of popular sentiments and passions which it is most essential it should understand and be early made acquainted with" (ibid.: 480–481). The value of the fourth estate as a "safety valve" is thus underscored, not least its capacity to moderate "discontent by allowing it to vent, in expending the energies and exposing the weaknesses and fallacies of demagogues, and in thus preserving the peace and order of society through the joint securities of freedom and of justice" (ibid.: 481). In contrast with critics insisting the fourth estate amounted to little more than an instrument advanced by a governing class to articulate its interests, Reeves was convinced that journalism was the most effective means to expose social injustices in the name of the publics it represented.

Viewed from the vantage point of today, these laudable observations about the virtues of the fourth estate risk seeming anachronistic, if not outright disingenuous in the eyes of critics. Today, the ideal of the fourth estate often appears to serve as a form of shorthand to register the conviction that press freedom is best measured by newspapers' independence from parliamentary influence. Advocates are steadfast in their belief that newspapers, even in the age of the Internet, remain uniquely charged with a noble mission of providing members of the public with a diverse marketplace of ideas to both inform and sustain their sense of the world around them. The performance of this democratic imperative, it follows, must be safeguarded from undue influence or impediments associated with power and privilege. In what amounts to a "system of checks and balances," newspapers underwrite a consensual process of surveillance—watchdogs nipping at the heels of the elite—in order to ensure political interests are held responsive to the shifting dictates of public opinion. Politics, in this sense, privileges for scrutiny partisan disputes between political parties, however, recurrently leaving the class politics of ruling elites' control over the press to one side.

In the next section, we shall begin to test the precepts that have given shape to these normative tenets of the fourth estate by focusing on the UK press's recent behavior through the spotlight cast by Leveson. Of particular interest will be the issue of newspaper independence, recognizing from the outset that much depends on how it is defined—and who is doing the defining—in relation to the ethical questions at the heart of the Inquiry.

YET ANOTHER ROUND AT THE LAST CHANCE SALOON?

It wasn't by chance that the press had been drinking for more than two decades in the last chance saloon. Alongside the uncovering of genuine public scandals, as for example the *Daily Telegraph*'s revelations in 2009 about the chronic abuse of parliamentary expenses, there have been numerous cases of overt press intrusion. Princess Diana was widely seen as being hounded by the tabloid press—particularly paparazzi—during and after the break-up of her marriage to Prince Charles until her death in 1997. In 2008, the *News of the World*, which was later to be closed by owner Rupert Murdoch because of the hacking revelations, ran a story about the head of Formula 1, Max Mosley, that was headlined: "F1 Boss has Sick Nazi Orgy with Five Hookers." In subsequent issues the newspaper accused Mosley of acting out Nazi death camp fantasies. Mosley duly sued the parent company,

News Group Newspapers, for gross invasion of privacy and won £60,000 in damages, the highest in recent newspaper history. When it came to the Leveson Inquiry, Mosley was at pains to point out in his testimony that ordinary members of the public had no such remedy because only one percent of the population could probably afford to take a newspaper to court over defamation or breach of privacy.

It is not difficult to see why titles at the "popular," "tabloid" end of the press spectrum spiraled out of control. It is part cultural, part economic. There has been a rich tradition of "naming and shaming" broadly at odds with the more circumspect "elite" culture of "serious," "quality" journalism made apparent by diverse voices addressing the Leveson Inquiry. To name and shame has long been associated with the *Daily Mail* but it often underlies much of what fills the columns of the *Sun*, the *Express* and to an extent the *Daily Telegraph* (Petley 2013: xiv). Paul Dacre, editor in chief of the *Daily Mail*, firmly believes the practice is a "vital element in defending the parameters of what are considered acceptable standards of social behaviour." In a speech to the Society of Editors in 2008, Dacre maintained that the press had the "freedom to identify those who have offended public standards of decency—the very standards its readers believe in—and hold the transgressors up to public condemnation" (Dacre 2008). The Max Mosley story alleging linkages between the FI chief to prostitutes and Nazis was typical of the genre. Ultimately such naming and shaming sells newspapers, as do "kiss-and-tell" stories, ever more important in the digital era when traditional business models based on advertising revenue have all but collapsed. Increasingly tabloids have used celebrity gossip, elaborate stings, checkbook journalism and scandal to prop up sales and, as evidenced by the success of the MailOnline, capture the online market and its advertising potential.[5]

New depths, however, were plumbed with the revelations in 2011 by the *Guardian* newspaper that the phone of murdered schoolgirl Milly Dowler had been hacked by *News of the World* reporters. Outraged public opinion, as noted earlier, prompted Prime Minister Cameron to respond by setting up the Leveson Inquiry to assess how best to fix a system of press self-regulation widely perceived to malfunction. According to the Inquiry's September 14, 2011 news release, its remit was to investigate:

> the culture, practices and ethics of the press, including contacts between the press and politicians and the press and the police; it is to consider the extent to which the current regulatory regime has failed and whether there has been a failure to act upon any previous warnings about media misconduct.
>
> (2012b: 1)

The Inquiry went on until June 2012, with 337 witnesses called and about 300 other statements made. The balance between the public's right to know and the public's right to privacy was at the heart of the hearings, a conflict that had in preceding years gained prominence because of the inherent clash of rights in Articles 8 and 10 of the European Convention on Human Rights.[6] The press has long struggled to define both public interest and privacy, often preferring to avoid hard and fast rules to leave the definition at best vague. The Editors' Code of Practice (2012) built into the current self-regulatory regime of the Press Complaints Council (PCC) states that the public interest includes, but is not confined to:

1. Detecting or exposing crime or serious impropriety;
2. Protecting public health and safety;
3. Preventing the public from being misled by an action or statement of an individual or organization.

It adds that there is a public interest in freedom of expression itself. The code on privacy (ibid.) is slightly less clear:

1. Everyone is entitled to respect for his or her private and family life, home, health and correspondence, including digital communications;
2. Editors will be expected to justify intrusions into any individual's private life without consent. Account will be taken of the complainant's own public disclosures of information.

By way of comparison, in broadcasting the British Broadcasting Corporation (BBC) is subject to a different regulatory regime through the government-approved media regulator Ofcom. Here the BBC tries to draw a balance between the conflicting rights in its editorial guidelines, stating:

> When using the public interest to justify an intrusion, consideration should be given to proportionality; the greater the intrusion, the greater the public interest required to justify it.
>
> (2014: Section 7)

Given the delicate balancing act, it was hardly surprising that when Lord Justice Leveson opened the hearing he focused on this very issue. Drawing on language of the fourth estate, he stated:

> The Inquiry must balance the desire for a robustly free press with the rights of the individual, while, at the same time, ensuring the critical relationships between the press, parliament, the Government and the police are maintained. The press provides an essential check on all aspects of public life. That is why any failure within the media affects all of us. At the heart of this Inquiry, therefore, may be one simple question: who guards the guardians?
>
> (2012c: 1–2)

The subsequent evidence was at times little less than spectacu\
terness against the press poured out. That bitterness was also di\
the PCC, a voluntary body controlled by newspapers and magazine\
in 1991 as the successor to the Press Council. Both bodies had bee\
as weak, ineffectual and failing to investigate properly the wrongdoir of
the press. Actor Hugh Grant, called before the inquiry, said the license the
tabloid press had used to expropriate the right to privacy was "a scandal
that weak governments have allowed to continue for too long." In harrow-
ing testimony, Milly Dowler's mother told the inquiry that when some of
her daughter's voicemails were deleted, it had given her false hope she was
still alive. The parents of three-year-old Madeleine McCann, who had gone
missing in Portugal in 2007, were also witnesses, revealing how the *Daily
Express* had, in the earlier words of media commentator Roy Greenslade
(2008), waged a "sustained campaign of vitriol" against them. As the proceedings drew to a close and speculation grew over the recommendations to
follow, it was clear that public opinion was hardening still further, increasing pressure on politicians to clamp down. An October 2012 YouGov poll
for the Hacked Off campaign found that 78 percent of respondents thought
newspapers should be regulated by an independent body established by law
to deal with complaints and decide on sanctions. Even a YouGov poll for the
Sun newspaper a few weeks later found 50 percent of respondents thought
that current press rules needed tightening up. In a ComRes poll on the day
of the Leveson Report publication, November 29, 2012, some 66 percent of
respondents said they had no trust in British newspapers.

The final 2,000-page report found that there was a need for an improved
self-regulation body (effectively a successor to the PCC) and that this, in
turn, should be overseen by a "recognition body." In making this suggestion, Lord Justice Leveson upheld persistent complaints that the PCC had
been ineffectual and lacked independence, essentially being in the pocket of
the newspapers. Lord Justice Leveson's comments could hardly have been
more scathing:

> I unhesitatingly agree with the Prime Minister, the Deputy Prime Min-
> ister and the Leader of the Opposition who all believe that the PCC
> has failed and that a new body is required. Mr Cameron described it
> as "*ineffective and lacking in rigour*" whilst Mr Miliband called it a
> "*toothless poodle.*"
>
> (2012a: Executive Summary, 14)

As John Lloyd, the director of journalism at the Reuters Institute for
the Study of Journalism at Oxford University, remarked shortly thereafter
(2013), the findings of the inquiry left Lord Justice Leveson with an unenvi-
able task: that of Canute telling the tide to stop.

The report recommended that the proposed new regulatory body to suc-
ceed the PCC would need to be independent from external influence—both

corporate and governmental—in respect of appointments and funding, and that it should have an arbitration and complaints handling mechanism for members of the public. Such a body should develop a new code of practice and issue guidance on what might be in the public interest and how to interpret it. Crucially, and on this single point most of the post-Leveson argument has focused, it was "essential that there should be legislation to underpin . . . and facilitate its recognition in legal processes" (2012a). While recognizing that this was the most controversial part of his recommendations, Lord Justice Leveson nonetheless argued that it could not be fairly characterized as statutory regulation of the press. He was at pains to point out that the majority of the press did good work but suggested that there were a significant number of instances where press reports failed to meet the acceptable standards of "integrity and propriety," reflecting the culture of some of the main titles. Journalist Joan Smith, who had suffered at the hands of the tabloid press herself, had made this point in her testimony to the Inquiry, identifying a gap between two cultures—one of the "serious press," which was responsible, evidence-based and concerned with issues facing society and another, a tabloid culture "so remorseless, (whose) appetite is so unable to be filled, that the people involved have lost any sense that they're dealing with human beings" (2012d: 39).

Almost at once, the report became a political football. Labour Party opposition leader Ed Miliband threw himself behind the Leveson recommendations, as did, albeit perhaps in more guarded terms, Deputy Prime Minister Nick Clegg, leader of the governing coalition Liberal Democrat party. "Changing the law," he said, "is the only way to give us all the assurance that the new regulator is not just independent for a few months or years but is independent for good" (Hansard 2012). Of the main three political parties, only Conservative Prime Minister David Cameron expressed his "concerns and misgivings" about passing new legislation to underpin the new regulator:

> The issue of principle is that, for the first time, we would have crossed the Rubicon of writing elements of press regulation into the law of the land. We should be wary of any legislation that has the potential to infringe free speech and a free press. In this House (of Commons), which has been a bulwark of democracy for centuries, we should think very, very carefully before crossing that line.
>
> (ibid.)

Press reaction saw sweeping condemnation from most of the "popular" newspapers, with the "serious" titles being more nuanced in their critique—although here too they came down against statutory underpinning of the regulator by a recognition body. Meanwhile the Hacked Off campaign welcomed the recommendations as "reasonable and proportionate." What followed was months of haggling, back room deals and brinkmanship, which led finally on October 30 2013 to the signing of a royal charter to establish an oversight or recognition body to ensure independent regulation. The decision to opt for a charter was a political compromise to bring the three major political parties together—a charter can, crucially, be introduced without statute. To try to blunt the sharper excesses of press criticism, it was decided that the charter could only be changed by a majority of two-thirds of both houses of Parliament, the Houses of Commons and Lords. But this fell far short of newspaper demands. Many vowed to challenge the charter in the courts and to ignore the new system, pressing on instead with establishing their own new regulator known as Ipso—the Independent Press Standards Organisation. By May 2014, many major national and regional newspaper publishers, barring the *Financial Times*, had signed up to IPSO (it remained to be seen whether *The Guardian* and *Independent* newspapers would join). The new body in turn moved relatively quickly to appoint its first chair, Court of Appeal judge Alan Moses. The result looked likely to be a classic stand-off between the newspapers and the government.

IMPLEMENTING LEVESON

Depending on which of the highly polarized views is adopted (that of the newspapers or Hacked Off), the royal charter either represents the end of 300 years of press independence and a fatal blow to the fourth estate, or it constitutes the mechanism required to uphold that ideal and make it work in practice. In this section, we will examine the case for adopting the Leveson proposals, and thereby arguments in favor of imposing tighter regulation with a statutory underpinning to enshrine and protect newspaper independence.

Certainly, taken at face value, the Leveson Report would appear to proclaim loud and clear the primacy of independence and, as observed earlier, Lord Justice Leveson himself did not interpret his recommendations as amounting to statutory regulation of press freedom (the precise meaning of the word "statutory" proving to be hotly contested in the ensuing debate). The report declares near the start of the first of its four volumes that "the importance of a free press to democracy is surely incontrovertible," although it concedes that the ostensibly obvious reasons why this is so warrant close consideration. In our reading, the report's authors appear to recognize that in order to support a call for tighter regulation, it would need to be shown that the behavior of the press within the current system of self-regulation does not support its ability to perform its democratic role—or, in other words, live up to the ideal of the fourth estate.

These tensions are discernible from the outset, namely where the Leveson Report calls on a historical conception of the newspaper press as the fourth estate to provide an initial framing of the principles at stake. An excerpt from a speech made by Winston Churchill in 1949 is cited to illustrate the quality of this freedom:

> A free press is the unsleeping guardian of every other right that free men prize; it is the most dangerous foe of tyranny. . . . Under dictatorship the press is bound to languish . . . But where free institutions are indigenous to the soil and men have the habit of liberty, the press will continue to be the Fourth Estate, the vigilant guardian of the rights of the ordinary citizen.
>
> (Leveson 2012a: Volume 1, 56)

Much of the ensuing discussion in the report's second chapter, "The Freedom of the Press and Democracy," provides a rationale for the fundamental nature of press freedom as it has evolved in the United Kingdom over recent centuries. Its significance was recurrently highlighted during the Inquiry's proceedings in two forms: "first, as a negative or 'default' argument (any interference with any sort of freedom must always be justified in a liberal democracy) and, second, as a positive argument (the press must be free to fulfil its important role)" (ibid.: 57). In striving to secure a basis to compare and contrast these contrary arguments, the value of this historical context—described as an "essential background"—quickly became apparent, not least in the "strength of feeling demonstrated by so many journalist witnesses" (ibid.: 58).

Briefly sketching several contours of press freedom's development from the advent of the printing press in 1476 onward, the report devotes particular attention to the dangers of suppression under state control, including with regard to licensing systems, criminal and seditious libel, "taxes on knowledge," bribes and official subsidies, amongst other measures, intended to undermine those campaigning to secure further independence for the press. By the early twentieth century, the growing consolidation of regional and national newspapers by powerful corporations proved to be a new form of limitation on this independence, the report maintains, such that by the interwar period these proprietors—"the press barons of the day"—exercised dominance over what was published. Next the focus shifts to consider government censorship during the Second World War, including the "now infamous" Defense of the Realm Regulations, which were used to close down radical newspapers. Further concerns regarding the persistent decline in press diversity are highlighted in relation to the three postwar Royal Commissions on the Press (1947–1949, 1961–1962, 1974–1977), as well as their inability to effect meaningful protections for journalists and editors from proprietorial control. The 1990 *Calcutt Report*'s recommendation to establish the Press Complaints Commission is noted in passing before the report pauses to observe that "great strides were achieved in securing legal protection for a free press" vis-à-vis the European Court of Human Rights, including its recognition of the duty of the press to act as an independent, public watchdog (2012a: Volume 1, 60).

This "watchdog" phrase reappears several pages later, when the report's authors underscore the vital roles to be undertaken by a free press committed to serving the interests of democracy, namely "enabling public deliberation" and through its "public watch-dog role, acting as a check on political and other holders of power." The press is capable of performing this latter responsibility, the report surmises, "because of its hard-won position as a powerful institution independent of the state, a position which earned it the nickname or sobriquet of the Fourth Estate amongst nineteenth century writers" (ibid.: 65). A brief section in Volume 2 elaborates upon this ideal:

> Thus, the very existence of a free press is invaluable in the sense that societies without such a press are invariably totalitarian regimes, which do not and cannot, countenance the type of scrutiny, which only an untrammelled Fourth Estate is capable of applying. Second, as many Core Participants have pointed out, a free press is the lifeblood of a mature democracy: it is an invaluable medium for the representatives of the people to get their message across, and an equally invaluable means both of examining the political message and holding the messengers to account.
>
> (2012a: Volume 2, 251)

The Leveson Report thus uses the ideal of the fourth estate as a normative yardstick, effectively equipping the Inquiry with a means to measure the relative performance of the newspapers under scrutiny.

Many of those who testified pushed the point even further, convinced that the behavior of newspapers had placed this ideal at significant risk. Typical of such voices was Mark Lewis, the lawyer for Milly Dowler's family, who stated:

> The intrusion in to the private lives and grief of others *distracts from the proper function of the Fourth Estate to keep the Third Estate in check*. Control by the press extends from not only what is printed to what is not printed in order to obtain commercial advantage, is the most sinister abuse of democracy. State control is wrong whether it is by this country or whether it is by a more powerful empire, the Murdoch empire.
>
> (cited in MailOnline September 19, 2011, emphasis added)

Lord Justice Leveson sought to be clear in his own argument that a statutory underpinning of self-regulation through a recognition body—as now in place through the royal charter—does not constitute statutory regulation of the press. In his summary, he stresses that no governmental powers to prevent newspapers from publishing material would be justified. On the contrary, he argues, these measures would "enshrine, for the first time, a legal duty on the Government to protect the freedom of the press." He added:

> What is proposed here is independent regulation of the press organised by the press, with a statutory verification process to ensure that the required levels of independence and effectiveness are met by the system in order for publishers to take advantage of the benefits arising as a result of membership.
>
> (Leveson 2012a: Executive summary, 17)

What counts as "statutory" thus assumes a very narrow definition, one intended to preserve newspaper independence in keeping with historical reasoning while, at the same time, striving to avoid openly antagonizing newspaper proprietors and their editors.

Critics were not convinced. As will be examined in the next section, certain voices in the press were skeptical—to put it mildly—about the merits of this case, pointing to what they considered to be seriously adverse consequences. Still, the argument that such a new system will be required to rein in the excesses of the press—and in so doing allow the fourth estate ideal to flourish—has won many supporters. In November 2013, more than 100 prominent figures from literature, the arts, science, academia, human rights and the law signed a declaration urging newspaper and magazine publishers to embrace the royal charter system. Crucially, they did not see it at odds with freedom of the press, stating:

> We . . . believe that editors and journalists will rise in public esteem when they accept a form of self-regulation that is independently audited on the lines recommended by Lord Justice Leveson and laid down in the Royal Charter of 30 October 2013. It is our view that this charter safeguards the press from political interference while also giving vital protection to the vulnerable. That is why we support it and that is why we urge newspaper publishers to embrace it.
>
> (Greenslade 2013a)

Among the 100 was *Guardian* journalist Nick Davies, whose reporting of the phone-hacking scandal pushed the issue into the public spotlight. Earlier, he had argued that criticism of the new system was no more than "froth on the lips of propagandists" (Davies 2012). He spoke of the nightmares that had *not* come true but added Leveson *was* a nightmare for the old guard of Fleet Street because for them "to lose control of the regulator is to lose their licence to do exactly as they please" (ibid.). He has won an unlikely ally in the shape of former *Sun* editor David Yelland. Speaking to mark the first anniversary of the publication of the Leveson Report, he said:

The party line is that Leveson and the royal charter that followed represent state regulation of the media. It is not true . . . what we witnessed, post-Leveson, was pure hysteria. The press simply does not understand that it became the very thing it is there to attack: a vested interest. It did not listen but instead censored the public debate about itself. And it tried to bully anyone who had the temerity to challenge the party line.

(Yelland 2013)

Victims and celebrities led by Hacked Off, disenchanted former editors such as Yelland and politicians who have sensed the public outrage have thus united to support the royal charter. A responsible press, they maintain, should not fear an independent referee. While most believe the Leveson Report requires further adjustment here and there (tinkering for some, a serious rewrite for others), it is for them the best chance to equip the press with the means of actually living up to the fourth estate ideal it so readily espouses.

CHALLENGING LEVESON

According to many critics, the Leveson Report and subsequent royal charter have already had a "chilling effect" on the press, not least because of its potential—to quote the *Financial Times*—to introduce "press law by the back door." Others, such as former BBC and ITV chairman Lord Grade, have argued that a line has already been crossed. Speaking at the 2013 Society of Editors conference just days after the royal charter had been sealed, Lord Grade said:

The current Royal Charter agreed by the three main parties with such approving noises from Hacked Off is a dangerous step too far. It enshrines the principle that Parliament has the right—however remotely—to intervene in the regulation of the press. And that, to me, is a red line. My key objection is that it gives Parliament not just a voice but a say in the regulation of the press. Parliament gets a say by voting. Imagine if a vote on press regulation had been going through Parliament at the time the Telegraph was exposing the scandal of MPs expenses?

He was certainly not alone in his criticism. In fact, an analysis by the Media Standards Trust (2013) showed that twenty-three out of the twenty-eight leader articles published in the last 100 days before the publication of the Leveson Report contained only negative statements about the inquiry. So much for balanced journalism when only three of the leaders contained both positive and negative statements (two offered no evaluation, while none contained purely positive statements). Since then, opponents have labeled the recognition body to be set up by the charter a sideshow and vowed to have nothing to do with it. But that may not be so simple.

The main fear expressed by the newspapers centers on the possible consequences, should they refuse to participate with the recognition body. Publishers outside its purview could face, at least in principle, exemplary damages in libel and privacy cases they lose, and be saddled with heavy financial penalties in libel actions *even when they win*. This provision (not spelt out in the charter itself, being the result of associated legislation, namely the 2013 Crime and Courts Bill), they argue, makes a mockery of statements by the likes of Deputy Prime Minister Nick Clegg that the new system is entirely voluntary. On the one hand, the Leveson system holds out the "carrot" of financial incentives for publishers who sign up and a measure of protection against excessive legal costs in libel actions; on the other hand, there is a clear financial penalty or "stick" for those who refuse to play by the new rules. As Lord Grade (2013) told the Society of Editors, there is "potentially a very large and very expensive stick available to beat up the press who don't like the look of the carrot."

A second major fear focuses on the charter's provision for three yearly cyclical reviews and, most significantly, "ad hoc reviews" of the self-regulator by the recognition body. Clause 8 of the second schedule of the Royal Charter on Self-Regulation of the Press (2013) states that such reviews may be carried out in two circumstances, namely if it appears that:

a) There are exceptional circumstances that make it necessary so to do, having regard, in particular, to whether there have been serious breaches of the recognition criteria;
b) There is a significant public interest in a review of the Regulator's recognition being undertaken.

As media commentator Steve Hewlett has pointed out (2013), the argument has come full circle. Who defines what the public interest is and under what criteria? In the eyes of critics, this could easily become regulation at one remove by the recognition body.

A third concern centers on the two-thirds parliamentary majorities required to change the charter. While this is theoretically designed to prevent politicians meddling with the system, skeptics say the one thing politicians can agree on is a shared desire to manage the press to advantage. Politicians' concerns have not only highlighted legitimate exposés, such as investigative work revealing how certain parliamentarians abused their expense accounts, but also those surfacing in murkier waters. *The Guardian's* recent reporting of documents leaked by U.S. computer specialist Edward Snowden detailing state spying on an industrial scale, for example, sparked outrage in Parliament. *The Daily Telegraph* has questioned whether the two-thirds majority would be adequate to prevent politicians voting to toughen further the royal charter:

Such a scenario is not unimaginable. *The Guardian's* recent investigation into state spying is exactly the kind of reporting that could spark a moral panic among politicians and give them cause to limit what the press can publish. If parliament can find the numbers to impose a royal charter upon the industry, it can also find the numbers necessary to censor it.

(Greenslade 2013b)

Some conservative members of parliament, such as former journalist Richard Drax, believe the two-thirds rule gives only an illusion of protection for press freedom. Drax is on record as saying that a simple amendment would allow a future government to sweep it away at any time with a single-vote majority (Greenslade 2013c). Large majorities, he said, were "not as rare as the charter supporters would have us believe."

Many of those steadfastly opposed to the Leveson Report's recommendations also argue that existing criminal laws are sufficient to bring newspapers into line. Would a more effective PCC have made any difference in the phone-hacking scandal, they ask, which after all could have been tackled—and is being tackled—through the courts? As Lord Grade (2013) remarked, "Phone-hacking is a criminal offence, like burglary. You don't deal with burglars by regulating them, you deal with burglars by 'banging them up.'" An appropriate sequel to the Leveson testimony has been playing out at London's Old Bailey court where, amongst others, two former editors of the *News of the World*, Andy Coulson and Rebekah Brookes, are on trial.[7] The "phone hacking trial" has been attracting sensational headlines as the day-to-day life of a tabloid newspaper is laid bare. If nothing else, the debate surrounding the Leveson Inquiry has served to highlight the fact that criminal laws are in place to cover a variety of offenses, including paying the police and public officials for stories. It is a point *The Economist* makes in a March 2013 editorial, highly critical of the Leveson Report, which accuses the government of making a "shameful hash" of press regulation:

Although the proposal involves bizarre institutional contortions to distance press regulation from the government, it raises the spectre of state regulation. To oppose this proposal is not to deny that much has gone wrong. Yet virtually all Fleet Street's worst abuses can be dealt with under existing law. Thanks to the scandals of the past few years, that law is now being enforced, and some 60 journalists face charges.

For *The Economist* and other critics, the proposals raise the specter that the new regulatory regime will become progressively more restrictive, conceivably to the point that the entire press will be bound by rules set in motion to cope with excesses of tabloid scandal-mongering. The royal charter, Lord Grade concluded, was a seriously flawed piece of parliamentary draftsmanship, with politicians comprehensively hijacked by a well-organized lobby group.

CONCLUSION: THE FUTURE OF
INDEPENDENT JOURNALISM

The issues at the heart of this chapter's discussion make apparent why questions regarding newspaper independence are so important to pursue. Much depends, as we have seen, on how "independence" is defined—and who is doing the defining—where the rhetorical ideals of fourth estate roles and responsibilities are concerned. The Leveson Inquiry's recommendations were intended to help narrow what is perceived to be a widening gap between these centuries-old values and the hard grind of actual practice today. Many of journalism's critics, no small number of whom are situated within its inner circles, have been ringing the alarm bell in the hope of provoking public debate. Leveson provided them with just the opportunity to express their deep misgivings, not least regarding the extent to which the press is recurrently complicit in upholding the very power structures it ostensibly strives to interrogate and challenge. Lofty rhetoric about steadfast commitments to fearless reporting notwithstanding, it is clear that in the current climate public trust will not be garnered as long as watchdogs are content to behave like lapdogs.

This is not to overlook instances where the newspaper press has succeeded in afflicting the comfortable while comforting the afflicted, to borrow a dusty phrase. Nor is it to deny that its corporate owners and their editors have mounted a robust defense of the status quo, refusing to countenance the charge that their publications may be found wanting in meeting their fourth estate obligations. The more thoughtful voices amongst them, however, recognize that the existing system of self-regulation is no longer tenable, its credibility being in tatters. Much work remains to be done to assess the viability of various proposed alternatives to the Press Complaints Commission, as noted earlier, with several prospective initiatives in early stages of development. Here it will be vital, in our view, to focus critical scrutiny on precisely what counts as "independence" at a time when newspapers are struggling to remain financially viable from one day to the next, some buckling under the strain of market forces as they scramble to secure a business model for the digital age.

Rhetorical appeals to fourth estate ideals almost always obscure how this mythology advances the interests of private capital, where the commercial pressures brought to bear on newspaper independence are just as serious as those of a partisan political or overbearing regulatory nature. Watchdogs do not bite their owners, as the saying goes. Editors of several titles have expressed their fears that hard-won reputations for reportorial integrity are being put at risk by these pressures; others have opted to refashion corporate priorities, blurring news and entertainment values into infotainment with an unwavering eye to bottom-line profitability. While managers talk of "reorganization," "downsizing," "concessions" and the like, news and editorial posts on some titles are being "concentrated," with remaining staff members compelled to "multitask" as they adopt greater "flexibility" with regard to their salary and working conditions. "Converged" content is being "repackaged" under the imperatives of "churnalism," a polite way of saying that its quantity—and, all too often, quality—is shrinking as "efficiencies" are imposed.

While the divisive debate over newspaper independence continues to revolve around differing views concerning journalism's normative relationship to government in the name of press freedom, these commercial pressures will continue to elude the attention they so clearly warrant. Now is the moment, we would argue, to be rethinking fourth estate ideals for today's realities, and in so doing strive to expand the parameters of these familiar debates to encourage richer, more diverse dialogues over how best to develop journalism's independence in the public interest.

NOTES

1. The phrase originated in the United States in the late nineteenth century but has been used metaphorically in Britain since the 1980s by politicians to warn that the press was risking the imposition of regulation.
2. The "Hacked Off" campaign was founded in July 2011 and quickly gained the support of a number of public figures, including actor Hugh Grant.
3. The phrase was widely cited, including by the *New York Times*, "Testimony in British Hacking Inquiry Takes Debate Beyond Murdoch's Empire," on November 21, 2011.
4. Interesting comparative studies concerning the emergence of newspaper independence ideals in other countries include Kaul (2003), Muhlmann (2010), Powe (1991), and Walker (1982), amongst many others.
5. The MailOnline topped 150 million users for the first time in October 2013. See http: www.theguardian.com/media/2013/nov/14/mail-online-monthly-browsers-top-150m (accessed May 8, 2014).
6. Newspapers are keen to claim their rights to freedom of expression under Article 10 but Article 8 also protects an individual's right to privacy, including privacy from media intrusion. The clash means that increasingly the courts are the arbiter (Petley 2013).
7. Brooks faces five charges in relation to allegations of conspiracy to hack phones, conspiracy to pervert the course of justice and conspiracy to commit misconduct in public office. Coulson is facing three charges in relation to allegations of conspiring to hack phones and allegations over a conspiracy to commit misconduct in public office when he was *News of the World* editor. Both have denied the charges.

REFERENCES

BBC. (2014) *Editorial Guidelines, Section 7—Privacy*. Available http: www.bbc.co.uk/editorialguidelines/page/guidelines-privacy-introduction/ (accessed May 8, 2014).

Calcutt, D. (1990) *Report of the Committee on Privacy and Related Matters*, presented to Parliament by the Secretary for State for the Home Department by command of Her Majesty, June 1990. London: H.M.S.O.

Carlyle, T. (1840) "The hero as man of letters: Johnson, Rousseau, Burns" (Lecture V, May 19). Available http: www.victorianweb.org/authors/carlyle/heroes/hero5. html (accessed May 8, 2014).

Dacre, P. (2008) Speech to the Society of Editors. Available http: www.pressgazette. co.uk/node/42394 (accessed May 8, 2014).

Daily Mail. (2013) "A judicial farce and a dark day for freedom," *The Daily Mail.* Available http: www.dailymail.co.uk/debate/article-2480711/DAILY-MAIL-COMMENT-A-judicial-farce-dark-day-freedom.html (accessed May 8, 2014).

Davies, N. (2012) "Leveson Report: A nightmare but only for the Old Guard of Fleet Street," *The Guardian.* Available http: www.theguardian.com/media/2012/ nov/29/leveson-report-nightmares-not-real (accessed May 8, 2014).

Fraser, N. (1990) "Rethinking the public sphere: A contribution to the critique of actually existing democracy," *Social Text* 25/26: 56–80.

Grade, M. (2013) "Society of Editors lecture," *Hold the Front Page* November 11. Available http: www.holdthefrontpage.co.uk/2013/news/lord-grade-delivers-the-society-of-editors-lecture/ (accessed May 8, 2014).

Greenslade, R. (2008) "Express and Star apologies to McCanns bring all journalism into disrepute," *The Guardian* March 19. Available http: www.theguardian. com/media/greenslade/2008/mar/19/expressandstarapologiesto (accessed May 8, 2014).

Greenslade, R. (2013a) "100 leading figures urge newspaper publishers to accept Royal Charter," *The Guardian* November 29. Available http: www.theguardian. com/media/greenslade/2013/nov/29/press-regulation-leveson-inquiry (accessed May 8, 2014).

Greenslade, R. (2013b) Newspapers Lament Signing of the Royal Charter on Press Regulation. Available http: www.theguardian.com/media/greenslade/2013/ oct/31/national-newspapers-press-regulation (accessed May 8, 2014).

Greenslade, R. (2013c) "Tory MP calls for bill of rights while backing publishers' new regulator," *The Guardian* December 5. Available http: www.theguardian. com/media/greenslade/2013/dec/05/press-regulation-press-freedom (accessed May 8, 2014).

Habermas, J. (1989) *The Structural Transformation of the Public Sphere: An Inquiry into a Category of Bourgeois Society* (originally published 1962). Cambridge: Polity Press.

Hansard. (2012) *House of Commons Debates* November 29. Available http: www. publications.parliament.uk/pa/cm201213/cmhansrd/cm121129/debtext/121129– 0003.htm#12112958000004 (accessed May 8, 2014).

Hazlitt, W. (1821) *Table-Talk: Essays on Men and Matters.* Available http: www. gutenberg.org/files/3020/3020-h/3020-h.htm (accessed May 8, 2014).

Hewlett, S. (2011) "PCC2 can learn a lot about privacy from TV," *British Journalism Review* 22, 4: 23.

Hewlett, S. (2013) "Could the Royal Charter force the press into political haggling?," *The Guardian* November 10. Available http: www.theguardian.com/ media/media-blog/2013/nov/10/press-regulation-royal-charter (accessed May 8, 2014).

Hunt, F. K. (1850) *The Fourth Estate: Contributions towards a History of Newspapers, and the Liberty of the Press.* (Volumes I and II). London: David Bogue.

Kaul, C. (2003) *Reporting the Raj: The British Press and India.* Manchester: University of Manchester Press.

Leveson, B. (2012a) *An Inquiry into the Culture, Practices and Ethics of the Press.* London: The Stationery Office. Available http: http://webarchive.nationalarchives. gov.uk/20140122145147/www.levesoninquiry.org.uk/about/the-report/ (accessed May 8, 2014).

Leveson, B. (2012b) *An Inquiry into the Culture, Practices and Ethics of the Press: News Release.* Available http: www.levesoninquiry.org.uk/wp-content/uploads/2011/11/Core-Participants-final-14.09.11.pdf (accessed May 8, 2014).

Leveson, B. (2012c*) An Inquiry into the Culture, Practices and Ethics of the Press. Transcript of Morning Hearing November 14 2011.* Available http: http://webarchive.nationalarchives.gov.uk/20140122145147/www.levesoninquiry.org.uk/wp-content/uploads/2011/11/Transcript-of-Morning-Hearing-14-November-2011.txt (accessed May 8, 2014).

Leveson, B (2012d) *An Inquiry into the Culture, Practices and Ethics of the Press. Transcript of Morning Hearing November 21 2011.* Available http: www.levesoninquiry.org.uk/wp-content/uploads/2011/12/Transcript-of-Morning-Hearing-21-November-20111.txt (accessed May 8, 2014).

Lloyd, J. (2013) "The two cultures," in J. Petley (ed.), *Media and Public Shaming: Drawing the Boundaries of Disclosure,* 217–222. Oxford: Reuters Institute for the Study of Journalism.

Macaulay, T. B. (1828) "Extract from a review of Henry Hallam's *The Constitutional History of England,*" *Edinburgh Review* 48, September: 96–169.

MailOnline. (2011) "Milly Dowler's family 'offered £3m settlement by News International' over Phone Hacking Scandal," *The Daily Mail.* Available http: www.dailymail.co.uk/news/article-2039266/Phone-hacking-Milly-Dowlers-family-offered-3m-settlement-News-International.html (accessed May 8, 2014).

Media Standards Trust. (2013) *Analysis: Press Coverage of Leveson.* Available http: http://mediastandardstrust.org/wp-content/uploads/downloads/2013/05/MST-Leveson-Analysis-090513-v2.pdf (accessed May 8, 2014).

Muhlmann G. (2010) *Journalism for Democracy,* translated by J. Burrell. Cambridge: Polity Press.

Petley, J. (2013) *Media and Public Shaming: Drawing the Boundaries of Disclosure.* Oxford: Reuters Institute for the Study of Journalism.

Powe L. (1991) *The Fourth Estate and the Constitution: Freedom of the Press in America.* Berkeley: University of California Press.

Press Complaints Commission (PCC). (2012) *Editors' Code of Practice.* Available at http: www.pcc.org.uk/cop/practice.html (accessed May 8, 2014).

Reeve, H. (1855) "The newspaper press," *The Edinburgh Review* October: 470–498.

Royal Charter on Self-Regulation of the Press (2013). Available http: www.gov.uk/government/uploads/system/uploads/attachment_data/file/254116/Final_Royal_Charter_25_October_2013_clean__Final_.pdf (accessed May 8, 2014).

The New York Times. (2011) "Testimony in British hacking inquiry takes debate beyond Murdoch's empire," *The New York Times* November 22. Available http: www.nytimes.com/2011/11/22/world/europe/prominent-british-hacking-victims-testify.html?_r=0 (accessed May 8, 2014).

Walker, M. (1982) *Powers of the Press: The World's Great Newspapers.* London: Quartet Books.

Yelland, D. (2013) "Leveson: Britain's press needs to learn humility—I should Know," *The Guardian* November 29. Available http: www.theguardian.com/commentisfree/2013/nov/29/leveson-humility-former-sun-editor-i-know (accessed May 8, 2014).

2 Differences of Kind and Degree
Articulations of Independence in American Cinema

Geoff King

If "independent" is always a relational term—implying independent *of* something, more or less specific—it is also often a *relative* quality rather than one that entails absolute or clear-cut distinctions between one thing and another. As far as American cinema[1] is concerned, the object in relation to which independence is defined is usually clear and quite easily identified: Hollywood. The major Hollywood studios, and their output (especially in their incarnation of recent decades, as parts of larger corporate media entities), are the single overwhelming object against which independence is set. That is to say, independent cinema is defined in relation to a particular commercial regime rather than any system of state regulation or interference, as is the case in a number of the other examples examined in this book. This occurs through discourses in which a number of similar values are often promulgated, however, in the sense that independence here also tends to connote a realm of freedom for the expression of viewpoints different from, or potentially opposed to, those associated with dominant institutions. As elsewhere, this is a domain in which "independent" is almost exclusively positive in the associations with which it is usually employed, as suggested in the introduction to this collection. In this realm, as in many others, it is a term that is heavily freighted with such resonances, which is one of the reasons why it has also been the subject of much heated debate and a concept in which powerful investments are often held. At the same time, however, independence here exists within a wide range of differences in both kind and degree and its celebration can also be viewed as the product of a particular cultural location.

If Hollywood is the all-encompassing point of comparison, against which independent cinema is usually defined, such a basis can also provide a source of difficulty in how exactly independence is conceived. "Independence" can be used in a relatively plain and factual sense, to designate a particular kind of operation outside that of the major studios. But it is difficult to restrict the term solely to the realm of literal denotation, so strong are the values—and especially the virtues—with which it is usually associated. Something similar might also apply in other national contexts, but this seems to be a particularly potent effect in a nation such as the United States, with a culture that has such a strongly self-conscious and self-congratulatory sense of its own historical achievement of independence. The celebration of the Declaration of Independence remains an active and prominent part of contemporary U.S. culture, along with a tendency for collective identification with the virtues associated with the term (however inappropriate that might seem to some critics of the American role in the world; see also the contribution to this volume by Daniel Kreiss, on the mobilization of such discourse in John Perry Barlow's *Declaration of the Independence of Cyberspace*). It is the loading of the notion of independence with such weight that makes it resonate with broader American discourses, and thus a topic of interest beyond the realm of particular kinds of cinema, but this can also complicate what exactly is understood as independent and in what manner.

The fact that Hollywood also looms so large, as effectively an American "national" cinema, also seems to give added resonance to the notion of independent cinema as something different but from within the same geographical space. Independence, as a term that can suggest a relative position within a particular locale, might have somewhat less discursive currency in countries or regions in which *any* nationally based production is likely to have the status of a Cinderella in comparison with the global dominance of Hollywood (which would apply in most cases other than Bollywood). In Britain, for example, any films made today without the involvement of Hollywood at some level might be seen as effectively independent in comparison with studio output, which seems likely to weaken the currency of the term in this context.

As essentially "non-Hollywood," the independent realm is extensive, a source of many resulting disputes about exactly what it has been taken to signify. Defined in these purely negative terms, independent cinema embraces a wide range of alternatives to the production of the major studios: from forms that bear no resemblance whatsoever to the familiar work of the commercial mainstream to others in which the grounds of distinction are much less clear cut. At one extreme, we could place various forms of avant-garde or experimental work, alongside other varieties of "underground" or otherwise highly alternative production, seen usually only by tiny audiences within very particular viewing contexts outside mainstream society. At the other, we find narrative features that share numerous qualities with those of their Hollywood counterparts, produced, distributed and circulated in varying degrees of distance from or proximity to the channels of the commercial mainstream. There are also many positions in between these, including, for example, works of commercial "exploitation" cinema of various kinds, including low-budget horror and action films. None of these very different manifestations of independence have anything essentially in common beyond their shared separation from Hollywood, which makes the concept of independent cinema in some ways not a very productive one, at least when taken in literal terms. It is not much more helpful than a conceit such as "overseas" or "foreign" cinema might be within the U.S. context. As identifiers of distinct quantities—bodies of work that might be expected to have some shared qualities—these are of questionable value. They are, in fact, more likely to mislead than to highlight points of commonality. That a film is non-Hollywood might tell us little more than that another is non-American; which is to say, not very much, given the huge variation found within either of these negatively defined categories.

A comparison with notions such as "overseas" or "foreign" cinema is a useful one, however, in that these are meaningful as *operative* categories, however limited (or in this case, also chauvinistic) they might be considered in literal terms. These are labels that are *in play* in the world, as part of the discursive sphere through which different kinds of cinema are often understood and their interrelations are mapped, at various levels, in popular, relatively more "serious" and also in some academic discourses. It is in this dimension rather than in any literal definition that independence is at its most powerful as a notion and in such terms that I primarily engage in this chapter. If we consider what independent cinema has been taken to signify in this sense, what we find is subject to both historical variation and plenty of debate within the contexts in which it has been most heavily deployed, particularly in recent decades. Across the history of American cinema, as Gregg Merritt (2000) suggests in his general survey of the terrain, the prevailing meaning of the term has shifted considerably and not always been positive in its connotations (it can, for example, mark a difference from Hollywood that is understood as one primarily of poor quality or shoddy workmanship). If media independence more generally is usually viewed as a positive or necessary quality—as, for example, a key dimension of an open/democratic society—resonances of this kind are not especially to the fore in many individual forms of independent cinema. The existence of scope for independence may still be important at this level, whatever particular manifestations might result, but many of these might not in themselves be likely objects of celebration on the basis of their broadly political or ideological merit.

DIMENSIONS OF INDEPENDENCE

It is necessary at this point to refine further a useful basis for defining independent cinema, to permit a more effective articulation of the different grounds on which difference from the mainstream/Hollywood can be understood. A definition based on a distinction from Hollywood can be taken in itself to embrace different dimensions of independence. The terms in which this is put are, initially, *industrial* in nature: a definition based on separation from a particular, established industrial regime. And the specifics of the industrial realm are an important part of most working definitions of the independent realm. We can identify independence, then, in specific areas such as the nature of the companies involved in the finance, production and/or distribution of films, and in other industry-level factors such as amounts of funding, access or otherwise to well-known performers (usually linked, of course, to funding), the types of theatrical release and marketing strategies that are employed, and so on. Difference from Hollywood also includes a great deal more than this, however, although other sources of difference are usually closely linked to these industrial factors. Difference from Hollywood also means difference at the level of the types of films themselves—without which, difference at the industrial level would be of vastly less interest or concern, with far less seemingly at stake. Separation from the studios *matters*, to those who engage in discourses surrounding independence in various ways, because it implies the existence—actual or potential—of films of a different nature from those produced by the studios. Difference from Hollywood in the nature of the films themselves can usefully be considered at two (also interconnected) levels: those of *form* and *content*. As well as being defined on an industrial basis, therefore, independence can be defined in terms of aesthetics and in terms of subject matter and its treatment—the latter of which can also amount to a definition in terms of the political-ideological dimension that tends to loom large in broader accounts of media independence.

That independence can be defined on these three levels (industrial, formal, sociocultural/political) seems now broadly to be accepted in academic understanding of this part of the film landscape, although the emphasis varies from one account to another (for more on this approach, see King 2005). Other commentators have disagreed, however, notably Merritt, who maintains that independence can only be defined in any clear manner in industrial terms, on the basis of separation from any involvement on the part of the Hollywood studios, or as he puts it, somewhat less specifically, "autonomous of *all* studios, regardless of size." Any other basis of definition, such as that independent films embody a different "spirit" or "alternative vision" from that of the mainstream, is declared to be too slippery. To impose such a limitation, however, is to ignore substantial dimensions of what is embraced by the term, and also the very nature of such territory, which is often precisely to *be* slippery, challenging and difficult to pin down in simple terms of black and white.

Independence is best understood as a relative rather than fixed quality, as suggested earlier. Independence—measured broadly in terms of difference from Hollywood—varies in both degree and kind. Particular examples—individual films or groupings of various types—can be more or less independent/different in their industrial location, context and strategies; in their aesthetic approaches; and in the meanings and ideological implications we might find in their substantive content. The degree of difference in each of these three domains might be closely correlated, or less so. The industrial realm tends to play a strongly conditioning role, setting certain limits of possible difference in most cases. Filmmaking of a radically independent variety in either form or content is generally only possible on the industrial margins, in operations freed from the limitations created by demands for large audiences and profitability. Filmmaking of a more modestly independent kind, in either respect, which might have a greater degree of commercial viability, if on a modest scale, can be found somewhat closer to the channels of the mainstream. If a distance from mainstream institutions is a requirement for radical aesthetics or politics, however, it is no *guarantee* of either of these—a key point for our understanding of how independence in this realm relates to broader notions of independence in the media.

Independent film can be entirely lacking in any distinct markers at the aesthetic or political level. For those who would valorize independence-as-difference, particularly in politically progressive terms, this is a crucial distinction. If Hollywood is considered broadly to be politically conservative, in the ideological implications of much of its output (see, for example, Ryan and Kellner 1990), a presence in the independent sector at the industrial level is, in itself, no guarantor of anything significantly different. Or, at least, of difference that would be defined as progressive in left/liberal terms. Radically left-leaning alternatives are, in fact, quite rare in the independent realm, although a wider range of independent productions might be considered to offer critiques of life within capitalism, patriarchy or racist society of a more implicit kind. The strongest examples of radical left politics in the American independent field would include some of the films of Haile Gerima, a member of what became known as the LA School in the 1970s, particularly features such as Bush Mama (1979) and Ashes and Embers (1982), which adopt the insurgent agenda of work that seems to dramatize a process of political awakening in terms that combine the dynamics of class and race. Very little other work of such an overtly political nature can be found, however, particularly in feature-length filmmaking that aspires to even the most marginal forms of commercial distribution. Most examples are in documentary form—a mode largely confined to the independent sector by default—notably including a number of films by Michael Moore that have reached much larger audiences than usual for this kind of material. More common is an implied critique of contemporary American life and/ or major institutions such as the family or suburbia, in independent features that are more likely to adopt modes such as satire and irony than to proffer alternative visions or prescriptions for social change (for example, Happiness [1998]). To a greater extent than work of an openly left-leaning orientation, independence has also created important space for filmmakers motivated by other political concerns, particularly those relating to issues of gender/sexuality and race/ethnicity, dimensions that have played a conspicuous part in some of the higher-profile manifestations of the sector in recent decades.

Much independent production might be considered to be largely apolitical or to share some broadly conservative implications found within Hollywood, including various schools of exploitation-oriented genre filmmaking. Some independent horror films, for example, might be interpreted as having radical potential, in what they imply about notions of the normal and the abnormal and how such categories might be blurred or undermined (for example, the vampire films *Martin* [1978] and *Habit* [1997]). But many are much more straightforward in their approach, seeking primarily to offer certain kinds of "thrills" to viewers on lower budgets than those typical of Hollywood (for example, *The* Evil Dead [1981] or *The Blair Witch Project*), sometimes with material that would be considered too "disreputable" for the preferred self-images of the studios (for useful case studies of some operations in this realm, see Perren 2013 and Wharton 2013). Independence is an arena chosen by some filmmakers, as a location within which to pursue more "personal" varieties of work, with lesser commercial constraints than those faced in the studio arena. This is an important part of the image—and romance—of independent filmmaking, and also part of the reality, although considerable constraint often still exists, most obviously at the level of available resources. But it is also a place chosen by others, filmmakers and those who are more business-oriented, as an opportunity space for enterprises that are more commercially intended. That is to say, it is constituted in part through the identification of gaps not filled by the studios that are available to be exploited, with profit as the primary motivation. The independent sphere also provides space for production of a kind that is politically distinct from Hollywood but motivated in terms that would be considered to be the opposite of progressive, as understood from left/liberal terms, including a thriving sphere of Christian production and circulation (see Russell 2013).

A similar range of possibilities exists in the aesthetic dimension, in which independence can be marked by differences at the level of the employment of key aspects of film form, such as narrative and audiovisual style. In work at the avant-garde or experimental end of the scale, we find explorations of the nature of the medium of the kind that would be associated with high modernism (examples include the work of Stan Brakhage). More commercially oriented independent features often employ aesthetics very close—or even more or less identical—to those of studio features, particularly in the use of familiar "classical"/canonical narrative structure and the basic visual orientation provided by established continuity editing schemas (if not always with the same polish as is available on larger budgets). In between, as in other dimensions, are various possibilities. Many titles now established as independent "classics" draw on formal qualities associated with works of international "art" cinema. These include claims for greater realism or authenticity than that of studio film, made through the employment of downplayed or de-dramatized narrative structures and/or the use of handheld visuals to create an impression of *verité*-style access to unmediated reality; qualities that can be linked closely to the political dimensions of films that might present visions of existence very different from those usually found in the products of Hollywood. They can also entail approaches marked as more artistically expressive in various ways—usually in renditions of subjective character experience (for more on all of these approaches, see King 2005, chapters 2 and 3).

THE INSTITUTIONALIZATION OF INDEPENDENCE

If independence can embrace so much variety (the above being only a very brief sketch of some of its parameters), debate about its exact meaning within the sphere of American cinema gained a particular currency in the period from the latter part of the 1980s onward, during which certain parts of the sector underwent a notable process of growth. Before this period, the term "American independent cinema" suggested something quite disparate and marginal: a number of more or less historically distant phases of avant-garde or underground work; the occasional narrative feature production, some of which gained greater prominence during the much-celebrated "Hollywood Renaissance" of the late 1960s to the late 1970s, in which the studios embraced some such work during a period of crisis; the output of exploitation-oriented outfits such as Roger Corman's New World Pictures; and so on. A number of factors led to an upsurge in independent feature production during the 1980s; most important of these was the advent of home video, which created a huge increase in demand for product that the studios were unable to meet. A number of new institutions came into existence, supporting and helping to consolidate what took on the appearance of a distinct and concerted movement, including new distributors and film festivals specializing in lower-budget films targeted to a niche art-house audience. The notion of American independent cinema, as something distinct and identifiable, gained wider and more sustained attention than had existed in the past, increasingly so by the early 1990s, partly as a result of the crossover success some individuals films achieved beyond the limits of the art-cinemas of the bigger cities and college towns (notable examples included *sex,* lies, and videotape [1989] and Pulp Fiction [1994]), and by the prominence gained by the sector's most visible institution, the Sundance Film Festival.

The main focus of this attention was a particular variety of independent film, what Yannis Tzioumakis describes usefully as "the low-budget, low-key quality film" (2013, 32). This is only one part of the broader independent spectrum, generally positioned as relatively "artistic" in style, without being close to the avant-garde or the experimental. It tended to be broadly alternative in politics, although often in the implicit manner suggested earlier rather than in more overt campaigning (the clearest cases of the latter related to issues of sexual orientation, particularly in the form of what became known as New Queer Cinema, and of race and/or ethnicity). This sector embraced a certain range—including that from the distinctly art-cinema-oriented to low-budget innovations within more commercial genres such as the crime thriller—but remained within a specific portion of the wider independent realm. Its prominence, however, was such that this kind of cinema was what the term "independent" came predominantly to signify in this period and afterward, one source of subsequent confusion and debate about how precisely the concept should be understood.

The increasing success enjoyed by some within this part of the independent landscape, and the increased prominence that resulted, began to increase the pressure on what the term "independent" was, could or should be taken to mean. During the 1990s, the discursive stakes were raised in much the same way as were those of the business itself, at a time when the unexpected crossover success of a number of hits (the likes of *Pulp Fiction* and *The* Blair Witch Project [1999]) created pressure within the industry for others to follow suit, rather than to be happy with the more modest returns that had characterized the business in the majority of cases. Pressure of this kind was seen as a threat to the distinctive character of the independent sector, or this part of it, at least. To try to build in crossover success from the start, rather than to take it as an extra, as icing on the cake, was perceived, rightly enough in many cases, to be to move in broadly conservative directions; to be more conventional, in all respects, including leaning more to the employment of familiar stars, with the upward budget pressure that would create, with its concomitant reduction in the scope for relatively more radical departure.

THE INVOLVEMENT OF HOLLYWOOD

The status of independence became seen as under threat during the 1990s, in other words, no more so than by the entry, stage-right, of the archenemy: Hollywood itself. Some of the studios played a part in the consolidation of independent institutions of the 1980s. Among the new distributors specializing in this material at the time were what became known as "classics" divisions, created first by United Artists in 1980 (no longer one of the majors but a struggling operation merged with the similarly fallen MGM) and subsequently by the big players Twentieth Century Fox and Universal. None of these lasted very long, which is probably why they were not seen as posing much of a threat to conceptions of independence at the time. They were followed in the 1990s, however, by a much more concerted series of studio moves into this territory, the creation of new entities such as Sony Pictures Classics and Fox Searchlight and the high-profile takeover of existing independent players, the most prominent of which was the 1993 purchase by Disney of Miramax, which had become a dominant force in the sector at the time, largely through the success of individual titles such as *sex, lies, and videotape* (1989), *The Crying Game* (1992) and *Pulp Fiction* (see King 2009; Perren 2012; Tzioumakis 2012).

The Disney takeover of Miramax had the appearance of a classic instance of commercially based threat to media independence. Disney was not only one of the six major Hollywood studios and, along with the others, part of a very large, consolidated multinational operation, but also perceived as the epitome of many of the worst traits of such entities, with its reputation for the output of bland, conservative "family"-centered material and for maintaining very strict global control over its various branded properties. If such corporations often figure prominently in general concern about media independence, in the broad dominance they exert over wide swathes of media and in their global power, the kind of initiative involved in this case was one in which any such sense of threat seemed all the more pointed, immediate and dramatic, in the act of buying out and gaining control over a previously independent operation. Not just that, but what also gave this takeover a particularly vivid character was the prospect of a company with the reputation of Disney—of all the studios—owning an independent that had built a reputation for the distribution or production of a number of relatively controversial titles (even if this was, in reality, largely the pursuit by Miramax of an exploitation-style strategy of deliberately courting controversy in an effort to gain unpaid-for publicity, as in the case of the gender identity "big secret" at the center of *The Crying Game*).

Far less "outraged" reaction greeted the more or less simultaneous takeover of the other largest independent distributor of the time, New Line, by media mogul Ted Turner, shortly after which another merger made New Line part of the huge Time-Warner conglomerate. This might have been an equally large foreclosure of independence, but did not signify as strongly within prevailing discourses relating to the concept because New Line was associated primarily with less valorized forms of independent film, its fortune being based on the success of the lower-status genre franchises of the *Nightmare on Elm Street* (1984–) and Teenage Mutant Ninja Turtles (1987–) series. The prospective loss of material of this kind to the studio-conglomerate realm did not tend to set off alarm bells, a further demonstration of the complexity of the independent realm and the differing levels of investment held in different kinds of non-studio production (the profits of these series did also enable New Line to invest in the creation of a more quality/art-film-oriented division, Fine Line Features, but this remained a minor part of the enterprise). Another, subsequent takeover that created some waves, but mostly restricted to those closer to the independent sector itself, was the takeover by Universal of Good Machine, producer of a number of key films of the New York independent scene, as part of its creation of its Focus Features division in 2002.

How much material difference takeovers such as these made to the viability of a distinct independent sector is generally difficult to measure with any certainty, although this would appear to be an important issue within the broader sphere of debate about media independence. Studio "specialty" divisions, as they became known, such as Miramax under Disney, Focus Features, Fox Searchlight and others were given varying degrees of autonomy, to operate without the approval of their corporate parents. These usually included the freedom to give the go-ahead to productions or purchases (in their role as distributors) up to certain budget ceilings. Key personnel were also retained in many cases, including Harvey and Bob Weinstein, founders of Miramax, who remained at the head of the Disney division, and David Linde and James Schamus, two of the three partners in Good Machine, who headed Focus Features. Studio interest in the independent sector was based primarily on a desire to share in some of the successes it had enjoyed, particularly the largest crossover hits, and this included a recognition of the importance of maintaining expert understanding of the specifics of this part of the film economy, rather than just reducing it to the same terms as the operations of their main divisions. This was a respect in which this wave of involvement differed importantly from the earlier period of generally unsuccessful "classics" divisions. A significant degree of independence was maintained, therefore, but for many this represented an uncomfortable blurring of the lines.

While the most obvious reaction from within the sphere of independent filmmakers and their supporters was a strong expression of disapproval of studio involvement in the sector, there were also considerable benefits for those involved in the creation of these new entities, or the changed status of existing operations such as Miramax. Under the wings of Hollywood, specialty divisions gained greatly increased access to resources, including not just finance but also, importantly, access to the powerful distribution and sales networks of the studios, sources of considerable advantage in the marketplace. This immediately raised more concerns, of course, about the impact of this on the status of the remaining unaffiliated independents, whose position was very much weaker. Miramax, especially, and notoriously, soon gained a reputation for bullying behavior in the marketplace for distribution rights to new independent features, the resources of Disney permitting it to outbid competitors and to dominate the competition (Biskind 2004: 156–157). This had a number of consequences that were seen as further threats to the capacity of parts of the independent sector either to remain in existence or to maintain previous degrees of difference from the mainstream in their orientation. In the face of the wave of buying started by Miramax, other specialty divisions and larger free-standing independents were effectively forced to increase the extent to which they invested in the production end of the business in order to gain access to features at an earlier stage in the process. This marked an important change of emphasis. This part of the business had until this point been founded primarily on distribution and a model based on the purchase of distribution rights to completed features. Investment in production is a very different kind of enterprise, involving greater risk than the identification of finished products that are seen as having commercial potential within the independent realm. Greater risks of this kind were viewed as leading to attempts to reduce risk in other ways, generally by favoring properties that appeared to be safer commercial bets, particularly through the increased use of stars (Biskind 2004: 160).

It is not really possible to measure any impact of this kind, and it is always easy to risk overstating how much more challenging or different parts of the independent landscape might have been in this period were it not for the involvement of the studio specialty divisions, a common hazard in some of the more rhetorical discourses surrounding the independent field. There have been occasions, however, on which clear-cut lines were established, markers of distinction of what can or cannot be permitted under the ambit of the studios: moments that throw into clear light some of what can be at stake in questions of precise degrees of media independence. These usually involve refusals by studio corporate parents to allow the distribution of certain individual titles, examples of what cannot be digested by even the semiautonomous divisions of such entities. A number of high-profile instances involved Miramax during its ownership by Disney. Miramax was required to create a new, separate, company to distribute the controversial youth-sex drama *Kids* in 1995, after it received an NC17 rating, a category the company was contractually disallowed from handling as a part of Disney. The religious comedy *Dogma* (1999) was personally bought back from the company by the Weinsteins, and sold to the independent Lion's Gate Entertainment, as a result of pressure put on Disney by a number of Catholic organizations. Greater controversy, because of its more overtly political dimension, greeted the abandonment of Miramax's planned release of Michael Moore's provocative documentary *Fahrenheit 911* (2004), following Disney pressure reportedly linked to its corporate interests in Florida (the company was accused of fearing that its involvement with the film would threaten tax breaks it received in the Disney World state, where President George W. Bush's brother Jeb was governor).

This appears to be the stuff of real and direct threat to media independence, resulting from corporate involvement in the sector, although even here some caution is required in the interpretation of such events. None of the films involved in these interventions can be said to have suffered in their ability to reach audiences as a result of such interventions. Quite to the contrary, it is almost certainly the case that they benefited from the considerable free publicity that resulted. The outcome at this level, if not the intention or conscious motivation, was very similar to that which Miramax had deliberately engineered in the numerous previous occasions in which it had courted controversy through acts such as challenging ratings decisions before the Disney takeover.

Whether or not the studio specialty divisions had any right to be described as part of the independent sector became a much-debated issue, as is perhaps unsurprising. They seemed a clear breach of any definition based on being "not Hollywood" and, for many, were firmly to be excluded. Their state of semiautonomous existence under the studio umbrella remained somewhat ambiguous, however. In any bottom-line account, they were likely to be seen as interlopers, cuckoos in the nest, part of the broader attempt of conglomerate-media-owned Hollywood to co-opt almost every potentially attractive source of profits that it could control. As far as the films that they handled are concerned, however, it is not so easy to argue for any simple basis of exclusion. A case can certainly be made that the specialty divisions have tended, on the whole, to cherry-pick within the broader range of independent feature production: to pick up for distribution or invest in productions of relatively greater commercial potential. Films from the specialty divisions are, on average, more likely to feature known star performers than those from unattached distributors, the presence of such figures often being taken as a key marker of more commercial/conventional status. They are also, arguably, more likely to feature relatively stronger deployment of conventions from familiar genres such as romantic comedy, and generally to be broadly more conservative in nature. In terms of their narrative strategies, they might be more likely to avoid entirely downbeat endings—another quality often taken as a marker of independent status, in its refusal of one of the most familiar of ameliorative Hollywood clichés. A fairly common feature of films from specialty divisions, I have suggested elsewhere (King 2009), is the mixed-resonance ending: one that leaves a positive resolution possible but not actually enacted, a way of having the best of both worlds that might be taken as symptomatic of this part of the film landscape more generally (as, for example, in the romantic comedy-drama Sideways [2004]).

These are only very approximate markers of the status of the realm of the specialty divisions, however, within which considerable space for variation exists, along with sizeable overlap with the qualities of films from unattached independents. The specialty divisions have handled some films the textual qualities of which are more or less indistinguishable from those distributed by the fully independent. Larger degrees of departure from mainstream routines are more likely to be found beyond the realm of the specialty divisions and a broad correlation can generally be identified between textual features and industrial location—but this does not amount to an entirely fixed, one-to-one relationship. This, again, suggests the requirement for nuanced understandings of media independence that allow for distinctions of such kinds to be made, in relation to differing degrees of independence in particular circumstances.

Distinctions also need to be made here between different examples of the studio-owned divisions. Sony Pictures Classics (SPC) is notable, for example, for handling a range of films much closer in textual qualities to those of the unattached independents, including a significantly larger number of more art-house-oriented and/or foreign-language titles. This is a case in which distinctiveness of output can be related quite directly to institutional arrangements, SPC being the specialty division in which the greatest autonomy from the studio parent was given to the heads of the division, on the basis of their established track record. Other divisions such as Miramax under Disney, Fox Searchlight and Focus Features have tended more strongly to target larger, crossover audiences. As much as in textual qualities, it is in fact in strategies in areas such as marketing and distribution that differences can often be identified between the studio divisions and the fully independent. A characteristic tendency of the specialty divisions, at least with what they see as their most promising releases, is to open them relatively wider than the norm for the independent sector, and to expand them more rapidly and to substantially larger numbers of screens if they perform successfully. This amounts to something of a hybrid between typically studio and typically independent approaches, and it is as a hybrid that this realm is usefully known, as suggested by the term "Indiewood."

Given the suspicion with which they were often treated by commentators invested in the perceived virtues of independence, it was no surprise that a generally celebratory tone was struck by some when the studios made a partial withdrawal from the sector toward the end of the first decade of the twenty-first century. This was a process begun by Time Warner in 2008 when it closed its specialty division, Warner Independent Pictures, as part of a reorganization that also involved the shutting of New Line and its more independent-leaning wing at the time, Picturehouse. Paramount also put an end to its Paramount Vantage label. Most notably of all, Miramax underwent a number of radical changes, following the earlier departure of the Weinsteins, who sold their stake in 2005, being downsized and eventually sold in 2010 to a group of private equity investors. A number of substantial players remained in place, particularly Fox Searchlight and Focus Features, but these moves were widely interpreted within industry and media circles as marking a retreat by the majors from the independent arena and as underlining some of the problems faced by this part of the American film business, particularly those created by excessive competition for what was perceived to be a finite specialty market.

"TRUE INDEPENDENCE"?

The response of many to the rise of the specialty divisions, and to their apparent or at least partial fall, provides a useful focus through which to examine more closely the manner in which investments in the notion of independence have been expressed in this part of the media landscape. If the studio-owned divisions are the negative object in prevailing discursive frameworks, the positive, in many accounts, is a conception of the "truly independent" to which this is counterposed. So, what is it to be "truly" independent, and what are the broader cultural resonances of such a construction? In concrete terms, to be truly independent is to be *entirely* independent. That is, initially, to have no ties to Hollywood of any kind. But it might also be taken a good deal further, if put in such strongly idealized terms. We might return here to Merritt's comment about the absence of ties to "*all* studios, regardless of size," which might be taken to include even very small industrially organized production enterprise. True independence might only be manifested by the effectively do-it-yourself level of operation, the usual condition of existence for the avant-garde and the underground. This might also be applied to the micro-budget level of independent feature fiction production, an approach that became popularized in the early 1990s in the context of films costing initial sums starting at around US$20,000 for work on 16mm (about US$33,000 in 2012 prices, adjusted for inflation). The difficulty with a concept such as this is that it can keep being chased further and further back, in increasingly restricted terms. As far as cost is concerned, feature productions have been completed for increasingly smaller sums, as low as, say, $7,000 on film for Primer (2004), and far less—almost nothing, if the labor of those involved is not included (an issue considered in other contexts in Section 2)—for some feature-length works on digital video.

Ultimately, of course, there is no such thing as *absolutely* true independence, in the sense of any form of cultural production that is 100 percent lacking in dependence on anything of any sort; not just institutions and resources, but ideas, concepts and basic frameworks of some kind within which to operate—not even for the single-person filmmaker or even for those operating in the most rarified and abstract territory. But it is possible, particularly in the era of ever-more affordable digital production tools, for something entirely independent to be achieved in more normal usages of the concept. The downside of very strong independence of this kind is that it tends to be accompanied by independence from more desirable quantities such as reaching an audience or achieving any revenue, an issue explored elsewhere in this collection. There are exceptions and occasional breakthroughs, but in general a broad inverse correlation can be established between degree of independence and likelihood of reaching substantial numbers of viewers (and the commercial returns that tend to be associated with the latter). The Internet has provided new potential channels of distribution. It has, for the first time, made it possible for filmmakers to distribute their work directly, without dependence on any of the usual institutions, but it remains very difficult to find an audience in this manner. Numerous new institutions have come into existence in this online domain, but beyond the largely free-for-all status of fora such as YouTube and other unregulated video-sharing sites, those that have the greatest capacity to reach an audience, or to produce any financial returns, tend to entail various forms of gatekeeping that in some ways replicate those of more traditional channels (King 2013, chapter 2). It is notable, though, that some of the most effective uses of new online initiatives, including crowd funding and the organization of screenings on a house-party model, have been in the most politically oriented parts of the independent arena, particularly documentaries such as the work of Robert Greenwald.

The problem, as often expressed by contemporary commentators such as Ted Hope, producer of many independent features, is finding a territory between the domains of the specialty divisions and an ultra-low-cost realm in which it is difficult to sustain any kind of viable business or career (see numerous posts on Hope's blog *Hope For Film*, online at www.hopeforfilm. com). A prevalent claim by figures such as Hope and others in the early 2010s was that the independent sector of the kind that became institution- alized from the 1980s was in crisis, its established model no longer viable, largely for reasons such as excessive competition resulting in increased spending on marketing, in the attempt to reach a limited audience for mate- rial of this kind. Whether or not this really constituted a significant change in the general fortunes of the sector is open to question, however, as I have argued elsewhere.

The independent sector certainly faced problems during the 2010s, not least feeling the general pinch accompanying the recession that followed the global financial crash of the late 2000s. It is debatable whether the situ- ation was qualitatively different from previous periods of difficulty faced by independent cinema, however, such as the aftermath of the stock mar- ket crash of 1987 or other financial setbacks and general fluctuations of fortune, or the generally parlous state in which much of the independent sector has *always* existed, even when a steady supply of breakout hits has been achieved. Another way of approaching this is to consider the notion of "crisis" to be of significance here, as much a part of the discursive rhetoric surrounding this territory as in relation to any specific difficulties in any par- ticular moment. *Really* to be independent, in a certain sense, in this context, is to occupy something like a permanent state of crisis and instability, rather than to reach too great a degree of the kind of stability that results from institutionalization, the latter carrying potential connotations such as rigid- ity, conformism to conventions of its own and, ultimately, inauthenticity. Notions of independence are strongly associated, in many media contexts, with notions of the authentic representation of whatever phenomena are not considered to be represented in this manner under conditions of dependence on dominant power, whether the latter is commercial or political in form. A key question that results is: how much institutionalization can occur with- out this being viewed as, in some way, a threat to notions such as "true," "real" or "authentic" independence? Or, from a purist perspective, whether or not *any* significant institutionalization can be approved?

A concern with the authenticity credentials of independent cinema is easy enough to understand, as part of the discursive regime that is in play in this territory. The independent sector has undoubtedly grown and become increasingly institutionalized, especially since the 1980s, and it not surpris- ing that some of its members or supporters might have viewed some of this with a degree of suspicion, particularly the involvement of the Holly- wood studios considered earlier. The level of investment that is sometimes expressed in notions of a more "true" or "authentic" independence suggests that something more is involved, however, than just a coolly logical response to concrete events on the ground. What appears to be involved here is some- thing akin to a defense of a particular faith, in a discursive context that has more than a little in common with some of the central tenets of Puritanism, a context applied in a similar manner to the realm of indie music by Wendy Fonarow (2006).

"INDEPENDENT," "INDIE," "INDIEWOOD" VERSUS "MAINSTREAM": DIFFERENCES OF KIND AND DEGREE

Investments of this kind are also in play in the choices of terms used to designate these parts of the film landscape, any of which inevitably risk becoming loaded with particular weightings and associations. The term "independent" is often used quite loosely and generally, but also on some occasions given a more protected status that seeks to signify something more specific and valorized. "Independent" is sometimes distinguished from the diminutive "indie," a term that is also in widespread use in this domain but the connotations of which vary according to usage. The two are sometimes used entirely interchangeably and to signify much the same, but not always. In some uses, "indie" signifies something valued less highly than "independent," being taken to refer to those forms of independence that are considered to be less authentic. As well as being a diminutive, and so initially suggestive of weaker status, "indie" has also been used to demarcate the particular part of the landscape that has been seen by some as representing a lesser quality than independence. It has been employed to suggest a variety of independence, particularly from the mid-1990s, that is seen as having become a conscious confection, designed to fit an institutionalized marketplace, rather than a form of independence that would, ideally, be created with no such prior consideration of its status as a particular form of commodity, even if one aimed at a niche market (an ideal that seems somewhat mythical and utopian, as if such work is ever created in a vacuum). "Indie" has also been used by some to designate the output of the specialty divisions, a further source of negative connotations and also of some confusion, given the usage of the term "Indiewood" also to indicate the same terrain. "Independent," when used in relation to such other terms, can come to suggest something stronger and more steely in nature, less subject to the suspicious slidings toward the conventional, the confected or the co-opted than the likes of indie or Indiewood.

My own terminological preferences are as follows, expressed here because it seems important always to define exactly how any of these labels are used in any particular context. I use "independent" to refer to the inclusive realm of all non-Hollywood cinema, as has been the case earlier in this chapter. "Indie" is a useful term with which to distinguish the particular variety of independence that came to prominence from the 1980s, as sketched earlier, partly because it came into broader circulation during this period in relation to this part of the landscape. There is no necessary reason why it should be defined in this way, but such usage also has the merit of suggesting some connections between these types of independent film and some broader aspects of contemporary American culture that go under the name of "indie," particularly the realm of indie music, where some similar issues are involved in relation to notions of authenticity, inauthenticity and selling out (the context of David Hesmondhalgh's contribution to this volume). "Indie" seems to me usefully to capture this sense of a wider cultural nexus, a dimension explored further by Michael Newman (2011), although it might, arguably, be considered to be less American-specific in some of its connotations ("indie" might be a term used more often in relation to certain kinds of British music and some other media, for example, than as a descriptor for lower-budget British films).

This is far from an area of agreement among academic authorities on the subject, however. Yannis Tzioumakis separates out "independent" and "indie" as distinct historical phases *within* the post-1980 variety of independent cinema while Alisa Perren uses the latter to identify the arena of the studio specialty divisions, which I find more usefully designated as Indiewood (another term the connotations of which are often decidedly negative, initially framed in a discursive gesture designed to de-valorize some forms by emphasis on the belittling "wood" component and its associations with the domain of the studios). The basis on which such terminology is chosen is related, in all of these cases, to the grounds on which independence is being considered. The distinctions made by Tzioumakis and Perren appear to be related to their primary focus on the industrial level, one that, for me, results in too narrow a usage of the term "indie" and that misses some of its broader cultural resonance. That agreement on the exact usage of such terms is absent among academics can be taken as further testament, however, to the loaded nature of the concepts that are involved, ones that do not lend themselves, despite our best efforts, to an entirely cool analysis absent of any investments of its own.

There are many value judgments inherent in the investments made in notions such as independence, or the distinctions made between one form of independent production and another, in film as elsewhere. To valorize independence over the world of corporate-owned studio production (or the "truly" independent over the "indie" or the products of Indiewood) might seem to be an unproblematic good, from a broader political viewpoint. But the way such differentiations are made tends also to be part of an elitist process of social distinction marking of the kind classically analyzed by Pierre Bourdieu (1984). To favor works of independent status might be to strike a blow for democracy and openness, but it is also to mark oneself as "superior," through the exercise of resources of cultural capital that are as unevenly divided as their economic equivalents. The contentious nature of definitions such as independent, indie and/or Indiewood is, to a significant extent, rooted in their relative or contested positions within broader cultural taste hierarchies—each of these being able to claim at least some degree of superiority through its opposition to the larger negative reference point constituted by the Hollywood mainstream.

In the case of American cinema, the notion of the "mainstream" does correspond to a reasonably solid form of opposition, rather than merely serving the purpose of imaginary chimera or mythical other. The Hollywood mainstream, although often used as a form of shorthand, is a quite coherent concept, denoting both a globally dominant industrial regime and a series of textual approaches against which independence can meaningfully be defined, even if only in varying degrees and with some limited space for departure within studio production. But the grounds on which these distinctions are made remain hierarchical and deeply rooted in unequal access to cultural capital. If some varieties of independent or indie film signify "quality" for their target audiences, primarily from the well-educated middle class, often middle-aged (the same ranks, often, as academics, myself included), it is worth remembering that they might suggest rather different qualities ("boring," "cheap," "rubbish," for example) to others whose taste preferences are closer to those of the studio products designed for a broader and often more youth-oriented market. We might want to valorize independence on important grounds of opposition to the control of dominant oligopolies such as that constituted by the Hollywood studios. But we should also remember that what goes under the name is both variable, contested and often designed to suit only a particular range of socially grounded taste patterns.

NOTE

1. I use the terms "cinema" and "film" interchangeably in this chapter, in their generally established usages, rather than to refer specifically, respectively, to either a particular site of exhibition or to the use of either celluloid or video media.

REFERENCES

Biskind, P. (2004) *Down and Dirty Pictures: Miramax, Sundance, and the Rise of Independent Film*. New York: Simon and Schuster.

Bourdieu, P. (1984) *Distinction: A Social Critique of the Judgement of Taste*. London: Routledge.

Fonarow, W. (2006) *Empire of Dirt: The Aesthetics and Rituals of British Indie Music*. Middletown: Wesleyan University Press.

King, G. (2005) *American Independent Cinema*. London: I. B. Tauris.

King, G. (2009) *Indiewood, USA: Where Hollywood Meets Independent Cinema*. London: I. B. Tauris.

King, G. (2013) *Indie 2.0: Change and Continuity in Contemporary American Indie Film*. London: I. B. Tauris.

Merritt, G. (2000) *Celluloid Mavericks: A History of American Independent Film*. New York: Thunder's Mouth Press.

Newman, M. (2011) *Indie: An American Film Culture*. New York: Columbia University Press.

Perren, A. (2012) *Indie, Inc.: Miramax and the Transformation of Hollywood in the 1990s.* Austin: University of Texas Press.

Perren, A. (2013) "Last indie standing: The special case of Lions Gate in the new millennium," in G. King, C. Molloy and Y. Tzioumakis (eds.), *American Independent Cinema: Indie, Indiewood and Beyond*, 108–120. Edinburgh: Edinburgh University Press.

Russell, J. (2013) "In Hollywood but not of Hollywood: Independent Christian film-making," in G. King, C. Molloy and Y. Tzioumakis (eds.), *American Independent Cinema: Indie, Indiewood and Beyond*, 185–195. Edinburgh: Edinburgh University Press.

Ryan, M. and Kellner, D. (1990) *Camera Politica: The Politics and Ideology of Contemporary Hollywood Film.* Bloomington: Indiana University Press.

Tzioumakis, Y. (2012) *Hollywood's Indies: Classics Divisions, Specialty Labels and the American Film Market.* Edinburgh: Edinburgh University Press.

Tzioumakis, Y. (2013) "'Independent,' 'Indie' and 'Indiewood:' Towards a periodisation of contemporary (post-1980) American independent cinema," in G. King, C. Molloy and Y. Tzioumakis (eds.), *American Independent Cinema: Indie, Indiewood and Beyond*, 28–40. Edinburgh: Edinburgh University Press.

Wharton, S. (2013) "Welcome to the (neo) grindhouse! Sex, violence and the indie film," in G. King, C. Molloy and Y. Tzioumakis (eds.), *American Independent Cinema: Indie, Indiewood and Beyond*, 198–209. Edinburgh: Edinburgh University Press.

3 From Independence to Independents, Public Service to Profit

British TV and the Impossibility of Independence[1]

James Bennett

> . . . it's a brutal, horrible business. The media and creativity in general
> are impossible. I mean TV independence is impossible and factual TV
> independence is impossible. I mean they're all impossible.
>
> —CEO of UK Independent TV company
> (Interview 40, December 5, 2011).[2]

Independence has been a central, guiding ideal in the history of British television. It has produced a system populated by both commercial and noncommercial public service broadcasters and producers: from the advent of the BBC in 1922, as a corporation independent of commerce, then to ITV's independence from the BBC's state-sanctioned monopoly in 1955, through to the establishment of Channel 4 in 1982 as a publisher-broadcaster designed to usher in a new commercial independent production sector. The various regulatory and policy structures of the following thirty years have, in turn, been largely concerned with sustaining and growing this independent sector. But the ideal of independence has also seen the British television industry marked by tension and compromise, between the ideals of political independence on the one hand, and the free market and economic and entrepreneurial independence on the other. Spanning these opposing views has been a concern with creating a public service broadcasting system that guarantees both editorial independence and the production of quality, innovative and diverse programming. As Edward Buscombe notes,

> Independence is not, by any means, the only goal of public service broadcasting. Indeed, from one perspective this is a means to an end. Independence is necessary so that a more fundamental purpose may be achieved, that of providing the public with the kind of information they need in order to discharge their full roles as citizens.
>
> (2000: 12–13)

The attempt to meet these ideals, whilst at the same time ensuring the growth of commercial broadcasting and production, has seen a gradual elision between the terms "independence" and "independents," whereby the former has been replaced by the latter: the entrepreneurial, profit-driven "Indie" television production sector that stands outside the central, public service broadcasters but who remain largely dependent on these organizations for their livelihood. Independence has therefore created a tension between public service and profit that continues to shape the experience of British television. For those in the production sector, attempting to reconcile these contradictory impulses can be an impossible undertaking.

This chapter examines the impossibility of that task for producers in the current British television landscape, drawing on interview and ethnographic work from a two-year study of factual producers in the independent sector. Whilst the wider study included an analysis of digital media companies and multiplatform producers (see Bennett, Medrado and Strange in this volume), here I focus on data drawn from our interviews with more than fifty workers spanning thirty independent television production companies, as well as commissioners and producers from the BBC and Channel 4.[3] Placing this study in historical relief against the way ideals of independence have shaped key developments in the organization and regulation of broadcasting, I suggest that despite the impossibility of independence noted earlier, it remains an important and utopian ideal that motivates many of the companies and individuals working across the sector.

Yet within television and media studies more generally, the centrality of independence is little acknowledged. Whilst Paul Bonner and Lesley Aston devote a six-volume history to independent television in Britain, it sheds little light on what being "independent" might mean, let alone what (competing) notions of "independence" might be in play (2003). Alternatively, studies have tended to focus on a single, "independent" institution or sector: such as Cathy Johnson and Rob Turnock's collection on ITV (2005), or the more industry-orientated accounts of the history of Channel 4 and the independent production sector it brought to life (Brown 2007; Darlow 2004; Potter 2008). The lack of attention to independence as an overarching and fundamental concern across developments in British television history is, I argue, a result of a range of historical and often contradictory slippages and extensions of the notion of independence, whereby opposing camps have mobilized its rhetoric in the service of competing aims and ideologies. In what follows I first describe the role independence played in the origins of British broadcasting and the BBC, before tracing how this notion was deployed with contrasting aims and ideals at stake in the coming of ITV and then Channel 4. I then turn to a more detailed study of independent production companies and the "horrible business" that has resulted. Independence, I suggest, has come to mean creative and editorial freedom in order to meet public service ideals of quality, diversity and innovation. However, in emphasizing economic independence from state control and monopoly there has also been a corresponding drive within the industry toward de-unionization and individuation under the neoliberal rhetoric of autonomy and flexibility.

The ideal of independence therefore can be understood to operate relationally as a series of incremental oppositions: between monopoly and free market, high culture and popular culture, mass culture and radical innovation, nonprofit and market liberalism, left-wing and conservative forces. And yet, despite the impossible and contradictory system that results, we nevertheless find a strong pull for many producers toward public service that provides hope, as I set out in the introduction to this volume, that independence might still fulfill some of the democratic and social ideals it has long been associated with.

ORIGINS, IDEALS AND COMPROMISE: PUBLIC SERVICE BROADCASTING AND THE BBC'S COMMERCIAL INDEPENDENCE

> Broadcasting was one of a number of areas . . . in which special pleading by powerful interest groups was disguised as high-minded commitment to some greater good. So anyone who queried, as I did, whether a licence fee . . . was the best way to pay for the BBC, was likely to be pilloried as at best philistine and at worst undermining its "constitutional independence."
>
> (Thatcher 2001: 51)

The BBC's funding by the license fee, paid by all UK television households, has long underpinned its independence from both commercial and political forces. However, it was forged by a range of historically and culturally specific conjunctural factors (Turner 2011) and, upon closer inspection, remains more contingent than first appears. Thatcher's long-standing attack on the Corporation throughout the 1980s and early 1990s is but one such instance that demonstrates the precarious and contested nature of this independence. More recently, the hastily renegotiated license fee settlement between the Corporation and the incumbent Conservative-Liberal Democrat government in 2010 continues to evidence how the BBC's independence remains far from settled.

Yet such independence was one of the main objectives of Lord John Reith's, the founding director general of the BBC, initial conception of broadcasting as a public service. His priority was to establish the independence of the BBC as free from any form of interference: both political and commercial. Paddy Scannell's well-worn history of public service broadcasting details how the crucial step in this conception was taken by the Sykes Committee's report on the regulation of broadcasting, which defined it as a "public utility," to be "regarded as a valuable form of public property" (quoted in Scannell 2000: 46). As such, the committee concluded that "the control of such a potential power over public opinion and the life of the nation ought to remain with the State," but insisted, nevertheless, that the Company was to be independent of the government to avoid "suspicion that it was using its unique opportunity to advance the interests of the political party in power" (quoted in Paulu 1961: 8). Up until this point British broadcasting had been run by the British Broadcasting Company, a consortium of radio manufacturers, which held a monopoly license for the commercial exploitation of the medium.

However, in the years that followed the Sykes Committee's report, Reith pushed forward this ideal of independence as a governing ethos for broadcasting. In the shift from the British Broadcasting *Company* to a publicly owned, not-for-profit British Broadcasting *Corporation* set up by royal charter in 1927, Reith won an ideological battle to promote the BBC as an entity run not only at arm's length from commerce but also from the state. The BBC that emerged was therefore free from its then commercial masters (the radio manufacturers) *and* government. Thus it would be able to put the public interest (or public good) in place of private, commercial imperatives or party political pressures. Such a system was set in stark contrast to the widely held view of the U.S. system as "chaos" created by the compromise between progressives and the almost "untrammelled pursuit of private profits" (Hilmes 2003: 26–27). As Graham Murdock crudely puts the distinction, "the British solution was built around the assumed needs of . . . citizens rather than consumers" (2000: 119). Hilmes's later work has demonstrated how these oppositions were demonstrative of the fact that American commercial and British public service broadcasting needed each other to legitimate themselves in their own territories (2012).

However, the BBC's newly enshrined independence was always and already a compromise. Glen Creeber has noted,

> although not *directly* controlled by the state, the future of the BBC ultimately lay in the hands of the government that continued to periodically renew its licence to broadcast and determine the cost of its licence fee—a practice that continues to this day.
>
> (2003: 23, emphasis original)

This compromise would see the BBC supervised by a board of governors appointed by Parliament in return for a monopoly to be exercised "with the maximum of freedom which parliament is prepared to concede" (Paulu 1961: 9). As Tim Wu has argued in relation to commercial monopolies of communications media, such "control of communications" was only granted in the name of the "greater [national] good" (2010). For the Reithian BBC, therefore, the brute force of monopoly was to be exercised in the national interest, which was often aligned not only with the interests of those in power, but also with ideals of quality. In this sense, public service broadcasting can be seen to have emerged as part of a wider "model of the public utility or public corporation . . . as an alternative to both direct government control and private enterprise" in the early twentieth century, which promised independence from both state and market and the use of scarce national resources for the public good (Curran and Seaton 1997: 113–115).

As a result, Reith's principle of independence had strong appeal to those in government. This was particularly true after the BBC's coverage of the 1926 General Strike, during which it prevented trade union leaders from accessing the airwaves whilst giving ample coverage to the Conservative government. As Lord Reith explained of this bias: "Since the BBC was a national institution, and since the government in this crisis were acting for the people . . . the BBC was for the government in this crisis too" (quoted in Scannell and Cardiff 1991: 33). The freedom promised by independence in broadcasting's early conception, therefore, was primarily defined in opposition to the free market and the pressures of commercialization, adopting the rhetoric of editorial independence even as it was compromised in the name of public and national interest. As Wu argues of radio broadcasting in the 1920s, both the United States and United Kingdom built systems based on earnest ideals of national betterment and quality, underpinned by two different notions of freedom that privileged the liberal market on one side of the Atlantic and monopoly on the other. But, in each setting, "the medium would never be more hopeful or high-minded" (2010). This hope and high-mindedness remains, I argue, in the way independence continues to function in the United Kingdom's television industry, but it is equally shaped by the compromises agreed at the outset of broadcasting.

Indeed, the ideal of independence as editorial freedom from both commerce and government forces grew in the years of the BBC's monopoly, particularly as a result of the BBC's coverage of World War Two. Andrew Crisell describes how the BBC resisted attempts to make it accountable to the Ministry of Information as a weapon of propaganda. Instead, the BBC "maintained a measure of independence from the various government departments," with its "willingness to tell unpleasant truths [meaning] that it could not be as closely associated with the government as, fairly or unfairly, as it had been in pre-war years" (Crisell 2005: 66). An editorially independent ethos during the war thus functioned to insure a more institutionally secure independence after it. So much so that by 1945 the BBC had so parted ways with the narrow view of editorial independence to be exercised in the national interest promulgated by Reith that Winston Churchill believed his own electoral defeat was, in part, due to unfavorable BBC coverage (ibid.: 84).

However, given the continuing role of Parliament in appointing the board of governors and setting the license fee, such independence was never absolute. As we shall see, the BBC's precarious independence from government has often come back to haunt it at key moments in the development of

British broadcasting history. To be sure, just as the BBC had won greater independence from government during the late 1940s, by the turn of the new decade, it came under fire from those seeking to establish a rival commercial service. For the proponents of the new "Independent Television" channel, economic independence from government would act as a guarantor of creative and editorial freedom, against the staid and elitist monopoly of the BBC. The Corporation's response enlisted its status as not-for-profit against the rhetoric of the free market to defend its monopoly on the grounds of its other public service claim to the national interest: that of creating quality programs that the market was incapable of producing. This duality, between public service and profit, quality and mass market, became the next key factor to shape the meaning of independence in British television.

PUBLIC SERVICE AND COMMERCIAL INDEPENDENCE: ITV AND FREEDOM FROM GOVERNMENT MONOPOLIES

ITV began broadcasting in 1955, but the lead up to its establishment was characterized by a "battle between those with commercial and ideological interests in the expansion of television services, and those who feared the impact of commercial forces on British cultural life and public service broadcasting" (Johnson and Turnock 2005: 16). Here, the advocates of a new commercial broadcaster mobilized a conception of independence that was almost the antithesis of the Reithian position established during the first half of the twentieth century. In an argument that would be repeated with the coming of satellite and cable television in the late 1980s and early 1990s independence meant, first and foremost, freedom from state control. In turn, this would promise freedom for the viewer. As Tim O'Sullivan has shown, those in favor of a commercial second television service "argued it was unacceptable for the BBC to continue with the 'brute force of monopoly.'" Commercial competition would represent "enterprise for industry and 'choice' for viewers—a means of liberating control from the patronising and 'out of touch' constrains of the BBC" (2003: 32). The *Beveridge Report* of 1951 had made the case for a new commercial network funded by spot advertising which, taking the lesson from the U.S. experience of distancing quality output from sponsored programming (Curtin 1995), it was hoped would ensure greater editorial independence for producers from advertisers' concerns. The service would also be aimed at the popular and regional markets, away from the upper middle-class taste codes, the South East, and London-centric associations of the BBC. Whilst most support for a commercial service came from the side of business and advertising that stood to gain financially from such a channel, the charges of elitism and what Beveridge termed "Londonization" of the BBC (quoted in ibid.), saw a peculiar coalition of commercial and left-leaning forces that "favoured the modernising tendencies of commercial television in one crucial respect. It would provide a place for the popular culture that was excluded from the public service regime of the BBC" (Ellis 2000: 54). As such, ITV's independence would be particularly defined not only in terms of commercial independence, but also in terms of localism, with its structure of regional franchise holders designed to promote diversity of voices against the hegemony and mainstream of the centralized, London-based BBC. This argument, which linked independence with diversity, returned with the advent of Channel 4 three decades later (as Aymar Jean Christian explores in Chapter 7, the alignment of independence with diversity continues in today's online independent TV market).

However, there remained a concern that commercialization would also bring about a dumbing down of programming and a reduction in quality through an appeal to the mass market. These fears were summed up in the charge that a commercial ITV would lead to the "Americanization" of British television. Here economic independence was once again pitted against the ideals of public broadcasting serving the "national interest." Crisell notes, however, campaigners for a commercial ITV effectively mobilized this ideal of independence against the Corporation:

> The term "independent," said to have been thought up by Norman Collins, was a mischievously clever one. It damaged the BBC, Collins's former employer and sworn enemy, since if ITV was so-called because it was independent of government control the implication was that the BBC was not. In practice too, "independent" became a handy euphemism for "commercial," which had connotations of greed and vulgarity.
> (Crisell 2005: 91)

As a result, the ITV that emerged was one that was primarily in hock with ideals of the free market and independence from government. And yet, ITV's independence was no more absolute than the BBC's before it, with a number of compromises reached in its regulatory and commercial structure. Thus, awarding of regional ITV franchises would be overseen by a newly established Independent Television Authority (ITA), whose membership was not only appointed by Parliament in a similar arrangement to the BBC's board of governors, but as Johnson and Turnock point out, was also "drawn from the same pool of people" (2005: 18). In turn, the ITA was responsible for ensuring programming remained of sufficiently high quality whilst concerns over excessive profits were dealt with by the imposition of a levy on revenues above a set level (Medhurst 2003: 41). Such conditions meant that ITV was not a solely commercially driven station, but was rather "an extension of public service broadcasting, not an alternative" (Scannell 2000: 51). Independence, in the ITV that emerged, therefore was hybrid in a range of often competing and contradictory impulses: public service and commercial; popular and decentralized; free market and regulated.

Many have argued that the arrival of ITV ushered in a new era of populism and competition in British broadcasting history, with the BBC

positioned as adopting a "knee jerk" response by introducing a more popu-
list tone. However, as Jamie Medhurst (2003), Su Holmes (2007) and others have demonstrated, the BBC's turn to populism preceded the advent of
competition and may have enhanced public service broadcasting through
providing a more universally accessible service in terms of its address. For
example, competition in news programming led the BBC to further drop
its government-friendly approach to reporting and absolute commitment
to strictly factual, formal journalism. Such an approach had emphasized a
stance that was free from editorializing and limited, in terms of balance, to
a narrow consensual spectrum of acceptable opinion between the moderate
left and right. In its place came a style of interviewing that was markedly
less obsequious and more inquisitive, with Grace Wyndham Goldie launch-
ing *Tonight* by supporting a skeptical approach in which "it was not always
necessary to be respectful; experts were not invariably right, the opinions of
those in high places did not have to be accepted" (quoted in Crisell 2005:
100). Independence was, once again, a valued editorial attitude on both
sides of the duopoly.

However, by 1960 the government's *Pilkington Report* into the state of
broadcasting found that the "public service compact" (Bennett, Strange,
Kerr and Medrado 2012) had been undermined rather than furthered by
competition. Instead, a "cosy duopoly [had emerged] in which the ITV programme companies were significantly protected from the marketplace . . .
[and both] were regulated by a public service broadcasting remit interpreted
by staff who had commonly worked for both the BBC and ITV" (Johnson
and Turnock 2005: 24). The report came down firmly in favor of the BBC
with the ITA chided for "equating quality with box office success, and was
scathingly condemned for its inability to 'understand the nature of quality or of triviality, nor the need to maintain one and counter the other'"
(quoted in Scannell 2000: 18). As Johnson and Turnock suggest, the *Pilkington Report* "essentially . . . argued that the responsibilities of a public
service broadcaster could not be reconciled with the profit motive of commercial television" (Johnson and Turnock 2005: 24). Despite this warning,
these two contradictory impulses were, again, to fundamentally underpin
the next significant shift in the meaning of independence and public service
broadcasting in UK television with the advent of Channel 4: a not-for-profit
public service broadcaster to be supplied by a for-profit independent production sector.

INNOVATION, DIVERSITY, PROFIT AND PUBLIC SERVICE: CHANNEL 4 AND THE EMERGENCE OF THE INDEPENDENTS

Channel 4 (C4) is, by all accounts, a strange hybrid public service-commercial
broadcaster that incorporates a range of ideals about independence and public service broadcasting. The outcome of the *Annan Report* in 1979, which

as Medhurst has noted, "redefined the role of public service broadcasting altogether," the Corporation commenced in 1982 with a remit for diversity, innovation "and satisfying the needs of the full range of groups in society" (2003: 42). The report argued: "Our society's culture is now multi-racial and pluralist. . . . The structure of broadcasting should reflect this variety" (Annan quoted in Hartley 1992: 68). Funded by advertising, but to sell no advertising itself (this was to be done by the regional ITV companies), C4 was envisioned as editorially independent of both government and market-place, at the same time as it was to usher in a new era of entrepreneurial-ism and free-marketerism in television. As a (somewhat bastard) child of Thatcherism, C4 was part of a wider process of deregulation that aimed "to 'set business free' from bureaucratic, essentially government controls . . . to 'let the market decide.' Private enterprise was the panacea for perceived public service inefficiency" (Crisell 2005: 222–223). The drive for diversity in program form coming as a result of the *Annan Report* was therefore coupled with a drive toward diversifying and multiplying the quantity of production companies, with an implicit belief that the latter guaranteed the former. Here the rhetoric of industrial independence was employed to fos-ter formal and sociopolitical forms of independence. C4 was to produce quality, innovative, alternative programming that addressed minorities—in terms of race, ethnicity, class and taste—away from the mainstream, mass and popular culture of the duopoly.

This would be achieved through C4's unique publisher-broadcaster sta-tus, producing no programs in house and instead commissioning at least a quarter of its output from an independent television production sector that C4's creation would stimulate (the rest was to come from ITV production companies). As with the advent of ITV, a strange coalition of the progressive left and the free-market right was responsible for the latest public service broadcaster on the block. Veteran television producer Michael Darlow's account of the period reveals that the largely left-wing campaigning Channel 4 Group hitched its wagon to Thatcher's 1979 Conservative Manifesto and rebranded itself as a purveyor of "a free market in ideas," even as it looked to promote more radical and diverse programming (Darlow 2004). In this process, however, the importance of financial independence began to take (further) sway in shaping public service broadcasting in the United King-dom. The notion of independence came to be both embodied, and yet ulti-mately replaced, by independents. As I go on to show, such a structure was arguably a formula for dependence and crisis rather than independence and freedom. This elision between independence and independents has harmed the formal and sociopolitical ideals of independence promised by the advent of Channel 4 and the "Indie" sector.

The concern with independence in the structuring of British television I have traced had, until this point, treated distribution and production as an undifferentiated remit of the broadcasters, focusing only on issues of edito-rial and economic independence. As Peter Goodwin notes, this meant that when C4 arrived, the industry "was a vertically integrated one . . . there were only a handful of independent television production companies ('independent,' that is, of the broadcasters)." Independents had produced major hits for the broadcasters—such as Sapphire's production of *The Adventures of Robin Hood* (1955–1959) for ITV—but estimates suggest they contributed "less than 1 per cent of the programme output of either BBC or ITV" (Goodwin 1998: 15). The publisher-broadcaster model of C4 created a crucial stimulus to the development of dozens and soon hundreds of television production companies. As Bonner and Aston detail, at the outset of Channel 4, new chief executive Jeremy Isaacs received "dozens of calls daily from people who called themselves independent producers. But what did that mean?" (2003: 39–40). There was little experience within the sector of actually producing programs outside of the BBC and ITV. These experiences of working within the "mainstream," therefore, would impact the ideals of economic, sociopolitical and formal independence strived for in the new broadcasters' and independent sector's creation.

In terms of the sociopolitical, the reliance on émigrés from the existing broadcasters to establish new independent companies meant that C4 did not necessarily usher in a new era of production diversity in terms of the ethnicity, class, sexuality or gender of program makers (Merck 2013). Nevertheless, various accounts of the early years of the channel depict it as the halcyon days of both the broadcaster and the new indies that provided its content (Hobson 2008). Maggie Brown (2007) and John Ellis (2003) have suggested that the new broadcaster did tap into what they described as a creative frustration of producers working within ITV and the BBC at the time. Drawing in "radicals from the film industry and independent cinema . . . [C4 provided] a substantial platform for left-wing ideas that were being squeezed out of other media, especially the BBC, by the prevailing orthodoxies of Thatcherism" (Ellis 2003: 96). As consensus in Britain broke down, the possibility of retaining traditional notions of balance was no longer viable and C4 instead emphasized balance across the schedule: something that was largely impossible to prove, enabling space for more opinionated and political programming (Ellis 2013). Independence here, therefore, was enlisted to ensure quality through diversity of ideas and program makers. Geoff Mulgan, summarizing debates about quality during the 1980s, notes that diversity provided one of several ideals of quality through the inference that a "broadcasting system of high quality must offer a wide range of programmes" (Mulgan 1990: 32). Certainly the early history of the channel and the independent sector provided a wide range of new topics that hadn't been explored on UK television before, from primetime series about black and Asian Britons to the first gay and lesbian programming through to the emergence of "yoof" television later in the decade (O'Neil 2014). As long-term producer and academic John Wyver has argued, in the "heady early days of Channel 4 . . . it was possible—as it had hardly been before—to produce distinctive and challenging programmes that worked in original ways . . . these programmes exhibited a sense of cultural independence" (2013: 117). At the same time, however, and as Wyver himself admits, the fact that most of the production base was comprised of former ITV and BBC producers meant there was little formal experimentation within this newly emergent independent sector (ibid.; Graham 2013).

In relation to economic independence, C4's publisher-broadcaster structure proved to be far less robust in terms of providing financial security. In turn, this arguably further undermined the kinds of formal and sociopolitical independence envisaged at the broadcasters', and independent sector's, creation. From the outset, independents would not only be charged with making new kinds of programs, but also turning a profit from these productions in a manner completely unfamiliar to the UK television industry. In an arrangement nearly as complex as that established to sell advertising on the new channel, independents would be forced to rely on a negotiated and largely standardized "production fee" for their profit margin, which was calculated at a fixed percentage of the budget. This was, undoubtedly, a precarious business. As Jeremy Isaacs informed the aspirant independent producers assembled for their first ever briefing in 1982, "nobody but a fool makes television programmes that are not pre-sold, in my view . . . That way lies bankruptcy" (quoted in Bonner and Aston 2003: 45). There was significant risk in this system that editorial independence would mean working for free, rather than freedom. As such, the system thus brought dependence rather than independence to the newly formed sector. As John Ellis has argued, "such a system . . . effectively ensured there was no such thing as the independent sector. A system that involved one-off payments for one idea selected from perhaps dozens that Indies offered to the broadcaster was no model for a business structure" (2013: 113).

Despite manifold changes in the economic arrangements of the sector, discussed later in this chapter, many current producers argue that it has been impossible to create an independent sector. As one long-term producer explained during an interview, this is because Indies "don't control the outlet of their product and consequently are wholly dependent upon the decision making priorities . . . of the broadcasters." As this interviewee went on, the independent sector is better understood as "the dependent sector" (Interview 73). Whilst the advent of C4 may have heralded a massive boom in the number of Indies producing television programs, few of these were financially robust. For example, by the time of the next large-scale review of public service broadcasting, *The Peacock Report* in 1986, Channel 4 had bought programs from 360 independents. Only thirteen of these companies received revenues of more than £1m, and 239, or 66 percent, made just one program for Channel 4 that year. A similar percentage (67 percent) received less than £100,000 each in revenues from the broadcasters (Bennett and Kerr 2012). In such circumstances, the freedom of independence left independent companies in a precarious position, often lurching from one financial crisis to the next.

The realities of such uncertain financial footing for many independents were, however, concealed by both the sheer growth of the sector in terms of number of businesses and the overall economic success of Channel 4. These factors, combined with wider shifts in the ideological and political terrain encapsulated by the *Peacock Report* in 1986, meant that by 1992 the independent sector had expanded to more than 1,000 companies whilst the broadcaster itself had demonstrated it could stand on its own two feet, no longer requiring the subsidy from ITV advertising revenues. The *Peacock Report*, however, was to mark a significant shift in the approach to broadcast regulation by treating broadcasting as a commodity and viewers as consumers rather than citizens (Scannell 2000). Combined with the success of C4, it enabled the Thatcher government and its supporters to mobilize ideals of independence associated with the free market against the monopoly of the BBC's license fee:

> Staffed by just 267 people, compared with the BBC's 23,000, [C4] was starting to sparkle as hundreds of small businesses—independent programme producers—demonstrated that they could make public service programming more cheaply than the BBC and ITV. Despite Mrs Thatcher's dislike of the sexually frank material . . . She saw Channel 4 as a shining example of private enterprise in action.
>
> (Brown 2007: 119)

The emphasis on efficiency, however, came at a double cost to the role of sociopolitical and financial independence of public service broadcasting: in both the independent sector and the broadcaster itself. First, in terms of programming form, John Ellis has argued that in the late 1980s and early 1990s, public service broadcasting, as represented by the BBC and C4, came increasingly under "threat from Thatcherism and privatisation." The impact on program makers, independent and in-house, was "more timid programme making . . . Outspoken documentaries were replaced by 'fly on the wall' documentaries, observing the lives of institutions . . .[which] promoted no general conclusions about the state or society: this was left up to the viewers" (2000: 161–162).

Second, the emphasis on economic competition in television production "exerted a downward pressure on broadcasting costs, in particular by weakening the trade union organisation in the industry which had flourished in the large, vertically integrated organisations of the duopoly" (Goodwin 1998: 34). The *Peacock Report*, particularly in its recommendation that both the BBC and ITV should be subject to an independent production quota of 40 percent, underlined the importance of independents to the United Kingdom's public service broadcasting system: not as a source of diversity and independence of voice, but rather as a source of neoliberal entrepreneurialism and efficiency. Arguably, such an outcome fulfilled Thatcher's vision all along. She had come to power at the same time as a devastating technicians' strike at ITV, which saw the unions win large pay raises. The resulting strength of the unions' position in the broadcasters caused Thatcher to describe the duopoly as "the last bastion of restrictive practices" (Thatcher 2001: 51). Up until this point, "the unions [had] ensured similar working practices in both institutions" (Johnson and Turnock 2005: 24).

The elision between independence and independent here came to mean working with the freedom of the market, including from the constraints and perceived restrictive practices of the unions and workplace regulation. The impact on conditions within the sector, continuing to the present day, was immediate and profound. As Goodwin notes, "freelancing has, from the start, been the norm in independent production. But by the mid-80s it was also becoming significant in most other fields of television employment" (1998: 160). By 1989 39 percent of workers were freelance or on short-term (less than one year) contracts; by 1993, this had risen to 54 percent. Skillset, the UK industry body for skills and training in creative media, estimates this is now as high as 60 percent. The overall impact on career paths for television producers has been to make them more unstable, particularly for women (Paterson 2001; Skillset 2012; Ursell 2000). The result, for some, has been the creation of a "morally sick" sector, incapable of reaching the impossible ideals of independence discussed at the outset of this chapter:

> [T]he independent sector has simply been the instrument of a national economic policy to reduce the cost of production. . . . Pay scales are down, working conditions are atrocious, exploitation is massive, training levels have fallen through the floor . . . the crisis in the independent sector and in broadcasting, created by this dependency of the independents whilst simultaneously leaving them to come to terms with the economic limitations and the removal of all employment legislation from the sector, means that we've created a really quite sick, I mean sick, morally sick, in terms of economic health, a very sick, sector.
>
> (IV73)

As Bennett, Medrado and Strange discuss in this volume, work on the moral economy of media work can demonstrate that such an account is too totalizing a description of what working life is like for many inside creative industries. Nevertheless, as Hesmondhalgh and Baker's study of work in the UK television production has suggested, flexible, precarious and individuated work has become the norm within an industry that has led to a great deal of self-exploitation (2008).

And yet, the independent sector continued to grow in importance and size throughout this period and beyond: in 1990 a quota was imposed on the BBC and ITV that required a minimum of 25 percent (measured by volume of hours) of all non-news programming be commissioned from independents. For the BBC, this figure now stands as high as 50 percent as a result of 2007's Window of Creative Competition (competition, that is, with in-house

BBC producers). The legislative concern with safeguarding the economic security of the independent sector arguably reached something of a nadir in 2003, however, with the *Communications Act*. As part of the Labour government's concern to promote the creative industries (see O'Connor 2007), the Act "essentially reversed the rules of programme ownership so that secondary and overseas rights would now revert to the production companies themselves rather than to broadcasters (after the contractually agreed number of terrestrial and digital transmissions)" (Bennett and Kerr 2012: 223). Such policy further stimulated competition and growth in the sector, which is now comprised of more than 700 companies, including a rising number of horizontally and vertically integrated and often internationally owned media conglomerates called "Superindies."

As a result, the sector "has grown from a cottage industry 10 years ago to a record-breaking world leader with revenues of more than £2 billion," according to the chief executive of its trade body, John McVay (PACT 2014). However, this is largely powered by a small group of Superindies that, according to PACT's own figures, saw the top eleven independent production companies account for £1070bn of market revenue between 2002 and 2006 (North and Oliver 2010: 22). Such growth means that the role of independents has shifted far beyond a concern with ensuring independence, as a form of editorial freedom or diversity, in public service broadcasting. Thus, although Channel 4 had been absolutely "decisive in creating, virtually from scratch, the independent production sector," by the mid-1990s the sector had already "outgrown its Channel Four origins" (Goodwin 1998: 33). By the mid-2000s independents were no longer seen as merely a part of public service television provision, but had instead become a central lynchpin in the promotion of the United Kingdom's creative industries as a major source of economic growth for the country.

Such growth, however, has called into question the original role envisioned for independents and may have even reversed the relationship of dependency between broadcaster and sector. As one interviewee complained, "you can be an independent producer and have a turnover of £500million a year . . . Channel 4 was set up to support new production companies . . . but now money is just flowing back to huge corporations that own independent production companies" (IV86). As a C4 senior executive admitted, the impact of "better [IP] rights position under the so called terms of trade," as a result of the 2003 *Communications Act*, led to the sector becoming more "aggregated and consolidated," causing the broadcaster to commission "the so called Superindies, who are much bigger than traditionally Channel 4 would have worked with" (IV50). In combination with a growing reliance on "up-scaling of factual content," through high-budget formatted programs, this has made it "very, very difficult to find small companies with the scale to do" the kinds of programs the broadcaster relies on (ibid.). In turn, the economic power of Indies, and Superindies in particular, has left C4 at their mercy in many respects. Maggie Brown's history of the broadcaster details how during the mid-2000s it had become entirely dependent on *Big Brother* for its ratings and profits, "sapping the ability to innovate." Alongside other big formats, such as the Superindie-produced *Wife Swap*, these programs "soaked up funds and lessened pressure on the handful of dominant programme suppliers to Channel 4 to put their creative thinking caps on" (Brown 2007: 4). As a result, C4 had become "over-dependent on" Superindies' formats and on *Big Brother* in particular, "undermining political support for the channel" (ibid.).

In the growth of the independent sector, therefore, independence has been elided by the free market success of independents. As a result, the tension between profit and public service that has shaped the role of independence in UK television has been placed into sharper relief, raising questions about the extent to which independents can fulfill the citizenry aims of broadcasting, such as quality, diversity, innovation and editorial independence set out in the quote from Buscombe at the start of this chapter. I turn to this issue in the concluding section in order to understand the extent to which independence remains important within the independent sector, and the structure of public service broadcasting more widely in the current UK context.

INDEPENDENTS: PUBLIC SERVICE, PROFIT AND IDEALISM

People woke up to the fact that if you [created] sustainable formats you could make money.

(IV67)

The fact is that I'm not really in it for the money. That does sound disingenuous because obviously I want to make a living. And I do make a living and the people who work here get paid, [but] they would probably get paid more elsewhere. We don't make a huge amount but we make enough. I employ a lot of people so if I was just in it for the money I wouldn't make documentaries.

(IV68)

These two quotes represent divergent views within the industry as to the role of independents in the United Kingdom's current public service broadcasting landscape. On the one hand, there are those who perceive content creation as "all a commercial proposition for the indie" (IV43) regardless of whether it is for a public service or commercial client. For others the creative freedoms, drive for editorial independence and to bring new and diverse stories to the screen has remained paramount, often at the expense of growing revenues. Yet the idealism of the second quote is tinged with pragmatism: the company must turn a profit for him and his employees to make a living. In this view, profit is not irreconcilable with public service, but it does entail compromises—both in terms of how much workers might be paid as well as what kinds of content might get (adequate) funding.

In this final section I suggest that understanding the pragmatism of such independent producers helps to appreciate the continuing role that independence can have in the United Kingdom's television industry. In particular, I focus on the relationship amongst profit, single documentaries and individualism. Here profit can be understood as a form of pressure on editorial independence in the face of the drive to create returnable and saleable formats; "singles," as a form of quality documentary, which bring diverse voices and story to the screen in a manner long associated with public service broadcasting; and the drive to individualism as a description of the working conditions within the sector. Our study concentrates on factual production because, as Brown notes, C4 "could never afford large quantities of home-grown drama, [so] is, at heart, a factual channel" (2007: 141). Whilst a study of another genre of production may yield different results, this is certainly not necessarily so: the companies we examined as part of the study produced a wide variety of content outside of factual programming forms.

Here I argue that rather than see compromise as an absolute failure, independence remains an important ideal that provides a strong motivation for those working in the sector because of its utopian impossibility. Thus whilst David Lee's otherwise admirable study of the public service ethics of producers in the independent sector concludes that the "values that inspired the creation of the independent sector" have been shifted away from as the independent sector has consolidated and come under ownership of commercial investors, looking for a return (Lee 2011: 168), I suggest that a compact between independents and public service broadcasters nevertheless remains (see Bennett et al. 2012).

The 2003 *Communications Act* and resultant terms of trade placed what many perceive as an inexorable pressure to produce returnable and exploitable formats at the expense of editorial independence and challenging, quality or experimental programming. The United Kingdom is the largest exporter of television formats in the world, with the independent sector contributing 72 percent of the United Kingdom's formats in 2009 (PACT 2011: 14). As Lee's study found, the "commissioning focus [is now] on the commercial return, and popular formats, rather than on one-off documentaries" (2011: 160). Summarizing a broadly held position by many within the industry and, indeed, historians of British television, Ellis argues that the departure from radical and innovative program making was assuaged by the emphasis on formats that emerged in the new millennium (2013). Recalling the fears about ITV's introduction of commercialism, more than one independent producer suggested that the result of the drive to formats is "an entrepreneurial situation . . . a race to the bottom: the lowest common denominator" (IV61). Interviewees, particularly television producers with long histories in the sector, complained of a lack of risk and innovation in a commissioning process dominated by formats: "that is where you pitch your films: nothing challenging" (IV68). As Aymar Jean Christian's essay in this volume suggests, the process of commissioning in broadcasting television can mitigate against innovation because, as another interviewee explained, "you can innovate away, but actually if you don't sell it, there's no point in innovating" (IV12). Independent production did not mean editorial or commercial independence as program makers remained at the behest of commissioners and an ever-expanding international market for sales. This emphasis on formatting, therefore, had significant impact on the way independents were organized as businesses and the creative freedoms experienced within them.

The primacy placed on the economic returns made possible in the new free market of intellectual property exploitation meant companies looked to consolidate, merge or position themselves for a buyer. This led, in a number of instances, to "a refocus in programming away from blue chip documentary to factual-entertainment: "'the fatted calf was being prepared,' as one interviewee put it" (IV76) (Bennett et al. 2012: 38). The drive to profits also reduced editorial control and independence, turning television companies into "sausage factories" (IV75), churning out "battery television" (IV79). As this producer went on to describe, an obsession with formats had adverse effects on working conditions:

> They built cutting rooms without windows in their offices, which to me said it all about how they viewed production: for me the cutting room is actually the epicentre of creativity because it is where the film is essentially made.
>
> (IV79)

Such "format factories" (IV94) meant producers were put under pressure to tell stories that fitted a preordained structure including, in one notable example, inventing a mythical IRA plot that might have been responsible for a well-known London fire. Overall, there was a concern that an overemphasis on formats undermined the promise of the independent sector as a space for formal innovation, editorial freedom and quality programming.

This anxiety about a withdrawal from quality took the form of a perceived co-contamination of attitudes toward and funding for one-off documentary films. Barry Dornfeld's study of public service production cultures notes a "folk history" of the long form single documentary as "a prominent genre in public television" (1998: 43). Most interviewees—from both the broadcasters and the independent sector—concurred with this "folk history" of the role of such programming in public service broadcasting, but also noted a long-term withdrawal from "singles." As Ellis has argued, the pull toward formats is contrary to "Channel 4's established practice of short runs and frequent change [that made] continuous innovation" its distinctive brand of public service independence (Ellis 2000: 162). Indeed, 32 percent of interviewees from television independents in our study considered singles to be the highest form of public service broadcasting. The shift away from what many perceive as the diversity of voices, challenging and innovative nature of such programming has threatened the "wholesale destruction of [specialist factual as] a successful genre in television" (IV73). Such a view seemed confirmed by the perspective held by commissioners at both C4 and the BBC. Thus at the BBC, one commissioner spoke of there being

> absolutely no desire to make single films . . . they are really difficult, they require quite a lot of specialist attention and the budgets aren't gigantean and the prize of profits is not going to be as great as coming up with the next *Apprentice*.
>
> (IV63)

Similarly at C4, commissioners spoke of Superindies looking simply at "the mark up that you can make from the various different genres of television and a single factual film does not generate income . . . It can't be sold globally" (IV50). As another concurred, "if you've got a head office in LA, or wherever, . . . you do not want [producers] sitting in an edit for weeks doing singles—its never going to sell [overseas] and the format is never going to sell" (IV94).

In combination with the move toward de-unionization, freelance and short-term contracts in the labor market discussed in the previous section, the drive toward profits from format production have all exerted downward pressure on the conditions for individual workers. As many studies of the industry have attested, self-exploitation and precarious labor are the hallmarks of television production where creative freedom is increasingly equated with working for free. As one interviewee explained:

> [T]he industry is terrible at looking after people. . . . What happens is that because budgets are tight, people are made to work obscenely long hours, people in television are sometimes exploited, especially junior people . . . now there's a culture where that's a kind of accepted thing.
>
> (IV93)

In such a milieu, craft, creativity, editorial independence and the ability to make quality programming all come under threat. In such a view "television is no longer a craft industry, where the self-belief of dedicated individuals in a privileged work situation will ensure that quality programmes are made" (Ellis 2000: 162). Indeed, many complained of a deskilling in the industry: "in a ratings driven market [there has been] a significant diminution of the craft of filmmaking, of camerawork" (IV91). David Lee's study suggests that although evidence of a care for craft might remain, it is largely squeezed by predominant attitudes within the industry that are increasingly "neo-liberal in flavour, favouring enterprise, commercialism, competition, flexibility and individualism," largely replacing "established television production values orientated around craft, quality and public service" (Lee

2011: 157–160). Moreover, such conditions have actually diminished the diversity of voices within the industry. As working for free, or at very low wages, becomes a norm to "make it" within the independent production sector, the pool of people with the financial and cultural capital to risk such conditions becomes invariably smaller. Skillset's 2012 survey of the sector indicates that just 7.5 percent of the total television workforce comes from black, Asian and minority ethnic backgrounds (2012). Here, it seems, the primacy of independents' commerciality seems to have truly replaced ideals of independence.

And yet, despite the emphasis on format sales and the withdrawal of funding for one-off documentaries, a desire to produce films that "make a difference" (Bennett 2015) persists within the sector. Such an ethos continues to be motivated by ideals of independence that underpinned the foundation of C4 and the independent sector. Thus producers spoke of creating challenging, one-off programming as "projects of passion rather than of profits" (IV91). Throughout our study there were numerous examples where companies and individuals were willing to put public service and editorial independence on the same footing as profits. For individuals, Lee's study of television producers found a "Neo-Reithian" ethic of production existed as a counter-discourse to the individualization and deskilling of television work. Similarly our study found workers willing to swap some aspects of security and economic reward for the independence of creative and editorial freedom to make public service-orientated programming. Here, as David Hesmondhalgh's work has shown, "to treat these positive components of creative work as mere sugar coatings for the bitter pill of precariousness is surely too dismissive of the genuinely positive experiences that some creative workers have in their jobs and careers" (2010: 282). Instead, we need to understand that workplace and creative autonomy can be highly valued by individuals and enable them to produce "good work, in the sense of work that contributes to the common good" (ibid.). Such commitments, however, required companies to make a similar investment in the belief of editorial independence and public service as a production culture, realigning the priorities between profit and public service I have thus far traced across the industry.

One such example was found in Lambent Productions, a small Brighton-based independent company specializing in one-off documentaries. Emma Wakefield, the CEO, has argued powerfully for the importance of this approach in a special issue of *Critical Studies in Television* on Channel 4's thirtieth anniversary:

> Lambent, as an independent production company whose first concern is to make a profit, has an ethos—a production culture—that is underpinned by public service broadcasting. When we set Lambent up we wanted to make films that made a difference: to make television that matters. This ethos inspires and underpins everything we do: … our

content . . . how we collaborate . . . our staff . . . how we define and structure the company, and informs our goals and ambitions. And the bridge between the business and the creative side—between the PSB purpose and the profit—is value.

(Wakefield 2013: 124)

Such an approach informed what kinds of projects the company was willing to work on, and although this did require an inevitable compromise, this compromise was taken in relationship to the size of profits rather than their editorial independence or public service ethos. As Wakefield reflected, such programming did not make a huge profit—but as the quote at the head of this section suggests, many in the sector are not in it for the money. Thus another managing director opined, "if you want to make money become an estate agent" (IV34). Nevertheless, in such a view, public service and profit are not incompatible:

It's not easy; there are tough choices here and sometimes those choices cost us. Purpose does come before profit, but profit can—and does—come from work that is riven with a PSB ethos. When that work has value beyond the budget though, it makes the profit that much sweeter.

(Wakefield 2013: 126)

Indeed, for others, the relationship between public service and profit, broadcaster and independent was symbiotic. In the same issue of *Critical Studies in Television*, Alex Graham has rejected the tension between profit and commerce as a fanciful vision of "artists dragged kicking and screaming into the marketplace and *forced* to make consumer product." Instead, he argues, we should understand that most television producers want to exploit the mass potential of the television marketplace in order to tell their stories to the widest possible audience. Graham—then the CEO of a much larger independent company, Wall-to-Wall, which was purchased by a Superindie in 2007—suggested that their biggest commercial success was also "the 'perfect' public service" program (Graham 2013: 115). He rightly points out that this format, *Who do you think you are?*, has won plaudits for making British and world history, along with genealogy, accessible, fun and informative to audiences around the globe. Such instances, whilst rare, are worth highlighting because they circulate as highly visible stories within the industry that suggest the utopian ideals of editorial independence, public service and profit may not be impossible. But the elision between independence and independents has made their achievement harder to conceive. As Aymar Jean Christian discusses in Chapter 7, independent television production remains a fragile concept, but one in which we can continue to invest hope for its potential to produce innovative, diverse and challenging content.

NOTES

1. My thanks to Paul Kerr in the writing in this chapter, whose knowledge of early broadcast history and the independent sector was invaluable.
2. Interviewees are referred to by interview number—1–105—throughout this chapter in the format: IV1–105.
3. This research was conducted as part of the Arts & Humanities Research Council project "Multiplatforming public service broadcasting," AH-H018522-2. For a full discussion of methodology and findings, see Bennett et al. 2012.

REFERENCES

Bennett, J. (2015) "Public service as production cultures: A contingent, conjunctural compact," in M. Banks, B. Connor and V. Mayer (eds.), *Production Studies: Volume 2*, forthcoming. London & New York: Routledge.

Bennett, J. and Kerr, P. (2012) "A 360° public service sector? The role of independent production in the UK's public service broadcasting landscape," in G. F. Lowe and J. Steemers (eds.), *Regaining the Initiative for Public Service Media: RIPE@2011*, 219–236. Gothenburg: Nordicom & University of Gothenburg Press.

Bennett, J., Strange, N., Kerr, P. and Medrado, A. (2012) *Multiplatforming Public Service Broadcasting: The Cultural and Economic Role of UK Television and Digital Independents*. London: Royal Holloway.

Bonner, P. and Aston, L. (2003) *Independent Television in Britain, Volume 6: New Developments in Independent Television, 1981–92, Channel 4, TV-am, Cable and Satellite*. Basingstoke: Palgrave MacMillan.

Brown, M. (2007) *A Licence to be Different: The Story of Channel 4*. London: BFI Publishing.

Buscombe, E. (2000) "Introduction," in E. Buscombe (ed.), *British Television: A Reader*, 3–22. Oxford: Oxford University Press.

Creeber, G. (2003) "The origins of public service broadcasting," in M. Hilmes (ed.), *The Television History Book*, 22–26. London: BFI Publishing.

Crisell, A. (2005) *An Introductory History of British Broadcasting*. London and New York: Routledge.

Curran, J. and Seaton, J. (1997) *Power Without Responsibility: The Press and Broadcasting in Britain*, 4th edition, London and New York: Routledge.

Curtin, M. (1995). *Redeeming the Wasteland: Television Documentary and Cold War Politics*. New Brunswick: Rutgers University Press.

Darlow, M. (2004) *Independents Struggle: The Programme Makers Who Took On the TV Establishment*. London: Quartet.

Dornfeld, B. (1998) *Producing public television: producing public culture*. Princeton, NJ: Princeton University Press.

Ellis, J. (2000) *Seeing Things: Television in the Age of Uncertainty*. London: I. B. Tauris.

Ellis, J. (2003) "Channel Four: Innovation in form and content?," in M. Hilmes (ed.), *The Television History Book*, 95–98. London: BFI Publishing.

Ellis, J. (2013) "From new born to last gasp? Channel 4 and the independent sector," *Critical Studies in Television* 8, 1: 111–113.

Goodwin, P. (1998) *Television under the Tories: Broadcasting Policy 1979–1997*. London: BFI Publishing.

Graham, A. (2013) "Cowboys or indies?," *Critical Studies in Television* 8, 1: 113–116.

Hartley, J. (1992). *Tele-ology: Studies in Television*. London and New York: Routledge.

Hesmondhalgh, D. (2010) 'User generated content, free labour and the cultural industries', *Ephemera: Theory & Politics in Organization* 10, 3/4: 267–284.

Hesmondhalgh, D. and Baker, S. (2008). "Creative work and emotional labour in the television industry," *Theory, Culture & Society* 25, 7–8: 97–118.

Hilmes, M. (2003) "The origins of commercial broadcasting in the US," in M. Hilmes (ed.), *The Television History Book*, 26–30. London: BFI Publishing.

Hilmes, M. (2012) *Network Nations: A Transnational History of British and American Broadcasting*. London and New York: Routledge.

Hobson, D. (2008) *Channel 4: The Early Years and the Jeremy Isaacs Legacy*. London: I. B. Tauris.

Holmes, S. (2007) "'A friendly style of presentation which the BBC had always found elusive?' The 1950s cinema programme and the construction of British television history," in H. Wheatley (ed.), *Re-viewing Television History: Critical Issues in Television Historiography*, 67–81. London: I. B. Tauris.

Johnson, C. and Turnock, R. (2005) "From start up to consolidation: Institutions, regions and regulation over the history of ITV," in C. Johnson and R. Turnock (eds.), *ITV Cultures: Independent Television Over Fifty Years*, 15–35. Maidenhead: Open University Press / McGraw Hill.

Lee, D. (2011) "Precarious creativity: Changing attitudes towards craft and creativity in the British independent television production sector," *Creative Studies Journal*, 4, 2: 155–170.

Medhurst, J. (2003) "Competition and change in British television," in M. Hilmes (ed.), *The Television History Book*, 40–44. London: BFI Publishing.

Merck, M. (2013) "Channel 4, public service broadcasting and diversity: The Paralympics and *Out on Tuesday*," *Critical Studies in Television* 8, 1: 121–124.

Mulgan, G. (ed.) (1990). *The Question of Quality (Vol. 6)*. London: BFI Publishing.

Murdock, G. (2000) "Money talks: Broadcasting and public culture," in E. Buscombe (ed.), *British Television: A Reader*, 119–142. Oxford: Oxford University Press.

North, S. and Oliver, J. (2010) "Manager's perceptions of the impact of consolidation on the UK independent television production industry," *Journal of Media Business Studies* 7, 2: 21–38.

O'Connor, J. (2007). *The Cultural and Creative Industries: A Review of the Literature*. London: HPM and Arts Council England.

O'Neil, M. (2014) Digital Spray: Channel 4, Innovation and Youth Programming in the Age of New Technologies. Unpublished PhD thesis. University of Portsmouth.

O'Sullivan, T. (2003) "Post-war television in Britain: BBC and ITV," in M. Hilmes (ed.). *The Television History Book*, 30–35. London: BFI Publishing.

PACT (2011) *Submission to DCMS Communications Review*. Available http: www. pact.co.uk/support/document-library/documents/.

PACT (2014). "TV and film recognised for economic power," www.pact.co.uk/about-us/news/tv-and-film-recognised-for-economic-power/#sthash.Ohg43l8I.dpuf.

Paterson, R. (2001) "Work histories in television," *Media, Culture & Society* 23, 4: 495–520.

Paulu, B. (1961) *British Broadcasting in Transition*. London: Macmillan.

Potter, I. (2008). *The Rise and Rise of the Independents: A Television History*. London: Guerilla Books.

Scannell, P. (2000) "Public service broadcasting: The history of a concept," in E. Buscombe (ed.), *British Television: A Reader*, 45–62. Oxford: Oxford University Press.

Scannell, P. and Cardiff, D. (1991) *The Social History of British Broadcasting (Vol 1.)* Oxford: Blackwell.

Skillset. (2012) *TV Labour Market Intelligence Digest 2011*. Available http: http://creativeskillset.org/assets/0000/6016/TV_Labour_Market_Intelligence_Digest_2011.pdf.

Thatcher, M. (2001) "Margaret Thatcher: The Downing Street years," extracted in B. Franklin (ed.), *British Television Policy: A Reader*, 50–53. London: Routledge.

Turner, G. (2011) "Convergence and divergence: The international experience of digital television," in J. Bennett and N. Strange (eds.), *Television as Digital Media*, 31–51. Durham, NC: Duke University Press.

Ursell, G. (2000) "Television production: Issues of exploitation, commodification and subjectivity in UK television labour markets," *Media, Culture & Society* 22, 6: 805–825.

Wakefield, E. (2013) "All shapes and sizes: Plurality, diversity, regionality," *Critical Studies in Television* 8, 1: 124–126.

Wu, T. (2010) *The Master Switch: The Rise and Fall of Information Empires.* Available http: www.capitolreader.com/sum/10211-masterswitch.pdf.

Wyver, J. (2013) "The same, only different: 'Cultural independence' and Illuminations," *Critical Studies in Television* 8, 1: 117–118.

4   Popular Music, Independence and the Concept of the Alternative in Contemporary Capitalism

David Hesmondhalgh and Leslie M. Meier[1]

INTRODUCTION: MUSIC, INDEPENDENCE AND FREEDOM

The concept of independence has been more important in popular music than in any other cultural form. In this chapter, we examine the changing ways independence has operated in the music industries since the 1950s, and just as importantly, among popular music audiences and in associated worlds of informal, amateur and semiprofessional musical production. In particular, we argue that digitalization and the Internet, widely hailed as producing new forms of autonomy in professional music making, have also created new modes of dependence.

As in other cultural industries, the term "independents" in the world of music usually refers simply to organizations that are not "corporations," understood as vertically integrated, well financed and *big*. Like most cultural industries the recording industry, which we focus on here,[2] has tended to take the form of an oligopoly of large companies with a very large market share, based on domination of distribution, financing and manufacture, coexisting with myriad smaller companies dealing mostly in geographical and/or cultural niches. Music independents tend to operate in market niches of which large record companies are unaware, or in which they are uninterested. Their lower operating costs and local operations make them well suited to capitalize on the fact that music making takes place everywhere in the world, takes vastly divergent forms, and is often relatively cheap, and even free—it costs nothing to sing.

However, the economics of the cultural industries under capitalism disproportionately rewards big hits (because of the relationship of fixed to marginal costs) and the creation of stars who effectively act as brand names in markets where it is difficult for buyers to know what kinds of pleasures they might be getting in advance from any individual cultural product. These are conditions that favor larger companies, and there has always been a strong tendency toward oligopoly and vertical integration in the cultural industries. At the same time, low operating costs and small workforces mean that many tiny record companies have often been able to survive on sales of hundreds rather than hundreds of thousands. So even though a very small group of large corporations (the ownership and composition of which changes from time to time) has dominated the recording industry for decades, both within particular nations and continents, and globally, these behemoths have coexisted alongside a massive number of independents, which are highly varied in their size, operation and motivations. They include substantial but privately owned companies (i.e., not listed on stock exchanges) that compete with the majors, yet also often coexist with them, entering into joint ventures of various kinds (Hesmondhalgh 1996). There are also thousands of "micro-independents" offering every conceivable flavor of musical taste, often to no more than a few hundred aficionados. The smaller enterprises often grow out of local scenes of music making and associated businesses (instrument and record shops, places of entertainment serving as venues etc.) and may not even be legally registered—in much of the world, cultural businesses primarily exist in the "informal economy" (Hunter et al. 2013).

What's more, independents have played a more crucial role in the history of recorded music than in, say, the history of film or book publishing. Although many well-known stars and recordings were contracted to major record labels, certain independents have been celebrated for their key role in a range of genres. Examples from U.S. popular music history include the role in jazz of labels such as Prestige, Riverside and Blue Note; in soul of Motown, Stax and Atlantic; in hip-hop of Def Jam, Death Row and Cash Money; in rock of Sun, Elektra and Sub Pop. The stars and recordings issued by these labels include some of the most prestigious in the history of music.[3]

What is also striking about the concept of independence in popular music, compared with its manifestation in other cultural forms, is the remarkable degree to which aesthetic-political hopes have been invested in independent record companies, especially in genres that are understood by their followers (including intermediaries such as journalists) to have social and cultural significance beyond musical pleasure or beauty, such as jazz, rock, soul and hip-hop. Institutional musical independence has been very strongly linked to ideas of aesthetic, institutional and political *alternatives*: to the idea that independence might contribute to the formation of different and better ways of organizing cultural production and consumption, and society itself.

Why has this been the case? A key context here is the relationship, in some everyday popular musical discourse, of independence as an institutional and organizational matter to more fundamental ideas about artistic *freedom*, which are in turn related to the hugely complex and disputed notion of *autonomy*. And music is a realm in which such ideas about artistic freedom and autonomy have been felt to matter a great deal. This fact derives from post-Enlightenment conceptions of the aesthetic as a vital realm of experience. In the wake of perceptions that religious thought could no longer act as a secure source of knowledge, the aesthetic came to be understood as a realm where the instrumentalism of science and the pursuit of wealth could be countered, providing access to more meaningful truths about being. Crucially, music was given a privileged place within such post-Enlightenment aesthetic thought because of its supposedly special links to subjectivity, often felt to be manifest in its power to express, arouse or instill emotion (see Hesmondhalgh 2013a). Such thinking, when combined with critiques of industrialism, helped to produce the idea that creativity and commerce were antagonistic to each other. Versions of that idea are often naïve and ill thought out, and are often dismissed by sniffy theorists as "romantic." But many versions hint at real contradictions and struggles over culture in societies where capitalism provides the main way economic life is conducted. Of course, creativity can flourish in capitalist conditions. Yet there remains a sense that the pursuit of profit can, and often does, inhibit culture's capacity to suggest routes to emancipation. Most music recorded and sold by "independent" record companies is far removed from such grand ideas of artistic freedom and autonomy. Yet popular music independence cannot be understood without considering changing discourses of "the alternative," of alterity.[4]

In that wider context, musical independence provides a testing ground for the achievements of vernacular cultural opposition in the era of neoliberalism. It offers a chance to assess the ability of the artistically and politically committed to provide a real and lasting alternative to prevailing ways of making music and doing business. Our story is essentially one of the rise and fall of musical independence as it was conceived by the counterculture.[5] But, as will become apparent, our conclusions are not entirely cynical or pessimistic.

DISCOURSES OF INDEPENDENCE AND THE "ALTERNATIVE"

The recording industry, like other major cultural industries such as television, expanded rapidly in the 1950s and 1960s, as leisure time and spending increased, at least in the global north. The major record companies were primarily consumer electronics producers who had entered into the recorded music industry (and often the radio business) as something of a sideline, such as RCA, Philips and EMI. The rapid growth of the recorded music business in the 1950s allowed the most successful majors to become international oligopolies. At the same time, new cultural meanings were being attached to popular music. Popular music's connections to emotion, sentiment and sexuality made it central to a new political economy based on individualism and consumerism. The links to sexuality and the breaking of boundaries between sacred and profane, and to complex trajectories of "race" and youth, also made certain musical forms the object of a new politicization. This was the kind of interpretation offered in the burgeoning worlds of musical criticism and cultural commentary (made possible by the growth of other cultural industries, such as newspapers, books and magazines) and in the new and expanding universities, filled with baby boomers.

By the time of the 1960s counterculture, the companies that dominated the recording industry were seen by growing phalanxes of young, middle-class, educated listeners as exemplars of modern bureaucracy, as hegemonic purveyors of mass culture. In an era of critiques of "mass culture" (see Ross 1989 for a survey) and "organisation man" (Whyte 1956), middle-class countercultural youth made strong distinctions between the hip and the square, between rebellion and everyday passive conformity. Starting with jazz, and then applying similar ideas to folk and rock, the proponents of a new cultural politics of music saw such genres as instances of vibrant, youth-oriented popular music that the organization men of the large record companies had then appropriated and made safe, to be sold to the masses alongside the mainstream entertainment of "show business," bland musicals and moronic teenage pop (Chapple and Garofalo 1977). In this context, the small record companies responsible for key recordings in postwar jazz, R&B, soul and so forth (see earlier in this chapter) began to be understood by the newly developing countercultural commentariat as rebels against the corporate oligopoly, as defenders of musical integrity, authenticity and expression against commodification and co-optation. Perceived in this way, they became part of rock culture's mythologization of popular music history. Even where it was known or suspected that independent labels were involved in appalling (often racist) rip-offs of the artists whose output they recorded, this was overlooked or implicitly forgiven, on the grounds that this was evidence of a gritty American hucksterism (a view apparent, for example, in the work of journalists such as Nik Cohn—see Cohn 1970). The fact that, from the 1960s, the major record labels were handling aesthetically and politically challenging music was seen as a sign of their intention to dilute and/or capture the music's potential (Chapple and Garofalo 1977).

AFTER PUNK: THE HEYDAY OF ALTERNATIVE INDEPENDENCE AND ITS APPROPRIATION

A key development in the changing meaning of independence in popular music was the emergence of punk and "new wave" in the late 1970s. Those influenced by punk thinking inherited and transformed a version of the countercultural discourses outlined earlier. They set themselves vehemently against what they saw as the complacency of the counterculture, but drew on countercultural ideas to do so. According to punk thinking, rock had lost its power, partly because its stars had become rich and out of touch with the vernacular vitality that gave popular music its energy and legitimacy. Musical independence was essential to restoring that vigor. In spite of the rise of a number of independent labels in the mid-1970s with links to the punk scene, such as Stiff and Chiswick, the two most important UK punk acts signed to majors—the Sex Pistols to EMI and the Clash to CBS (later bought by

Sony).[6] The Pistols had nihilistically rejected hippie principles concerning boundaries between art and commerce (along with much else), whereas the Clash's politics were didactic and politicized—so they were lambasted for signing to CBS.[7] In the United Kingdom and in the United States (where the Clash's debut album sold 100,000 copies on import alone) the debate about such "selling out" helped to fuel the growth of a new generation of labels, inspired by the Do-It-Yourself ethos of punk, a politics and an aesthetic of access and mobilization, expressed (among many examples) in one fanzine's diagram of guitar chords (A, E and G), accompanied by the words "this is a chord, this is another, this is a third—now form a band" (reproduced in Savage 1991: 280) and in the band Desperate Bicycles' invocation: "It was easy, it was cheap, go and do it" and in their publication of their own recording costs on a record sleeve (Reynolds 2005: 97). As we pointed out earlier, far more than film and television, and even print, popular music can be based on relatively cheap means of production and access costs, especially in situations where audiences affiliate themselves with an aesthetic of rawness and energy rather than sophistication and complexity. This is partly what has made popular music more amenable to an ethos of DIY independence than any other cultural industry, especially in certain genres. By the early 1980s, as sales of recorded music slumped in the global recession of the time, post-punk independents had created alternative distribution networks for recordings that formed a significant challenge to the multinationals. There were increasing cultural and institutional connections between myriad local punk and post-punk scenes around the world.

The formation of these alternative networks was achieved by a much more reflexive and socially aware critique than that provided by the rock counterculture (see Hesmondhalgh 1997; Reynolds 2005: 92–110). The organic intellectuals of post-punk inherited the '60s counterculture's romantic opposition of art to commerce but added to it a recognition of the politics of musical production and circulation—the problem of getting products to audiences. In the United Kingdom, the influential music press began, from 1979, to publish charts of the best-selling independent products, providing an alternative measure of popularity to the standard top 40 or 50 lists that then occupied a central place in the music industries (see Fonarow 2006: 30–33). It was in these circumstances that the term "indie" evolved, initially in the United Kingdom: uniquely, a musical genre term that, as an abbreviation of "independent," referred to production and distribution, and was therefore an encapsulation of the political-aesthetic hopes invested in small and decentralized recording industry institutions. The term was later applied to other media, to comics, to literature, to cinema and to "indie culture" as a whole (see Oakes 2009).[8] In the realm of popular music, the terms "alternative rock" and "alternative pop" were more widely used in the United States in the 1980s and 1990s. Indie was more often used in the United Kingdom and usually referred to music with a nostalgic, pop-based aesthetic. But the terms have shifted over the years, especially since the term "indie" began to be used more globally, and it would take a separate book chapter to track the changing nuances of "indie" and "alternative" and the relations between them (see Fonarow 2006: 40 for one differentiation). This suggests how closely intertwined the two concepts have been in popular music.

Especially in the early 1980s, the music associated with these notions of institutional and aesthetic independence was rich, diverse and innovative (see Azerrad 2001; Reynolds 2005). In the words of one noted writer, it "felt like one long rush of endless surprise and inexhaustible creativity. You were constantly anticipating the next twist, the latest leap forward" (Reynolds 2005: 517). By the early 1990s, musicians inspired by this aesthetic environment, and who had emerged from punk and post-punk independent labels and associated "scenes" (REM, Nirvana, U2), were achieving huge international success on "independently managed" subdivisions of major labels, or on independents such as Island, which now had such close ties to the majors that they were essentially part of them. Yet indie/alternative rock and pop had entered into institutional, aesthetic and political crisis. During the 1990s, important labels such as Rough Trade and Factory had gone bankrupt, following years of chaos and/or conflict over the need to move toward more "professional" ways of working (Hesmondhalgh 1997; King 2012). Although systems of independent distribution established in the post-punk era remained in place throughout the 1990s, they had lost their link to post-punk notions of independence, and many labels had entered into close financing, distribution and marketing partnerships with the corporations, by now thriving in the era of the compact disc. The socialist and anarchist movements whose thinking helped to shape post-punk independence had sustained defeat after defeat. Although a system of "micro-independents" (Strachan 2007) and an international punk underground (O'Connor 2008), based on principles of autonomy and doing it yourself continued, and even thrived in the 1990s, the cross-class nature of the punk moment venerated by indie culture had evaporated. Indie and alternative rock/pop had become, to use the language of sociologist Pierre Bourdieu, the preferred musical tastes of the dominated fraction of the dominant class—that is, those who had relatively high levels of cultural capital, but relatively low economic capital, compared with others in the same social class.[9] In the United States, alt rock became "college music," disseminated relentlessly on college radio stations (Kruse 2003: 10). In the United Kingdom, one wing of post-punk developed an alternative pop aesthetic based on a critique of the sexism and machismo of hard rock and heavy metal, much of it based on a celebration of childhood and a desexualized appreciation of '60s pop and psychedelia (Reynolds 1989), critically—but sympathetically—elaborated the various aesthetics at play in this classic form of indie. By the mid-1990s, that aesthetic had become detached from any notion of political and cultural opposition (Hesmondhalgh 1999). "Britpop" tied indie aesthetics to a nostalgic English nationalism and reverence for a canon of mainstream rock. At times, this was insipid and at its worst conservative, though the raucous hedonism of bands such as Oasis drew some working-class fans back to the indie tradition, and it became part of mainstream rock. Indie and alternative rock were by now symptomatic of an increasingly backward-looking, retrospective culture.[10] By the turn of the century, even the most committed fans would be hard pressed to argue that indie and alternative musical culture was in any meaningful sense "independent" of, or "alternative" to, anything much (see Azerrad 2001: 493–501) except in various underground manifestations often known only to a few thousand enthusiasts. Bands in the indie and alternative traditions became increasingly pragmatic about having their work placed in an advert or on a film and television soundtrack, allowing a steady stream of rights income (see Klein 2009)—an issue that we discuss later in this chapter. Meanwhile, the key indie media institutions (networks of record shops, live venues and radio stations, plus what remained of the declining alternative music press) started to act as something close to niche-oriented entertainment outlets.[11]

Of course, there were other developments in popular music outside the world of rock, in its mainstream and indie versions. But none of them had much of an explicit relationship to the notion of independence, other than the obvious desire on the part of individual acts to maximize "artistic control" and income. In Europe, while electronic dance music and rave culture had offered a new moment of subcultural alterity in the late 1980s and early 1990s, they largely eschewed alternative notions of institutional independence (Hesmondhalgh 1998), and by 2000 had faded as forces for aesthetic innovation beyond small niches. Hip-hop was as reliant as most other genres on independent institutions to maintain a flow of new, challenging styles, but its pragmatic—even cynical—refusal of a politics of production meant that hip-hop independent institutions were often without any commitment to providing any long-term institutional alternative.[12]

A NEW TYPE OF CAPITALISM?

These developments of course suggest that "indie" and "alternative" rather rapidly became misnomers, and it's possible to see them as confirmation of an old story, whether in its academic or vernacular form, of co-optation and "selling out," about how challenges to hegemonic, dominant forms of culture inevitably get absorbed under capitalism. But what happened to indie and alternative music is arguably symptomatic of some broader changes in the relationship between business on the one hand and political, cultural and aesthetic opposition on the other, in a way that has significant implications for the very concept of "media independence."

As we have seen, the rock counterculture linked a critique of corporate business to alternative aesthetics, and punk took up in earnest the challenge of providing an alternative institutional infrastructure to that of shareholder-led multinational entertainment conglomerates. Yet the counterculture also fostered a new kind of capitalism that was more willing than ever to produce goods and services that at least purported to be critical of capitalism and/or modernity. One version of this story is told by Thomas Frank (1998) in his book *The Conquest of Cool*. Frank, examining in particular the businesses of advertising and clothing, shows how countercultural notions of hipness and coolness became integral to new forms of consumer capitalism during the 1960s.[13] In a fuller sociological analysis, Luc Boltanski and Eve Chiapello (2005) have outlined a new spirit of capitalism that emerged in the 1960s. Their account differentiates two principal ways capitalist societies have been criticized—social critique and artistic critique. Social critique emphasizes poverty, inequality, the opportunism and egoism of private interests, and the destruction of social bonds brought about by capitalism. Artistic critique, with its roots in bohemianism and romanticism, instead stresses capitalism as a source of disenchantment and inauthenticity, and the limits it places on freedom, autonomy and creativity (Boltanski and Chiapello 2005: 35–38). Boltanski and Chiapello trace how, faced with a crisis of legitimacy and motivation in the late 1960s, under pressure from both the social and artistic critiques (coming together in the events of 1968 in France and across much of the world), capitalist institutions responded by validating the artistic critique, especially critical demands for autonomy in working life. Measures aimed at providing security for workers were replaced by measures aimed at relaxing hierarchical control and allowing people to fulfill their individual potential (Boltanski and Chiapello 2005: 190). Boltanski and Chiapello's analysis provides a way to understand the fate of alternative culture and media independence in the era of the Web. For, as we shall see, the 1990s and 2000s saw these phenomena, based on the artistic critique, more and more validated and appropriated by capitalist organizations, and increasingly divorced from social critique (the theme of countercultural movements, capitalism and independence is explored further in Daniel Kreiss's chapter in this volume).

THE STATE OF INDEPENDENCE IN THE ERA OF THE WEB: A DUAL SYSTEM

In the 2000s, the recording industry faced a crisis not seen since the early 1980s and perhaps since the 1930s (Hesmondhalgh 2010). The majors made a series of mistakes in meeting the digital challenge, and were presented as outdated behemoths by journalists (Knopper 2010 is just one account of this kind). The continuing popularity of guitar music laid the basis for great success by some independent labels with roots in the post-punk world (such as XL and Domino). But the kind of hopes that were once invested in small record companies had migrated to new Web-based forms: commentators, musicians and fans increasingly sought, and foresaw, a better and more just musical future in networked forms of digital distribution. They saw in the declining revenues of the corporate record companies and the larger "independents" that seemed to offer less and less of a genuine alternative evidence of the democratizing power of the Internet.

As the dust has settled on what remains of the recorded music industry after the earthquake of digitalization, two main types of popular music independence remain. The first involves fairly well-established large independents (almost akin to mini-majors in the U.S. film business, or the super-indies of the European television industry—see the chapters from King and Bennett respectively in this volume), many of them with close financing, distribution and other connections to the majors, selling various versions of alternative music, some but not that much of it distinguishable from the products of major record companies. The second is a world of amateur and precarious semiprofessional musical production, including the continuing world of underground scenes and micro-independent institutions. This second type of independence is able to draw upon a remarkable range of new production technologies and digital distribution mechanisms (see Hector Postigo's chapter in this volume on new modes of amateur-independent production in gaming). However, in spite of considerable hype about initiatives such as crowd funding, the new digital technologies have failed to offer a sustainable and meaningful institutional alternative to corporate capitalism (in its cultural-industry and IT forms). As we shall show in the remainder of this chapter, the hopes invested in new forms of alternative independence in the new digital musical world were just as, if not more, misplaced than those of their countercultural and punk-influenced predecessors.

Crucial to understanding musical independence, and indeed media independence in general, in the twenty-first century is the new shape of the cultural industries that emerged in the first decade. This was marked by the following features:

- a widespread belief that the "old" cultural industries, based on analog forms of cultural production, were being displaced by new forms enabled by the IT and mobile telecommunications sectors, and a related sense of crisis in the record companies that had been the center of musical production and distribution for more than five decades;
- the increasing use of branding, sponsorship and other ways of maximizing revenue, such as cross-media use (the use of songs in advertising or on soundtracks), sales of merchandise and an increasing premium on live musical experiences;
- an intensification of existing patterns of cultural labor markets, based on the "over-production" by higher education systems of workers ready and willing to work in cultural production, drawn by the idealism of "living for art" (and therefore particularly inclined to an interest in independent and alternative musical activity), increasingly sure that such a life was possible because of new digital distribution

technologies, and yet competing for fewer and fewer resources based on the kinds of direct sales that might best provide the autonomy they craved.

In what follows, we shall see how these various features have affected popular music making in recent years, and notions of musical independence.

THE DIGITALIZATION CRISIS AND WEB UTOPIANISM

The dominance of the major record label system had largely hinged on these companies' control over distribution and unrivalled access to sales and marketing resources. So there were good reasons to see the proliferation of digital platforms for promoting, discussing, sharing and selling music as a catalyst for a renewed wave of musical independence. In the digital media environment, independent musicians have been granted considerable creative control and, in many cases, a new ability to retain ownership of their copyrights. Armed with home studios and Internet connections, aspiring recording artists can self-produce and self-release sound recordings—a situation that has led many to suggest that digital technology has allowed for a "democratization" of popular music production and the destabilization of entrenched industrial structures (Hracs 2012: 455–456, Young and Collins 2010: 344–345). Widespread access to digital music retailers (iTunes, Google Play), video platforms (YouTube, Vevo), streaming sites (Bandcamp, SoundCloud, Spotify), social media sites (Facebook, Twitter), and "fan management," sales and marketing sites (Nimbit, Topspin), combined with fan e-mail lists collected at live performances, means that aspiring and star artists alike can directly interact with and disseminate music to audiences. The popular and academic discourses that we characterize as "Web utopianism" conflate the availability of this suite of new tools—in many ways a positive development—with the "flattening" of the music marketplace overall. Such perspectives argue that popular music's gatekeepers and "middlemen" have been displaced in the Internet age and that the major record companies are increasingly irrelevant and, hence, en route to financial ruin (for an overview and critique, see Burkart and McCourt 2006: 1–3, 37, 44–45; Rogers 2013: 2–4, 8–9). What is typically missing from such accounts is recognition or understanding of decisive ways that music industry power remains tied to access to capital, financing and marketing support, and how this has allowed for the continued dominance of the majors across platforms old and new. In the digital era, the corporate structures that independents work through and against have become increasingly complex.

Today, the indie moniker invokes a diverse range of approaches to producing and promoting music. This wide spectrum ranges from more traditionally organized large independents that in many ways resemble their major label counterparts[14] to DIY approaches that involve self-financing and self-releasing music—the inheritors of the micro-independents. In their efforts to build sustainable careers, smaller-scale and larger-scale independent artists have explored business partnerships with technology, media and consumer brands. Musical independence continues to be circumscribed by one very important factor: financing. As pointed out by Damian Kulash, the lead singer of independent band OK Go (formerly signed to EMI) and a champion of new business models available to independent and unsigned artists, "one part of the old record industry that no one seems to know how to replace [is] the bank. . . . Even if there are newer, more efficient models for distribution and promotion in the digital era, there aren't many new models for startup investment" (Kulash 2010). Because of the continued centrality of marketing, distribution and financing ("the bank") in the new music industry, independence from the majors is entangled with a new reliance on Silicon Valley and Madison Avenue: the IT and marketing industries. Today, indie no longer necessarily signals an anti-corporate ethos; instead, it is routinely bracketed as a more modest anti-major label stance. This new version of indie culture has been readily accommodated inside neoliberal capitalism, as labels and artists have remade themselves according to the requirements of new music industry gatekeepers.

It is perhaps unsurprising that prominent utopian accounts of digital music models originate from researchers, entrepreneurs and writers involved in the Internet and IT industries. The ideas of *Wired* magazine founding editor Kevin Kelly and former *Wired* editor in chief Chris Anderson, for instance, have circulated widely in independent music industry circles. Of particular relevance to a discussion of musical independence are Anderson's (2006) "long tail" thesis and Kelly's "1,000 true fans" (2008) idea, given that both argue for the viability of small-scale music production and herald the decline of the major label system anchored by hit singles and blockbuster albums. The long tail refers to a demand curve in which a handful of hit releases produce the overwhelming majority of sales (the head) while the vast majority of titles released are niche products that sell in much lower volumes (the long tail). Anderson (2006: 24) claimed that online distribution had produced a new parity between hits and niche media products sold in low volumes, due to a radical reduction in costs associated with manufacturing, distribution and bricks-and-mortar retailing. Kelly, meanwhile, argued that an artist able to attract a following of 1,000 "true" fans willing to spend $100 per year on an artist's music-related products could generate an annual income of $100,000 (Kelly 2008). Both accounts reflect a lack of familiarity with the risks, costs, contract terms and financial challenges characteristic of the cultural industries, especially major and independent record production. For instance, the costs of pressing and shipping physical albums were not prohibitive in the first place, compared with recording and marketing; the recording industry has always been marked by low reproduction costs relative to those other costs (see Garnham 1990: 160–161; Hesmondhalgh 2013b: 29).

It is true that widespread access to digital technologies has generated considerable fragmentation across the music marketplace. However, the proliferation of Anderson's niches and Kelly's "microcelebrities" has actually had a very different effect than their theses suggest: major labels' intensified reliance on hits and stars whose music and personae are capitalized on more fully across multiple platforms and revenue streams (see Marshall 2013; Stahl and Meier 2012). Interestingly, while Anderson's (2006) book comes with a ringing endorsement by Google CEO Eric Schmidt, the same executive later pointed out that "while the tail is very interesting, the vast majority of revenue remains in the head. . . . While you can have a Long Tail strategy, you better have a head" (in Resnikoff 2013). A tremendous array of unsigned, independent and major label music may find audiences large and small today, but corporations able to aggregate music-related content and monetize corresponding niche audiences still benefit most in the contemporary music industry, with juggernauts such as Google able to profit from hits (the head) *and* non-hits (the long tail).

Indeed, under new music industry models, major and independent music companies have been joined by Internet industry giants such as Apple and Google—transnational corporations strongly positioned to capitalize on the global market for digital media "content" by way of digital retail, streaming and advertising businesses. Because of the massive reach of such companies and the tremendous competition for music audiences today, the choice *not* to work with these Internet giants is not feasible for many independent record companies and unsigned artists. Independents are systemically disadvantaged vis-à-vis the current Big Three major record companies—Sony Music Entertainment, Universal Music Group and Warner Music Group—when it comes to negotiating deals with these companies now central to digital promotion and distribution.

A recent dispute between independent record labels and Google's YouTube, formerly a key avenue for indie circumvention of the major label system, illustrates this dynamic. YouTube is threatening to remove and block the massive catalog of independent music and video from its Web site if indie labels do not agree to new licensing terms tied to its new advertising-free, paid service (Sisario 2014b). Deals with the Big Three reportedly are already in place, but the independents have rejected what they see as "inferior terms" (Sisario 2014b).[15] In this case, the financing, distribution and marketing deals established between indies and majors during the 1990s actually have hampered the bargaining position of the independents. The majors' purported practice of including within their market share figures copyrights owned by independent labels but distributed via the majors' distribution companies, the indies argue, has allowed the majors to command higher royalties, minimum guarantees and advances (Sisario 2014b).

There is growing concern that "access to the online marketplace controlled by a few has become a privilege affordable only by the biggest and richest players" (Sisario 2014b), with Worldwide Independent Network chief executive Alison Wenham going so far as to claim that with "the growth of the Internet, what was to be a utopian leveling of the playing field, a democratization for all, what is actually happening is a form of cultural apartheid" (in Sisario 2014b). The vision of the Web optimists has begun to lose its luster.[16]

Google's interest in and influence over the digital music industry is likely to grow.[17] Adopting a similar tack, Apple recently acquired Beats, an audio product company and music streaming service spearheaded by hip-hop star Dr. Dre and record producer-entrepreneur Jimmy Iovine. These technology companies not only aggregate media content but also wider portfolios of media-related businesses. They resemble major corporations such as Sony and Universal Music Group's parent company, Vivendi, which have interests spread across the media, telecommunications and Internet industries. The power of the Big Three on the one hand and of the Internet giants on the other derives from their ability to invest in digital enterprises *en vogue* today and to continue to adapt to ever-changing market conditions via acquisitions, mergers and joint ventures. Independent record companies do not benefit from the same access to capital and are not able to spread their risks across multiple ventures in the same way.

Unsigned artists do not necessarily need to turn to independent labels for support in this digital media environment, however. Many independent and unsigned artists interested in retaining ownership of their copyrights have turned to a different set of companies in their quest for funding and marketing exposure: advertisers and brands. "Lifestyle" brands have been drawn to independent music and the idea of independence—as an attitude, vibe or sense of cool—that indies still are seen to represent.

BEYOND WEB UTOPIANISM: BRANDING, SPONSORSHIP AND CROSS-MEDIA EXPLOITATION

Record companies and recording artists have long forged sponsorship, endorsement, licensing and various cross-promotional deals with consumer brands. Youth-targeted brands historically have been particularly interested in the star power of and massive audiences attracted by Top 40 artists, as was the case with Pepsi's deals with Michael Jackson and Madonna in the 1980s and with the Spice Girls and Britney Spears in the 1990s. Beginning in the first decade of the twenty-first century, however, brands began to take increasing interest in independent artists. According to John Cohen, co-CEO of New York lifestyle marketing firm Cornerstone, "When we started in the '90s, it was still considered sacrilegious for bands to work with brands"—a markedly different situation than was the case a decade later, during which time he claims that "selling out" became "buying in" (in Billboard 2009). Marketing boosterism aside, it is true that as new fissures in the major label system became visible, brands presented themselves as indie allies to aspiring artists who sought alternative avenues into the music marketplace.

Licensing popular music for use in television commercials was part of the picture, as advertisers positioned themselves as "hero to the damsel-in-distress of the struggling artist" and were "portrayed as a champion of music that might otherwise be unheard" (Klein 2009: 60). This was especially so in the case of Apple's iPod and iTunes commercials, which featured artists such as Feist (2007) and the Ting Tings (2008). Advertising spots were reimagined as an alternative to commercial radio as a way of "breaking" artists, the so-called new radio (see Klein 2009: 59–78), as were music placements in television shows and video games. Advertising agencies such as Leo Burnett have even hosted showcases for emerging artists (Beltrone 2012).

In their efforts to gain credibility with their target markets, lifestyle brands went a step further. The notion that "lifestyle brands are becoming the new record labels" (Sisario 2010) was entertained by music industry commentators and artists—albeit for a relatively brief time. Alternative metal band the Melvins released music through Scion/AV, an "art and music project" tied to the Toyota automobile brand (Sisario 2011). Alternative hip-hop act the Cool Kids and indietronica act MNDR released music through Mountain Dew's Green Label Sound (Barshad 2011). Rum brand Bacardi signed Groove Armada to a one-year deal (Brandle 2008) in its effort to capitalize on the links between electronic music, club culture and alcohol. A key reason why such arrangements were welcomed by many independent and unsigned artists was that most lifestyle brands were not interested in owning artists' copyrights. Label-like deals with brands typically involve "few strings" (Sisario 2010) and, as explained by the Cool Kids' Mikey Rocks, there "was no Green Label Sound exec sitting in the studio, telling us what to do" (in Barshad 2011). An idea of independence surfaced that was bound up with proprietary concerns—the aim of owning one's own music rather than relinquishing those rights under a record deal—coupled with the long-standing desire to limit label interference in the creative process. Brands, meanwhile, wanted to glean some of the "cool factor" tied to an indie aesthetic and attitude; their interests in music were limited to its usefulness as a marketing and promotion tool—not as a core business asset.

While corporate sponsorship of festivals and concerts is nothing new, in the approaches adopted by brands such as Virgin Mobile, Coca-Cola and Budweiser, the brand assumes the role of "curator," not simply sponsor. Brand involvement is not limited to the inclusion of logos; these companies confer to themselves a prominent position more akin to the headlining acts. Branded live music experiences allow for the conversion of the collective enjoyment of music into a source of brand value (see Carah 2010). The spirit of independence tied to popular music is invoked. Take this case from Virgin's Right Music Wrongs campaign, through which the brand ostensibly (and paradoxically) sought to rescue "real" music from a world sullied by excessive commercialism:

> It is time to make a stand and support just causes. It is time to stand up, jump about and be counted. It is time to remember that out there, in garages, basements, bedrooms, studios, once smokey bars, stadiums and in fields across the country, real people are playing real music with real purpose. . . . Real music is the Sex Pistols playing badly . . . Sigur Ros standing on a hillside in the Icelandic wildness sound checking to a herd of sheep. [Real music] can be quiet and considered, or loud and obnoxious but it is not artificially sweetened, mass produced, celebrity seeking mediocrity with a marketing plan at its core.
>
> (campaign quoted in Carah 2010: 21)

This is a classic instance of the incorporation of the artistic critique discussed by Boltanski and Chiapello (2005)—and it echoes Thomas Frank's (1998) account of the conquest of cool. A distancing from the idea of the marketing plan becomes yet another marketing pitch, as does the idea of musical independence. Even Lollapalooza, the key U.S. alternative rock festival in the 1990s, now features "fully branded" stages, sponsored bag checks and various brand "activations" (Hampp 2012). It is increasingly difficult to opt out of brand-sponsored or curated live music opportunities. According to Howlin' Pelle Almqvist of the Swedish group The Hives, participants in Budweiser's Made in America festival, "Maybe ten years ago, we could go on tour and play nothing that was sponsored. But nowadays, if we said, 'We don't play anything that's sponsored,' we'd get no shows" (in Greenburg 2012). Independent artists ranging from experimental rock group Dirty Projectors to hip-hop collective Odd Future participated in Budweiser's festival in 2012.

Critique of commercial culture and celebration of rebellion are evident across popular music's mainstreams and margins, but this is largely divorced from any commitment to social justice movements, and implicit cross-class and cross-ethnic aesthetic alliances.[18] There is artistic critique, but social critique is distinctly muted, to use Boltanski and Chiapello's terms. Brands' attempts to gesture toward and capitalize on such critiques underline the fact that audiences remain frustrated with crude capitalist approaches to cultural production and have a desire for alternative approaches. But the avenues of music marketing, financing and distribution that have allowed for circumvention of the major label system have tethered indies to new commercial and promotional logics. In so doing, they have dealt a critical blow to the notion of musical independence as it was imagined by the counterculture and post-punk. The story of the new indie grafts neatly onto critical accounts of the ways that contemporary capitalism's "flexible" production systems, sophisticated marketing techniques and capacity to personalize have catered to audiences' desire for diversity and difference, but in so doing, also have engendered expanded proprietary involvement in cultural production (Harvey 1990, 2005). We have not seen the removal of music's intermediaries but instead a game of musical chairs, in which new gatekeepers have emerged. The new indie's embrace of Silicon Valley and Madison Avenue demonstrates the depth of mistrust felt toward the majors. It also suggests a misunderstanding regarding the ways that companies that (primarily) operate outside the music industries—and are similarly bottom-line oriented—view music and musicians: as an asset to be leveraged. Gains in independence from the majors have been shadowed by new forms of financial, commercial and promotional dependence.

Loosening the grip of traditional gatekeepers over popular music production and distribution has not made sustaining a career in the music industry any easier. Web utopians hail crowdsourcing as a new form of financing, but freedom from the majors has impelled musicians to remodel themselves and their careers according to more entrepreneurial terms and to take on new forms of promotional work (see Meier 2015; Morris 2014; Powers 2013; Scott 2012). In what has become a fiercely competitive music marketplace, these artists must personally assume what can amount to considerable financial risk, as alternative rock artist David Lowery points out: "The artist pays for the recording, the artist pays for all publicity, promotion and advertising. . . . The artist absorbs the costs of touring. . . . [T]he new model makes the artist absorb all the risk" (in Digital Music News 2012). Today, independents must find ways to "monetize creativity at a time when the value of recorded music is at an all-time low" (Young and Collins 2010: 353). Revenues from sound recordings, tours and related merchandise are still monopolized by a select few stars, and artist revenues from newer sources, such as music streaming, remain paltry (see Byrne 2013; Sisario 2013).

In this context, some independent artists are even revaluating their anti-major label stances. The case of Trent Reznor (of Nine Inch Nails) had been heralded as an example of the viability of the independent self-releasing model (after parting ways with Universal), but he has since returned to the majors, signing a deal with Columbia/Sony—a decision largely based on the benefits of having "a team of people who are better at that [marketing] than I am, worldwide" (in Hogan 2012). Annie Clark, a rising star who records as St Vincent, recently signed a deal with a major label imprint, explaining that "the music industry is the wild, wild west now and the labels of 'indie' and 'major' don't mean the same things that they did 20 years ago . . . If people think that they still do mean those things then they're working off an old paradigm" (in Ugwu 2014). "Going it alone" in a music marketplace marked by considerable change has produced a new set of challenges for working artists. What explains this reversion to the majors? It is that major labels and their marketing departments appear to offer some artists a reprieve from the demands of what former artist Alina Simone characterizes as "forced entrepreneurship" and the accompanying "incessant self-promotion" (Simone 2013).

REINVIGORATING MUSICAL INDEPENDENCE

The goals of musical independence and alterity have faced two serious problems in the twenty-first century. One is that from the 1960s onward, new forms of business started to become aware of the need to incorporate critique and opposition into their practices, and by the 1990s had become accomplished at this. The second is that the ascendance of neoliberalism (an overused but still indispensable term) meant that musicians, fans and intermediaries were operating in a context where certain features of business that would previously have been frowned upon by musicians critical of corporate ethics and aesthetics were increasingly embraced, or at least accepted with a pragmatic sigh. We see the results of these changes in the new state of the music industries analyzed earlier. Exciting and interesting music of course continues to exist, but a widely shared sense of aesthetic stasis among rock, indie and hip-hop musicians and audiences may not be unrelated to these developments.

Yet it may be too soon to give up on independence even in the era of marketing, branding and established independents. Many music independents have offered interesting and powerful aesthetic interventions; some have even offered more politicized, ethical and sustainable ways of running cultural businesses. The idea of the alternative still has some power to invoke a notion of democratized cultural production. It implies the need for greater levels of institutional and aesthetic autonomy from corporate commercial aesthetics, and from financialized neoliberal capitalism. This is about doing things differently, with greater attention to human freedom and social justice. Without such a language, however inflected by romanticism and misunderstanding, we are left only with existing capitalism and its hugely problematic ways of organizing production, consumption and labor. That system may be complex and contradictory, but it is also fundamentally flawed. We need better culture, and better means of cultural production. Even if various forms of musical alterity failed to realize their visions, we should not cynically assume that all such efforts are doomed to failure. The question is: can new forms of musical independence emerge, alongside new forms of critique, in the years and decades ahead, imbued with hope but freed from the naiveties of digital optimism?

The current moment calls for a revisiting and perhaps redefinition of what independence means and could mean for popular music. The abundance and diversity of independent music available today speaks to successes in terms of indie's aesthetic ambitions. As the contours of the challenges associated with the new music industry have come into sharper focus, so too have understandings of the dilemmas faced by working musicians. Washington, DC-based musician advocacy organization The Future of Music Coalition has produced important research on American artists' changing revenue streams, incomes and health insurance needs (see futureofmusic.org). Ideas regarding how independent musicians might be treated more fairly have begun to circulate. The Worldwide Independent Network's "Fair Digital Deals Declaration," "which aims to level the playing field between indie labels, major labels and online platforms such as YouTube, iTunes and Spotify" and involves a label pledge to increase transparency with artists, has secured more than 700 signatories from independent record companies from twenty-three countries (Michaels 2014). Such collective approaches arguably point to an ethic and an ethics at the heart of early DIY approaches—independence gained through collaboration—and may suggest one route to meaningful institutional change. The promise and perils of the new music industry are hotly debated by commentators and fans as well as industry representatives—a passion ostensibly tied to widespread belief that popular musical independence matters. Ongoing dialog and critique will continue to shed light on the complexity of cultural production in the digital age and spur different ideas regarding how independence might be expressed and achieved.

NOTES

1. With thanks to Jennifer Carlberg for research assistance, and to Lee Marshall, Bethany Klein and the editors of this volume for their comments.
2 "The recording industry" is sometimes used as a synonym for "the music industry" and this reflects its particular importance. Many analysts, including ourselves, prefer to use the term "music industries," which would always include recording, music publishing (which refers to the control of certain rights rather than the publication of sheet music) and the live music sector, and would sometimes include the musical instruments sector.
3. Some of the most famous company names in popular music were, for many years, independents, before their takeover by corporations, including a number of examples from the list in this paragraph.
4. Alterity, unlike the adjective "alternative," is not a term that fans and industry folks would use, but at least it is a viable noun, unlike "alternativeness."
5. Our focus is on the Anglophone world. But see Ho (2003) on the Taiwanese independent sector and Luvaas (2013) on Indonesian indie.
6. The Pistols were dropped because of a moral panic in the powerful UK newspapers about punk, and were eventually signed by the independent Virgin label, which at that time was seen as countercultural. The Virgin business empire that

grew out of that hippie record label embodies key characteristics of the new spirit of capitalism that we discuss later in this chapter.

7. Jon Savage's 1991 book *England's Dreaming* remains the definitive history of the emergence of British punk from 1975 to 1978. For further details on debates and controversies about punk, independence and "selling out," see, among many others, Dale 2012, and relevant sections in biographies such as Gilbert 2004 and Gray 2003.

8. Book-length analyses of indie include Kruse (2003), who concentrates on its places and spaces, Fonarow (2006) on its aesthetics and rituals, Bannister (2006) on its gender politics, and Harris's fine journalistic study of "Britpop" (2003). King (2012) provides a history of the labels, mainly focused on the United Kingdom; see also Cavanagh (2000) on Creation Records.

9. See Hibbett (2005) for a Bourdieusian analysis of indie rock.

10. The opportunities afforded by the Internet to make much of the past available with a few mouse clicks would later intensify this trend (see Reynolds 2010).

11. One consistent element here was that indie retained its "whiteness" (see Straw 1991 for a comparison of alternative rock and electronic dance music in terms of their politics of place and cosmopolitanism). Indie/alternative audiences were often suspicious of hip-hop, electronic dance music, R&B and other forms popular among nonwhite audiences (see also Bannister 2006; Fonarow 2006).

12. See Quinn (2005) for a nuanced discussion of the business politics of one key strand of hip-hop, gangsta rap.

13. See also McGuigan (2009) and Pountain and Robins (2000).

14. For instance, Concord Music Group, an independent company with interests spread across the recording and music publishing industries, captured an 8.9 percent share of the U.S. independent label market in 2013 (Danova 2013: 25). The company releases jazz, R&B, blues, Latin, world, classical, and pop and rock music.

15. Of particular concern is a "negative most-favored nation clause" that purportedly enables YouTube to lower rates for all labels if it is able to agree to lower rates with any one label (Sisario 2014b).

16. A wave of indie criticism also has surfaced in relation to licensing terms and payments offered by on-demand licensing services such as Spotify, from which the majors have benefited disproportionately (see Byrne 2013; Sisario 2013).

17. For example, Google recently acquired music streaming and recommendation site Songza (Sisario 2014a).

18. See Halnon 2005 for an analysis of the commodification of the "alienation experience" offered by artists such as Eminem and Marilyn Manson.

REFERENCES

Anderson, C. (2006) *The Long Tail: How Endless Choice Is Creating Unlimited Demand*. London: Random House.

Azerrad, M. (2001) *Our Band Could Be Your Life: Scenes from the American Indie Underground, 1981–1991*. London: Little, Brown.

Bannister, M. (2006) *White Boys, White Noise: Masculinities and 1980s Indie Guitar Rock*. Aldershot: Ashgate.

Barshad, A. (2011) "Can Mountain Dew save the music industry?" *Vulture.com*, August 12, available http: www.vulture.com/2011/08/can_mountain_dew_save_ the_musi.html (accessed April 4, 2014).

Beltrone, G. (2012) "Behind the music: Call it borrowed authenticity or just plain good marketing, but brands are reaching out to indie bands, and both are coming out ahead," *Adweek*, March 20, available http: www.adweek.com/news/advertising-branding/behind-music-138995 (accessed April 29, 2014).

Billboard. (2009) "The decade in music: Business trends—top 10 trends of the decade," *Billboard.biz*, December 19. Available http: http://gateway.proquest.com.proxy1.lib.uwo.ca:2048/openurl?url_ver=Z39.88–2004&res_dat=xri:iimp:&rft_dat=xri:iimp:article:citation:iimp00719970 (accessed January 25, 2011).

Boltanski, L. and Chiapello, E. (2005) *The New Spirit of Capitalism*. Elliot, G. trans. London: Verso.

Brandle, L. (2008) "Bacardi, Groove Armada toast to 360 deal," *Billboard*, March 28.

Burkart, P. and McCourt, T. (2006) *Digital Music Wars: Ownership and Control of the Celestial Jukebox*. Toronto: Rowman and Littlefield.

Byrne, D. (2013) "David Byrne: The Internet will suck all creative content out of the world," *The Guardian*, October 11, available http: www.theguardian.com/music/2013/oct/11/david-byrne-internet-content-world (accessed January 19, 2014).

Carah, N. (2010) *Pop Brands: Branding, Popular Music, and Young People*. New York: Peter Lang.

Cavanagh, D. (2000) *The Creation Records Story: My Magpie Eyes Are Hungry for the Prize*. London: Virgin.

Chapple, S. and Garofalo, R. (1977) *Rock 'n' Roll Is Here to Pay: The History and Politics of the Music Industry*. Chicago: Nelson-Hall.

Cohn, N. (1970) *Awopbopaloobop Alopbamboom: Pop from the Beginning*. London: Paladin.

Dale, P. (2012) *Anyone Can Do It: Empowerment, Tradition and the Punk Underground*. Farnham: Ashgate.

Danova, A. (2013) "Facing the music: Changing technology and consumer behaviour dampen industry growth." *IBISWorld Industry Report 51221 Independent Label Music Production in the US*, January.

Digital Music News. (2012) "I'm a successful artist and here's why things have never been worse," *Digital Music News*, February 14, available http: www.digitalmusicnews.com/permalink/2012/02/14/Cracker (accessed June 8, 2014).

Fonarow, W. (2006) *Empire of Dirt: The Aesthetics and Rituals of British Indie Music*. Hanover, CT: Wesleyan University Press.

Frank, T. (1998) *The Conquest of Cool: Business Culture, Counterculture, and the Rise of Hip Consumerism*. Chicago: University of Chicago Press.

Garnham, N. (1990) *Capitalism and Communication: Global Culture and the Economics of Information*. London: Sage.

Gilbert, P. (2004) *Passion Is a Fashion. The Real Story of the Clash*. London: Aurum.

Gray, M. (2003) *The Clash: Return of the Last Gang in Town*. London: Helter Skelter.

Greenburg, Z. O. (2012) "Jay-Z's Made in America Festival: A crosspromotional bonanza," *Forbes*, September 4, available http: www.forbes.com/sites/zackomalleygreenburg/2012/09/04/jay-zs-made-in-america-festival-a-crosspromotional-bonanza/ (accessed April 5, 2012).

Halnon, K. B. (2005) "Alienation incorporated: 'F*** the Mainstream Music' in the mainstream," *Current Sociology* 53, 3: 441–464.

Hampp, A. (2012) "Dolla-palooza: Why more brands than ever are flocking to Lolla," *Billboard.biz*, August 4, available http: www.billboard.biz/bbbiz/others/dollapalooza-why-more-brands-than-ever-1007751152.story (accessed March 14, 2014).

Harris, J. (2003) *The Last Party: Britpop, Blair and the Demise of English Rock*. London: Harper Perennial.

Harvey, D. (1990) *The Condition of Postmodernity: An Enquiry into the Origins of Cultural Change*. Cambridge, MA: Blackwell.

Harvey, D. (2005) *A Brief History of Neoliberalism*. Oxford: Oxford University Press.

Hesmondhalgh, D. (1996) "Post-Fordism, flexibility and the music industries," *Media, Culture and Society* 18, 3: 468–488.

Hesmondhalgh, D. (1997) "Post-punk's attempt to democratise the music industry: The success and failure of rough trade," *Popular Music* 16, 3: 255–274.

Hesmondhalgh, D. (1998) "The British dance music industry: A case study in independent cultural production," *The British Journal of Sociology* 49, 2: 234–251.

Hesmondhalgh, D. (1999) "Indie: The aesthetics and institutional politics of a popular music genre," *Cultural Studies* 13, 1: 34–61.

Hesmondhalgh, D. (2010) "Music, digitalisation and copyright," in P. Golding and G. Murdock (eds.), *Unpacking Digital Dynamics*, 63–80. New York: Hampton Press.

Hesmondhalgh, D. (2013a) *Why Music Matters*. Malden, MA: Wiley-Blackwell.

Hesmondhalgh, D. (2013b) *The Cultural Industries*. 3rd ed. London and Los Angeles: Sage.

Hibbett, R. (2005) "What is indie rock?" *Popular Music and Society* 28, 1: 55–77.

Ho, T. H. (2003) "The social formation of Taiwan's Mandarin popular music industry," PhD thesis, Lancaster University.

Hogan, M. (2012) "How Radiohead inspired Trent Reznor's return to major labels," *Spin*, October 15, available http: www.spin.com/articles/trent-reznor-david-byrne-major-labels-destroy-angels-radiohead/.

Hracs, B. J. (2012) "A creative industry in transition: The rise of digitally driven independent music production," *Growth and Change* 43, 3: 442–461.

Hunter, D., Lobato, R., Richardson, M. and Thomas, J. (eds.) (2013) *Amateur Media: Social, Cultural and Legal Perspectives*. New York: Routledge.

Kelly, K. (2008) "1,000 True Fans," The Technium blog, March 4. Available http:www.kk.org/thetechnium/archives/2008/03/1000_true_fans.php (accessed November 1, 2013).

King, R. (2012) *How Soon Is Now? The Mavericks and Madmen Who Made Independent Music, 1975–2005*. London: Faber and Faber.

Klein, B. (2009) *As Heard on TV: Popular Music in Advertising*. Burlington, VT: Ashgate.

Knopper, S. (2010) *Appetite for Self-Destruction: The Spectacular Crash of the Record Industry in the Digital Age*. New York: Soft Skull.

Kruse, H. (2003) *Site and Sound: Understanding Independent Music Scenes*. New York: Peter Lang.

Kulash, D. (2010) "The new rock-star paradigm," *Wall Street Journal*, eastern edition December 17, available http://online.wsj.com/article/SB100014240527 48703727804576017592259031536.html (accessed January 25, 2014).

Luvaas, B. (2013) "Exemplary centers and musical elsewheres: On authenticity and autonomy in Indonesian indie music," *Asian Music*, 44, 2: 95–114.

Marshall, L. (2013) "The 360 deal and the 'new' music industry," *European Journal of Cultural Studies* 16, 1: 77–99.

McGuigan, J. (2009) *Cool Capitalism*. London: Pluto Press.

Meier, L. M. (2015) "Popular music making and promotional work inside the 'new' music industry," in K. Oakley and J. O'Connor (eds.), *The Routledge Companion to the Cultural Industries*. New York: Routledge.

Michaels, S. (2014) "Over 700 independent labels sign fair digital deals declaration," *The Guardian*, July 16, Available http: www.theguardian.com/music/2014/jul/16/700-independent-labels-sign-fair-digital-deals-declaration-youtube-spotify (accessed July 17, 2014).

Morris, J. W. (2014) "Artists as entrepreneurs, fans as workers," *Popular Music and Society* 37, 3: 273–290.

Oakes, K. (2009) *Slanted and Enchanted: The Evolution of Indie Culture*. New York: Henry Holt and Co.

O'Connor, A. (2008) *Punk Record Labels and the Struggle for Autonomy: The Emergence of DIY*. Lanham, MD: Lexington Books.

Pountain, D. and Robins, D. (2000) *Cool Rules: Anatomy of an Attitude*. London: Reaktion.

Powers, D. (2013) "Now hear this: The promotion of music," in M. McAllister and E. West (eds.), *The Routledge Companion to Advertising and Promotional Culture*, 313–325. New York: Routledge.

Quinn, E. (2005) *Nuthin' But a "G" Thang: the Culture and Commerce of Gangsta Rap*. New York: Columbia University Press.

Resnikoff, P. (2013) "Google chairman: The future is the exact opposite of the long tail. . .," *Digital Music News*, July 22, available http: www.digitalmusicnews.com/permalink/2013/07/22/longtail (accessed April 4, 2014).

Reynolds, S. (1989) *Blissed Out: The Raptures of Rock*. London: Serpent's Tail.

Reynolds, S. (2005) *Rip It Up and Start Again: Post-punk 1978–84*. London: Faber.

Reynolds, S. (2010) *Retromania: Pop Culture's Addiction to its Own Past*. London: Faber.

Rogers, J. (2013) *The Death and Life of the Music Industry in the Digital Age*. New York: Bloomsbury Academic.

Ross, A. (1989) *No Respect: Intellectuals and Popular Culture*. London: Routledge.

Savage, J. (1991) *England's Dreaming: Sex Pistols and Punk Rock*. London: Faber and Faber.

Scott, M. (2012) "Cultural entrepreneurs, cultural entrepreneurship: Music producers mobilising and converting Bourdieu's alternative capitals," *Poetics* 40: 237–255.

Simone, A. (2013) "The end of Quiet Music," *New York Times*, September 25, available http: http://opinionator.blogs.nytimes.com/2013/09/25/the-end-of-quiet-music/ (accessed June 6, 2014).

Sisario, B. (2010) "Looking to a sneaker for a band's big break," *New York Times*, October 10, available http: www.nytimes.com/2010/10/10/arts/music/10brand.html?pagewanted=all (accessed April 4, 2014).

Sisario, B. (2011) "Backing indie bands to sell cars," *New York Times*, September 27, available http: www.nytimes.com/2011/09/28/business/media/toyota-scion-is-backing-indie-bands-to-sell-cars.html?_r=0 (accessed June 3, 2014).

Sisario, B. (2013) "Defining and demanding a musician's fair shake in the Internet age," *New York Times*. September 30, available http: www.nytimes.com/2013/10/01/business/media/defining-and-demanding-a-musicians-fair-shake-in-the-internet-age.html?_r=0&pagewanted=print (accessed January 19, 2014).

Sisario, B. (2014a) "Google in deal for Songza, a music playlist service," *New York Times*, July 1, available http: www.nytimes.com/2014/07/02/business/media/google-buys-songza-a-playlist-app-for-any-occasion.html?_r=0 (accessed July 1, 2014).

Sisario, B. (2014b) "Indie music's digital drag," *New York Times*, June 24, available http: www.nytimes.com/2014/06/25/business/media/small-music-labels-see-youtube-battle-as-part-of-war-for-revenue.html?_r=0# (accessed June 25, 2014).

Stahl, M. and Meier, L. M. (2012) "The firm foundation of organizational flexibility: The 360 contract in the digitalizing music industry," *Canadian Journal of Communication* 37, 3: 441–458.

Strachan, R. (2007) "Micro-independent record labels in the UK: Discourse, DIY cultural production and the music industry," *European Journal of Cultural Studies* 10, 2: 245–265.

Straw, W. (1991) "Systems of articulation, logics of change: Scenes and communities in popular music," *Cultural Studies* 5, 3: 361–375.

Ugwu, R. (2014) "Backstage with St. Vincent: New style, new label and a bold new album," *Billboard.com*, February 24, available http: www.billboard.com/articles/news/5915666/backstage-with-st-vincent-new-style-new-label-and-a-bold-new-album (accessed July 1, 2014).

Whyte, W. H. (1956) *The Organization Man*. New York: Simon and Schuster.

Young, S. and Collins, S. (2010) "A view from the trenches of music 2.0," *Popular Music and Society* 33, 3: 339–355.

5 A Vision of and for the Networked World

John Perry Barlow's *A Declaration of the Independence of Cyberspace* at Twenty

Daniel Kreiss

Governments of the Industrial World, you weary giants of flesh and steel, I come from Cyberspace, the new home of Mind. On behalf of the future, I ask you of the past to leave us alone. You are not welcome among us. You have no sovereignty where we gather.

We have no elected government, nor are we likely to have one, so I address you with no greater authority than that with which liberty itself always speaks. I declare the global social space we are building to be naturally independent of the tyrannies you seek to impose on us. You have no moral right to rule us nor do you possess any methods of enforcement we have true reason to fear.

John Perry Barlow—*A Declaration of the Independence of Cyberspace*, 1996

John Perry Barlow wrote his famous *A Declaration of the Independence of Cyberspace* in Davos, Switzerland on February 8, 1996 while attending the World Economic Forum. In passionate prose, Barlow both gave voice to and crystallized a set of themes that had been circulating in the social worlds he traveled through as a lyricist for the Grateful Dead in the 1970s, an early member of the Whole Earth 'Lectronic Link (WELL), founding member of the Electronic Frontier Foundation and writer for *Wired* magazine. Barlow and his fellow travelers believed in the power of information technologies to create an independent mind and media space free from the terrestrial strictures of government, bureaucracy, institutions and law. In this new (Cyber) space, psychologically whole individuals were already gathering in new forms of collectivity supported by media and governed only by an emergent sense of "ethics, enlightened self-interest, and the commonweal." Cyberspace was giving rise to an independent, technologically enabled, disembodied and stateless "civilization of the Mind" (Barlow 1996).

The *Declaration* is a product of a particular time and, as cultural historian Fred Turner (2006) has extensively documented, the collision of the unlikely actors, technologies and media forms that gave rise to a "New

Communalist" vision of cyberspace as an independent society of conscious-ness. Turner shows how the New Communalists, unlike the New Left during the 1960s and 1970s, turned away from politics in the streets to head back to the land, living out alternative forms of community on communes equipped with Cold War tools from the *Whole Earth Catalog*. By the early 1980s, with the collapse of the communes, the terrestrial frontier had transformed into Barlow's "electronic frontier," as personal computers and networked systems such as the WELL became the new locus of projects for alternative forms of community building. Experiments in mediated sociality were also the outgrowth of the new, unstable, freelance economy in the technology development hub of California's Silicon Valley, where networking and gifting became essential to securing future paid work. The electronic frontier metaphor helped these homesteaders imagine their work as a project of independence and new world making, even as they lived out their economic lives in precarity. It was from this social world that the *Declaration* emerged in 1996, hot on the heels of Barlow's cofounding of *Wired* magazine in 1993, itself a publication with techno-utopian cultural stylings. The *Declaration* joined *Wired* as an artifact that both codified and distilled the particular ways of imagining cyberspace that emerged from these networks, making their metaphors for technologically enabled social life visible to wider publics. And, like *Wired*, the *Declaration* encoded a particular vision that aligned sweeping socioeconomic changes with libertarian dreams of cyber independence.

In the years since their crafting, the cultural artifacts of the New Communalists, from the *Whole Earth Catalog* and *Wired* magazine to Barlow's *Declaration*, have influenced how computer programmers, policy makers, engineers, journalists and scholars think about the Internet and its relationship to society and the state. Among these artifacts, the *Declaration* has served as a particularly visible and markedly portable media object around which people from disparate fields gathered and found frameworks for understanding their own domains and cultural tools to challenge extant institutions. For some outside of the networks that converged to create it, the *Declaration* provided a language to interpret experiences of technological change. For others, it served as a rhetorical tool that could be used to animate and achieve the aims of a broad economic, social and political project of "cyberlibertarianism" that exists in many forms (Golumbia 2013), or more narrow deregulatory aims (Turner 2006). For still others, the *Declaration* served as a foil through which to critique a particular cultural and social vision (Flichy 2007) or propose new frameworks for interpreting social and technical change (Goldsmith and Wu 2006).

Although twenty years later it is now a historical artifact rather than an actively cited manifesto, Barlow's *Declaration* forms part of the discourse that constitutes how we imagine the Internet. Robin Mansell argues that Barlow's *Declaration* can be located in the "prevailing social imaginary of the information society," with its suggestion "that the state should not be involved in Internet governance because this will discourage innovation and the creativity needed to sustain a flourishing Internet system" (2012: 155). Barlow's *Declaration* neatly encapsulates the belief that the Internet is an independent, self-generating and adapting system best left to its own evolution outside of the meddling of governments, bureaucracies and laws that seek to influence its development toward particular ends. At the same time, in Barlow's formulation, the normative desirability of an emerging social order and ethics is neatly entwined with the free functioning of markets for information goods.

While the *Declaration*, and the other founding documents of the *Wired* era, may no longer be actively cited and referenced, they form part of the cultural backdrop that both produces and constrains the ways that social actors imagine technologies and their relationships with society. It is this cultural vision that courses through high-profile contemporary projects of independent, utopian new world making such as WikiLeaks and open-source technical production. In its initial formulation, WikiLeaks was conceived by founder Julian Assange as a nationless, cosmopolitan, information liberator that could take down massive state governments through radical projects of transparency waged from an independent and autonomous networked space. The outcome was, however, very different, as Assange encountered the continuing presence and expansive reach of the state, and needed old institutional allies—news organizations—that have proved markedly enduring and symbolically powerful (indeed, perhaps nothing speaks to the importance of institutions as much as the fact that Assange now also remains dependent on diplomatic asylum in the Ecuadorian embassy in London). For the open source movement, the imaginaire of which the *Declaration* is a key tributary, enables hackers to envisage their labor in romantic and creative terms, independent of the industry that subsidizes and profits from it.

In sum, this chapter argues that there is a myth of independence that courses through the *Declaration* and the dominant Internet imaginary it helped give rise to. Barlow's *Declaration* is performative, an attempt to conjure into being a media space that was independent from the political, economic and legal systems of terrestrial life. In the end, however, independence was always a myth, a utopian animating vision that elided all of the ways that media are always premised on interconnection. It was the defense department's funding and high-technology economy of the Valley that gave rise to cyberspace, and the latter shaped the tenuous labor practices that undergirded a romantic vision of digital independence. In the case of WikiLeaks, Assange learned that independence must be premised on institutional support. Ironically, it was legacy media organizations that could function relatively independently of the state through the symbolic power of the fourth estate and legal codes that seek to protect it. Open source software programmers, meanwhile, realize their independence to code only through forms of material subsidy offered by large corporations.

The resonant myth of independence is, as James Bennett sets out in this volume, a "vision that promises to fulfil that which is perceived to be missing." It was both economic uncertainty and the longing for a more communal, egalitarian and ultimately nonhierarchical society that was behind the New Communalist ethos (Turner 2006). For Assange, independence meant the absence of democratic checks on the state and the institutional power of organized economic interests. For many contributors to free and open source software projects, it is the desire for un-alienated labor and freedom from the strictures of the property rights that can stifle human creativity.

All are laudable goals, but they are premised on a myth of independence that leads us to misdiagnose all the ways that media spaces are *always* entangled in economic relations, governmental and regulatory structures, and the workings of institutions. As Bennett (this volume) notes, utopian visions of independence matter in the world. They matter when people such as Assange believe they can go it alone in an independent networked media space and face the institutional power of states. The ways that imagining practices of coding as neoliberal critique matter when they work to preclude consideration of neoliberal subsidy. Myths of independence shape not only how we imagine the possibilities and potentials for Internet governance, but also the industries that supply much of our digital infrastructures. These myths matter when they shape desires to live in stateless worlds, devalue existing institutions such as news organizations as outmoded and outdated, or make organized wage labor seem passé (see Khiabany's chapter for more on this issue).

This chapter proceeds in three parts. I begin by historicizing Barlow's *Declaration*, drawing on the work of Turner to show how this famous statement of independence emerged from, helped make visible and distilled the understandings and rhetoric of a particular sociocultural formation. In the process, I provide a critical reading of the document, showing how the *Declaration* makes certain understandings of independence, technology, freedom and social order visible, while eliding the complex workings of economic, political and social power in play within networked space. I then chart the *Declaration*'s specific influence as a media object, showing how it was taken up by a variety of technologists, practitioners and scholars. Third, I show how the animating ideas of the *Declaration*, and the New Communalists more generally, are resonant today in the ways the myth of independence served the emancipatory aspirations of WikiLeaks and helped the free and open source movement to entwine working for freedom with working for free.

Ultimately, this chapter is concerned with how aspirations for normative ideals of and empirical beliefs in independence elide analysis of the relationships that exist between networks and entrenched institutions. The independence of cyberspace was ultimately an aspirational ideal that could be rhetorically invoked and performed but not enacted. For WikiLeaks, it was the instability of the network form vis-à-vis powerful institutions of government and journalism that led to the recasting of its tactics and mission. For hackers in free and open source communities, the forms of institutional subsidy that underpin collaborative gifts of code are elided in ways that limit political critique. Similar to Mansell's project of creating new imaginaries to open a productive space to recast dialogue, this chapter hopes to offer an alternative imaginary that highlights the interaction of networks and institutions, and critiques both understandings and values of independence.

IMAGINING AND ASSERTING THE INDEPENDENCE
OF THE ELECTRONIC FRONTIER

To understand Barlow's vision for an independent cyberspace requires detailing the social, cultural and technical worlds that the *Declaration* emerged from. Many of the ideas in the *Declaration* had already been circulating for nearly thirty years when Barlow penned his influential statement. For example, the *Declaration*'s use of the frontier metaphor to conceptualize cyberspace, which Barlow helped come up with during his cofounding of the Electronic Frontier Foundation in 1990, has a rich history. As Turner details, the electronic frontier metaphor "capped a long process by which the countercultural and cybernetic ideas that had informed the Whole Earth publications for two decades had migrated into the digital arena" (2006: 172). The frontier metaphor helped networked information workers with precarious employment in a rapidly changing economy imagine their lives in terms resonant with countercultural critique and aspirations of mobility and independence (Turner 2006: 173). In the *Declaration* and other writings, Barlow imagined the cyberspace frontier as a space of back-to-the land freedom, where information workers lived at the margins of the military and corporate bureaucracies that structured off-line social and professional life.

In this vision, cyberspace was a refuge, an independent, alternative space that had to be fought over and protected much like early frontier towns. It was the perceived threat of governmental persecution that gave rise to Barlow's writing of the *Declaration*, which simultaneously rhetorically *describes* an independent cyberspace and attempts to *perform* it into being by declaring independence. Responding to the *Telecommunications Act* of 1996 and the ongoing arrests and prosecutions of hackers, Barlow declared that cyberspace was an "act of nature" and asserted its independence, ironically from the very heterarchical entanglements of the military, university, commercial and political worlds that had given rise to computer networking over the preceding two decades (Abbate 2000). Within this independent cyberspace was an unfolding project of democratic new world making. In claiming the specific mantle of "Jefferson, Washington, Mill, Madison, DeToqueville, and Brandeis," Barlow situates cyberspace within a discourse of "liberty" and "freedom and self-determination" (see DiMaggio et al.

2001). Even more, within cyberspace order will be emergent. Barlow argues that governance will "emerge" "from ethics, enlightened self-interest, and the commonweal"—a vision of direct democracy (Jenkins and Thornburn 2003) that would not be out of place with many of the participatory democratic projects of the 1960s and indeed, more contemporary movements such as Occupy Wall Street (Kreiss and Tufekci 2013).

This project of democratic world making worked across many registers. Barlow's *Declaration* performs the rhetorical work that enabled different social actors to gather around this ideal of a utopian, independent cyberspace, forging a cultural space that supported the advancement of projects ranging from libertarian statelessness and anti-censorship practice to building new social tools and protecting "the wealth of our marketplaces." As Turner argues, in the context of *Wired* magazine:

> Thanks in part to a confluence of extraordinary economic, technological, and political currents, its technocentric optimism became a central feature of the biggest stock market bubble in American history. Its faith that the internet constituted a revolution in human affairs legitimated calls for telecommunications deregulation and the dismantling of government entitlement programs elsewhere as well.
>
> (Turner 2006: 208)

The interpretative flexibility of Barlow's *Declaration* mirrors the worlds within which it, and publications such as *Wired*, were crafted. As Turner explains, by the 1990s the New Communalist ethos of the communes was wedded to the "technological and economic legitimacy of the computer industry" and fused with a libertarian desire for smaller government (Turner 2006: 219). The elite among the New Communalist network, Barlow included, cycled between the worlds of Silicon Valley, media publishing and the corridors of power in Washington, DC, particularly those of Gingrich's new right revolution. "Independence" here also works as part of a libertarian imaginary, unlike its usual articulation from the political left (see King, this volume). Indeed, part of the appeal of the New Communalist cultural style was its fundamental malleability as a social vision of egalitarianism and claims for the technological means to secure it; technologically enabled commerce and sociability alike could be harnessed into fostering psychologically whole individuals and a new world order. Liberation through unfettered markets, along with the romance of high technology, was particularly appealing to the new right generation.

This was as much a social vision as it was a response to the demands of the new economy. Barlow himself was, as Turner notes, a refugee from an older economy as his Wyoming cattle ranch failed. Those in his cohort experienced different, if no less dramatic, shifts in the economy of the Valley. Denizens of early sites such as the WELL were often networking for their daily bread, as the deinstitutionalization of the computing profession made

for twenty-first-century piecework with an ever-advancing set of requirements for technical mastery, high risk and uncertainty, and a lack of stable
benefits and income.

These shifts were made all the more palatable by the ability to imagine
this new mode of work on the margins as liberating and free, even subver-
sive. In his study of the New Economy during this era, Andrew Ross noted
the ways workers in technology communities believed they were playing by
different rules: "In the Valley's technology startups, an anti-authoritarian
work mentality took root, and over time it grew its own rituals of open
communication and self-direction, adopting new modes and myths of independence along the way" (Ross 2004: 9–10). As Thomas Streeter has noted,
even the use of the term "cyberspace" offers "a taste of rebel-hero selfhood"
(Streeter 2006: 123). The myth that cyberspace was actually independent
contributed to the mistaken belief that the New Economy was independent
from old financial institutions. All of which meant that cultural longings for
more humane workplaces and practices eased the blending of personal time
and work time and acceptance of deferred wages. Meanwhile, the reliance of
New Economy companies on stock valuations left employees newly vulnerable to market and technological changes.

THE *DECLARATION* AS A MEDIA ARTIFACT
OF THE INTERNET IMAGINARY

As the preceding discussion makes clear, the *Declaration* can be historicized
and socially located as emerging from a distinct social and cultural world
(see also Jordan 1991; Streeter 2011). This was a world that, as Turner
(2006) persuasively argues, was highly influential in shaping the very ways
that we understand online social interaction in terms of "virtual communities," not marketplace transactions; networked computers as the agents of
personal and social liberation not social control; and the Internet as a space
apart for collaboration that exists independently from the terrestrial strictures of government and bureaucracy. Even more, this cultural framework
for understanding the Internet has influenced technological development,
spurred investment in technology companies, shaped regulatory policy and
created a cultural style that has drawn thousands to the technology industry
and contributed to the current cultural cache of "nerds" and computing
culture.

Indeed, in the years since its publication the *Declaration* has served as a
crystallizing document that made these cultural stylings visible and portable
to wider publics. The *Declaration* works simultaneously as a manifesto and
set of rhetorical resources that computer programmers and other Internet
advocates drew on in the course of debate—even while at times disavow-
ing its utopian language. In essence, the *Declaration* became a media object
through which a range of social actors found new languages and frameworks

for articulating their experiences and understanding technological change. Even more, it offered a powerful framework for imagining and working toward normative ideas of cyberspace. For example, the *Declaration* is cited hundreds of thousands of times across a vast sea of journals, magazines and Web sites. According to Wikipedia, more than 40,000 Web sites have reprinted the document. Within the technology community, designers, gamers and programmers have all drawn on its metaphors in popular writings in the years since its publication.

Perhaps as a result of its wide cultural reach, the *Declaration* has also been an extraordinarily contested object. In her decade retrospective, Morrison (2009) offers a trenchant textual criticism of its rhetorical strategies, showing how while the *Declaration* resonated in the mid- and late-boom 1990s, its sweeping claims increasingly became the subject of derision in the years since. Even more, Morrison argues that Barlow's utopian rhetoric undermined the sorts of "specific coalition-building and lobbying which might have rendered the declaration more effectual in the long run, and less easily dismissed as a silly artifact of a long gone moment of naïve idealism" (Morrison 2009: 66). Within the scholarly literature, for instance, the *Declaration* is now often perfunctorily cited as a footnote to early technology culture and its extreme rhetoric (Jenkins 2014) and misguided regulatory thinking (Goldsmith and Wu 2006; Morozov 2012; Murray 2007; Slane 2007; Tehranian 2007) during the early boom years of Silicon Valley.

Other scholars, however, have shown how the categories of thought in the *Declaration* continue to resonate culturally. A number of scholars situate the *Declaration* within a broader cultural turn toward cyber-libertarianism (Dahlberg 2001; Golumbia 2013) and utopianism (Burns 2008). Brown and Duguid (2000: 66) note that Barlow developed the idea of the "information worker" posited against industrialization. Zittrain (2008) cites Barlow as offering both an early critique of intellectual property and a cogent forecast of the distinctiveness of ideas in the knowledge economy. Corrin, Bennett and Lockyer (2010) argue that the *Declaration* was the first use of the term "native" to describe generational shifts in computing.

Despite their disparate substantive areas of interest, these scholars all point to the ways that the *Declaration* contributes to the broader "imaginary" of the Internet. The idea of the "imaginary" has a long history in social analysis (for a contemporary review, see Mansell 2012). Most broadly, the concept relates to the ethos, orientations and structures of feeling that make certain forms of action and social organization possible and legitimate. Analyzing imaginaries reveals how people see themselves and their societies, how they situate and ascribe meaning to their practices in the world, the values they have and what they consider to be a meaningful social life and the expectations they have of and for others. Importantly, while there are dominant imaginaries, alternatives open up the possibility of subverting or altering those entrenched, shared understandings that routinely shape social life.

A number of scholars have applied the concept of the imaginary to the ways that people understand, make sense of and experience technologies, mediated social life and the possibilities for alternative practice. For these scholars, Barlow's *Declaration* is often a touchstone for discussions of the cultural ideas that animate technical practice, as well as scholars' own categories for analyzing those practices and the effects of technologies. For example, Patrice Flichy situates Barlow's *Declaration* within what he calls the "internet imaginaire," the collective sociological imagination of the medium that spans entire professions and sectors, as well as users. Flichy argues that this imaginary shapes Internet adoption, the design of applications and architectures and the frameworks for understanding and valuing the types of actions technology affords. The discourses of imaginaires constitute "the utopias and ideologies associated with the elaboration and possibly the diffusions of technical devices, and the description of an imaginary virtual society" (Flichy 2007: 13). The imaginaire of the Internet, for instance, helps guide the creation of particular technical systems and their design characteristics. Designers and engineers have to invest technologies with value and meaning and situate them within cultural frameworks for them to be taken up, even as they are guided by ideological frameworks that legitimate particular conceptions of design and use.

Flichy argues that Barlow and his fellow travelers became the cyber-elite that offered an imaginaire sweeping in its implications. As it circulated through their media objects such as the *Declaration* and *Wired* and national popular media, the "cyber-imaginaire" offered a new way of thinking about the relationship between individuals and their societies, the distinctions between body and mind, and politics and marketplaces. For Flichy, Barlow and others were:

> specialists of discourse who produced the information society *imaginaire* in the mid-1980s. This was not only the *imaginaire* of a technical project or information highways of the Internet . . . but that of a new society whose relationships with individuals, the state, and the market were changing. The digerati's discourse presented us with new forms of politics and economics, and a new definition of the self that emerged with the digital revolution.
>
> (2007: 104)

Similarly, Mansell (2012) locates the *Declaration* in the dominant imaginary of the Internet focused on economic growth and free markets. This imaginary, along with another on collaborative production, converges around allowing the Internet to independently govern itself—an idea that is remarkably resonant with Barlow's *Declaration*. Indeed, Barlow's manifesto ties together both the idea of exogenous technological change—which Hartley, Burgess and Bruns (2013: 2–3) describe broadly as "turbulent relations across a range of different media"—as a key driver of social innovation and the difficulty of controlling these changes. It also encodes an idea of the wealth that technological changes make possible, as well as the emergent forms of collaboration that will supposedly humanize these changes. While Mansell's concern is ultimately with "creating the means of encouraging a new social imaginary with more diverse choices involving neither the excesses of hegemonic governance from above with its neoliberal ideology of the market nor naïve trust in the generative power of dispersed online communities as a means of governance from below" (Mansell 2012: 184), I now analyze how the idea of media independence has shaped particular forms of activism and analysis.

In the first case I analyze WikiLeaks, which was marked by the failure to reconcile the persistence, legitimacy and power of institutions with a world of networks, at least in its early stages. In the second, I argue that there is a widespread elision of the subsidies provided by the capital arrangements that underpin collaborative technical production. While Barlow's *Declaration* is twenty years old, I argue that these two cases reveal a similar failure to analyze the institutional and economic worlds that are entwined with our experiences of being online. That is, how our freedoms are often premised on particular relations of *dependence*, in the first case on the institutional resources and legitimacy of the institutions of journalism in confrontations with state power, in the second on subsidies provided by large corporations to open source laborers.

THE MYTH OF INDEPENDENCE: ANTI-INSTITUTIONALISM AND THE DREAM OF STATELESS INFORMATION

> The first serious infowar is now engaged. The field of battle is WikiLeaks. You are the troops.
>
> —John Perry Barlow, quoted in
> *The Washington Post*, December 4, 2010

Barlow's dream of digitally enabled, stateless cosmopolitanism continues to animate projects of democratic renewal two decades later. Barlow makes a simultaneous claim of, and for, the un-governable nature of cyberspace and the Internet more broadly given its supposed "innate" independence from the material world (see Barney 2000). Despite skepticism toward Barlow's rhetoric, almost two decades after Barlow's *Declaration* this claim is alive and well as a dominant way that we imagine digital technologies.

This is apparent in Julian Assange's launch of his global technological effort to undermine conspiratorial authoritarian state efforts to control information flows (see, for instance, Assange 2006). The principals behind WikiLeaks explicitly framed the project as a stateless informational effort, one designed to leverage the decentralized structure of the Internet to undermine the effective functioning of institutional power. While interpreters such as press scholar Jay Rosen (2010) called WikiLeaks "the world's first state-less news organization," it was closer to Barlow's vision of an emergent and distributed social order premised on nonhierarchical collaboration than anything as stable as a "news organization." Indeed, Rey (2011) analyzes the political theory of Assange, revealing his deep distrust of all institutions and championing of "individuals" and "small voluntary associations"—language resonant with Barlow's *Declaration*. WikiLeaks was conceived as a networked project that would enforce accountability over states and power over institutions through transparency, brought about by independent actors.

WikiLeaks was formulated within an imaginary that entails both anti-institutionalism and the general failure to appreciate the persistent role of institutions in shaping social life or to analyze the role of individuals vis-à-vis those institutions. For example, the most extensive empirical study of WikiLeaks to date (Beckett and Ball 2012) reveals how the project struggled to define itself throughout its history, undergoing a series of phases where it served as a neutral file repository, a utopian technological social movement, a radical press outlet and finally a partner to the professional press. WikiLeaks was launched in late 2006. The original site was built according to a Wikipedia model, where users could comment on documents and edit the site, and leakers could anonymously upload information. The site accorded with Assange's theory that information and transparency can provide accountability over powerful institutions (see Rey 2011). In its first few years, the site released, generally unedited, some high-profile information leaks, such as vice president candidate Sarah Palin's e-mails and e-mails between prominent climatologists. In April 2010, WikiLeaks took on more of the trappings of an advocacy press outlet, releasing documents and videos about the killing of two Reuters journalists by an American Apache helicopter in Iraq under the title "Collateral Murder." WikiLeaks also issued an edited seventeen-minute film and sent correspondents to Baghdad to report the story. Collateral Murder drew international attention to the site. Soon after, WikiLeaks began publishing classified documents leaked by Private Bradley (now Chelsea) Manning—including the Afghan War and Iraq War Logs and diplomatic cables. In publishing these, WikiLeaks actively collaborated with media partners (such as *The New York Times*, *The Guardian* and *Der Spiegel*). By the end of 2010, WikiLeaks was under extraordinary pressure by the United States and other governments. Many of its commercial infrastructure providers such as Amazon, EveryDNS and PayPal had severed ties with the site, resulting in a financial and organizational crisis.

As Beckett and Ball argue, this organizational evolution occurred partly as a response to the instability of the network form itself when faced with state power. This power was manifest in the state's ability to reach through the commercial institutions, such as server hosting companies and PayPal, which provided WikiLeaks's critical infrastructure. As such, Beckett and Ball suggest, networked efforts are often ill equipped to confront well-established institutions:

> WikiLeaks has made us reconsider how politics and journalism work. It also makes us think again about its future. But ultimately its real value may be to show that the very nature of journalism and news has changed from a socio-economic structure that produces journalism as an object, to a contestable, unstable networked process, especially in its relation to power.
>
> (Beckett and Ball 2012: 13)

The very flexibility and deinstitutionalization that Barlow celebrated—and social theorists such as Manuel Castells (2009) proclaim to be the great strength of informational networks—are precisely what led to WikiLeaks's power being so fleeting and Assange's ultimate embrace of powerful press institutions to disseminate the diplomatic cables that caused an international sensation. Lacking resources, WikiLeaks needed the professional press to deal with the massive amounts of material to be verified, filtered, made meaningful and redacted where necessary. And, it was the publicity that professional journalism organizations could secure that Assange desired in the wake of WikiLeaks's failures at independent crowdsourcing efforts: "Assange and others had grown disillusioned with the site's original intention to simply publish material in the hope Internet users would sift through it for stories. They wanted more high-profile results and a more direct way of achieving them" (Beckett and Ball 2012: 50). Finally, and most important, was WikiLeaks's relative weakness when up against organized interests wielding symbolic and material power. It was only when WikiLeaks was able to leverage the established institutional forms of professional, national news organizations—including the ways they serve as mediators between governmental officials and national publics in ways that both recognize as legitimate—that Assange could make progress toward his goals.

Even that was short lived, which reveals that independence is always in crisis, a point that a number of other chapters in this volume have made (see chapters from Bennett, King and Khiabany in this volume). WikiLeaks faced incredible retaliation from the U.S. government, pro-government hackers and commercial infrastructure providers. With deteriorating and even hostile relationships with its former collaborators among institutional journalism outlets around the embassy cables, WikiLeaks was marginalized. Even more, WikiLeaks lacked much in the way of infrastructure, a defined organization and routinized financial and symbolic resources that would have helped it independently weather the onslaught of public criticism and state pressure. In the end, WikiLeaks proved little match for the institutional forces arrayed against it.

WikiLeaks encoded a stateless, informational and democratic vision that courses throughout documents at the founding of contemporary digital culture, such as the *Declaration*. This is a vision of an independent networked world that is as subtly appealing as it is doomed to fail. The deep irony here is that despite proclamations of independence WikiLeaks, like Barlow's "civilization of the mind," was itself bound by both nation-states and civil societies (and the politics of social media platforms themselves, which Poell and van Dijck explore in this volume). In a cogent analysis Yochai Benkler, the foremost scholar of the networked society, argues that WikiLeaks:

> forces us to ask us how comfortable we are with the actual shape of democratization created by the Internet. The freedom that the Internet provides to networked individuals and cooperative associations to speak their minds and organize around their causes has been deployed over the past decade to develop new networked models of the fourth estate. These models circumvent the social and organizational frameworks of traditional media, which played a large role in framing the balance between freedom and responsibility of the press. At the same time, the WikiLeaks episode forces us to confront the fact that the members of the networked fourth estate turn out to be both more susceptible to new forms of attack than those of the old, and to possess different sources of resilience in the face of these attacks. In particular, commercial owners of the critical infrastructures of the networked environment can deny service to controversial speakers, and some appear to be willing to do so at a mere whiff of public controversy. The United States government, in turn, can use this vulnerability to bring to bear new kinds of pressure on undesired disclosures in extralegal partnership with these private infrastructure providers.
>
> (2011: 311)

The ethos at the heart of the *Declaration*, and the particular imaginary of the Internet of which it is a part that posits both the independence and ungovernability of cyberspace and order through emergent forms of collaboration, proved a powerful animating force in projects such as Assange's WikiLeaks. As in other domains of institutional life, however, this particular dream of independent statelessness proved fleeting, information warfare decidedly subservient to established state power.

THE MYTH OF INDEPENDENCE: DISAPPEARING LABOR

> You have not engaged in our great and gathering conversation, nor did you create the wealth of our marketplaces. You do not know our culture, our ethics, or the unwritten codes that already provide our society more order than could be obtained by any of your impositions.
> —*A Declaration of the Independence of Cyberspace*

The cultural objects of early cyberculture, such as *Wired*, enabled technologists to imagine their work as a social and creative activity. As Barlow's rhetorical slide from "conversation" to "marketplace" to "culture" and finally "society" in the *Declaration* makes clear, in New Communalist rhetoric there are heterarchic regimes of value. The personal and social shaded into economic and democratic registers rather quickly. As Turner (2006) points out, this cultural work enabled the early information workers on sites such as the WELL to imagine their online interactions in terms of social and cultural renewal while eliding the underlying economic contexts in which they took place. By the 1990s, the *Declaration* as well as other artifacts of the time enabled participants to cast their networking in terms of building new social ties and creating new forms of community, while also engaging in relationship building to survive the piecework of the Valley and rapid technological churn of the information economy. Indeed, for the vanguard of the cyber-elite it was not just about survival but fortune, which in turn fashioned the *Declaration* into a cultural resource for those espousing a particular brand of libertarian, new right politics premised on individual liberty and economic freedom from governmental interference. For example, the *Declaration* expressly frames the independence of cyberspace in the context of protecting liberty, while roundly ignoring the institutional economic work that was taking shape to support and facilitate the "transactions, relationships, and thought itself" of cyberspace.

Cyberspace, in Barlow's attempt at a performative declaration, is independent from the economic, material basis of the terrestrial economy, in addition to the regulatory regimes of states. This form of thought, which involves bracketing digital social relationships and cultural production off from their economic and regulatory underpinnings, is echoed in the dominant imaginary of our own time. This is particularly apparent in the context of free and open source technical production around projects such as the operating system Linux. The ability to imagine the collaborative spaces and software of the Internet as a commonweal, while generally eliding the ways they are circumscribed by a set of structural material relations, is a cultural achievement, one made possible by the imaginary of the Internet. Two decades after Barlow's cyber manifesto, the basic premise of imagining social life online separate from the economic structures that give rise to it continues to animate how practitioners and scholars talk about such things as collaborative behavior on digital networks.

For example, in his study of the annual Burning Man event's importance to the economy of Silicon Valley, Turner argues that "commons-based peer production depends on particular structural and ideological scaffolding" (2009: 76). While a technological commons provides opportunities for collaboration, it is premised on forms of material subsidy that ensure participants can make a living. Even more, it requires an ideological framework that allows participants to imagine themselves in particular ways and motivates contributions of gifts to the commons, whether that is the WELL,

Wikipedia or the repository of code that is Linux. And yet, in keeping with the logic of the gift (Bourdieu 1990), no one can name the material under-pinnings of the symbolic economy of the gift if it is to continue to work.

This cultural dynamic is clear in the dominant ways we have for imagin-ing open source technical production. A decade before Barlow's *Declaration*, in 1984, a new mode of collective labor and technical production was being forged by programmer Richard Stallman: free software. Stallman helped assemble a group of hackers and computer programmers who saw them-selves threatened by the expansion of intellectual property rights within the computer industry under the banner of a free operating system called GNU. Aside from its technical properties, it was the cultural ideal of freedom that created collective identity around GNU. Free software provided users with a reverse form of copyright called the GNU General Public License that grants users the ability to share, modify and redistribute the operating system, pro-vided that future uses remain under the same license (see Kelty 2008 for a full discussion). In the ensuing decade, a host of free software tools such as Linux and Apache grew in prominence.

Many scholars have explored Stallman's innovations in free software and his motivation to undermine the regime of intellectual property rights, as well as its intersections with decidedly more business-friendly "open source" software. Programmer and cultural entrepreneur Eric Raymond, who is prominent in the open source movement and authored a number of its key texts, stripped much of the ideological valence from free software's powerful critique of intellectual property rights in favor of a distinctly capital-friendly open source approach (Berry 2008). For open source proponents, the rheto-ric was distinctly about the "corporate discourse of technical efficiency and market power" rather than the ethical precepts of free software in "sharing, freedom, and collaboration" (Coleman 2012: 82). Although they developed from within different cultural worlds, Raymond's cultural work served as a complement to Barlow's own rather market-friendly *Declaration* that was also prompted, in part, by a perception of overbearing state intervention—both of which serve to illustrate the dominant imaginary of the Internet where "state intervention is unlikely to benefit anyone who believes in free-dom and democracy" (Mansell 2012: 156).

Aside from the fact that free and open source software took shape in reac-tion to the expansion of government-secured intellectual property, it is sig-nificant that the cultural understandings of the movement *require* the elision of the material forms that support sociability and creative cultural practice online. To demonstrate that software could be produced outside of a com-pensatory model required giving up claims to be directly compensated for labor. Indeed, in order to advance a critique of intellectual property, labor *must* proceed without compensation—spurred on by any number of poten-tial motives, from the thrill of the hack to altruism and sharing. Produc-tion without compensation, as Coleman argues, drawing on Latour's work, operates "as a 'theater of proof' that economic incentives are unnecessary to secure creative output" (2012: 185). Labor must be gifted voluntarily to the collaborative network, based solely on the individual free desire for technical efficiency and achievement. As Weber (2004) noted in his study of open source, nonmonetary forms of compensation, collective identity and external enemies such as Microsoft motivate participation and keep collaborative projects together.

For some interpreters, this is a radical political critique. Coleman argues that free software represents a "targeted, if not wholesale, critique of neoliberalism in challenging intellectual property law" (2012: 11), even as there is an "aesthetic" of hacking that enacts a "romantic sensibility" (2012: 4) undermining the liberal values and the self it is premised on. The freedom of the hacker is "the utopian promise of unalienated labor, of human flourishing through creative and self-actualizing production" (Beebe quoted in Coleman 2012: 15).

On another reading, we can see this "romantic sensibility" as a potent cultural achievement, similar to the crafting of the discourse that enabled New Communalists such as Barlow to imagine their informational labor as forms of self-expression and community building—even while there were differential economic returns on digital labor. For one, similar to the logic of the gift economy, the subsidies on which voluntary gifts are premised are often completely absent from discussion of these communities' political and social values. All forms of collaborative production—especially those that take advantage of the lowered costs of the Internet—are premised on having:

> sufficient material, social and psychological resources already in hand to take the time to join such communities. If they do not have those resources, participation in the group must generate sufficient material value to replace the work they otherwise would have to do to keep body and soul together.
>
> (Turner 2009: 76–77)

Coleman notes, in a composite life history, the growing financial independence of young hackers "thanks to lucrative information technology jobs as a programmer or system administrator that gave him the financial freedom, the 'free time,' to code for volunteer projects, or alternatively paid him explicitly to work on free software" (2012: 26). This includes, in some cases, working for firms such as IBM, Red Hat and Hewlett-Packard that directly subsidize particular contributions to open source projects. In this sense, the freedom to work for free is premised on a material subsidy granted through the structure of the technology industry, an industry full of billion-dollar firms such as IBM that profit off this code (for a discussion, see Coleman 2012: 191–193).

The issue is that the value of free software is differentially returned. For some, compensation is indirect, such as through the hiring of hackers who make contributions to free and open source projects by firms that monetize what was gifted from those acting according to other social and psychological motives, such as to realize the expressive freedom of coding. For those outside of the direct compensatory system, voluntary contributions are often premised on other forms of subsidy that secure material needs, such as jobs outside of the computing industry (or voluntary contributions are made in anticipation of gaining more permanent employment in the future, as Ross [2013] details). Either way, the value that firms derive from open source technologies far outstrips the returns that hackers achieve—a point that Stallman himself made repeatedly, as he hoped that "programmers would be paid for their labor" (Coleman 2012: 82).

Even more, the aesthetic of hacking and romantic sensibility that animates it can work ideologically to motivate "working for free." An ethos of productive freedom and a romantic sensibility translates into economic value. Ironically, independently working *with* and *for* freedom is, in essence, working *for* free—given that free and open source software projects often fail to provide direct compensation and job security. This is a point that Andrew Ross (2006) has made: communities of hackers have a very limited degree of labor consciousness. And, while scholars such as Coleman have shown the value of the legal and contextual knowledge these communities develop, in addition to their broader critiques of intellectual property, what is clear is that the relationship of capital to the common and the way that cultural understandings spur people to gift their labor is generally left outside of the political critique of the free and open source software movement.

CONCLUSION: THE *DECLARATION* AT TWENTY

At twenty years old, Barlow's *Declaration of the Independence of Cyberspace* is both an artifact of an earlier, headier time, and an important tributary of our current cultural understandings of the digital age. It was a powerful rhetorical invocation (and simultaneously a failed performative enactment) of the independence of cyberspace—premised on forging a utopian world apart from the terrestrial governments, laws, marketplaces and institutions that gave shape to the inequalities of our own social world. At its most idealistic, the *Declaration* is a clarion call for stronger forms of democracy and community, greater individual liberty and expressive freedom. And yet, it is a deeply flawed document. Cyberspace never was—and never could be—independent from the governing institutions, economic structures and cultural and social worlds that gave rise to it. Indeed, cyberspace has always been dependent on those worlds for its very existence and form.

As the case studies of WikiLeaks and free and open source software make apparent, the myth of independence works ideologically to elide the complex embeddedness of all social action (online and off) in larger structures of economic and cultural power. Ideas of independence undermined WikiLeaks's political effectiveness, at least initially, even while the enduring power of states, national journalistic outlets, commercial platforms and cultural ideas of the press's obligations to society was clear. Assange's idea of independent, deterritorialized and stateless information ultimately undermined WikiLeaks's ability to build enduring alliances with powerful and socially legitimate institutions. At the same time, the aesthetic sensibilities of free and open source software enable hackers to imagine a world apart where they pursue the expressive practice of coding for intrinsic reasons, and forget the deeper ways they are still imbricated in the logics of neoliberalism.

Ultimately, despite attempts to create new independent media—cyberspace, WikiLeaks and open source software—free from the strictures of the market and state, we may be too quick to turn away from the "old media" that often can be more "independent" of other powerful institutions. Ironically, legacy media's institutional entanglements with the state are often its positive sources of freedom. It is difficult to imagine similar attacks on professional journalistic outlets as those experienced by WikiLeaks, at least in the United States, because they have evolved institutionally to have certain legal, ethical and regulatory safeguards positively guaranteed by the state—such as the courts (see Allan and Jukes's chapter in this volume). New media sites such as WikiLeaks lack those safeguards and forms of institutionally secured independence. Meanwhile, open source laborers may trade as much freedom as they gain when they turn from the old to the new economy—the freedom to earn a living from their labor or freedom to be paid a minimum wage, both of which are secured by state regulations.

REFERENCES

Abbate, J. (2000) *Inventing the Internet.* Cambridge, MA: MIT Press.
Assange, J. (2006) *State and terrorist conspiracies.* Online. Available http: http://cryptome.org/0002/ja-conspiracies.pdf (accessed October 30, 2013).
Barlow, J. P. (1996) *A Declaration of the Independence of Cyberspace.* Online. Available http: http://homes.eff.org/~barlow/Declaration-Final.html (accessed October 30, 2013).
Barney, D. (ed.) (2000) *Prometheus Wired: The Hope for Democracy in the Age of Network Technology.* Chicago, IL: University of Chicago Press.
Beckett, C. and Ball, J. (2012) *WikiLeaks: News in the Networked Era.* Malden, MA: Polity Press.
Benkler, Y. (2011) "Free irresponsible press: Wikileaks and the battle over the soul of the networked fourth estate," *Harvard Civil Rights-Civil Liberties Law Review* 46: 311–397.
Berry, D. M. (2008) *Copy, Rip, Burn: The Politics of Copyleft and Open Source.* London: Pluto Press.
Bourdieu, P. (1990) *The Logic of Practice.* Stanford, CA: Stanford University Press.
Brown, J. S. and Duguid, P. (2000) *The Social Life of Information.* Cambridge, MA: Harvard Business Press.
Burns, M. E. (2008) "Public service broadcasting meets the Internet at the Australian Broadcasting Corporation (1995–2000)," *Continuum: Journal of Media & Cultural Studies* 22: 867–881.

Castells, M. (2009) *Communication Power.* New York: Oxford University Press.

Coleman, G. (2012) *Coding Freedom: The Ethics and Aesthetics of Hacking.* Princeton, NJ: Princeton University Press.

Corrin, L., Bennett, S. and Lockyer, L. (2010) "Digital natives: Everyday life versus academic study," In L. Dirckinck-Holmfeld, V. Hodgson, C. Jones, M. de Laat, D. McConnell and T. Ryberg (eds.), *Proceedings of the 7th International Conference on Networked Learning 2010.*

Dahlberg, L. (2001) "Democracy via cyberspace: Mapping the rhetorics and practices of three prominent camps," *New Media & Society* 3: 157–177.

DiMaggio, P., Hargittai, E., Neuman, W. R. and Robinson, J. P. (2001) "Social implications of the Internet," *Annual Review of Sociology* 2001: 307–336.

Flichy, P. (2007). *The Internet Imaginaire.* Cambridge, MA: MIT Press.

Goldsmith, J. L. and Wu, T. (2006) *Who Controls the Internet?: Illusions of a Borderless World.* Oxford: Oxford University Press.

Golumbia, D. (2013), "Cyberlibertarianism: The extremist foundations of digital freedom," *Uncomputing* September 5.

Hartley, J., Burgess, J. and Bruns, A. (eds.). (2013) *A Companion to New Media Dynamics.* New York: John Wiley & Sons.

Jenkins, H. (2014) "Rethinking 'Rethinking Convergence/Culture,'" *Cultural Studies* 28: 267–297.

Jenkins, H. and Thornburn, D. (eds.) (2003) *Democracy and New Media.* Cambridge, MA: MIT Press.

Jordan, T. (1999) *Cyberpower: The Culture and Politics of Cyberspace and the Internet.* New York: Routledge.

Kelty, C. M. (2008) *Two Bits: The Cultural Significance of Free Software.* Durham, NC: Duke University Press.

Kreiss, D. and Tufekci, Z. (2013) "Occupying the political: Occupy Wall Street, collective action, and the rediscovery of pragmatic politics," *Cultural Studies-Critical Methodologies* 13: 163–167.

Mansell, R. (2012) *Imagining the Internet: Communication, Innovation, and Governance.* New York: Oxford University Press.

Morozov, E. (2012) *The Net Delusion: The Dark Side of Internet Freedom.* New York: Public Affairs.

Morrison, A. H. (2009) "An impossible future: John Perry Barlow's 'Declaration of the Independence of Cyberspace,'" *New Media & Society* 11: 53–71.

Murray, A. (2007) *The Regulation of Cyberspace: Control in the Online Environment.* New York: Routledge.

Nakashima, E. and Cody, E. (2010, December 4). "Wikileaks struggles to keep its site active online." Available http: www.washingtonpost.com/wp-dyn/content/article/2010/12/03/AR2010120306804.html (accessed March 30, 2014).

Rey, P. J. (2011) "Julian Assange: Cyber-libertarian or cyber-anarchist." *The Society Pages.* Online. Available http: http://thesocietypages.org/cyborgology/2011/11/08/julian-assange-cyber-libertarian-or-cyber-anarchist/ (accessed October 30, 2013).

Rosen, J. (2010) "The Afghanistan War Logs released by Wikileaks, the world's first stateless news organization." Online. Available http: http://archive.pressthink.org/2010/07/26/wikileaks_afghan.html (accessed October 30, 2013).

Ross, A. (2004) *No-collar: The Humane Workplace and Its Hidden Costs.* Philadelphia, PA: Temple University Press.

Ross, A. (2006) "Nice work if you can get it: The mercurial career of creative industries policy," *Work Organisation, Labour and Globalisation* 1: 13–30.

Ross, A. (2013) *Real Love: In Pursuit of Cultural Justice.* New York: Routledge.

Slane, A. (2007) "Democracy, social space, and the Internet," *University of Toronto Law Journal* 57: 81–105.

Streeter, T. (2011) *The Net Effect: Romanticism, Capitalism, and the Internet.* New York: New York University Press.

Tehranian, J. (2007) "Infringement nation: Copyright reform and the law/norm gap," *Utah Law Review* 2007: 537–550.

Turner, F. (2006) *From Counterculture to Cyberculture: Stewart Brand, the Whole Earth Network, and the Rise of Digital Utopianism.* Chicago, IL: University of Chicago Press.

Turner, F. (2009) "Burning Man at Google: A cultural infrastructure for new media production," *New Media & Society* 11, 1–2: 73–94.

Weber, S. (2004) *The Success of Open Source*, vol. 368. Cambridge, MA: Harvard University Press, 2004.

Zittrain, J. L. (2008) *The Future of the Internet: And How to Stop It.* New Haven, CT: Yale University Press.

Section II

Working with Freedom or Working for Free

6 A Moral Economy of Independent Work? Creative Freedom and Public Service in UK Digital Agencies

James Bennett, Niki Strange and Andrea Medrado

This chapter investigates media independence at two interconnected levels: first, our study is concerned at a macro level with independent digital media companies working in the United Kingdom's multiplatform public service sector; second, we are interested at a micro level in the independence afforded individual workers within those companies. In particular, we aim to investigate how the rhetoric of independence functions to provide a space in which both companies and creative labor can be understood, and more importantly, *understand themselves*, as working with freedom. Moreover, and in turn, we argue that this creative freedom is utilized and valued by those individuals and companies for the ability it provides them to do "good" work (Hesmondhalgh and Baker 2011). For those working in the digital agencies we studied, the condition of independence was vital to the ability to carry out this "good" work—in the cultural products and the modes of working undertaken. Here independence functioned as an ideal that enabled companies and individuals to reconcile public service and profit, by providing the freedoms to create "good" work that "made a difference." Informed by scholarship on the "moral economy" of creative work (Banks 2006; Keat 2000; Lee 2012; Sayer 2007), we argue that such a moral economy operates within the sector as a form of workplace ethics to guide the way many companies and individuals navigate the compromises and crises that come hand in hand with independent media work. Thus different forms of self-exploitation and precarious and emotional labor are accepted within the digital independent media sector precisely because of the desire to work with a creative freedom that fulfills the utopian promise of media independence: to create a better, more just and open society.

This chapter is divided into five parts. Following an introductory section that sets out an understanding of the relationship amongst scholarship on independence, "moral economies" and labor in creative industries, we then provide a brief discussion that delimits the boundaries of the digital independent sector under examination and the methods employed. In the third and fourth sections, we turn to examine how public service broadcasting (PSB) and digital culture produce a moral economy that mixes ethics from both spheres to operate on both a macro and micro level, guiding the practices of companies and workers within this sector. In so doing, we trace the nexus between independence and a moral economy, which provides the focus for our concluding section.

At a macro level, the companies we studied form part of an expanding sphere of "independents" supplying the two main UK public service broadcasters, the BBC and Channel 4, with multiplatform content. These companies' independence, therefore, is primarily defined in terms of the creative freedom, efficiency and speed of the free market set in opposition to the mainstream, slow, bureaucratized and state-sanctioned public service broadcasters. At the same time, however, such companies also subscribe to notions of public service and not-for-profit work as forms of independence from media conglomerates' drive for revenue and capital above all other concerns. Similarly to James Bennett's chapter on independent television within this volume, these companies must therefore turn a profit at the same time as fulfilling public service remits—often drawing on the moral economy we find in this chapter to balance inherent tensions between these competing impulses at the same time as maintaining their independence. On a micro level the moral economy is important for understanding that ethical concerns guide how individuals navigate independence as a promise of autonomy and working with freedom, at the same time as it exposes them to precarious working conditions.

Over recent years, the notion of a moral economy within creative industries has gained traction as a counter to more pessimistic accounts of creative work. This "moral economy turn," as David Lee terms it (2012), takes place in response to the post-Foucauldian scholarship of earlier studies of creative labor, which provided too totalizing an account of conditions under neoliberalism, particularly the way workers were seen to be duped by the glamour of creativity. That is, analyses by Ross (2004), McRobbie (2002) and others tended to suggest that individuals suffered self-exploitation and precarious and insecure labor conditions in exchange for doing "creative work": something that should be valued more highly than the rote, repetition and drudgery of industrial or office labor. However, such scholarship argued that "creative work" was itself a doctrine of neoliberalism that served to bootstrap workers' free time and thoughts in the name of providing "flexible" working conditions that actually enhanced corporate efficiency and reduced company overheads (Caldwell 2011). Most importantly, therefore, the post-Foucauldian analysis drew attention to how such an exchange took place within the broader shifts of neoliberalism, whereby the emphasis on the entrepreneurial self equally required punishing regimes of self-regulation, self-exploitation, flexibility and precarity. Such conditions seemed particularly rife in the digital workplace, where Andrew Ross's study found that creativity worked as a discourse that promised "oodles of autonomy along with warm collegiality," but also enlisted "employees' free-est thoughts and impulses in the service of salaried time" (Ross quoted in Hesmondhalgh and Baker 2011: 72).

The turn to the concept of the moral economy has attempted to complicate some of these visions about the nature of creative work. As Lee usefully explains, this "does not necessitate a radical 'break' in thinking from the earlier post-Foucaldian studies . . . [but] rightly puts emphasis back onto ethics, practices and agency" (2012: 482). Importantly, such work does not deny that capital can exploit labor in the terms discussed earlier. In our study we were acutely aware of workers being enlisted in what Ross has termed "work you can't help doing." Similarly to David Lee's study, the creative workers we interviewed and spent time with were

> not merely "entranced" by the lure of creative work . . . Rather, they [were] highly aware of the negative aspects of their mode of working lives. They use work as a means to find "self-realization," but their desire for autonomy does not blind them to the structural conditions that determine their working experiences.
>
> (Lee 2012: 482)

Work on moral economies provides a corrective to some of the overdetermined studies of creative labor that, "at their worst . . . see the forces of neoliberalism at work behind every apparently moral action," by supplying evidence of how individual labor's agency informs creative work (Kennedy 2012: 12). As Helen Kennedy explains it, such a perspective provides a counter to neoliberal views of self-regulation that see it as inherently "problematic, resulting in individualized and individualistic work practices," and instead draws attention to the way self-regulation can also be ethically motivated (ibid.: 20). Thus Mark Banks shows how notions of volunteerism, investment in local communities and concern with the conditions of labor that lower-end workers inhabit inform business and work practices across a range of creative industries (2006).

This critique chimes well with Hesmondhalgh and Baker's close analysis of individual autonomy and the nature of good and bad work within the creative industries. Invoking Blauner's conception of alienation and Keat's definition of "decent work," Hesmondhalgh and Baker map out "good work" as including autonomy, interest, sociality, self-esteem, self-realization and security (2011: 31). Importantly, they identify engagement in the creation of products that "'*promote aspects of the common good*' as a feature of good work in the cultural industries" (quoted in Kennedy 2012: 41). Drawing on Georgina Born's study of the "situated ethics and aesthetics" of BBC television producers in documentary, drama and current affairs, they argue that such an approach "crucially puts the emphasis on the *positive possibilities* of cultural production, by asking when its powers might be used 'responsibly, creatively, inventively in given conditions and when not'" (Hesmondhalgh and Baker, quoting Born, 2011: 74). Their work calls attention to the possibility of what John Caldwell has termed "critical industrial practice" within the industry: that is, self-reflexivity in the processes, aesthetic choices and economics of production. As Caldwell explains, "industry theorizes its presence in moving image form, even as it teaches the audience at home by publicly circulating insider knowledge about the televisual apparatus" (2006: 103). Critical of work that dichotomizes economism and textualism, Caldwell's approach invites us to consider the cultural outputs—in our case, the texts of multiplatform production—as performances of context. In this instance, we suggest that it is possible to understand these texts as negotiations of media independence: between profit and public service, as well as between working with freedom and working for free. Thus, just as Born does not claim that industrial reflexivity always results in better television, we concur with Hesmondhalgh and Baker's approach that paying attention to such practices nevertheless remains a "key analytical task" in order to "consider how the reflexivity, intentionality and agency of cultural producers conditions the creativity and innovation possible within a given medium" (Hesmondhalgh and Baker 2011: 74).

Recent work by David Lee (2011, 2012) and Helen Kennedy (2012) has taken up this call in areas particularly pertinent to this study: public service broadcasting and Web design. Here we find a strong correlation between "good work" and its products and a moral economy. Describing a "neo-Reithian" ethics of production that governed the practices of many workers in the United Kingdom's independent television sector, Lee argues that they "care about the product that they are working on and they carry out creative work not just for the 'glamour' but also because they want to inform, educate and have a positive impact on society" (2012: 487). Such an analysis has strong resonances with our own study of the United Kingdom's television and digital independent sector, where we found a commitment to creative products that could "make a difference" in society—discussed further later in this chapter (Bennett et al. 2012). Similarly, Helen Kennedy demonstrates that ethical concerns of Web design workers can not only lead to pro bono work and hostile responses to exploitation, but also a commitment to designing sites that provide accessibility for disabled users and adhere to a set of standards that focus on "good practice." Kennedy's analysis usefully draws our attention to the way a moral economy might emerge not just from individual worker agency and the values they bring in to the workplace from their non-work lives (as in Banks's 2006 study), but is also conditioned by overarching and shared culture across an industry. As Kennedy explains, the ethics of Web design are conditioned at an industrial level by the original conception of the Web by Sir Tim Berners-Lee and other founding figures, such as John Perry Barlow (discussed in Daniel Kreiss's chapter in this volume). This vision of the Web placed openness and freedom at the heart of digital cultural work to create an "open, interoperable and accessible medium, whose power would lie in its 'universality'" (Kennedy 2012: 9).

Outside of literature on creative industries labor, the concept of a moral economy has circulated in studies of digital culture—most prominently coming from the work of Henry Jenkins, who suggests a "moral economy of information" emerges with participatory culture: "that is, a sense of mutual obligations and shared expectations about what constitutes good citizenship within a knowledge community" (Jenkins 2006: 136). As Jenkins and Josh Green expand, this moral economy generates a set of "social expectations, emotional investments, and cultural transactions that create a shared understanding between all participants within an economic exchange" (Green and Jenkins 2009: 214). In developing the notion of a moral economy in the chapter that follows, we suggest that the companies and individuals we studied exhibit an ethos that can be understood via the intersection of these differing debates and definitions of moral economies, that is, from studies of both digital culture and creative labor. But we also suggest they are conditioned by a vision of public service broadcasting similar to that found by Lee in his study. What emerges, therefore, is a hybrid moral economy of digital independents informed by the ethics of individual workers, including a commitment to ideals of independence, a shared ethos from digital culture and a commitment to public service broadcasting that emphasizes the production of goods that do not simply exist for profit, but seek to "make a difference" in society (Bennett 2015).

Having set out the parameters of the moral economy debate and independence, we now provide a more detailed description of the sector under examination and the methods utilized for this study before returning to the relationship amongst public service, digital culture, moral economies and independence.

THE DIGITAL INDEPENDENT SECTOR

The companies focused on in this chapter were based in London and Brighton and were part of what we term the "multiplatform public service production ecology" of UK television (Bennett et al. 2012). Multiplatform here is understood as content that is commissioned and created to produce an integrated or connected experience across multiple platforms, including television, rather than simply content re-versioned for different platforms, such as television programs available on demand via catch-up services such as BBC iPlayer, Hulu or 4oD. Moreover, "multiplatform" is a term specific to the strategies emerging through the United Kingdom's public service broadcasters to position themselves in the newly emerging digital mediascapes of the "noughties." It springs from the BBC's and Channel 4's experimentation with digital content at the start of the millennium and their eventual enshrinement in official strategy during the middle of the decade, through to a perceived decline and withdrawal at the end of the 2000s (see Bennett and Strange 2014; Chitty 2013; Strange 2011). The shift to multiplatform represented a belief that delivering integrated content across new digital platforms could "enhance the delivery, scope and meaning of PSB, renewing it for the digital age. In turn, these strategies required a plethora of new content, services and applications to be developed by both in-house and independent producers" (Bennett and Kerr 2012: 224). As Bennett and Kerr go on to suggest, such a shift brought with it both pressures and opportunities for the United Kingdom's independent production sector: "most notably in the development of digital divisions by existing TV Indies as well as enabling new entrants into the market in the form of digital agencies who may supply some of this multiplatform content" (ibid.: 225).

The sector is therefore a complex hybrid of public service broadcasters, television companies and stand-alone digital agencies together with integrated TV and digital companies alongside what have been termed "Superindies": horizontally and sometimes vertically integrated television, digital and post-production conglomerates that emerged during the period in response to changed IP ownership laws.[1] Nevertheless, at the heart of this sector lie the BBC and Channel 4, who commission much of the multiplatform content produced. The digital independents studied, or digital agencies as they often term themselves, all made multiplatform public service content for the BBC and Channel 4, either through direct commissions with the broadcasters or via subcontracting arrangements with television independents who were already producing broadcast programs that required a digital component. However, many digital agencies either existed long before the PSBs became involved in commissioning and creating digital, multiplatform content or are engaged in a much wider—and often more commercial—industry, making applications, software, Web design and other creative work for a range of clients beyond the PSBs. As a result, not only do such companies often come from more overtly commercial backgrounds, but they also often have more tacit relations with public service broadcasting than their independent television counterparts discussed by Bennett in this volume. Such digital agencies would therefore seem to sit well with Angela McRobbie's identification of a "second wave" of the independent cultural production sector that is "more aggressive, commercially driven [and] in hock to the free market and global multinationals" (quoted in Banks 2006: 459). The digital agencies we studied, therefore, formed part of a sector that was independent—and free—from the tightly controlled world of the public service broadcasters themselves, even as they relied on them for some of their work. Indeed, often such companies are positioned at the forefront of the United Kingdom's creative industries and the push for growth for corporate and self-entrepreneurialism that stands in contradistinction to old models of state-funded media (O'Connor 2007).

The notion that PSB might operate as a moral economy on these companies' actions might, prima facie, seem dubious. However, we found a strong commitment within these companies to undertaking work that "made a difference"—seeking to bring about social change for a democratic, more open and just society. Such an ethos informed what projects and clients companies worked with and, in turn, the working lives and conditions of those within such companies. As one managing director explained in relationship to his company's client list, "there are lots of people who we wouldn't want to work with for the most ethical reasons" (IV46). Thus the vast majority, if not all, of the digital agencies we studied made content not only for Channel 4 and the BBC, but also a host of other non-broadcast public service organizations, public sector clients, galleries and charities. As we discuss later in this chapter, whilst such work was rarely pro bono, companies' decisions of which work to undertake or pitch for were based as much on ideals of "good work," including creating for the "common good," as they were on profit margins. Moreover, these companies also evidenced a culture that was based on a particular vision of the Internet and digital culture. Andrew Ross's study of work in U.S. digital agencies suggests how such companies emerged out of a "distinctive community . . . bound by a fierce loyalty to shareware, freedom of information and the ethos of cooperation" (Ross 2004: 12). This mix between commercial and public service work, as well as the *conditioning* provided by the open and democratic imaginings of digital culture was crucial to their investment in the moral economy of the sector (see Daniel Kreiss's chapter in this volume on the Internet imaginaire of early Web pioneers).

Methodologically, this chapter emerges from an AHRC-funded two-year study of the United Kingdom's multiplatform public service production ecology in which more than 100 interviews were conducted across television, digital, Superindie and integrated companies, alongside regulators and broadcasters.[2] At the macro level here, we focus on the twenty-nine interviews that took place with employees working in the fifteen digital agencies studied within this wider sample. Interviewees were drawn from across the spectrum of roles within these companies, from CEOs and managing directors, through to producers, designers and researchers. These companies comprised a range of different business configurations: one of these was a truly integrated digital-TV hybrid, two companies were existing television companies that had developed large and successful digital divisions, two were part of wider Superindie conglomerates (including one of the TV companies with a digital division), whilst the other eleven were stand-alone digital agencies producing software, applications, design and a range of bespoke solutions to clients. At the micro level, we draw on forty weeks of ethnographic data collected from four differently sized independent production companies: first, a medium-sized London digital agency that had software, video and audio divisions; second, a medium-sized London TV company with a small digital division, staffed mainly by freelancers; third, a small Brighton-based television independent that worked primarily on television productions, occasionally branching out into quite limited forms of multiplatform productions, primarily through re-skilling the existing television staff or relying on the broadcasters' in-house teams to supply the digital components; finally, a large and integrated television and digital company that had a sizeable digital team, although significantly smaller than its television division, which was also part of a Superindie.

It is worth making a short point about the authors' relationship to the objects and fields of study here. Collectively we all worked on the research project for its two-year duration, but each of us had a different role and relationship with the digital independents in the study that inform our analysis. All three members of the team conducted interviews; however, whilst James Bennett led the overall project, his encounters with individuals from the sector were limited to participation in trade events and interviews. Niki Strange, on the other hand, approached the sector against the backdrop of a ten-year work history in digital agencies, where she had primarily been employed as a business development manager—experiencing both freelance and more permanent work during this period. Her own experiences in choosing which companies to work for, which clients to work with and how her non-work life values influenced her practice within the production ecology inform the arguments here. In contrast, Andrea Medrado spent ten weeks in each of the four different independent companies detailed earlier. The experience of all three researchers provides a detailed understanding of the sector and the individuals within it, as well as a rich interpretative framework for the analysis that follows.

A MACRO MORAL ECONOMY: FREEDOM FROM PROFIT AND COMPETITION

In this section we explore how a combination of a commitment to public service and to a particular vision and ethos of digital culture has produced a moral economy of the digital independent sector that guides what independence means and how it is valued, both economically and culturally, by the companies involved. As Henry Jenkins and Josh Green have argued, key facets of this digital moral economy include aspects taken from fan communities such as collective intelligence, collaborative and open source production, the importance of the gift economy and what Axel Bruns terms "permissive regimes of engagement" (Bruns quoted in Jenkins and Green 2009). However, whilst Jenkins's and Green's concern with a moral economy was to "bridge between the historically separate spheres of audience studies and industry research" in order to understand how the "moral economy which governed old media companies has broken down and there are conflicting expectations about what new relationships should look like," we posit no such radical break here (2009: 214). Moreover, and in line with Helen Kennedy's study of Web design, we suggest that aspects of this digital moral economy actually inform the business and labor practices of companies working within this sector. In this section, therefore, we suggest how participatory culture values—such as collective intelligence, networked collaboration and open source production—interact with public service as an ethos that is concerned with "making a difference," social good, ethics and quality.

In interviews, we often found workers drawing on particular notions of digital culture that conditioned the way their companies operated. As one senior executive told us:

> Parts of digital culture, creative ideas, open source culture, [our company] has been careful to start thinking in that way, in house we foster collaborative relationships, we've got hacker culture.
>
> (IV24, March 2, 2011)

During the participant observation of the company involved, we observed this "open source" and collaborative culture in operation. In particular, the company opened its office space to digital start-ups for free to help them get off the ground, even if those companies might eventually become competitors. As the senior executive explained at the end of our period of ethnographic research:

> I made a really conscious decision to make sure that guys like [company X] had good space for free, because it's good having them around. . . . Another company which we could have [seen as a rival], which we are now strong competitor wise, but we gave them some desk space in their very early days.
>
> (ibid.)

Such an approach brought a different atmosphere to the company, and helped its employees produce better work: "it is a cliché but we started doing a lot better when we started throwing our doors open and letting people join in our process from outside" (IV104). As he went on to explain, such an ethos benefited the sector as a whole when conceived as a network whose vibrancy brought collective intelligence through sharing, rather than simply competition. As another employee present at the meeting recognized, being open like this connected the company to networks that they couldn't otherwise leverage: "so when we are really struggling to get this one skill which is really hard to find, it tends to be easier with them around, because there is a bigger network in the office" (ibid.). Here the production cultures and economics of independence are understood as a network, which can be sustained through a moral economy of mutual collaboration and open source approaches to production.

This notion of an open and collaborative network was connected to a "gift economy," which companies employed as part of the way ideals from digital culture informed their business practices. Whilst Jenkins, Ford and Green's *Spreadable Media* (2012) focuses on gifting as a practice between fans that governs media industries' relationships with them—such as the act of "fansubbing" in anime subcultures—drawing on Marcel Maus and Lewis Hyde's original conception of the gift economy, they usefully point to the way that such economies are "socially rather than economically motivated and

[are] not simply symbolic of the social relations between participants; it helps to constitute them" (Jenkins et al. 2013: 67). As Jenkins reflects elsewhere, Hyde's conception of the gift economy invokes an obligation to give, accept and reciprocate, suggesting how participants undertake "a commitment to good relations and mutual welfare" (Jenkins and Green 2009). In contrast to mere economic value, gifts have "worth" that might not only be "aligned with meaning as it has been discussed in cultural studies" (Jenkins et al. 2013: 68), but also community and mutual obligation. Thus one interviewee told us of an example of the gift economy operating between companies that indicated how such bonds and community operated as a form of moral economy in the digital independent sector. Working on a multiplatform production that required a last-minute and significant change to its digital code in order to make the product work, the interviewee told us, they turned to a rival digital agency for help, who they knew owned a piece of code that would perform the function they required. Rather than acting out of competition, however, the rival company sold them the code for a nominal £1 fee. This, the interviewee rationalized, was on the basis that whilst it wasn't possible to provide the code entirely on open source terms, in order to protect their long-term investment in intellectual property, the collective intelligence and vitality of the sector was enhanced by such sharing (IV99).

Arguably, such gifting may be partly understood as a response to what Kennedy describes as the "the inescapable openness of the code that is used to build the web: it is impossible not to give away HTML" (2012: 73). However, not all code is as open as the HTML Kennedy discusses and, indeed, proprietary software code is what underpins much of the digital economy— from software giants such as Microsoft through to the smaller digital agencies we studied. The gifting we saw, therefore, is better understood as part of the moral economy that places worth on independence by digital companies: that is, the rival company understood that it was in the best interests of the sector as a whole if robust and quality products were produced, on time, if the PSBs were going to continue to make investment in independently produced multiplatform content and services. Paradoxically, such an ethos also placed a primacy on the value—or worth—of independence in terms of the free market, whereby the independent sector as a whole was perceived as more agile, responsive and, indeed, creative than the "linear legacies" of television-orientated (Bennett and Strange 2014), slow-moving, overly bureaucratized, central public service broadcasters. Digital agencies, in particular, tended to value their independence in this regard because of what Kennedy discusses as the fast-paced nature of digital work (2012: 76). Thus independents, to many working in the sector, were better at delivering public service value because they were more efficient, creative and diverse than broadcasters who commissioned them.[3]

This gifting and open source philosophy extended to companies' relationship with their audiences. Green and Jenkins posit that in the shifting contours between industry and audience inherent in participatory culture there exist both prohibitionist and collaborative responses from the media industries. The former, they suggest, attempts to lock down intellectual property by aggressively pursuing any and all infringements as well as by housing content in walled gardens and strongly delimiting the terms of use on which audiences can engage with content. In Green and Jenkins's approach to the new relationships between audiences and fans in web2.0, such practices are out of kilter with an emergent moral economy. Drawing on Hector Postigo's (2007) study of modding within game cultures, such a view positions ethically and morally inflected breaches of copyright by fans as legitimate, often on the basis that fans understand "that games companies benefit economically from their labor" (Jenkins and Green 2009). However, whilst large multinational games companies may permit such activities in order to generate hype around their titles (see Postigo in this volume), this says little of how smaller, independent companies manage the contradictory pulls between their roots in the digital culture of open sharing and the need to produce a financial return in order to secure their continuing economic survival and independence.

In this context, the strength of the moral economy of digital independents was startling. These companies often positioned, and fought, the broadcasters' approach to intellectual property as needlessly prohibitionist, complaining of contracts that locked down rights and distribution for periods that would exhaust any social or economic value from the PSBs' investments. One company even bartered away some of its rights in order to develop a distribution model based on piracy for a game aimed at teaching UK boys about the Battle of Hastings: "Our distribution plan was to allow it to be pirated, to be ripped and for people to put it on their own sites" (IV51, August 8, 2011). Whilst some in the industry questioned such a model in the face of an emerging micro-economy of casual gaming, the chief executive argued that the approach had generated far more value and worth than a prohibitionist approach. Thus the game had recorded more than 30 million plays and whilst not all players fitted within the target demographic of C4's public service remit, the high visibility of the game meant that the core user group was more likely to encounter the game, for example, via reviews or game-fan networks that drove up its visibility on search engines, making it the top search result in Google for "Battle of Hastings" for well over two years. Finally, such visibility transferred to the agency itself, which could be leveraged to win more work and maintain its status as an independent company: one trusted by a growing community of gamers.

In any moral economy, however, the relationship between profit and community is a vexed issue. Axel Bruns sets outs the fundamental problem:

> If the host of the community takes the content generated by that community and realizes profit from that content, the creators of that content will immediately be afflicted with a number of conflicting feelings.
>
> (quoted in Bennett 2011: 348)

Such tensions, however, are further exacerbated by the condition of independence more generally and the specific pulls felt between public service and profit in the digital agencies we studied. To take the general condition of independence first, Aymar Jean Christian has pointed out that the digital strategies of entertainment industries, and their independent offshoots, can stray "far from the discourse of subcultures, from the affective and moral economies of fandom" to gain attention in the competitive online world. Instead, they often "try to marshal the marketing potential of marginal communities into an independently sustainable commercial market" (2011). The decision not to try and monetize, sell to or sell out a community, therefore, is part of the moral economy of independence that we found conditioned the business practices of the sector. Of course, the decision not to monetize such communities cannot simply be explained by altruism alone: the relationship between public service and profit was also imperative here. Here we found a commitment to producing content that "makes a difference"— with nearly 50 percent of our digital producer interviewees describing their understanding of PSB as producing content that "makes a difference" by educating people about particular topics, raising awareness of social issues such as alcoholism, bullying or domestic abuse or providing tools that might help change antisocial or unhealthy behavior. In turn, well over 60 percent of interviewees understood PSB to motivate which projects and clients they worked with.

Nevertheless, balancing such a commitment to public service at the same time as ensuring profitability—necessary for the survival and growth of the company—remained a constant point of conflict and crisis in the independent sector's delivery of multiplatform projects for PSBs (Bennett et al. 2012; Bennett and Medrado 2013). As one managing director suggested in response to a question regarding whether there was an ethical dimension to decisions about what kind of projects they did:

> Creative freedom is what matters . . . it's nice if they do good things, like the Big Knit or whatever, it makes you feel better, because it is a nice thing you can be doing. But at the end of the day, I personally have to [take] quite a pragmatic view: it's ultimately people's jobs . . . it might not extend to selling arms, so there is a line. [pause] Although there might be a nice arms dealer. . . .
>
> (IV62 September 27, 2011)

Whilst, in this manager's view, creative freedom and the need to produce profit outweighed all other concerns, such a perspective was rare in the way digital independents negotiated the tension between PSB and profit. More uniformly, response and tactic displayed evidence of the sector's hybrid public service-digital moral economy.

For many companies, this was as simple as eschewing and highlighting what they called the "snake oil salesmanship" of some approaches to the "dark arts of analytics," whereby companies would employ ethically dubious tactics to search optimization, such as fake reviews, inbound links from fake satellite Web sites and bamboozling clients with too much data (IV46; see also Andrejevic 2013). For others it meant it was inappropriate to sell advertising against particularly sensitive material—such as health advice or campaigns to do with more sustainable food and environmental practices—or to make the user data collected from such sites available to use for commercial purposes: such as targeted marketing and tracking of preferences (IV19 20, 30, 31, 38, 46, 80, 105). It also motivated partnerships with nonprofit organizations to further a particular charitable cause, or build public knowledge through research collaborations with universities. One such instance of this form of critical industrial practice occurred in a company we studied making a multiplatform health project. Here they utilized their strong program brand to invite viewers of the show to take an autism test on the associated Web site that was designed by university researchers. This partnership meant dedicating considerable production time to covering the topic in the program, helping build the online application and then ensuring the data was held securely for the researchers. For the researchers, the partnership meant they were able to reach a much wider audience and conduct testing on a mass scale never before thought possible. Independence, as a moral economy hybrid of digital culture and PSB, therefore meant not only freedom from an overriding call to free market economics but also a concern with producing work for the common or public good. We turn to this issue in more detail now as we examine how the moral economy informed the work lives and creative freedoms of the individuals involved in the sector.

A MICRO MORAL ECONOMY: FREEDOM TO DO AND PRODUCE "GOOD WORK"

At a micro level, this hybrid moral economy of public service and digital culture informed how and why individuals valued the creative freedoms afforded by working within the digital independents we studied. As with the company's need to negotiate the pulls of public service and profit, the moral economy of digital independence helped individuals navigate their conditions of employment and the kinds of products they made. Such navigation enabled workers to make sense of and pick a way through the dualisms within which Hesmondhalgh and Baker argue autonomy and cultural production are largely understood to take place:

> They are usually expressed as between some kind of contrastive pairing: for example, between art and capital; art and commerce; culture and commerce; creativity and commerce; culture and commodity.
>
> (2011: 77)

Drawing on Mark Banks, they argue that "we need to think of creativity-commerce or art-commerce relations in terms of a triad, composed of orientations toward creativity, commerce and the social." Doing so, Hesmondhalgh and Baker suggest, may enable us to understand "the degree to which creative workers seek not only to live an aestheticised life, but also actively seek to intervene in social relations" (ibid.). Generally studies of creative labor have tended to emphasize that different aspects of "good work" are traded off against each other, whereby conditions of security, self-realization, decent hours and pay are swapped for autonomy, interest, sociality and even the investment in making "good" cultural products. Whilst we don't suggest it is possible to "have it all," in this section we look at how the values and beliefs that individuals bring to the workplace actively inform their conception and commitment to good work, including attempts to intervene in social relations, as well as how the organizational structures within companies further condition and complicate this moral economy.

It is useful to start by considering the conditions of employment within the digital sector. Taken as a whole, there is a tendency toward freelance and casualization, with individuals experiencing the precarious conditions and various forms of self-exploitation discussed in other studies of digital work (McRobbie 2002; Ross 2004). Whilst we want to acknowledge such problematic conditions, we also found evidence of different practices that were guided by a moral economy of digital independence. At the extreme end of such practices, we found examples where companies described themselves as "wilfully overstaffed," retaining people on longer-term contracts in preference to freelance because of their belief in ethical employment practices (IV104). This led employees to appreciate a culture of openness and security that meant "members of staff are not constantly job hunting" (FN May 13, 2011). At other agencies internships were never offered without pay or without a clear and reciprocal arrangement with universities as part of interns' degree structures, including an undertaking by company staff to lecture on interns' degree courses. As the digital managing director explained, an ethical approach to employment meant their relationship with employees was a "two way street" (IV105). Long-term contracts and hiring interns meant it was "worth us investing in training for them," whilst employees then tended to "care about the company [which] means that they are more likely to stay for longer." In turn, this enabled the company to not only build up a portfolio of different skill sets but also encourage and grow a company ethos and shared approach to doing things. For individuals working in digital independents that bought into the moral economy described in the previous section, however, working with freedom did not necessarily mean working for free.

In such companies the creative freedom and potential of individuals was fostered as part of an ongoing concern with professional development. Here employees were well aware of the notion that the flexible conditions of the new economy often mean that creativity was nurtured only for companies to "grab it and desperately try to make money out of it and make you work harder and harder and harder" (FN May 27, 2011). They contrasted this approach to an atmosphere that encouraged creativity and working with freedom, allowing staff to borrow equipment to make their own video or music projects (FN May 13, 2011). Equally, senior members of staff took an interest in this creativity without attempting to bootstrap employees' labor. Thus the company's director regularly set aside time to read a junior producer's film script, making recommendations in terms of storyline and how to go about pitching it in the wider industry. Work in these companies was set in stark contrast to the general conditions of freelancing experienced by many in the sector. More widely it was felt that freelancing inhibited creativity because it reduced the scope for individuals to make the mistakes necessary to learn through the creative process "and, as a freelancer, you're not hired for a short period of time to make mistakes . . . Employers are not willing to take their time and invest in people" (FN June 6, 2011).

These differing approaches to employee relationships and contracts produced very different production cultures between companies we observed. Thus whilst the digital agencies fostered an ethos of collaboration, not only between companies, but within them as well, the television companies of similar size tended to emphasize strict role boundaries. Workers within digital companies talked of a culture that was "quite open . . . I would feel comfortable asking anybody for help or thoughts on stuff." In turn, such a collaborative and open culture gave workers autonomy so that working with freedom meant having the ability to "work outside of your job description or your strict role," in order "to get involved with something different" and gain experience (FN February 27, 2012). In comparison, we found little or no collaboration between people working in different projects—the emphasis on freelance and short contracts meant that workers in the same office space rarely knew each other's names, as there was "no time to introduce people and ask who they are. With a freelance culture, everyone gets on with their job" (FN May 31, 2011).

The emphasis on collaborative workplaces in digital independents echoes many previous studies of such work cultures that emphasize flattened hierarchies in companies' organizational structures. Such structures have, however, generally been understood in the negative terms of neoliberalism— whereby a seeming emphasis on sociality within the workplace often creates a gendered barrier to career progress by demanding Friday night drinks and informal networking and by presenting an opaque career path that women, in particular, find harder to navigate given the continued unequal division of domestic labor (Gregg 2007). However, such an emphasis on nonhierarchical work cultures can also be understood in relationship to the practices—and politics—of alternative media (see Bennett's introduction to this volume). Here alternative media's distinction from the mainstream is often proclaimed in terms of their nonhierarchical organizational structures. Thus Kejanlioglu suggests that alternative media, apart from being non-dominant and counterhegemonic, are also defined by their "non-hierarchical organiza-tion, flexible operation, openness to make their audience producers . . . and experimental aesthetic forms" (Kejanlioglu et al. 2012: 275). Such a defini-tion echoes the emphasis Bailey, Cammaerts and Carpentier (2007) place on the networked, rhizomatic nature of alternative media. These descriptions are readily applicable to the way creative workers value the role of indepen-dence in the digital workplace. Thus one senior producer explained, "it is not really a hierarchal company. If you are good at what you are doing and you work hard, you are pretty much left to do it. And developed to be able to do it better" (FN May 27, 2011). This was a view that junior staff also shared: "CEOs, MDs, directors are friendly and accessible, they don't shut themselves, they take an interest in everyone" (FN May 13, 2011).

More importantly, such working conditions within digital independents weren't just in the service of generating a more creative workplace but also related to the desire to intervene in social relations, often in counterhege-monic ways. Thus at one digital agency, the nonhierarchical organization of the company was utilized to draw in and share experiences of school bully-ing to help create a game designed to enable teens to navigate the transition from junior to senior school. This structure was indicative of a more widely shared investment in a culture of play within digital agencies that, again, didn't just enlist people's freest thoughts and creativity in the service of com-pany time, but also produced radical and experimental aesthetic forms, such as a video game for blind people. Overall, these conditions of employment suggest how a belief in a moral economy conditioned not just the business practices of companies, but also their employee relations. Independence did not, therefore, necessarily mean precarious employment and self-exploitation, but could also foster creative freedoms, potentialities and ethics within com-panies as a "two-way street."

In turn, individuals also brought a string of concerns from their non-work life into the workplace and their working lives. Such ethical concerns informed what companies people wanted to work for in terms of not only the conditions of the workplace, but also a concern to make "good" cultural products. As one managing director explained:

> We do lots of work with not for profits and charities and we are known for that a bit. And a lot of people when they come for job interviews . . . they say "that's one of the reasons I want to work with [your company]."
>
> (IV46)

Here workers within digital independents placed a high value on how the cultural goods they created matched up with their own ethical interest in "making a difference" in society, which was often aligned with PSB. As one digital producer put it:

> I work for [Company] because I think you can feel proud of the out-put, I would not be comfortable working for a company that was

making . . . like game show entertainment stuff, we do an element of that, but we work on [multiplatform] when you get the feedback and potentially save peoples' lives.

(FN February 13, 2012)

Concern with "making a difference" meant that individuals would often tolerate and, indeed, embrace flexible working conditions. Whilst neo-Foucauldian accounts tend to position such flexibility as a form of self-exploitation and precariousness, arguably such descriptions are too monolithic to explain how a moral economy can operate at a micro level. Here independence—as flexibility, autonomy and even working for free—was valued by employees for the opportunity to explore their ethical concerns: from volunteering to act as a mentor for new companies and freelancers within the sector, in an ethos of collective intelligence and cooperation, through to undertaking pro bono work for charitable organizations.

At one company, an ethos of such volunteerism and commitment to the PSB moral economy of "making a difference" filtered through into the company's orientation around projects that had social good at their core. Here the production manager worked with vulnerable children, which was only possible because of the autonomy and freedom in her work life, whilst the development producer acted as a community councilor on the weekends. This interest in social issues often shaped or coincided with the kinds of projects the company took on, becoming a key business asset for the company because it meant that such employees "were really plugged in the communities and that feeds back into production because they have a handle of what life is about rather than being stuck in an ivory tower" (FN September 21, 2011). As David Lee has argued, particularly for people working in PSB, work identity is strongly shaped by a moral core, a desire to change society and "to get people to think about the world we live in" (2012: 480).

This ethical concern with what got made extended to the way individual employees understood the relationships with their audiences—drawing on the participatory culture ethos that Jenkins and Green describe as "recogniz[ing] and respect[ing] consumer engagement while demanding respect in return" (2009: 223). Thus one digital producer working on a health project talked about how the company emphasized "responsible procedures" in terms of how they interacted with the online community. Here the hybrid moral economy of digital and public service cultures produced a rewarding experience for the individual because it enabled him to feel like his work was valuable, making a difference, by offering support to vulnerable people:

if we see worrying messages, we get . . . their details and get back to them with support groups and that is the rewarding thing: you can really press it and chase it, prevent someone from committing suicide.

(FN February 20, 2012)

Of course, whilst many found satisfaction in the "good work" produced in their working lives, tensions nevertheless remained. Thus for the same worker, it was difficult to reconcile this preference for producing projects that had a "positive impact on people's lives" with some makeover programming made at the company, "which they dubbed 'dubious' in terms of the company's professed PSB values" (Bennett and Medrado 2013: 107). Whilst a degree of "emotional labor" (Hesmondhalgh and Baker 2011) was certainly necessary to reconcile or put aside such contradictions, the conditioning of digital media independence suggested how a moral economy operated at a micro level to guide how individuals navigated such tensions, crises and compromises in their working lives. As Ulrich Beck has argued, even within the small scale of individuals' lives, including their working lives, people attempt to "realize a more perfect democracy in miniature" by mobilizing an ethical approach to their cultural production (Beck and Willms 2004: 67).

CONCLUSION: A MORAL ECONOMY OF DIGITAL WORK

Accounts of labor within the digital media industries have tended to emphasize the way they operate as neoliberal models of work that encourage flexibility, insecurity, self-exploitation and precariousness in exchange for an ideal of creative freedom. We hope to have shown, however, that whilst some of these negative conditions may exist the creative freedom that they are swapped for is not only complex, but far from the only concern of companies and individuals. Our study suggests that a moral economy of digital independence conditions how that creative freedom is understood and valued by the sector, resulting in an investment in business practices that foster an open source, networked and collaborative approach alongside working conditions that promote ethical practices of employment and relationships with user communities. Whilst these conditions are often premised on a shared view of digital culture, they are also underpinned by a PSB ethos committed to producing content that "makes a difference." Moreover, such an investment is often mutually beneficial to companies and their employees in terms of fulfilling their desire for good work, and work that is profitable.

Just as Mark Banks's study of moral economies hoped that paying attention to the way the neoliberal push for workers to "be independent" and "think for themselves" may produce results that are "unanticipated and unwelcome by government" (2006: 100), our study has demonstrated how an industry often positioned at the vanguard of creative entrepreneurialism is often concerned with practices and ethics that run counter to the goals of neoliberalism. This moral economy operates as something of a hybrid economy that indicates the way independent media work often fuses different values and arrangements, bringing together values of public service broadcasting on the one hand and digital culture on the other. To be a digital independent, and to work within that sector, therefore entails complex negotiations between profit and public service, creative freedom and insecurity, which can be underplayed if we don't pay attention to both the micro and macro effects of such a moral economy. Compromises in the way individuals and companies seek to achieve and understand media independence should not, therefore, be understood merely as failures of independent media. Instead, we can see such compromises as a productive site of good work—both in terms of the cultural products made and the conditions of labor experienced.

NOTES

1. In particular, the reversal of intellectual property ownership laws by the 2003 *Communications Act* had made the production of television formats, with their potential for international sale, especially profitable. For a more detailed discussion of the history and structure of the sector, see Bennett and Kerr 2012.
2. This research was conducted as part of the Arts & Humanities Research Council project "Multiplatforming public service broadcasting," AH-H018522-2. For a full discussion of methodology and findings, see Bennett et al. 2012. Interviewees are designated by number—represented IV1–104—in order to maintain anonymity. For a full explanation of methodology, see Bennett et al. 2012.
3. See also David Hesmondhalgh and Sarah Baker's astute discussion of the marketization of broadcasting in the United Kingdom (2011: 95–98).

REFERENCES

Andrejevic, M. (2013) *InfoGlut*. New York: Routledge.
Bailey, O. G., Cammaerts, B. and Carpentier, N. (2007) *Understanding Alternative Media*. London: Open University Press/McGraw Hill.
Banks, M. (2006) "Moral economy and cultural work," *Sociology* 40, 3: 455–472.
Beck, U. and Willms, J. (2004) *Conversations with Ulrich Beck*. London: Wiley Blackwell.
Bennett, J. (2011) "Architectures of participation: Fame, television and web2.0," in J. Bennett and N. Strange (eds.), *Television as Digital Media*, 332–357. Durham, NC: Duke University Press.
Bennett, J. (2015) "Public service as production cultures: A contingent, conjunctural compact," in M. Banks, B. Connor and V. Mayer (eds.), *Production Studies: Volume 2*, forthcoming. London and New York: Routledge.
Bennett, J. and Kerr, P. (2012) "A 360° public service sector? The role of independent production in the UK's public service broadcasting landscape," in G. F. Lowe and J. Steemers (eds.), *Regaining the Initiative for Public Service Media: RIPE@2011*, 219–236. Gothenburg: Nordicom & University of Gothenburg Press.
Bennett, J. and Medrado, A. (2013) "The business of multiplatform public service: Online and at a profit," *Media International Australia* 146, February: 103–113.
Bennett, J. and Strange, N. (2014) "Linear legacies: Managing multiplatform production cultures," in D. Johnson, D. Kompare and A. Santos (eds.), *Making Media Work: Cultures of Management in the Entertainment Industries*, 63–89. New York: New York University Press.

Bennett, J., Strange, N., Kerr, P. and Medrado, A. (2012) *Multiplatforming Public Service Broadcasting: The Cultural and Economic Role of UK Television and Digital Independents*. London: Royal Holloway.

Caldwell, J. T. (2006) "Critical industrial practice branding, repurposing, and the migratory patterns of industrial texts," *Television & New Media* 7, 2: 99–134.

Caldwell, J. (2011) "Worker blowback: User-generated, worker-generated and producer-generated content within collapsing production workflows," in J. Bennett and N. Strange (eds.), *Television as Digital Media*, 283–310. Durham, NC: Duke University Press.

Chitty, A. (2013) "How multiplatform PSB stopped trying to change the world and grew up (but got smaller)," *Critical Studies in Television* 8, 1: 126–130.

Christian, A. J. (2011) "Fandom as industrial response: Producing identity in an independent web series," *Transformative Works and Cultures* 8, 2011. Available http: http://journal.transformativeworks.org/index.php/twc/article/view/250/237.

Green, J. and Jenkins, H. (2009) "The moral economy of Web 2.0: Audience research and convergence culture," in J. Holt and A. Perren (eds.), *Media Industries: History, Theory, and Method*, 213–225. Oxford: Wiley Blackwell.

Gregg, M. (2007) *Works Intimacy*. Cambridge: Polity Press.

Hesmondhalgh, D. and Baker, S. (2011) *Creative Labour: Media Work in Three Cultural Industries*. London: Routledge.

Jenkins, H. (2006) *Fans, Bloggers and Gamers: Exploring Participatory Culture*. New York: New York University Press.

Jenkins, H., Ford, S. and Green, J. (2012) *Spreadable Media: Creating Value and Meaning in a Networked Culture*. New York: New York University Press.

Jenkins, H., Li, X., Domb Krauskopt, A. and Green, J. (2009) "If it doesn't spread, it's dead (part four): Thinking through the gift economy," blog post at *Henryjenkins.org* February 18, 2009. Available http: http://henryjenkins.org/2009/02/if_it_doesnt_spread_its_dead_p_3.html.

Keat, R. (2000) *Cultural Goods and the Limits of the Market*. London and New York: Routledge.

Kejanlioglu, D. B., Coban, B., Yanikkaya, B. and Kokslan, M. E. (2012) "The user as producer in alternative media? The case of the Independent Communication Network (BIA)," *De Gruyter Mouton Communications* 37, 3: 275–296.

Kennedy, H. (2012) *Net Work: Ethics and Values in Web Design*. Basingstoke: Palgrave MacMillan.

Lee, D. (2011) "Precarious creativity: Changing attitudes towards craft and creativity in the British independent television production sector," *Creative Industries Journal* 4, 2: 155–170.

Lee, D. (2012) "The ethics of insecurity: Risk, individualization and value in British independent television production," *Television & New Media* 13, 6: 480–497.

McRobbie, A. (2002) "Clubs to companies: Notes on the decline of political culture in speeded up creative worlds," *Cultural Studies* 16, 4: 516–531.

O'Connor, J. (2007) *The Cultural and Creative Industries: A Review of the Literature*. London: HPM and Arts Council England.

Postigo, H. (2007) "Of mods and modders chasing down the value of fan-based digital game modifications," *Games and Culture* 2, 4: 300–313.

Ross, A. (2004) *No-collar: The Humane Workplace and Its Hidden Costs*. Philadelphia, PA: Temple University Press.

Sayer, A. (2007) "Dignity at work: Broadening the agenda," *Organization* 14, 4: 565–581.

Strange, N. (2011) "Multiplatforming public service: The BBC's 'bundled project," in J. Bennett and N. Strange (eds.), *Television as Digital Media*, 132–157. Durham, NC: Duke University Press.

7 Indie TV
Innovation in Series Development

Aymar Jean Christian

I spent five years interviewing creators of American Web series, or independent television online,[1] speaking with 134 producers and executives making and releasing scripted series independent of traditional network investment. No two series or creators were ever alike. Some were sci-fi comedies created by Trekkers, others urban dramas by black women. Nevertheless, nearly every creator differentiated their work and products from traditional television in some way. Strikingly, whenever I asked if any particular creator inspired them to develop their own show independently, I heard one response more than any other: Felicia Day.

Indie TV creators revere Day for her innovation in production and distribution: she developed a hit franchise, *The Guild*, outside network development processes. *The Guild*, a sitcom about a diverse group of gamers who sit at computers all day to play an MMORPG in the style of *World of Warcraft*, ran for six seasons, from 2007 to 2013, and spawned a music video, DVDs, comic books and a companion book, as well as marshaled the passions of hundreds of thousands of fans. By the end of its run, *The Guild* had amassed more than 330,000 subscribers on YouTube, although it could also be seen on other portals.

In my work I have seen *The Guild* emerge as central to the online indie TV industry's case for itself as antidote to what ails Hollywood. Day initially pitched to networks, which all passed. "People loved it, but said it was too 'niche,'" Day said early in its development (Au 2007). The niche she refers to is gamers, but in other interviews Day has remarked on how production companies with network ties also mistreat women and actors, even when they are also producers:

> I think it's very hard in Hollywood for women—in Hollywood, you're [treated one of two ways:] Either as an actress, so you look really pretty and perfectly polished and you're treated as eye candy, like an object ... I've had some professional studio meetings, and the ones where I really got glammed up, I've had questions like, "You didn't really write that script, did you?" I've actually had a couple of producers or executive people ask me that to my face. ... Unless you're

in Hollywood, you don't really understand how actors are treated—
either like dirt, or you're a god, and there's no in-between.

(Ryan 2010)

The Guild, created by and starring a woman and featuring leads cast
from various ethnicities, ages and body types, is Day's response to everything that's wrong with corporate television development: its tendency to
marginalize and undervalue storytelling, workers, identities and fans in pursuit of profit. So Day produced the first season of *The Guild* on her own,
with a small but plucky team of fans. She published it via the Internet, and
gamers—who spend hours a day online—started to champion it. When Day
put out a call for money to complete the first season, 550 individuals helped
her raise it via PayPal (Goldberg 2011). At the same time, fans were joining
the production, donating their labor or locations. One such fan was Jenni
Powell, who would become one of the most influential Web television producers. Powell got her start on the early Web hit *lonelygirl15* but moved up
the ranks on *The Guild*. Powell met Day in a chat room and told her how she
got her start as *lonelygirl15*'s lone production assistant doing "80 different
things." Day gave Powell a list of tasks and Powell joined season two as the
head production assistant and Day's part-time assistant. By season three she
was an assistant director. "Literally the show was built by the fans," Powell
told me.[2]

Fans helped Day bridge the gap in financing long enough for her to negotiate a remarkable, if modest, development deal with Microsoft, who signed
on as the semi-exclusive distributor of *The Guild* (at the time, Microsoft
sought original programming for its Xbox console and MSN network), and
Sprint, who signed on as a sponsor. Day retained ownership of her show,
with enough money to make it, if not enough to get rich off it. *The Guild*'s
fans never left, following Day from comic-cons, industry festivals and Twitter, where she amassed more than 2 million followers, allowing her to use
her celebrity power to manage *The Guild*'s disparate connections between
fans, industry and media (Ellcessor 2012).

Any consideration of the value and function of the independent television
market must contend with who has power in corporate series development
and how power is brought to bear in making decisions. In traditional television, network development executives shape series pitched by producers
and their companies, but executives' clients are advertising agencies, executives at media conglomerates and, by extension, shareholders of media companies. Despite the incredible rise of fandom and independent television
series production, a small group of network executives continues to hold
sway over the supply (creative production), consumption (fans or audiences)
and financing (brands) of television content. This power imbalance and its
inefficiencies were less visible before deregulation expanded the number of
channels and original series on cable and the Internet. Today it has grown
irksome to nearly everyone involved in the development process, including

the decision makers themselves. Studying the upfront buying process in the mid-2000s, Amanda Lotz found it in "crisis . . . with many in the industry expressing open dissatisfaction in public forums, one-on-one conversations, in trade press articles and as evidenced by the creation of an industry discussion group to formally reconsider the process" (Lotz 2007a: 550). Central to the crisis was the vast amount of pitches for extremely limited slots (constrained production), declining ratings for new shows (the challenge of creating new fans) and brand dissatisfaction with the reach and attention of commercials (Lotz 2007a).

Indie TV producers, during the period Day's *Guild* franchise spans (roughly 2007–2013), inverted these dynamics, placing power in development in the hands of creative workers, their fans and brands. By "indie TV" I describe an undercounted segment of producers who create mostly short-form serials and release them through YouTube, Vimeo or other online platforms for Web distribution. They comprise amateurs, film students and graduates and television professionals (inside and outside Hollywood unions, above and below the line) who produce video for themselves, their communities or, most rarely, for independent and corporate online and TV networks. This sector is defined by limited access and amounts of capital, which predominantly takes the form of algorithmic advertising, licensing, crowd-financing, subscription or sponsorship. Extremely undercapitalized, the indie market nevertheless models the kind of open and diverse TV ecosystem the deregulated landscape was intended to fertilize, before corporations purchased profitable distribution channels, increasing the scale of production but not always wages, creative freedom or audience and brand input. This chapter uses three Web series—*High Maintenance*, *Whatever this is* and *Easy to Assemble*—alongside my wider study, to explore the pilot process and upfront financing, which support networks' access to US$70 billion in television advertising. I will show how pilot production, upfront monetization and audience selling are ill suited to an age of online networking and market fragmentation; how network control over programming falls short of balancing art, culture and commerce; and how independent television development supports innovation in series creation by empowering producers, fans and brands frustrated with network control. I outline how independent production in online TV creates more innovative and open TV storytelling through three interconnected concerns: creative ownership with "free" labor, a "highly ambivalent" political project to counteract exploitation in corporate employment (Hesmondhalgh 2010: 280–282; Hesmondhalgh and Baker 2011); diversity, through the power of self-representation and community-led development; and authenticity, by working directly with sponsors to support producer-led stories. The indie TV market is massive, comprising thousands of series, and by the late 2000s and early 2010s, its most innovative projects inspire some television networks to develop them, most notably Abbi Jacobson and Ilana Glazer's *Broad City*, which premiered in early 2014 to strong ratings and reviews.

Few Web series achieve that level of success, however, and development deals rarely result in series orders and the promise of good work—working with freedom for fair reward—elusive in independent media. Nevertheless the cases in this chapter show how independent production works toward a utopian system where workers, audiences and sponsors pilot new shows.

THE PILOT PROCESS AND THE POLITICS OF DISTRIBUTION

Independence from Hollywood in film, television or music is best understood through differences in production and distribution, even though most scholars employ aesthetic and cultural critiques of independently produced texts. As Geoff King argues in this volume, the aesthetics and ideologies of independently produced texts can vary in degree and kind from their mainstream counterparts, along a continuum of industrial strategies and locations (see King's essay in Chapter 2 of this volume). My understanding of the online video market supports King's assertion that indie aesthetics and ideology do not differ from Hollywood as often as their industrial locations, contexts and strategies, where difference can almost always be found. Many Web series deviate from Hollywood aesthetics to produce stories fractions of the length of traditional television. Yet, like in corporate television and film, heterosexual, middle- and upper-class white men overwhelmingly produce the most visible and profitable productions in the online video market, which tend to be ideologically heteronormative, even misogynistic (Wotanis and McMillan 2014). The Internet marketplace accommodates independents whose production, storytelling and distribution strategies push against inequalities and the status quo. My work posits those differences can be instructive, a way of understanding Hollywood's industrial inefficiencies and inequalities, with potential but largely untested implications for television's aesthetics, ideology and economic and social role (Christian 2013a; 2013b).

If industrial practices are essential to differences between Hollywood and independent producers, I argue we must consider those practices that dominate the development of new series on traditional television: the pilot process and upfront advertising sales. The pilot process includes the pitching of thousands[3] of new series, and the production of its first episode, presented to brands and advertising agencies at the upfronts in May, where 75 to 90 percent of ads are sold to finance the rest of the season. Piloting and upfront ad sales govern nearly all of U.S. broadcast scripted television development—that of CBS, NBC, ABC, Fox and the CW. Sales for those networks represent half of all TV series monetization, totaling around US$9 billion annually (Lotz 2007a). A slightly greater number of cable channels now comprise the other half of the annual haul, a result of the rapid growth in interest in cable programming from brands and advertisers over the 2000s (Crupi 2013).

These cable channels, most owned by conglomerates with ownership stakes in broadcast production (series) and distribution (channels), increase market share by controlling costs, filling schedules with cheap reality television produced by nonunion contracts while greenlighting a few costlier, more often union, productions to attract big financiers and press attention. In the latter case they tend to give producers more creative control—for shows like *Louie*, *Portlandia* or *Girls*—or rely heavily on developing series with passionate fan bases in other media—for franchise shows like *The Walking Dead* (graphic novel), *Game of Thrones* (series of novels)—and from sports. When cable networks release original shows they pilot fewer and are more likely to commission straight to series.[4] For several years corporate online networks like Yahoo and Hulu, and multichannel networks on YouTube, worked to replicate upfront selling through the Newfronts, run by marketing firm Digitas in its early years and moving to the Interactive Advertising Bureau (IAB).[5] The online networks' lack of brand recognition as original program distributors, however, meant channels catered heavily to the perceived needs of brands, producing uninspiring content from mostly Hollywood producers and a few YouTube personalities in its earliest years. For 2013 the IAB estimated Internet advertising revenue at US$43 billion, more than broadcast television's US$40 billion, but video advertising, which delivers the highest rates for Web television, comprised just US$3 billion (IAB/PricewaterhouseCoopers 2014).

Despite the increase in competition from corporate channels on cable and the Web, broadcast networks have maintained and, in some years, increased the size of the pilot market and upfront ad sales. Amanda Lotz shows how upfront financing of series "remains remarkably steadfast" for a number of reasons, including legacy relationships between networks and advertisers, the perceived value of broadcast television compared to other channels for advertising, and the broadcasters' continued, albeit waning, ability to attract audiences larger than other channels on cable and the Web (Lotz 2007a: 556). The upfront process developed over decades, starting in the 1960s, to accommodate the needs of networks, brands and their agencies. It favors the networks: brands purchase time on series that have not been tested with audiences and without data on what rates other brands are paying; networks establish base rates for brand clients to guarantee a relatively stable amount of sales each year; the scarcity of programming, particularly for "hit" networks, incentivizes agencies to spend high and bid quickly; and scatter markets—where ads are sold at a discount during the run of the season—provide networks an outlet for monetizing slots that haven't sold upfront or if programs underperform (Lotz 2007a).

Buoyed by the relative strength of the upfront market, networks increased the size and scale of pilot production, even as success rates for pilots did not rise in kind. Film L.A., which coordinates and processes permits for film and television in Los Angeles, has counted the number of television pilots in production since the 2004–2005 season. That year, 124 pilots were produced,

101 of them in Los Angeles. Pilot production dropped under 100 from 2007 to 2009, following the recession and Writers Guild of America strike, but by the 2012–2013 season production rebounded to a record 186 pilots, 96 filmed in Los Angeles, most of those sitcoms. Accounting for the remaining jump in production were dramas; the vast majority were shot outside Los Angeles in New York, Canada (Vancouver and Toronto) and Atlanta, which offer financial production incentives to help companies offset costs: "Often, this means financial concerns trump creative concerns when deciding where to shoot" (Film L.A. 2013). The total amount broadcasters spent on pilots produced remained stable, despite increased competition for advertising campaign dollars. Film L.A. estimated networks and production companies spent US$309 million on pilots in 2005, dipping to US$207 million in 2009 but rebounding to US$278 million in 2013 (Film L.A. 2013).

Continued brand investment in traditional television buoys the market for financing and producing new shows and allows networks to maintain control over who gets to make television and what kinds of stories audiences see. Networks have had this power for most of their history, and it has been fraught with uncertainty, and by extension, conservatism, about what kinds of productions audiences want. Because of this uncertainty, networks "develop[ed] ways to control both supply and demand—supply in order to smooth its workings, demand so that it remains of a sort the networks are set up to satisfy" (Gitlin 1983: 14). By controlling the supply (production) and demand (advertising, range and type of stories audiences can see) networks have avoided drastic shifts in revenue year to year and curtailed advertisers' interest in migrating to other platforms. But the process is antithetical to story creation. Todd Gitlin, in his analysis of television development during the beginning of the multichannel transition around 1980, characterized the pilot process as a "slow 'no' . . . the business of satisfying executives who have to satisfy other executives—all with opinions about the mass market" (Gitlin 1983: 26). Because of limited distribution through broadcast networks, the effect of network control in series development has been to limit storytelling possibilities (ibid.: 29). Risk avoidance declined with increased competition from series on cable, paving the way for morally and narratively complex series from *Arrested* to *Community*, *Lost* to *Scandal* (Creeber 2004; Mittell 2006). But an unconventional program receiving a series order remains an exception to the rule, and typically possible only when pitched by elite producers with lucrative multiyear development contracts or with multiple projects in development or production (Ettema 1982; Turow 1982).[6] The loosening of rules over program and network ownership increased the number of executives who could say "no" to projects while limiting the bargaining power of the independent producers who write them because networks own multiple channels. The result has kept diversity stagnant among television's producers, where employment for women and racial minorities has barely risen—from 2007 to 2012 women comprised 27–28 percent and racial minorities just 10–11 percent of all television writers, according to the Writers Guild (Hunt 2014). This is despite the growth in production and existence of network diversity programs (Bielby and Bielby 2002; Bullock et al. 2008; Christian 2013b; Shah 2013). Network ownership structures make it difficult for executives to satisfy multiple constituencies—producers, brands, audiences. Empowered with balancing what is marketable, engaging and artistically or culturally valuable, networks only occasionally satisfy all three, and prioritize marketability in service of a media conglomerate's chief goal: profit. Indie TV productions work toward balance, although they cannot guarantee the stable working conditions corporations provide when they do invest accordingly (see James Bennett's discussion of the movement to "independents" in Chapter 3 of this volume).

INNOVATION IN SERIES DEVELOPMENT AND CHALLENGES TO NETWORK CONTROL

In their quest for creative fulfillment, indie TV producers like Felicia Day intervene in corporate control over new series development. First episodes or seasons of indie TV shows are best thought of as pitches and pilots, which, if successful, can sustain themselves through producer, fan or brand support. The development of independent Web series intervenes in network control over producers in the pitch process, their control over intellectual property and labor once the series airs, over what audiences watch through pilot selection, and over the process of monetizing audiences through crowdsourcing and brand sponsorship. In each case, indie TV offers an "innovation." Here, I am extending Stuart Cunningham's argument that innovation in creative industries is best defined beyond traditional Schumpeterian terms of new products and modes of production to include "the application of those ideas for realized or potential economic, social or public benefit" (Cunningham 2013: 4). This framing of innovation "provides a value-driven orientation to productivity and, ultimately, quality of life, rather than merely a cost-efficiency driver for intervention," a foil to investment-driven innovation that dominates digital technology product development (ibid.: 7).

In its ideals, and often in practice, the indie TV marketplace values creative producers first, whose work inspires fans and sponsors. As such, indie development redefines the value of television away from the needs of network intermediaries and toward those who drive the commercial television system with their labor, attention and capital. Within the indie TV market, producers labor to create value for: writers, producers and actors, through ownership of intellectual property, narrative experimentation and engagement with cultural politics; for audiences, through storytelling shaped and financed by communities; and for brands, by creating stories that appeal to communities specific enough to meet increasing demand for complex and targeted marketing and publicity campaigns.

Where online indie TV producers focus on maximizing creative value, networks value advertising volume and price, but both are under pressure in the post-network marketplace (Lotz 2007a: 557). Advertising agencies deliver to networks brands and payment for time on new and returning series, time that networks (must) value more than the agencies. In return brands get the audiences they value more than the network (audiences in different sizes/configurations), and agencies get fees and a continued relationship with their clients and the networks. As new technologies allow audiences to bypass commercial spots, as ratings on broadcast networks decline,[7] brands are starting to question the value they pay for TV time. The threat—the heart of the "crisis" in television—is declining value for advertising from brands and viewership from fans. Both influence each other, driving revenue down, albeit slowly.

Media studies have explored challenges to the process of corporate network piloting in financing, audience behavior and distribution (Jenkins, Ford and Green 2013; Lotz 2007b; Rizzo 2007; Tussey 2014). Yet scholars have understudied the role of independent production in bridging competing industry stakeholders' needs through alternative practices and values. By considering the alternatives to the pilot process, I expose the limits of corporate television's power to raise capital while supporting writers, audiences and innovation. As Lotz argues of proposals to restructure upfront financing: "A different method of purchasing [e.g., an all-'scatter' market] would reallocate capital and value throughout the television industry in ways likely to affect the programming produced" (Lotz 2007a: 555). I argue indie TV creators are already reallocating capital and value, responding to Hollywood's tightening labor market on the supply side along with demand from brands and audiences. As will be shown, the types of programs produced are different from traditional television, including a consistent theme of individuals struggling and surviving, often humorously, the pressures of contemporary corporate capitalism.

The rest of this chapter explores what online indie TV series development looks like when producers, their fans and interested brands spearhead development. What I found were greater degrees of creative freedom and ownership in production, greater agency from fans and audiences in the development of new and the perpetuation of existing series, and series more responsive to the needs of TV's sponsors.

PRODUCER-DRIVEN DEVELOPMENT: CREATIVE OWNERSHIP, EXPERIMENTATION AND CULTURAL POLITICS

The story of television's hidden innovators is as complex as it is thrilling. Consider the JankyClown Productions team, or, the "Jankies," and their hit series, *High Maintenance*. *High Maintenance* started when Katja Blichfeld, a casting director best known for her Emmy Award-winning work on *30 Rock*, her husband, Ben Sinclair, and his manager, Russell Gregory, realized they had access to great actors and an idea they could execute. Each episode of *High Maintenance* takes viewers into a different New York apartment or locale and introduces them to a stressed-out group of people in need of weed. "We just want to get inside the apartment and meet these characters," Russell Gregory told me in an interview (Christian 2013d). Those characters were mostly actors with film and TV credits, but few, if any, starring roles. Blichfeld realized she was in a unique position to showcase great, undiscovered talent she couldn't cast or could cast but only in small roles: "A lot of the people who I loved either I never got to cast, or I would cast them, and it was like a two-line part that would be funny and have impact but I would always know that actor was capable of way more than anyone was seeing," she told me (Christian 2013d).

High Maintenance became a hit indie Web series, with hundreds of thousands of views on Vimeo and a number of critical raves, including from myself in *Indiewire* and Rachel Syme in *The New Yorker*, largely, I argue, because of this innovation (Syme 2013). The series took a source of labor undervalued in the corporate system—actors—and gave them creative work, including the ability to write or shape the story. Lack of access to seasoned acting talent, who expect to be paid, hinders many indie Web series, which more often rely on new or unprofessional talent to save money for other aspects of production.[8] The *High Maintenance* team cast great comedic talent, many of them indie producers themselves. In "Olivia," one of the series' most popular episodes, Heléne Yorke (*Masters of Sex*, *30 Rock*) and Max Jenkins play chatty hipster-grifters. While both had tiny parts on *30 Rock*, their comedic chops are on full display—Jenkins's talents previously carried Karina Mangu-Ward and B. Hodgson's Web series *Gay's Anatomy*. Noted indie TV creator Michael Cyril Creighton—whose series *Jack in a Box* explores the sad life of actors and was the first indie series reviewed by *The New York Times*—wrote and starred in a *High Maintenance* episode, "Helen," playing a character markedly more depressed and complex than his *30 Rock* cameo as a sales clerk for a Brooklyn clothing store owned by Halliburton. Hannibal Buress, a rising comedian who also appears in *Broad City* (the indie series and the Comedy Central show), plays a version of himself grappling with racism and violence.

Producer-driven development involves a team of creative and technical workers collaborating on a project—investing labor time for an unguaranteed pay-off, or "sweat equity"—in the hope it finds an audience or a buyer, in form of a network or brand. Most Web series are initially produced in this way; entire series have been filmed using this kind of precarious labor. While most Web series are made by producers, just as in television, I distinguish producer-driven development as the creation of series whose "pitches" must be executed to communicate their effectiveness, or whose stories are too complex or outré to get brand or audience participation in preproduction. Producer-driven series need audiences, networks or brands, eventually, but because of the distinctiveness of their pitch, the creative team will make one or more seasons of the show without any interest from the aforementioned stakeholders. Indeed, some series go years without spreading widely but instead focus on craft in the hope of selling to distributors on television and the Web. For limited financial reward, producers find in independent production some solidarity with other creative workers and "meaningful self-realisation . . . social respect and recognition," among other nonmonetary rewards critics of free labor sometimes miss (Hesmondhalgh and Baker 2010; see also Khiabany in Chapter 12 of this volume).

Successful producer-driven Web series reconfigure the scale and politics of the set to suit their storytelling needs. Blichfeld and Sinclair's essay for the "Indie TV Innovation" series on my *Televisual* site (tvisual.org) identified three reasons for their success: working with actors they like, working within their means and working with the flow (Blichfeld and Sinclair 2013). At the time episodes of *High Maintenance* cost between US$500 and US$800, they wrote, based on producers taking on multiple roles, inexpensive equipment rentals and condensed shoots (from sixteen hours to two days). Actors were not paid, but agreed because of the producer's reputation in television and the chance to play a role explicitly written to showcase their talents in ways traditional television series did not. Because the production is so lean, the team can configure the story to the realities of the shoot and the talent on set:

> Flexibility is a necessity, especially on a shoestring budget. That means everything we do is subject to change. For instance, when we heard winter storm "Nemo" was to hit NYC when we were planning to shoot, we incorporated the storm into our story. When a noisy Latin American street festival suddenly popped up outside of our shooting location, we wrote it in as a B-story to contrast the quiet isolation of that episode's A-story. We usually just write shooting scripts to convey the story and the imagery; but if a line of dialogue isn't working for an actor, or a shot doesn't look great to our DP, we ask the artists to change them to what they think would look or sound good, while still getting the story point or joke across. If the story is strong, than the script can undergo all kinds of on-the-fly changes.
>
> (Blichfeld and Sinclair 2013)

Here, Blichfeld and Sinclair highlight their ability to shape the story to their environment and redistribute creative ownership of the series to actors and crew, in order to save time and money and do what's best for the story. Traditional television workers tell similar trade stories, particularly after cost controls and technological changes shifted the pace and intensity of corporate production (Caldwell 2008). Those who work outside the constraints of mainstream narrative (episode style and length) and distribution (corporate financing and control) find creative ownership and freedom in balancing the demands of the production with those of workers, fans and/or sponsors. We might, therefore, describe this balancing act as a never-ending effort to create "good work" when it is in decline in Hollywood (see Strange, Medrado, Bennett, this volume).

Traditional television networks achieve such efficiency, when they can, through deep investments in intellectual property, established producers and marketing, but not necessarily by expanding creative freedom and ownership. Networks greenlight and develop pilots based on great ideas but control their execution to manage sales and audience reception. Series almost inevitably shift away from the creator's original intent—to varying degrees, based on the type of show and the clout of the producer—to meet network demands. Networks are aware of this and increasingly turn to producers willing to work with network-owned studios to develop ideas they can market (Sharma and Hagey 2013). The growth of complex television, as coined by Jason Mittell, has coincided with rising network participation in production (Mittell 2012–2013). The result is more complex "poetics," or format creativity on screen—Mittell eschews focusing on representation, or the cultural meanings of race, gender and sexuality, all under pressure in post-network TV—but less behind it, where producers now have less ownership of the fruits of their creative labor (chiefly, intellectual property).

High Maintenance intervenes in this issue of ownership, spreading it among creative stakeholders, but it also signals the possibilities for narrative experimentation and engagement with cultural politics when indie producers drive the development of new stories. Web series like *The Misadventures of Awkward Black Girl*, *Broad City*, and the shows on the Black & Sexy TV network, who are inking development deals with traditional television networks, adapted the sitcom genre for niche audiences and online networks like YouTube, telling stories in a shorter format that still inspired hundreds of thousands of fans and helped buttress the careers of its writers and talent. Issa Rae produced several episodes of *Awkward Black Girl* before turning to crowd-funding site Kickstarter to raise US$56,000 in 2011, nearly twice her ask, in the process dispelling long-held industry lore: that black women could not star in and produce a sitcom explicitly dealing with racism and misogyny. As a sign her innovation broke beyond indie communities; in 2013 she signed a development with HBO (with *The Daily Show* and *Bernie Mac Show*'s Larry Willmore executive producing), released other original series on her site and helped advance her writers' careers (writer Amy Aniobi, for example, created her own Web series, *The Slutty Years*, and earned a job writing for NBC's *The Michael J. Fox Show*. Dennis Dortch and Numa Perrier's Black & Sexy TV network's marquee series, *The Couple*, takes the opposite approach: a black romantic comedy that is at once intimate and arty, specific and universal; the team also announced an HBO development deal with Spike Lee in 2014. Abbi Jacobson's and Ilana Glazer's *Broad City* was itself an experiment in the craft of storytelling, held together by a consistent, efficient engagement with gender and New York social life; each episode was essentially a punch line (Glazer 2013). These are just a few of many examples of how producer-driven development drives innovation through narrative experimentation and engagement with cultural politics.

FAN-DRIVEN DEVELOPMENT: CREATIVES INSPIRE FANS INTO DEVELOPMENT

In lieu of network development, indie producers must turn to direct financing, either from fans or brands. In the mid- to late 2000s, crowd-funding emerged as an indispensable source of financing for indie creators. When fans drive development, they pledge their own money or labor (sharing and promotion) to support a particular story, genre, personality or production team.

Like many of New York's young creative class, Adam Goldman was an underemployed college graduate living in a gentrifying neighborhood in Brooklyn. Around him were writers, musicians, actors and cinematographers with lots of talent but no space to unleash it. Goldman saw opportunity. In 2012 he wrote *The Outs*, a drama about a group of young, sad, broke Brooklynites searching for connection and same-sex love. Goldman and his studio, Rascal Department, produced a twelve-minute pilot for *The Outs*, "State of the Union," which he used to raise US$1,000 on Kickstarter to make the next two episodes. His pitch? Help a team of creatives transform television with a sincere story about underrepresented experiences:

> Finally, you know that TV show you hate? . . . The one with the stupid people and the bad actors spouting dialogue that makes you cringe? Less of that, please. Vote with your dollars. Then maybe next time someone's going to put something like massively offensive, short-lived sitcom *Work It*[9] on the air, they'll think twice and produce something you'll actually enjoy. Makes sense, right?[10]

The pitch worked, and Goldman beat his goal by US$600. Three months later Goldman went to Kickstarter again to raise US$8,000 to finish the six-episode first season. He ended up raising US$22,000, enough to produce a forty-five-minute "Channukah Special," which premiered half a year later to a crowded room at Public Assembly in Williamsburg. While Goldman took meetings with television producers, he wrote another show, *Whatever This Is*, a six-episode, half-hour dramedy about a diverse group enduring the horrors and indignities of working as crew in New York's reality television market. When he executed his third Kickstarter campaign, he beat his goal and raised US$171,000, much of it before the pilot aired during the campaign in August 2013.[11]

How did Goldman raise six figures for an original dark comedy about inequality in media production? He capitalized on the lack of quality gay storytelling on television. On TV gay characters, if allowed to lead a show, were too often middle-aged, rich, white men stuck in mediocre sitcoms, and Viacom's niche network Logo was moving away from the gay market to reach "broader" audiences. Goldman's success demonstrates how fans are willing, even excited, to develop a new crop of TV showrunners from their communities. Goldman brought together a team of Brooklyn creatives—from on-screen talent to the shows' original music composer—to produce a "good gay show." Fans are aware such synergy is rare, and if they don't support it they will lose their stories.

Digital and cable distribution challenged television networks' ability to attract audiences to watch new series at scheduled times. Network financing presumes a certain number of people are going to watch a certain program at a certain time, but the growth in series production across platforms means audiences have more choices. Although Americans are watching as much, if not more, television than they ever have (Lafayette 2013), ratings for viewers in the key demographic (18–49), for individual shows and cumulatively, are declining on broadcast television. While they are rising on cable in some cases, genres that do not employ new union-backed writers, mainly sports, reruns and reality television, make up the bulk of the growth. New scripted series on cable often launch weakly and grow over seasons, although most still never come close to the ratings broadcasters amassed in the 1980s and 1990s, before cable was a significant threat. Creating successful scripted entertainment now necessitates inciting fans to actively seek out new programming; networks want engaged audiences but are used to serving bulks of casual viewers. Cable and corporate online networks, freed from broadcasters' profitable yet intractable practices, are having more success in this environment, challenging traditional development by greenlighting cheaper series where producers have more creative freedom (FX's *Louie*, HBO's *Girls*, Netflix's *Orange Is the New Black*, Amazon's *Transparent*, etc.) and picking up established franchises (AMC's *The Walking Dead*, HBO's *Game of Thrones*, Syfy's *Battlestar Galactica*, Netflix's *House of Cards* and *Arrested Development*). Online networks like Amazon and Netflix incorporate fan interest as data in development while pushing against TV's homogeneity with series like Jill Soloway's *Transparent*, about a father undergoing a gender transition, and Jenji Kohan's *Orange Is the New Black*, about a women's prison. On occasion, fans can end a series, as when Amazon scuttled its adaptation of *Zombieland* when fans negatively reviewed its pilot.

In the indie TV market the only successful shows are those good enough to motivate a production team to invest its time and talent, and those whose team can motivate either a sizable group of fans or brands to invest money and time for production and promotion. Success can take several forms. Auteurs like Goldman, Rae and Day—who write, produce and star in their work—have proven capable of mobilizing followers to give more and promote their shows. Series in genres underrepresented on television have also proven particularly adept at generating fan interest, and in many cases fans value the show more than the creators (campaigns exceed the ask). Dramas, or soap operas, particularly about underrepresented groups, have been able to crowd-fund for multiple seasons, including teen lesbian drama *Anyone But Me* and *Hustling*, about a biracial, bisexual ex-escort in New York. Fans with interest in specific action subgenres have also done well. Freddie Wong's *Video Game High School*, a youth action comedy about a high school where gaming is pedagogy, was for a long time the most crowd-funded series on Kickstarter: more than 5,600 people gave US$273,000 for its first season, more than twice the ask, and more than 10,000 people gave US$800,000 for season two, US$160,000 over the ask. Fan interest from gamers allowed Wong to bring in major sponsors. Martial arts series have similarly elicited significant interest: *Kung Fury*'s pitch, a send-up of 1980s cop films, incited 17,000 donations for US$630,000 for the first season, three times the ask, and *Awesome Asian Bad Gays*, a comedic take on the disposability of Asian villains in films from the same era, raised US$54,000 in 2012 for a first season. Successful crowd-funding campaigns respond to fan desires to see genres and subjectivities underrepresented in television storytelling.

Video stars who produce content quickly and cheaply can often amass enough fans to make money from algorithmic advertising. Mostly found on YouTube, these stars can sustain enterprises for years with a small crew, and can enter traditional or online network development based on the size of their audience. Lucas Cruikshank was one of the first to achieve this. His channel, *Fred*, about Fred Figglehorn, an adolescent too often "off his meds," was one of the first YouTube channels to reach 1 million subscribers, earning Cruikshank a string of three movies and one season of a television show released by Nickelodeon. *The Annoying Orange*, a similarly irreverent, juvenile cartoon about anthropomorphized produce, similarly amassed millions of subscribers in under two years and ran for two seasons on Cartoon Network. Off YouTube, Jake Hurwitz and Amir Blumenfeld, of *Jake and Amir*, spent years cultivating a passionate fan base on College Humor before signing deals with corporate television networks.

YouTube claims tens, if not hundreds, of thousands of channels monetize through ads on their videos, but most work incredibly long hours for what amounts to middle-class salary, at best. Few producers hoping to get a break become rich off "sweat equity." The market is far from its ideal, but the productivity of fan-driven producers and the range and depth of stories they create models a more representative television market. Self-representation, therefore, is the hope of independent television: fans develop stories that support a positive creative environment for producers marginalized by an industry that misrepresents them.

BRAND-DRIVEN DEVELOPMENT: CREATIVES INSPIRE BRANDS TO FUND ORIGINAL STORIES

In most cases fan funds are not enough to support shows for more than one season or those productions that want to pay union labor industry rates. So brands have become the other major source of financing indie TV through sponsorship and branded entertainment. Frustrated by viewers skipping expensive advertisements on linear television, brands have been using the Internet to distribute their own programming since around the turn of the century, when American Express financed *The Adventures of Seinfeld and Superman* and BMW released *The Hire*. Branded entertainment accelerated in the latter 2000s after the recession tightened budgets, streaming video grew in popularity and data showed online video viewers were more engaged than traditional television viewers (Friedman 2013; Moses 2013). Most of the recipients of these funds were short-lived network digital studios, advertising and marketing agencies and the independent production companies they contracted for work. From non-A-list actors to entrepreneurial executives, creative producers looking to increase their value in Hollywood supplied the labor brands needed to breathe life into advertising and marketing campaigns.

Unlike producer- or fan-developed series, brand-developed series do not give producers complete creative control. Branded series rarely offend, deviate from normative ideology or critique the companies who finance them, though there is considerable variation (McNutt 2014). In the context of post-network Hollywood development, however, where networks increasingly take stakes in intellectual property and manage storytelling through aggressive note giving, producers working with brands framed their participation as allowing for creative freedom and ownership. Brands needed writers to produce authenticity, because branding is more than a process of commodification: "it is a cultural phenomenon more than an economic strategy . . . [impacting] the way we understand who we are, how we organize ourselves in the world, what stories we tell ourselves about ourselves" (Banet-Weiser 2012: 4–5). Arguably, brands granted producers more creative control over narrative and character than corporate networks because they want to maintain relationships with consumers directly—where corporate TV networks focus on advertising agencies and their clients.

Early branded Web entertainment featured a marriage between independent production and corporate sponsorship. This has precedent in early American television, when corporations sponsored prestige dramas and game shows before dishonest practices allowed networks to take control by the 1960s (Anderson 1994; Hilmes 2014). In the 2000s, freedom from network interference drew independent producers to sponsors. In 2004 Illeana Douglas, an indie film fixture, pitched television networks a series based on a short film she shot with Jeff Goldblum, "Supermarket," about almost-famous actors working at a grocery store. The series never made it beyond a pilot, but IKEA contacted Douglas after seeing it, expressing interest in "a new, hip approach to their brand," Douglas said (Staff 2010). *Easy to Assemble* premiered in 2008, and "Supermarket" relocated to IKEA. IKEA invested only US$50,000 in the first ten-episode season, a sliver of the furniture maker's nine-figure global marketing budget (Dobuzinskis 2008). The per-season budget eventually increased to the mid-six figures, still a fraction of the broadcast sitcom season budgets that regularly exceed US$20 million. In return for less money, Douglas got creative control. When asked by *Fast Company* if IKEA ever censored what she wrote, Douglas said the company told her to change a line from ice cream to yogurt because that's what the company sells. "The first season was wildly experimental," she told *The Wall Street Journal* (Tuttle 2012). Her only note for the next season was to keep it "family friendly," a suggestion Douglas publicly disregards as significant, implying her original vision aligned with the brand's (Staff 2010). For Douglas and celebrity costars like Justine Bateman, creative control compensated for the lower investment. "Honestly I would rather be on the Web than be on television because I don't have any illusions that if this got picked up and went to network I would lose the creative control," she told *Reuters* (Dobuzinskis 2008). The series would eventually get a spin-off in *Spärhusen*, starring Douglas and Keanu Reeves as members of a fictional 1970s Swedish band. Within six months of its premiere *Easy to Assemble* garnered 800,000 views and 2,000 blog mentions, helped by exposure on IKEA fan sites (McClellan 2009). Subsequent episodes averaged views fewer than 10 million.

CJP Digital, a unit of New York marketing firm CJP Communications, helped the series attract such a wide viewership. Started by PR executive and actor Wilson Cleveland, CJP Digital helped launch and promote the best of branded Web entertainment from roughly 2006 to 2012, including *Easy to Assemble*, *The Temp Life*, *Suite 7*, *Leap Year*, *Bestsellers* and *The Webventures of Justin & Alden*. *The Temp Life* (2006–2011), created and produced by and starring Cleveland, and *Leap Year* (2011–2012), co-created by Cleveland with Yuri and Vlad Baranovsky, were its biggest critical and ratings hits. Funded by temp-staffing firm SFN Group (formerly Spherion), *The Temp Life* is a comedy about workers staffed through a "worst practices" firm, Commodity Staffing, which sends temps out on jobs like urinal maintenance and assisting a socialite with her Webcast. When the recession hit, the series picked up as more people started temping, and SFN chief executive Roy Krause, who was hoping the series would reach younger workers, said the show was the company's top marketing ploy and contributed to a bump in its stock (Hampp 2010). *The Temp Life* would eventually amass more than 100 million cumulative views across platforms (Manarino 2013). Cleveland used its success to support other indie TV workers. Cleveland packaged *Bestsellers*, from Susan Miller and Tina Cesa Ward, creators of indie hit *Anyone But Me*, with SFN as a sponsor, and he tapped Baranovsky, who had created *Break a Leg*, to script *Leap Year*, a drama about a Silicon Valley start-up chasing a US$500,000 pot of money, funded by small business insurance company Hiscox. Storylines were taken from traditional start-up struggles and led to an increase in interest and sales of Hiscox products (Lewis 2013).

Cleveland successfully pitched brands on original production with two strategies distinct from network development practices: advocating producers shape the story and avoiding advertising agencies for financing. Through CJP Digital, Cleveland approached the public relations departments of the brands he thought could sponsor his stories because PR executives are constantly trying to "earn" media—as opposed to paid media, that is, ads: "it's a lot harder to tell your story . . . They will always be receptive to things like this. They never get to do anything cool like the ad agencies do, so give them something different to do," Cleveland said in a Writers Guild of America East instructional video (Writers Guild of America East 2012). Public relations helps brands shape the story they want consumers to hear, and Cleveland saw an opportunity for skilled writers, actors and producers to help brands reach increasingly disengaged audiences through authenticity, the prime goal of brands in late capitalism (Banet-Weiser 2012):

> The way to always approach it is: how will this brand benefit from the story I can tell? Nine times out of ten they can benefit from being associated with something that's not a shill, and just telling a story. They don't need you need sell more cans of soda. They don't need you to sell more packs of gum. They have plenty of people who are paid a lot of money to do that. What they can never get across—what's harder to get across—is that actual brand story that you don't necessarily see in terms of a logo.
>
> (Writers Guild of America East 2012)

Here Cleveland argues that when producers' ideas can fit within brand campaign demands they can construct narratives with wider constraints than in traditional television. Cleveland contrasts advertising and logos with story, where creators can produce authenticity—a sincere connection to viewers—when given freedom or ownership over narrative. His producer-centered pitch to brands through alternative financing means worked, but the payout was small. SFN gave Cleveland less than US$1,000 to make the four-minute pilot for *The Temp Life* (Manarino 2013). Three seasons in, *The Temp Life* had a modest mid-five-figure budget, and production value was moderate (Hustvedt 2009); *Leap Year*'s budget for its second season was reportedly $400,000 through PR agency Prosek Partners (Lewis 2013).

Networks continue to have the upper hand in attracting campaign funds from brands, but they have not created long-running original branded series for the Web. Both NBC and ABC created digital studios for this purpose, but each only produced one or two series before shuttering.[12] Fox quietly launched and quickly shuttered a digital studio, 15 Gigs, around the same time, but restarted its efforts with Fox Digital Studios, which continues to produce new series, though nearly all have lasted less than a year.[13] Cable networks have experimented with releasing series produced by independent companies online but without brand integration, including AMC's marquee network AMC (*The Trivial Pursuits of Arthur Banks*) and sister network IFC (*Young American Bodies, Lizzie the Lezzie, Green Porno*). Traditional television networks have had an easier time finding financing for extensions of existing series, particularly NBC, which had extensive transmedia promotions for *Heroes*, and ABC, which did for *Lost*, along with a stellar but short-lived Subaru-sponsored series for *Happy Endings*.

What brand-driven development in the indie TV demonstrates are the limits, however small, of traditional television's upfront selling process. With more channels releasing more stories, networks are finding it challenging to make audience guarantees to brands; meanwhile brands want more data on who's watching because they don't trust their messages are getting heard. Frustrated, they are moving to data-driven methods online, with questionable legality and ethics; advertising networks and publishers are partnering with data management and marketing firms to share, trade and sell user data—information from demographics, searches, purchases, even health status—to target and monetize individual users (Turow 2012). In this environment indie producers and brands forged a productive, if tenuous, relationship, where brands granted them more— but not complete—creative control and a small bit of financing so writers could produce a sense of authenticity that might engage consumers as more than data.

THE POSSIBILITIES FOR RESTRUCTURING INDUSTRY

Network TV development dwarfs indie TV development in size and consistency. Major networks still command the bulk of funds for advertising in the United States and this is unlikely to change because of the decades-old process of piloting and financing series upfront. Yet this durable system becomes less so each year. The vertical integration and escalating size of media conglomerates has stifled diversity among producers, leading to a crisis of creativity in a global and fragmented media landscape, where consumers and brands have more choice.

The indie TV market allows new entrants to capitalize on these dynamics by empowering producers—creatively, if not financially—which excites fans and brands, who give modest sums to release series that speak to their communities or customers. This is, as a whole, an innovation, designed to benefit all those invested in original production. Critical scholars who ignore or dismiss it for its limited resources and impact fail to see how workers, fans and sponsors actively work to correct and improve the systems we critique. Indie markets are not only spaces for artistic experimentation and cultural reimagining but also for adapting industrial relations to support the needs of those entrenched decision makers neglect, underserve or undervalue. Independent media creation, however compromised and impossible, pushes media industries away from extracting value to supporting its growth by expanding creative ownership, community-led storytelling and authenticity in marketing campaigns. Restructuring industry is the hope of independent media.

NOTES

1. Series developed independent of corporations released via an open network, the Internet, which I will refer to as "independent television" or "indie TV."
2. Phone interview with Jenni Powell. August 31, 2009.
3. Estimates range from 2,000 to 3,000. See Chozik, 2011.
4. A practice some broadcast networks, most notably Fox, are starting to follow. See Andreeva, 2014.
5. http://iab.net/newfronts
6. This has been the case historically (see later in this chapter), but inequalities have been exacerbated as writing staffs cut back and are more egregious given possibilities to redistribute programs equitably across multiple channels. See Ettema 1982; Turow 1982.
7. Ratings for individual series, while rising, cannot match them—programs like AMC's *The Walking Dead* and Netflix's *Orange Is the New Black*, along with sports, aside.
8. Although SAG-AFTRA, like the Producers and Writers guilds, do offer new media contracts that allow production companies to pay talent below union minimums.
9. *Work It* was a very short-lived ABC show about two straight men who dress like women because women supposedly are easier to hire, a laughable premise in light of Hollywood's own diversity problems.
10. www.kickstarter.com/projects/236250953/the-outs
11. After *Whatever This Is* Goldman and his team branded Rascal Department as a producer of "groundbreaking web content with production values that rival traditional television programming," placing independent television development on a continuum where only distribution contexts—"traditional" broadcast and cable versus open digital distribution—not production value or levels of fan engagement define hierarchies of television. Press release. 2013. "'Whatever this is.' Season Finale Now Live." December 17.
12. www.imdb.com/company/co0215748/?ref_=fn_al_co_2; www.imdb.com/company/co0284326/?ref_=fn_al_co_1
13. www.imdb.com/company/co0365818/?ref_=fn_al_co_2

REFERENCES

Anderson, C. (1994) *HollywoodTV: The Studio System in the Fifties*. Austin: University of Texas Press.
Andreeva, N. (2014) "Fox's abolishment of pilot season: Practical guide to how will it work," *Deadline* January 13. Available http: www.deadline.com/2014/01/fox-no-pilot-season-how-will-it-work (accessed April 26, 2014).

Au, W. J. (2007) "NewTeeVee Pick: *The Guild*," *NewTeeVee* October 31. Available http: http://gigaom.com/video/the-guild (accessed April 26, 2014).

Banet-Weiser, S. (2012) *Authentic™: The Politics of Ambivalence in a Brand Culture.* New York: New York University Press.

Bielby, D. D. and Bielby, W. T. (2002) "Hollywood dreams, harsh realities: Writing for film and television," *Contexts* 1, 4: 21–27.

Blichfeld, K. and Sinclair, B. (2013) "When work isn't 'work' (*High Maintenance*)," *Televisual* April 4. Available http: http://tvisual.org/2013/04/04/when-work-isnt-work- high-maintenance (accessed April 26, 2014).

Bullock, V., et al. (2008) "Out of Focus—Out of Sync: Take 4: A report on the television industry." National Association for the Advancement of Colored People. Available http: http://courses.washington.edu/com201/COM%20201%20readings/ NAACP- Out%20of%20focus.pdf.

Caldwell, J. T. (2008) *Production Culture: Industrial Reflexivity and Critical Practice in Film and Television.* Raleigh, NC: Duke University Press.

Chozik, A. (2011) "The math of a hit TV show," *The Wall Street Journal* May 12. Available http: http://online.wsj.com/news/articles/SB10001424052748703864204576315240324571266 (accessed April 26, 2014).

Christian, A. J. (2012) "Newfronts 2012: Web networks take on television," *Televisual* April 30. Available http: http://tvisual.org/2012/04/30/newfronts-2012-web-networks-take-on- television/ (accessed April 26, 2014).

Christian, A. J. (2013a) "Valuing post-network television," *Flow* 17, 11. Available http: http://flowtv.org/2013/05/valuing-post-network-television-aymar-jean-christian-northwestern-university.

Christian, A. J. (2013b) "The black TV crisis and the next generation," *Flow* 18, 5. Available http: http://flowtv.org/2013/08/the-black-tv-crisis.

Christian, A. J. (2013c) Open TV: Rescue pilots from development hell," *Flow* 18, 8. Available http: http://flowtv.org/2013/10/rescue-pilots.

Christian, A. J. (2013d) "Critic's picks: 2013's best comedy web series, and 18 more you need to watch now." *Indiewire* December 19. Available http: www.indiewire. com/article/2013s-best-comedy-web-series-and-18-more-you-need- to-watch-now (accessed April 26, 2014).

Creeber, G. (2004) *Serial Television: Big Drama on the Small Screen.* London: British Film Institute.

Crupi, A. (2013) "Cable upfront haul passes the US$10 billion mark," *Adweek* October 21. www.adweek.com/news/television/cable-upfront-haul-passes-10-billion-mark-153290 (accessed April 26, 2014).

Cunningham, S. (2013) *Hidden Innovation: Policy, Industry and the Creative Sector.* St. Lucia: University of Queensland.

Dobuzinskis, A. (2008) "Stars tune-in to Web video, advertisers still shy," *Reuters* September 26. Available http: http://mobile.reuters.com/article/entertainmentNews/ idUSTRE48P93720080926?src=RS S-ENT (accessed April 26, 2014).

Donaton, S. (2005) *Madison and Vine: Why the Entertainment and Advertising Industries Must Converge to Survive* . New York: McGraw-Hill.

Ellcessor, E. (2012) "Tweeting @feliciaday: Online media, convergence, and subcultural stardom," *Cinema Journal* 51, 2: 46–66.

Ettema, J. S. (1982) "The organizational context of creativity: A case study from public television," in J. Ettema and D. C. Whitney (eds.), *Individuals in Mass Media Organizations: Creativity & Constraint*, 91–106. Beverly Hills/Dehli: Sage.

Film L.A. (2013) *2013 Television Pilot Production Report.* Los Angeles, CA: Film L.A.

Friedman, W. (2013) "Online video trumps TV in engagement, ad shifts," *MediaDailyNews* June 5. Available http: www.mediapost.com/publications/article/ 201835/online-video-trumps-tv-in-engagement-ad-shifts.html (accessed April 26, 2014).

Gitlin, T. (1983) *Inside Prime Time*. New York: Pantheon Books.

Glazer, I. (2013) "How two broads braved the web (*Broad City*)," *Televisual* April 29. Available http: http://tvisual.org/2013/04/29/how-two-broads-braved-the-web-broad-city (accessed April 26, 2014).

Goldberg, L. (2011) "Felicia Day: How a girl geek made it big on her own," *The Hollywood Reporter* July 20. Available http: www.hollywoodreporter.com/news/felicia-day- how-a-girl-212744 (accessed April 26, 2014).

Hampp, A. (2010) "If you build a web series around it, will they come?," *Advertising Age* August 9. Available http: http://adage.com/article/madisonvine-digital-entertainment/branded-entertainment-brands-flock-web-series/145276 (accessed May 15, 2014).

Hesmondhalgh, D. (2010) "User-generated content, free labour and the cultural industries," *Ephemera* 10, 3/4: 267–284.

Hesmondhalgh, D. and Baker, S. (2011) "'A very complicated version of freedom': Conditions and experiences of creative labour in three cultural industries," *Poetics* 38, 1: 4–20.

Hilmes, M. (2014) *Only Connect: A Cultural History of Broadcasting in the United States*, 4th ed. Boston, MA: Wadsworth.

Hunt, D. (2014) "Turning missed opportunities into realized ones," *The 2014 Hollywood Writers Report*. Available http: www.wga.org/uploadedFiles/who_we_are/hwr14execsum.pdf (accessed April 14, 2014).

Hustvedt, M. (2009) "Spherion-backed 'Temp Life' re-staffs for new season," *Tubefilter* September 10. Available http: www.tubefilter.com/2009/09/10/spherion-backed- temp-life-re-staffs-for-new-season (accessed April 26, 2014).

IAB/PricewaterhouseCoopers. (2014) "IAB internet advertising revenue report: 2013 full year results," Internet Advertising Bureau. April. www.iab.net/media/file/IAB_Internet_Advertising_Revenue_Report_FY_2013.pdf

Jenkins, H., Ford, S. and Green, J. (2013) *Spreadable Media: Creating Value and Meaning in Networked Culture*. New York: New York University Press.

Lafayette, J. (2013) "Nielsen: Time spent watching traditional TV up," *Broadcasting and Cable* June 10. Available http: www.broadcastingcable.com/news/technology/nielsen-time-spent-watching- traditional-tv/50055 (accessed April 26, 2014).

Lewis, T. (2013) "Small business-themed Web series helps drive extra sales," *PR Week* January 1. Factiva (PRWKUS0020130102e9110000p).

Lotz, A. (2007a) "How to spend US$9.3 billion in three days: Examining the upfront buying process in the production of US television culture," *Media, Culture & Society* 29, 4: 549–567.

Lotz, A. (2007b) *The Television Will Be Revolutionized*. New York: New York University Press.

Madrigal, A. C. (2014) "How Netflix reverse engineered Hollywood," *The Atlantic* January 2. Available http: www.theatlantic.com/technology/archive/2014/01/how-netflix-reverse-engineered-hollywood/282679 (accessed April 26, 2014).

Manarino, M. (2013) "Wilson Cleveland has a bright idea for web video," *The Video Ink* October 10. Available http: www.thevideoink.com/features/wilson-cleveland-has-a-bright-idea-for-web-video (accessed April 26, 2014).

McClellan, S. (2009) "Shops grow despite economic hardship; media agency report cards '08," *Mediaweek* March 16. Available http: www.adweek.com/news/television/media-agency-report-cards-08–101197?page=6 (accessed May 15, 2014).

McNutt, M. (2014) "On Hulu, the chicken enchilada comes before the egg," *AV Club* April 17. Available http: www.avclub.com/article/hulu-chicken-enchilada-comes-egg-203530 (accessed April 26, 2014).

Mittell, J. (2006) "Narrative complexity in contemporary American television," *The Velvet Light Trap* 58, 1: 29–40.

Mittell, J. (2012–2013) *Complex TV: The Poetics of Contemporary Television Storytelling*. MediaCommons Press.

Moses, L. (2013) "Some question just how great online video engagement is," *Adweek* September 16. Available http: www.adweek.com/videowatch/some-question-just-how-great-online-video-engagement-152403 (accessed April 26, 2014).

Rizzo, T. (2007) "Programming your own channel: An archaeology of the playlist," in A. Kenyon (ed.), *TV Futures: Digital Television Policy in Australia*, 107–131. Melbourne: Melbourne University Press.

Ryan, M. (2010) "Felicia Day slays the Internet with 'The Guild,'" *Chicago Tribune* (The Watcher blog) July 13. Available http: http://featuresblogs.chicagotribune.com/entertainment_tv/2010/07/guild-felicia-day.html (accessed April 26, 2014).

Salmon, F. (2014) "Netflix's dumbed-down algorithms," *Reuters* January 3. Available http: http://blogs.reuters.com/felix-salmon/2014/01/03/netflixs-dumbed-down-algorithms (accessed April 26, 2014).

Shah, B. (2013) "In the white room with black writers: Hollywood's 'diversity hires,'" *Defamer* December 20. Available http: http://defamer.gawker.com/in-the-white-room-with-black-writers-hollywoods-dive-1486789620 (accessed April 26, 2014).

Sharma, A. (2013) "Amazon mines its data trove to bet on TV's next hit," *Wall Street Journal* November 1. Available http: http://online.wsj.com/news/articles/SB10001424052702304200804579163861637839706 (accessed April 26, 2014).

Sharma, A. and Hagey, K. (2013) "For TV shows, it's seller's market," *Wall Street Journal* September 16. Available http: http://online.wsj.com/news/articles/SB10001424127887323342404579079352046677392 (accessed April 26, 2014).

Staff. (2010) "Illeana Douglas assembles the web's most beloved hit show—no allen wrench required," *Fast Company* September. Available http: www.fastcompany.com/1684019/illeana-douglas-assembles-webs-most-beloved-hit-show-no-allen-wrench-required (accessed April 26, 2014).

Syme, R. (2013) "Why web TV series are worth watching," *The New Yorker* September 9. Available http: www.newyorker.com/online/blogs/culture/2013/09/why-web-tv-is-worth-watching-high-maintenance.html (accessed April 26, 2014).

Turow, J. (1982) "Unconventional programs on commercial television: An organization perspective," in J. Ettema and D. C. Whitney (eds.), *Individuals in Mass Media Organizations: Creativity & Constraint*, 107–129. Beverly Hills/Dehli: Sage.

Turow, J. (2012) *The Daily You: How the new Advertising Industry Is Defining You and Your Worth*. New Haven, CT: Yale University Press.

Tussey, E. (2014) "Connected viewing on the second screen: The limitations of the living room," J. Holt and K. Sanson (eds.), *Connected Viewing: Selling, Streaming, & Sharing Media in the Digital Age*, 202–216. New York: Routledge.

Tuttle, B. (2012) "IKEA's hit web show: An entertaining ad," *The Wall Street Journal* September 7. Available http: http://online.wsj.com/news/articles/SB10000872396390444358404577609932125128046 (accessed April 26, 2014).

Vine, R. (2013) "*Zombieland*: When fan power turns bad," *The Guardian*, TV&Radio Blog. May 22. Available http: www.theguardian.com/tv-and-radio/tvandradioblog/2013/may/22/zombieland-tv-show-axed-fan-power (accessed April 26, 2014).

Wotanis, L. and McMillan, L. (2014) "Performing gender on YouTube," *Feminist Media Studies* 14, 6: 1–17.

Writers Guild of America East. (2012a) "Wilson Cleveland: How can I break into branded entertainment?" *Writers Guild of America East channel* January 19. Available http: www.youtube.com/watch?v=PYKLiTPw2q0 (accessed April 26, 2014).

Writers Guild of America East. (2012b) "Wilson Cleveland: What is branded entertainment?" *Writers Guild of America East channel* , January 19. Available http: www.youtube.com/watch?v=PYKLiTPw2q0 (accessed April 26, 2014).

8   Social Media and Journalistic Independence

Thomas Poell and José van Dijck

Do social media, such as Facebook and Twitter, facilitate or even enhance journalism's democratic functions? Current research suggests they do. Prominent scholars portray social media as key drivers of an emerging news ecosystem, which revolves around public participation and democratic accountability (Benkler 2006; Jenkins, Ford and Green 2012; McNair 2006; Shirky 2008). Social platforms have been hailed as potential saviors of professional news production, allowing journalists to find new sources and to engage directly with "the people formerly known as the audience," as well as trace their preferences and interests (Bruns 2008; Flew 2009; Gillmor 2004; Hermida 2011; Paulussen et al. 2007; Rosen 2006). Some scholars have argued that social media users and new computational techniques may relieve the press from part of its news reporting duties, leaving it free to concentrate on investigative journalism and quality news coverage (Anderson, Bell and Shirky 2012; Bruns 2011; Flew et al. 2012).

In the sections included later in this chapter, we argue that even if social media allow users to contribute information and observations to professional news production, these platforms do not in and of themselves facilitate journalism's proclaimed democratic role. In contrast to what most current research suggests, they are not *neutral* technologies that merely *enable* user activity. Instead, social platforms very much *shape* how users share information, curate news and express their points of view, as well as how these activities—in the form of social media metrics—start to play a role in the production and dissemination of news. If the agency of social media users is inimically bound up with platform technologies, what does this mean for journalistic independence?

This chapter critically interrogates claims of user empowerment by exploring how social media technologies and data become entangled with news selection, production and dissemination practices of major commercial news sites, such as *The Huffington Post*, as well as leading traditional newspapers, like the *New York Times* and *LA Times*. This inquiry reveals a general shift from editorial to algorithmic logic: from the judgments and choices of professionals to proceduralized machine choices (Gillespie 2014). We will show that this shift compromises, rather than enhances, democratic public communication. More specifically, we argue that the very mechanisms through which social media user activity affects the news process threaten both independent journalism and informed public debate. Instead of enhancing journalistic freedom and autonomy, the rise of social media intensifies the commercial pressures on journalistic independence.

A PROMISE OF RENEWAL

Throughout the twentieth century, journalism's role in democratic politics has primarily been associated with professional news media, also labeled as the fourth estate. Two partly overlapping fourth estate models have been formulated. The first model, based on an educational ideal, views the press as a vehicle for public debate in which different ideas and perspectives are exchanged until the common good prevails (McChesney 2004; Starr 2004). This ideal, which originates from nineteenth-century Britain, informed Jürgen Habermas's highly influential conceptualization of the bourgeois public sphere (Calhoun 1992; Habermas 1991). The second model, based on a representative democratic ideal, prescribes that news media should defend the public's interests, providing them with vital political information and keeping the government accountable to the public (Kovach and Rosentiel 2001; Muhlmann 2008).

What both models have in common is the idea that the press links representative government to its constituents, either by promoting public debate or by providing critical checks on government (Hampton 2010). To fulfill these functions, it is crucial that the press operates independently from both political and economic power. However, it is precisely at this junction where problems arise. Critics have pointed out that mainstream news media are strongly affected by commercial forces, as also becomes clear from Jukes and Allan's discussion of the Leveson Inquiry in Chapter 1 of this volume. Commercial pressure especially results from the incorporation of news media into large conglomerates and the constant necessity to maximize audience share and advertising revenue (McChesney 1999; Underwood 2001). Mainstream reporting is also shaped by political pressure, which in liberal democracies is exercised through journalists' structural dependency on government sources for vital political information (Barnett and Gaber 2001; Bennett, Lawrence and Livingston 2008; Schudson 1978; Tumber and Palmer 2004).

Growing public awareness of these political and commercial pressures has led to a decline in the cultural authority of professional journalists, a decline that has accelerated over the past decade as a result of the rise of social media. Many theorists see the development of social media-driven news practices as part of a larger shift "from a culture shaped by the logics of broadcasting toward one fostering greater grassroots participation" (Jenkins, Ford and Green 2012: xiv; see also Benkler 2006; Bruns 2008;

Castells 2009; Jenkins 2006; Shirky 2008). In journalism, this shift is said to take the form of a transition from industrial news production revolving around "gatekeeping" by professional editors to a process of "gatewatching," based on "open news story development" and the "communal evaluation" of news coverage (Bruns 2008: 71–76).

In light of the perceived changes in the news landscape, the "participatory culture" authors suggest that it is vital to rethink how journalism's key democratic functions should be fulfilled. They question the traditional role of the press as the fourth estate—the view that professional news organizations are the prime carriers of public debate and the key government watchdogs. Some theorists argue that instead of expecting the press and professional journalists to fulfill all these functions, it is time to shift the focus to the news ecosystem as a whole. As Anderson, Bell and Shirky contend: "We must move away from pinning our democratic hopes entirely on the Fourth Estate conception of the press. Public accountability must come, in part, from the networked news ecosystem itself" (2012: 75–76). To illustrate that this ecosystem already fulfills key democratic functions, scholars point to striking examples of social media users collectively reporting on and curating unfolding news events, such as natural disasters, political scandals and major protests (Bruns 2011; Hermida 2010; Murthy 2011; Shirky 2008, 2011). Others have demonstrated that data from social media and other online platforms open up new vistas for the analysis of user engagement in a system where audience measurement plays an increasingly important role in the news process (Anderson 2011; Usher 2013).

While we agree with the assessment that it is crucial to shift the focus from professional news organizations as pillars of the fourth estate to the news ecosystem as a whole, we are skeptical of the idea that social media technologies and the engagement of their users enhance public debate and facilitate democratic accountability. We are particularly critical of the assumption that online systems in general, and social media specifically, act as neutral technologies that enable users to participate in the news process and directly translate social media data through new analytic methods. As Gillespie points out, such an understanding of social media has been developed through the notion of the "platform" as a descriptive term for digital media intermediaries, which supposedly provide "open, neutral, egalitarian and progressive support for activity" (2010: 352). Resonating with the 1990s idea of the independence of cyberspace, as discussed by Daniel Kreiss in Chapter 5, the activity on social "platforms" is presented by scholars, by journalists, and most prominently by the social media corporations themselves as free from the kinds of governing mechanisms that characterize the "old media."

However, social media are far from neutral platforms. Through their technological architectures and through the values and interests inscribed in these architectures, social media very much steer user activity as well as the processes in which publics are constructed and relevance is determined

(Chun 2011; Gillespie 2014; Hands, Elmer and Langlois 2013). Instead of providing open, neutral, egalitarian platforms for social interaction, social media introduce new techno-commercial mechanisms in public communication, which intensify rather than neutralize the commercial strategies of the mass media (van Dijck and Poell 2013).

Building on these insights, the following sections explore how social media shape the contemporary news ecosystem. We will start by reviewing how social media have become entangled with the processes of news production, dissemination and reception. Drawing from this review, we will subsequently demonstrate how social media introduce techno-commercial mechanisms in these processes that potentially *undermine* journalism's ability to work with freedom and fulfill key democratic functions of independent media.

MAKING NEWS "SOCIAL"

To understand how social media shape today's news, it is vital to see how news organizations, journalists and users have engaged with platforms such as Facebook, Twitter and Google in the production, dissemination and reception of news. Mainstream news organizations and professional journalists have played a particularly important part in this regard. Today, virtually every news organization in the United States, as well as in other parts of the world, has a range of Twitter accounts and Facebook pages. Moreover, most journalists employ a variety of social media in their daily routines, but their efforts are largely focused on disseminating content (Blasingame 2011; Greer and Ferguson 2011). Surprisingly, this one-way communication approach is not typical only for news organizations, but also for the majority of journalists (Artwick 2013; Hedman and Djerf-Pierre 2013; Lasorsa, Lewis and Holton 2012). Except for a few prominent reporters, who are constantly twittering and blogging, most journalists use social media "to gather the news and find sources, and then report the news and drive traffic to websites" (Hermida 2013: 300). Thus, most superficially, making news "social" refers to the process of increasing news volumes through established social media platforms.

These content distribution efforts are certainly starting to pay off. The Pew Research Center observes a rapid growth in the number of Americans who follow the news through social media. In 2010, 9 percent of the total population received their news through social platforms. Two years later this share had risen to 19 percent (Sasseen, Olmstead and Mitchell 2013). Research by NewsWhip, a news aggregation and analysis service, confirms this trend. Tracing the number of Facebook likes, shares and comments for news articles from the top fifty online publishers worldwide, NewsWhip detects a huge increase: in August 2013 the content of the top publishers generated 117 million Facebook interactions each month, compared with just

45 million at the same point in 2012 (Quigley 2013). NewsWhip's research also shows that online-only platforms BuzzFeed and *The Huffington Post* have been particularly successful in generating user engagement. BuzzFeed can be considered the "most social" publisher with more than 13 million articles shared, liked and commented on in February 2014, directly followed by *Huffpo* with more than 6 million interactions. The top traditional news organizations, led by CNN, BBC and the *New York Times*, each generate about 2 million interactions (NewsWhip 2014).

While these numbers of news activity through social media are impressive, most people who receive news digitally still get it through other means. In a survey specifically focused on these digital news consumers, conducted in January 2012, Pew found that only 9 percent primarily gets news through Facebook or Twitter recommendations, whereas 36 percent get it by going directly to a news portal, 32 percent by querying a search engine and 29 percent by using an app or news aggregator (Mitchell and Rosenstiel 2012). Hence, social media have certainly not yet replaced more "traditional" ways of accessing news. Moreover, like social media, portals and search engines come attached with specific metrics to evaluate how news content is performing, as well as with particular tactics to maximize the circulation of this content. As will become clear, these tactics and metrics affect how journalism can fulfill its democratic functions.

It is not just news organizations that have invested in online news dissemination strategies to reach and mobilize millions of users. Social media platforms and their corporate owners have also strongly stimulated this development. Over the past few years, social media platforms have created guides and instructions specifying in detail how news organizations can maximize audience engagement with their content. For example, in its guide for journalists and newsrooms, Twitter highlights that user engagement grows when journalists include hashtags and URLs in their tweets, and when they regularly post updates on unfolding news events (Twitter 2013a). Facebook, on its "Media on Facebook" portal launched in May 2013, also urges news organizations to share breaking news updates. Moreover, it advises news organizations to visually enhance their stories with photos and videos, and to use "Facebook Insights" to "learn what content resonates with your audience, and optimize how you publish to your audience to grow your reach and engagement" (Lavrusik 2013a).

At the same time, social media corporations have technologically designed their platforms to optimize the distribution of content and boost social traffic. While most of these technological developments have not been specifically targeted at news, they strongly affect how news circulates. Most crucial has been the creation of social buttons, allowing users to "share," "like," "tweet" and "plus" content from across the Web (Gerlitz and Helmond 2013). In 2006, social news Web sites Digg and Reddit were among the first to develop such buttons, which can be placed on any Web site, enabling users to share content from their sites with aggregating sites. Following this example, Facebook quickly introduced a share button in 2006. Other platforms launched similar buttons in subsequent years. Today, a selection of social buttons—always including those of Facebook and Twitter—can be found on virtually every major news site. These social plugins allow news content to circulate far and wide. For example, in the case of Facebook, as Gerlitz and Helmond (2013: 1352–1353) have pointed out, clicking a share or like button not only makes external Web content available for "friends," but also for further liking and commenting within the Facebook platform itself.

Second, social media corporations have developed a range of technologies to promote content to be shared via their platforms. Because of such technologies, Twitter has morphed into a prominent real-time news network (Bruns and Highfield 2012; Hermida 2013; Newman, Dutton and Blank 2012). Particularly vital for the news process are the hashtag and retweet functionality as well as Twitter's trending topic feature. The practices of retweeting and hashtagging were originally developed by users and only later implemented in the platform's architecture. Hashtags are important for journalism, as they allow users to organize and access the real-time stream of reports and comments on unfolding news events. Retweeting, in turn, enables users to promote the posts they find relevant (Poell and Borra 2012). Both functions play a key role in Twitter's trending topic feature, which algorithmically identifies "topics that are immediately popular" (Twitter 2013b). As we will explain, trending topics play a central but also problematic role in the news selection process. By developing these information-organizing technologies, Twitter has clearly positioned itself as a news platform rather than just a transmission channel comparable to the telephone or telegraph (van Dijck 2012).

While Facebook has situated itself, both technologically and rhetorically, as a platform for social networking and personal conversation, it has started to make an effort to also facilitate and stimulate the dissemination of news. Beyond the recently launched Media on Facebook portal, the corporation has implemented some of the same news-oriented features in its architecture as Twitter. In 2013, Facebook integrated the hashtag functionality into its architecture, allowing users to click on a hashtag to access all related posts on a topic or event (Lindley 2013). In the same year, the company also announced that it would redesign its News Feed, separating streams of content into multiple categories, including All Friends, Photos, Music and Following (Lavrusik 2013b). The Following feature is particularly important to our inquiry because it is through this category that users receive news. With this redesign Facebook aims to consolidate its position as the leading social network for personal exchanges, while at the same time trying to become a more dominant force in the distribution of news. As Mark Zuckerberg stated: "We want updates from our friends, but we also want updates from publications" (Robertson 2013).

News organizations and social platforms are rapidly moving toward each other, mutually articulating each other's strategies and activities in the news process. The following sections will explore how the increasingly central role of social media in this process challenges journalism's proclaimed democratic functions. First, we discuss the tension between social media's technological mechanisms and journalism's democratic role. Second, we interrogate how these mechanisms become involved in the production and dissemination of news at mainstream news organizations.

ALGORITHMS AND METRICS

The rise of social media means that the ability to select news has partly shifted from professional journalists and news organizations to social media users, who select their own media diet interacting with their platforms and each other. As mentioned earlier, some theorists have interpreted this development as a democratization of the news process. User empowerment is, however, only half of the story. The mounting significance of social media platforms in the production and circulation of news means that users' input becomes encapsulated in technological configurations, which are controlled neither by news organization nor by social media users, but by these platforms' owners.

This development creates two interrelated problems for civic journalism—that is journalism as a catalyst for civic engagement (Rosen 1996). First, instead of merely connecting users with news content shared by friends, social media *select* and *prioritize* content by algorithmically translating user activity into "most relevant" or "trending" topics. What is relevant or trending is calculated through a combination of signals taken into account by the platform's algorithms (Bucher 2012; Gillespie 2012; van Dijck and Poell 2013). By including and excluding particular signals and giving them relative weight, algorithms impose a new knowledge logic, which "depends on the proceduralized choices of a machine, designed by human operators to automate some proxy of human judgment or unearth patterns across collected social traces" (Gillespie, 2014: 192). Algorithmic logic can be contrasted with traditional editorial logic, which is based on the judgments and choices of professional journalists. The question is how social media algorithmically shape the selection and circulation of news: "editorial" choices appear hidden in algorithms. Building on documentation provided by social media corporations, interviews in trade magazines and newspapers with software engineers and reverse engineering experiments, we can trace how the major social media platforms algorithmically sort the news.

We start by examining Facebook's influential news feed algorithm. Facebook includes both signals of personal interest and signals from its global user base in its algorithmic design. In a recent interview, Lars Backstrom, one of Facebook's News Feed engineers, made clear that the platform attempts to distinguish between different levels of affinity. It measures how close each user is to friends, people they follow, as well as to Pages and Groups. This measurement is based on personal interactions, but also on global interactions, which can outweigh personal signals. Backstrom explains: "For example, if we show an update to 100 users, but only a couple of them interact with it, we may not show it in your News Feed. But if a lot of people are interacting with it, we might decide to show it to you, too" (McGee 2013). Facebook is trying to strike a balance between private conversation and public communication, between mechanisms of personalization and popularity. In this algorithmic balancing act, time decay also plays a crucial role—recent interactions weigh heavier than older ones—allowing Facebook to identify and highlight trending topics to its users.

Twitter's trending topic algorithm is equally important to the news process. To understand how this algorithm identifies trends, it is helpful to briefly look at the controversy around Twitter's trending topics in the fall of 2011. During this period, the Occupy movement heavily relied on Twitter for its communication purposes. Yet, the movement's dominant hashtags, #OccupyWallStreet and #OccupyBoston, never trended in New York and Boston. Surprisingly, these hashtags did trend in other parts of the country, whereas less popular Occupy-related terms and hashtags made it into the trending topic lists of the two cities. Suspicious protestors subsequently accused Twitter of manipulating its trending topics. However, as Gilad Lotan has demonstrated through a reverse engineering experiment, no censoring appears to have taken place; ostensibly it was the "outcome of a purely algorithmic mechanism." To understand this, it is vital to notice that trending topics are not simply determined on the basis of the volume of tweets containing a particular hashtag or term. Instead, "the algorithm adapts over time, based on the changing velocity of the usage of the given term in tweets. If we see a systematic rise in volume, but no clear spike, it is possible that the topic will never trend" (Lotan 2011). On its blog, Twitter explains: "Topics break into the Trends list when the volume of Tweets about that topic at a given moment dramatically increases" (Twitter 2010).

In sum, both Facebook and Twitter's news-oriented algorithms clearly privilege breaking news stories in order to trigger user engagement and boost social traffic. Not coincidentally, this is exactly what the two corporations advise journalists and news organizations to do when using their platforms to disseminate content. A heavy predilection toward breaking and engaging news does not bode well for the dissemination of news content on complex political issues that play out over longer periods of time. It appears unlikely that complex and protracted content will be identified as "relevant" by social media's algorithms. Evidently, social media's sorting mechanisms do not necessarily correspond with journalism's role as a facilitator of informed public debate and democratic accountability.

The second challenge to journalism's democratic functions comes from the way social media boost the role of audience metrics in the news process, which has become increasingly central as a result of the development of online communication. While news producers, especially those depending on advertising, have always relied on third-party measurement firms to monitor viewers, readers and listeners, the networked infrastructure has rendered the quantified audience a reality (Anderson 2011; Napoli 2011; Usher 2013). As every online action generates a data trail, a wealth of information has become available, spawning a variety of measurement services. Traditional firms, such as Nielsen NetRatings and comScore, measure online media use by installing tracking software on the computers of a group of carefully selected Internet users, whose habits are extrapolated to reflect a broader population. Companies such as Google Analytics, Omniture, Hitwise and Quantcast track audiences through server data from news Web sites or traffic data from Internet Service Providers (ISPs) (Graves and Kelly 2010: 12).

Social media add a particularly valuable set of metrics to this data culling. These metrics not only provide insight in how people engage with available news content through social media, but also steer people's current news interests; in other words, they simultaneously measure and massage what topics are trending. Facebook and Google+, who enforce a real name policy, have the ability to combine these data with demographic details—such as age, gender, location and relational status—as well as so-called post-demographic data concerning users' tastes, interests and sentiments (Cheney-Lippold 2011; Rogers 2008). The rise of social media, as Andrejevic makes clear, opens up the realm of sentiment and emotion to "automated forms of mass quantification, collection, and mining" (2013: 91). While social media metrics are not necessarily representative of the larger population, they do, given the large number of social media users, cover a vital part of the online audience. Consequently, news organizations are particularly interested in social media metrics as instruments for targeting specific audiences through content personalization, and marketing these to advertisers.

Social media corporations, for their part, have made an effort to cater to the data needs of the news industry as well as those of other industries. Both Facebook and Twitter offer their own analytic tools to news organizations, allowing them to track audiences' content engagement and to know the demographics of their followers. Twitter's analytics tool, launched in 2013, yields basic metrics concerning numbers of mentions, retweets and replies, as well as the gender, location and interests of followers (Twitter 2013c). Facebook Insights is more advanced. It provides Facebook page owners not only with detailed metrics concerning the number of page likes, unique users engaging with the page and the demographics of these users, but also informs them when page followers were online each day of the week, and what type of post—for example, "status update," "photo" or "video"—generated the highest reach and engagement (Lee 2013). In addition, Insights offers demographic data on Facebook users' engagement with external Web sites, encouraging these sites to "optimize your content for sharing and better tailor your content to your audience" (Facebook 2013).

Especially important for the production of news are the social media data services that show the real-time news interests of users. For years, Twitter has been delivering such services to the industry through its "data resellers" Topsy, Gnip, DataSift and NTT DATA (Dwoskin 2013). These resellers have direct access to every tweet ever sent through the platform. Topsy, for example, provides "instant social insights" to news organizations and other clients concerning the frequency of "any term" or "top related terms"; it also identifies the most influential users for any topic. Topsy's metrics tell news organizations how "positive" users perceive a topic or "your brand," "where your topic is active" and what is trending in any given location and date range (Topsy 2013). In September 2013, Facebook also released two search tools specifically aimed at news organizations and marketers, yielding data on real-time social conversations triggered by news events (Goel 2013). One of the tools allows news organizations to perform keyword searches through public Facebook posts, while the other enables searches through private posts. The latter only pulls up aggregate anonymized data, but it does play to Facebook's strength by providing the basic demographic details of posters and commenters.

All in all, social media greatly contribute to the quantification of audiences and content. These metrics allow the news industry to trace the demographic composition and interests of individual users and how they engage with news content in order to target them more precisely. Such metrics-driven news production clearly compromises journalistic independence and, consequently, journalism's ability to function as the fourth estate, as it pressures journalists to cater to the interests and preferences of audiences instead of focusing on issues of general public concern. Of course, how this works out in practice very much depends on the operations of news organizations, which still produce most of the news.

THE OPERATIONS OF NEWS ORGANIZATIONS

Over the past decade, news organizations have become intimately familiar with Web metrics and processes of algorithmic sorting. Graves and Kelly (2010) point out that given the abundance of Web data and the different methods used to track audiences on the basis of this data, news organizations typically subscribe to a number of audience measurement services. They contend that Web metrics have become an integral part of American newsrooms' daily routines. Since the early 2000s, increasing numbers of Internet users have been accessing the news through search engines, resulting in a variety of search engine optimization (SEO) strategies developed specifically for the news industry. SEO and SMO (social media data and optimization) tactics are now fully integrated into most major news operations.

While various studies arrive at different observations on how Web metrics and SEO affect newsroom decision making, they all agree that audience-tracking data and SEO strategies have become a central aspect of news production (Anderson 2011; Dick 2011; Graves and Kelly 2010; Lee, Lewis and Powers 2012; MacGregor 2007; Usher 2013; Vu 2013). Although some journalists ignore these metrics or even actively resist them, it is clear that quantified audience tracking systematically pressures journalists and editors to be aware of, and adapt to, consumer tastes. Audience signals, either in the form of aggregate metrics or active users' comments and posts, are becoming central to contemporary news production.

Anderson (2011) argues that as a result of this development a fundamental change in the professional self-perception of journalists is evolving. Drawing from ethnographic studies at two local U.S. newspapers and a related news-aggregating Web site, he traces this change in the proliferating newsroom "rhetoric about active, empowered, generative audiences, a rhetoric that emerges in parallel to the increasing reliance on news metrics" (Anderson 2011: 564). He maintains that although quantified and active audiences are often regarded as contradictory forces, they may not be incongruous at all. In the newsrooms where he did his fieldwork, Anderson observed that news consumers were discussed as "creative, active participants in the news making process that needed to be simultaneously empowered, catered to, and captured for analytical purposes." He concludes that "audience empowerment . . . might be seen as laying the groundwork for a deeper reliance on audience metric data as a determining faction in news production" (ibid.).

We consider such interpretation of the relationship between Web metrics and audience emancipation to be highly problematic. It is symptomatic of the dominant current discourse, in which metrics are presented as natural traces or signals of audiences' interests and where social media are understood as neutral facilitators of these interests. As discussed in the second section of this chapter, not only do prominent scholars buy into the rhetoric of Web metrics as audience empowerment, but so do editors and journalists. Such understanding of platforms as neutral facilitators of Web conversation systematically understates the central role of social media platforms in processes of news selection and production. The following comment by *New York Times* editor Jim Roberts is typical in this regard: "To me the benefit of social is not just increasing page views but as a way of developing a more personal connection with your audience. You can talk to them, and they can talk to you" (Glaser 2011).

As we have stated earlier in this chapter, social media technologies are far from neutral facilitators and neither are data "natural" footprints of users. Social media do not simply enable user participation in the news, but algorithmically privilege particular user signals and types of content. Social media's sorting mechanisms push breaking and entertaining news, provoking bursts of user engagement. In addition, it is important to recognize that the social media practices through which users participate in the news process, such as "sharing," "retweeting," "hashtagging," "liking" and "following" are very much technologically shaped. These practices constitute the ways social media steer user participation. Therefore, social media metrics should not be seen as natural reflections of user interests and perceptions, but rather as algorithmic and technological interventions. Social media platforms effectively act as interfaces between news producers and the audience, shaping what content users get to see and how these users can engage with this content, and, subsequently, translating these mediated forms of user interaction into metrics useful to news organizations. Instead of enabling a direct dialog between the news industry and "the people formerly known as the audience," social media insert a technological layer that very much structures their exchanges. As such, both audiences and news organizations become *dependent* on social media platforms.

The impact of social media on the day-to-day operations of news organizations, and ultimately their ability to work as an independent fourth estate, becomes evident when we compare how both print-based newsrooms and Web-born news outlets deploy major platforms to trigger audience traffic around news content. Over the past few years, print-based news organizations and their journalists have increasingly relied on social technologies for disseminating content. However, this is not to say that simply all news content is tweeted or posted on Facebook, or that social media "conversations" spring up around any type of content. News producers are becoming increasingly apt at selecting and developing content that triggers social media engagement. In a 2012 interview, Alexis Mainland, social media editor at the *New York Times*, contended that "the cliché that a picture is worth 1,000 words rings especially true on social media sites. . . . We regularly find that images we share on Facebook are more popular and engaging than text" (Margolis 2012). Mainland makes clear that the *Times* carefully selects "sharable" content, which is expected to generate user traffic. Besides photos, this content includes "personal stories" and "breaking news."

Whereas the *New York Times* selects items primarily from its available content, the *Los Angeles Times* has taken its SMO strategies one step further by developing and promoting content on its Web site specifically aimed at triggering social media buzz. The newspaper has intensified the development of its Web site's blog section, where it presents breaking news in an "informal and conversational" manner. Frequently updating its range of blogs, such as *LA Now* and *Politics Now*, the *LA Times* gives readers the latest updates on unfolding new events, often without providing the supporting context. This live-blogging approach is combined with a deep integration of Facebook's commenting technology. Readers can leave comments via their Facebook logins, which means that their comments are cross-posted onto their Facebook profiles. As a result of these strategies, the *LA Times* saw a widely celebrated 450 percent increase in referrals from Facebook in 2011 (Ellis 2011; Fisher 2011).

The examples of the *NY Times* and *LA Times* suggest that the impact of social media on the operations of news organizations, even if it does not directly influence editorial decision making, actually shapes the style of journalism. The two newspapers' tactics to emphasize breaking news and boost social media user traffic is becoming widespread among mainstream media. Like the *LA Times*, a growing number of news organizations have embraced liveblogging. Many of these organizations and their journalists use social platforms, especially Twitter, to alert followers concerning breaking news and to engage them in an informal personal manner (Blasingame 2011; Greer and Ferguson 2011; Hermida 2013). Evidently, this is precisely the type of news activity rewarded by Facebook and Twitter's news-oriented algorithms, and in line with these companies' instructions given to newsrooms.

While SMO strategies shape content selection, production and distribution at the *NY Times* and *LA Times*, they are extremely moderate compared to the tactics employed by Web-born news outlets such as *The Huffington Post* (*HuffPo*). Rather than pursuing online user engagement as an additional objective besides news reporting, the news aggregator has turned SEO and SMO strategies into its core business, defining this organization's news operation in a number of ways.

First, *HuffPo* has so-called traffic editors whose job it is to scour the Web for popular search terms and trending social media topics, and make article recommendations on the basis of these terms and topics. A key component of this tactic is to develop real-time content during major unfolding news events, such as disasters or scandals (Shontell 2010). Jonah Peretti, one of the site's cofounders, explains how *HuffPo* applies a "swarming tactic" to become the top result on Google for trending topics: "when you think about something like Heath Ledger dying, *Huffington Post* would have five people writing a story, seeing what everyone else is writing and seeing every single breaking news. So aggregating from other sources, linking to other sources." This tactic results in a news page that does particularly well on search engines as it links to authoritative sources and is frequently updated. Peretti points out that existing SEO tactics were later enhanced by the introduction of Twitter and Facebook modules and data streams, ensuring continuous updating of breaking news pages (Nisenholtz 2013).

Second, in order for its content to go viral—that is, to circulate widely on social networks and receive a lot of comments and hits—*The Huffington Post* develops a massive stream. In 2010, Paul Berry, former chief technology officer (CTO), revealed that the site produces between 600 and 1,000 pieces of original content every day. Of all this content, between 10 and 100 articles go viral. According to Berry, *HuffPo*'s content management system is completely tailored to "capture the content that is going viral, and it is constantly optimized to double-down on whatever is working" (Shontell 2010). This strategy corresponds with the overall approach to the news process by AOL, the corporation that bought *HuffPo* in February 2011. A leaked document titled *The AOL Way* specifies how AOL plans to maximize its audience reach (Carlson 2011). The document models how day-to-day news production and distribution should take place on all AOL sites—a process that starts with a "Demand Module" identifying trending topics. Next, the traffic and revenue potential of a topic is calculated before the format gets decided. After the content has been produced, user engagement gets triggered through Twitter, Facebook, Reddit, Digg and AOL discussion boards. The document stresses that for each item of content, it is important to "ensure that social media/sharing buttons serve as prominent calls to action." Finally, the results of this first dissemination effort are fed back into the process to determine whether it is profitable to continue promoting particular content (ibid.). Social traffic has become a goal in itself.

Third, the *Huffington Post* further promotes social traffic by cultivating user comments and these efforts have paid off hugely. In 2012, the site received on average 25,000 comments every hour, with some content generating +100,000 comments (Sonderman 2012). Of course, these numbers first reflect *HuffPo*'s successful news production process built around trending topics and popular search terms as well as its viral distribution strategies. The large number of comments certainly also results from the way the site makes clever use of social media by allowing users to comment via their Facebook or Twitter logins, thereby cross-posting these comments to the respective platforms. Yet another contributing factor is the site's intricate reward system, which stimulates activity by handing out badges and privileges to users for frequently commenting on content and for sharing *HuffPo* stories on Facebook and Twitter. The news site awards a range of badges, including the "networker badge," "based on a commenter's popularity among other HuffPost commenters," the "superuser badge" for the amount of "HuffPost content the person shares outside of the platform" and the "community moderator badge," acknowledging the "commenter's reliability in tagging inappropriate material" (Jones and Altadonna 2012: 250). These strategies, in turn, enabled *HuffPo* to "personalize" the large amounts of comments, showing the comments of "friends" and "followers" above those of other users.

Our analysis of newspaper and born-digital newsroom practices shows how social media metrics and algorithms affect their daily operations. As news organizations embrace social technologies to disseminate content and enhance their audience reach, social media logic begins to work throughout the operations of these organizations. By selecting "sharable" content, focusing resources on real-time forms of journalism and by organizing, in the case of the *HuffPo*, news production around trending topics, news organizations are effectively retooling their selection mechanisms to fit social media algorithms. In this respect, the news process is shifting from an editorial logic to an algorithmic logic, bringing with it new forms of dependency. Evidently, we are currently witnessing only the beginning of such a shift. The majority of news organizations, including the *NY Times* and *LA Times*, still mostly operates on the basis of an editorial logic. Nevertheless, the extremely rapid growth of algorithm-driven and metrics-driven news organizations, such as the *Huffington Post*/AOL and BuzzFeed, suggests that change could come quickly.

CONCLUSION

Independent journalism was once thought to mean "independent from political and economic power" and "representing the interests of citizens." The fourth estate, according to its critics, had already compromised its independent position by aligning news reporting with economic interests and by succumbing to political power. The emergence of online user-driven platforms has been depicted as the antidote to this state of affairs, raising the prospect of neutral technologies "measuring" and thus reflecting the people's concerns. However, two problematic claims underlie the idea of social media enhancing journalism's democratic potential: that users are simply empowered by platforms and that platforms impartially reflect audiences' concerns and opinions. Both mutually enhancing fallacies have gained ground in part of the academic world and in the daily practices of news organizations, making them more, not less, dependent on commercial mechanisms.

We have argued in this chapter that user news practices and personalized content are shaped by social media's algorithms and translated as aggregate metrics to news organizations. In turn, these organizations, operating on the principle of attracting audiences for advertisers, can hardly afford to neglect social platforms if they want to survive in an online environment. Moreover, the commercial model of most news organizations enhances the logic propelled by social media to boost traffic by focusing on popular and breaking news to trigger users' attention. The strategies pushed by social media algorithms are, in this regard, not very different from those of the penny press in the late 1900s or the popular press in the 1980s, which were equally predicated on pushing large volumes of "fast" news. What is more troubling is the tendency of leading news organizations, including the *NY Times* and *LA Times*, to adopt a rhetoric that equates algorithmically elicited user activity to audience empowerment, implying that "social traffic" intrinsically enhances the democratic power of citizens. Social media users cannot be equaled to citizens or to producers of news. Much rather, they are the products of algorithmic steering, pushed toward particular content and sold to advertisers.

Independent journalism, we propose, needs not only to reflect on its independence from commercial and political forces, but also from social platforms and their users. The production of news is clearly impacted by the algorithmic predilections inscribed in search engines and social media, which drive users toward particular content. Making news "social" may not be a viable means to enhance the democratic character of the news process. To the contrary, social media logic may take over the last part of editorial autonomy that professional journalists ever held: the power to select content, items and issues regardless of their popularity amongst (mass) audiences and regardless of the particular interests of specific user aggregates. As such, this logic undermines journalism's ability to fulfill its key democratic functions of keeping governments accountable and facilitating informed public debate.

REFERENCES

Anderson, C. W. (2011) "Between creative and quantified audiences: Web metrics and changing patterns of newswork in local US newsrooms," *Journalism* 12, 5: 550–566.

Anderson, C. W., Bell, E. and Shirky, C. (2012) *Post-Industrial Journalism: Adapting to the Present—A Report*, Columbia Journalism School.

Andrejevic, M. (2013) *InfoGlut*. New York: Routledge.

Artwick, C. G. (2013) "Reporters on Twitter: Product or service?," *Digital Journalism* 1, 2: 212–228.

Barnett, S. and Gaber, I. (2001) *Westminster Tales: The Twenty-First-Century Crisis in Political Journalism*. London: Continuum International Publishing Group.

Benkler, Y. (2006) *The Wealth of Networks: How Social Production Transforms Markets and Freedom*. New Haven, CT: Yale University Press.

Bennett, W. L., Lawrence, R. G. and Livingston, S. (2008) *When the Press Fails: Political Power and the News Media from Iraq to Katrina*. Chicago, IL: University of Chicago Press.

Blasingame, D. (2011) "Gatejumping: Twitter, TV news and the delivery of breaking news," *#ISOJ Journal* 1, 2. http://online.journalism.utexas.edu/ebook.php.

Bruns, A. (2008) *Blogs, Wikipedia, Second Life, and Beyond: From Production to Produsage*. New York: Peter Lang.

Bruns, A. (2011) "Gatekeeping, gatewatching, real-time feedback: New challenges for journalism," *Brazilian Journalism Research* 7, 2: 117–136.

Bruns, A. and Highfield. T. (2012) "Blogs, Twitter, and breaking news: The produsage of citizen journalism," *Produsing Theory in a Digital World: The Intersection of Audiences and Production in Contemporary Theory* 80: 15–32.

Bucher, T. (2012) "Want to be on the top? Algorithmic power and the threat of invisibility on Facebook," *New Media & Society* 14, 7: 1164–1180.

Calhoun, C. J. (ed.) (1992) *Habermas and the Public Sphere*. Cambridge, MA: MIT Press.

Carlson, N. (2011) "Leaked: AOL's master plan," *Business Insider* February 1. www.businessinsider.com/the-aol-way (accessed October 15, 2013).

Castells, M. (2009) *Communication Power*. Oxford: Oxford University Press.

Cheney-Lippold, J. (2011) "A new algorithmic identity: Soft biopolitics and the modulation of control," *Theory, Culture & Society* 28, 6: 164–181.

Chun, W. H. K. (2011) *Programmed Visions: Software and Memory*. Cambridge, MA: MIT Press.

Dick, M. (2011) "Search engine optimisation in UK news production," *Journalism Practice* 5, 4: 462–477.

Dwoskin, E. (2013) "Twitter's data business proves lucrative," *The Wall Street Journal* October 7. http://online.wsj.com/news/articles/SB10001424052702304 441404579118531954483974 (accessed October 14, 2013).

Ellis, J. (2011) "Traffic report: Why pageviews and engagement are up at Latimes. com," *Nieman Journalism Lab* August 16. www.niemanlab.org/2011/08/traffic-report-why-pageviews-and-engagement-are-up-at-latimes-com/ (accessed October 14, 2013).

Facebook. (2013) *Insights*. https://developers.facebook.com/docs/insights/ (accessed October 15, 2013).

Fisher, L. (2011) "Who says social media can't bring you traffic? The LA Times shows how it's done," *Simply Zesty* August 18. www.simplyzesty.com/Blog/Article/August-2011/Who-says-social-media-can-t-bring-you-traffic-The-LA-Times-shows-how-it-s-done (accessed October 12, 2013).

Flew, T. (2009) "Democracy, participation and convergent media: Case studies in contemporary online news journalism in Australia," *Communication, Politics & Culture* 42, 2: 87–109.

Flew, T., Spurgeon, C., Daniel, A. and Swift, A. (2012) "The promise of computational journalism," *Journalism Practice* 6, 2: 157–171.

Gerlitz, C. and Helmond, A. (2013) "The like economy: Social buttons and the data-intensive web," *New Media & Society* 15, 8: 1348–1365.

Gillespie, T. (2010) "The politics of 'platforms,'" *New Media & Society* 12, 3: 347–364.

Gillespie, T. (2012) "Can an algorithm be wrong?" *Limn* 2. http://limn.it/can-an-algorithm-be-wrong/.

Gillespie, T. (2014) "The relevance of algorithms," in T. Gillespie, P. Boczkowski and K. Foot (eds.), *Media Technologies*, 167–194. Cambridge, MA: MIT Press.

Gillmor, D. (2004) *We the Media: Grassroots Journalism by the People, for the People*. Sebastopol, CA: O'Reilly.

Glaser, M. (2011) "Social media grows at NY Times, but home page remains king," *PBS* January 13. www.pbs.org/mediashift/2011/01/social-media-grows-at-ny-times-but-home-page-remains-king013/ (accessed October 17, 2013).

Goel, V. (2013) "Facebook offers new windows into social conversation," *New York Times* September 9. http://bits.blogs.nytimes.com/2013/09/09/facebook-offers-new-windows-into-social-conversation/?_r=0 (accessed October 12, 2013).

Graves, L. and Kelly, J. (2010) "Confusion online: Faulty metrics and the future of digital journalism." *Tow Center for Digital Journalism, Columbia University Graduate School of Journalism*, Accessed September 10, 2013. www.journalism.columbia.edu/system/documents/345/original/online_metrics_report.pdf.

Greer, C. F. and Ferguson, D. A. (2011) "Using Twitter for promotion and branding: A content analysis of local television Twitter sites," *Journal of Broadcasting & Electronic Media* 55, 2: 198–214.

Habermas, J. (1991) *The Structural Transformation of the Public Sphere: An Inquiry into a Category of Bourgeois Society*, Trans. T. Burger. Cambridge, MA: MIT Press.

Hampton, M. (2010) "The fourth estate ideal in journalism history," in S. Allan (ed.), *The Routledge Companion to News and Journalism*, 3–12. Abingdon, UK: Routledge.

Hands, J., Elmer, G. and Langlois, G. (eds.) (2013) "Platform politics," *Culture Machine* 14.

Hedman, U. and Djerf-Pierre, M. (2013) "The social journalist: Embracing the social media life or creating a new digital divide?," *Digital Journalism* 1, 3: 368–385.

Hermida, A. (2010) "Twittering the news: The emergence of ambient journalism," *Journalism Practice* 4, 3: 297–308.

Hermida, A. (2011) "Mechanisms of participation: How audience options shape the conversation," in J. B. Singer et al. (eds.), *Participatory Journalism: Guarding Gates at Online Newspapers*, 13–33. Chichester, UK: Wiley-Blackwell.

Hermida, A. (2013) "#Journalism: Reconfiguring journalism research about Twitter, one tweet at a time," *Digital Journalism* 1, 3: 295–313.

Jenkins, H. (2006) *Convergence Culture: Where Old and New Media Collide*. New York: New York University Press.

Jenkins, H, Ford, S. and Green, J. (2012) *Spreadable Media: Creating Value and Meaning in a Networked Culture*. New York: New York University Press.

Jones, J. and Altadonna, N. (2012) "We don't need no stinkin' badges: Examining the social role of badges in the Huffington Post," in *Proceedings of the ACM 2012 conference on Computer Supported Cooperative Work*, 249–252. ACM.

Kovach, B. and Rosentiel, T. (2001) *The Elements of Journalism*. New York: Crown Publishers.

Langlois, G., Elmer, G., McKelvey, F. and Devereaux, Z. (2009) "Networked publics: The double articulation of code and politics on Facebook," *Canadian Journal of Communication* 34, 3.

Lasorsa, D. L., Lewis, S. C. and Holton, A. E. (2012) "Normalizing Twitter: Journalism practice in an emerging communication space," *Journalism Studies* 13, 1: 19–36.

Lavrusik, V. (2013a) "Best practices for journalists on facebook," *Facebook* May 2. www.facebook.com/notes/facebook-journalists/best-practices-for-journalists-on-fac ebook/593586440653374?id=206736659338356 (accessed October 14, 2013).

Lavrusik, V. (2013b) "How the new news feed design improves content discovery," *Facebook*, March 7. www.facebook.com/notes/facebook-journalists/how-the-new-news-feed-design-improves-content-discovery/571743776170974 (accessed October 15, 2013).

Lee, A. M., Lewis, S. C. and Powers, M. (2012) "Audience clicks and news placement: A study of time-lagged influence in online journalism," *Communication Research*.

Lee, J. (2013) "An introduction to Facebook's new page insights," *Search Engine Watch* October 14. http://searchenginewatch.com/article/2300218/An-Introduction-to-Facebooks-New-Page-Insights (accessed October 17, 2013).

Lindley, G. (2013) "Public conversations on Facebook," *Facebook* June 12. http://newsroom.fb.com/News/633/Public-Conversations-on-Facebook (accessed October 15, 2013).

Lotan, G. (2011) "Data reveals that 'occupying' Twitter Trending Topics is harder than it looks!," *SocialFlow* October 12, 2011. http://blog.socialflow.com/post/7120244374/data-reveals-that-occupying-twitter-trending-topics-is-harder-than-it-looks (accessed September 10, 2013).

MacGregor, P. (2007) "Tracking the online audience: Metric data start a subtle revolution," *Journalism Studies* 8, 2: 280–298.

Margolis, L. (2012) "How The New York Times does social media," *Photoshelter blog* April 23. http://blog.photoshelter.com/2012/04/how-the-new-york-times-does-social-media/ (accessed October 12, 2013).

McChesney, R. W. (1999) *Rich Media, Poor Democracy: Communication Politics in Dubious Times*. Chicago, IL: University of Illinois Press.

McChesney, R. W. (2004) *The Problem of the Media: U.S. Communication Politics in the Twenty-first Century*. New York: Monthly Review Press.

McGee, M. (2013) "EdgeRank is dead: Facebook's News Feed algorithm now has close to 100K weight factors," *Marketing Land* August 16. http://marketingland.com/edgerank-is-dead-facebooks-news-feed-algorithm-now-has-close-to-100k-weight-factors-55908 (accessed October 14, 2013).

McNair, B. (2006) *Cultural Chaos: Journalism and Power in a Globalised World*. New York: Routledge.

Mitchell, A. and Rosenstiel. T. (2012) "The state of the news media 2012," *Pew Research Center*.

Muhlmann, G. (2008) *A Political History of Journalism*. Cambridge: Polity.

Murthy, D. (2011) "Twitter: Microphone for the masses?," *Media Culture and Society* 33, 5: 779–788.

Napoli, P. M. (2011) *Audience Evolution: New Technologies and the Transformation of Media Audiences.* New York: Columbia University Press.

Newman, N., Dutton, W. H. and Blank, G. (2012) "Social media in the changing ecology of news: The Fourth and Fifth Estates in Britain," *International Journal of Internet Science* 7, 1: 6–22.

NewsWhip (2014) "The biggest Facebook publishers of February 2014," http://blog. newswhip.com/index.php/2014/03/biggest-facebook-publishers-february-2014 (accessed April 1, 2014).

Nisenholtz, M. (2013) "Jonah Peretti," *Nieman Journalism Lab* March 7. www. niemanlab.org/riptide/person/jonah-peretti/ (accessed October 24, 2013).

Paulussen, S., Heinonen, A., Domingo, D. and Quandt, T. (2007) "Doing it together: Citizen participation in the professional news making process," *Observatorio* 1, 3: 131–154.

Poell, T. and Borra, E. (2012) "Twitter, YouTube, and Flickr as platforms of alternative journalism: The social media account of the 2010 Toronto G20 protests," *Journalism* 13, 6: 695–713.

Quigley, P. (2013) "Top social publishers August 2013: Sharing way up for all publishers, and BuzzFeed on top," *NewsWhip* September 26. http://blog.newswhip. com/index.php/2013/09/social-publishers (accessed October 10, 2013).

Robertson, A. (2013) "Facebook redesigns News Feed with multiple feeds and 'mobile-inspired' interface," *The Verge* March 7. www.theverge.com/2013/3/7/4075548/ facebook-redesigns-news-feed-with-multiple-feeds (accessed October 9, 2013).

Rogers, R. (2008) "Post-demographic machines," in A. Dekker and A. Wolfsberger (eds.), *Walled Garden*, 29–39. Amsterdam: Virtueel Platform.

Rosen, J. (1996) *Getting the Connections Straight: Public Journalism and the Troubles in the Press.* New York: Twentieth Century Fund Press.

Rosen, J. (2006) "The people formerly known as the audience," *Presshink*, June 27. http://journalism.nyu.edu/pubzone/weblogs/pressthink/2006/06/27/ppl_frmr. html (accessed February 20, 2014).

Sasseen, J., Olmstead, K. and Mitchell, A. (2013) "The state of the news media 2012," *Pew Research Center*. http://stateofthemedia.org/2013/digital-as-mobile-grows-rapidly-the-pressures-on-news-intensify/ (accessed October 5, 2014).

Schudson, M. (1978) *Discovering the News: A Social History of American Newspapers.* New York: Basic Books.

Shirky, C. (2008) *Here Comes Everybody: The Power of Organizing Without Organizations.* New York: Penguin.

Shirky, C. (2011) "Political power of social media. Technology, the public sphere, and political change," *Foreign Affairs* 90: 28–40.

Shontell, A. (2010) "Success secrets revealed from the media startup on steroids, Huffington Post," *Business Insider* October 7. www.businessinsider.com/secrets-from-the-startup-on-steroids-huffington-post-2010–10#how-do-you-make-content-go-viral-1 (accessed October 12, 2013).

Sonderman, J. (2012) "How the Huffington Post handles 70+ million comments a year," *Poynter* October 23. www.poynter.org/latest-news/top-stories/190492/how-the-huffington-post-handles-70-million-comments-a-year/ (accessed October 15, 2013).

Starr, P. (2004) *The Creation of the Media.* New York: Basic Books.

Topsy. (2013) "Topsy pro analytics features," http://about.topsy.com/products/ proanalytics/features/ (accessed October 15, 2013).

Tumber, H. and Palmer, J. (2004) *Media at War: The Iraq Crisis.* London: Sage.

Twitter (2010) "To trend or not to trend," https://blog.twitter.com/2010/trend-or-not-trend (accessed October 9, 2013).

Twitter (2013a) "Twitter best practices for journalists and newsrooms," https:// dev.twitter.com/sites/default/files/files_media/journalistsbestpractices_v2.pdf (accessed October 9, 2013).

Twitter (2013b) "FAQs about trends on Twitter," https://support.twitter.com/articles/101125-faqs-about-trends-on-twitter (accessed October 9, 2013).

Twitter (2013c) "Analytics," https://analytics.twitter.com/ (accessed October 9, 2013).

Underwood, D. (2001) "Reporting and the push for market-oriented journalism: Media organizations as businesses," in L. W. Bennett and R. M. Entman (eds.), *Mediated Politics: Communication in the Future of Democracy*, 99–116. Cambridge: Cambridge University Press.

Usher, N. (2013) "Al Jazeera English online: Understanding web metrics and news production when a quantified audience is not a commodified audience," *Digital Journalism* 3, 1: 335–351.

van Dijck, J. (2012) "Tracing Twitter: The rise of a microblogging platform," *International Journal of Media and Cultural Politics* 7, 3: 333–348.

van Dijck, J. and Poell, T. (2013) "Understanding social media logic," *Media and Communication* 1, 1: 2–14.

Vu, H. T. (2013) "The online audience as gatekeeper: The influence of reader metrics on news editorial selection," *Journalism*.

9 Playing for Work

Independence as Promise in Gameplay Commentary on YouTube

Hector Postigo

On March 5, 2011 a seventeen-year-old YouTube video game commentator posted on his channel a "thank you" video for his subscribers. In his video, the "commentator" panned the handheld camcorder close to his face and began to list all the good things that had come to him from his YouTube channel. With more than half a million subscribers (and growing) and a YouTube partnership that was increasingly generating revenue, this commentator noted that he had been able to afford his first new car, save enough money to go to college and even lend his parent some cash. Beyond being a "thank you," this user-generated video was a form of "set up" film, a genre that commentators use to show to their subscribers their gaming "set ups" letting their viewership see the extent of their "geekiness" or technophilic commitment. The "set-up" that this particular commentator was showing, however, was his new car—2011 Mercedes E350 Coupe, valued at almost 50,000 U.S. dollars. Quite an achievement for a seventeen-year-old whose only source of income came from a YouTube advertising partnership. In this chapter I focus on the independence of video gamers/fans who have converted their gameplay into work. I trace material and cognitive shifts among "YouTubers" producing commentary to first-person shooter video games from 2010 until 2012 when their content became increasingly popular.

The video game industry has grown into a major entertainment business in the decades since it began in earnest with the manufacture of home consoles and games for the personal computer. During that time the industry has expanded, developing novel technologies, games and business models. Video games, once confined to the personal computer, are now on mobile phones, mobile consoles and dedicated home consoles. Like other media businesses the industry has seen consolidation. Nintendo, Microsoft and Sony, for example, now dominate the home console market. Game development, the work of making games, has also experienced consolidation. Many formerly "independent" development companies are now housed under larger publishing businesses like Activision Blizzard, Electronic Arts, Sony and Nintendo.

This chapter explores independence in relation to individual workers' experiences of creative freedom and economic reward. Independence here is understood as an ideal that one can not only work free of a corporation's influence, alienating structures and routinized work processes, but also that one can engage in "passionate labor" that is at once personally fulfilling and financially rewarding. Such a view of independence has been important in the professional imaginary that frames game development as a career (Lange 2007; Perelman 2000; Postigo 2009). After all, if game designers and developers are anything, they are gamers first: men and women who ultimately want to turn their passions into a job. The notion of independence in one's work is not unique to the game industry but a value held by anyone who seeks creativity and fulfillment in work. Certainly, YouTube in its early years (before its acquisition by Google) traded exclusively on the notion of independent media production, leveraging user-generated content for value and positioning itself as the "celestial bullhorn" of amateur video production. No longer would video producers need transmission towers, access to satellite feeds or the transmission spectrum to massively distribute their even most whimsical creations. All they would need was a webcam and an idea. High-capacity mobile phone data towers and smartphone adoption ultimately afforded an even more expansive vision of video capture and distribution within a matrix of Web platforms, apps and mobile devices that has grown into a major media business.

Video gameplay commentators engage with the notion of independence as a "promise" for a particular form of creative labor. Video game commentators have come to call themselves "directors," the term denoting their transition from hobbyist—providing footage of their gaming experience on YouTube—to conscientious craftsperson—creating and purposefully formulating a novel entertainment experience. The use of the term "director" is primarily a custom of commentators who have been asked to join the YouTube partner program or signed content sharing contracts with Machinima.com to distinguish themselves from the wider commentary community. Their understanding of their place in leisure communities (video gamers) as labor and the "game industry" proper positions independence differently from how it has been understood in media industries. Their practices did not begin as interventions into an existing industry, but rather as corollary production to content and media platforms. Unlike other interventions in the name of creating independent media experienced in other systems (see Chapter 3 in this volume), their work was not an attempt to break the monopoly on game design or video game distribution. In other words, their form of independence did not reproduce the narratives produced by established media players, but borrowed them as raw material for their own form of entry into the industry. They created a whole new ideal of what the video game experience can be: a spectator sport.

Analysis of the most widely watched commentators, their videos, their communities and their practices, shows that while they started their

YouTube "careers" as independent producers of game-related content, they have, over the eighteen months of research conducted for this chapter, become deeply embedded in the processes and structures of the mainstream mass media industries. The independence of their work belies a deep reliance on audience tastes, platform business models (the video game industry's and YouTube's) and the dynamics of a consumer/producer community that takes place across digital networks, trade conferences and personal relationships. Their foray into media production has historically been a pursuit of a hobby with the promise of independence from otherwise alienating labor, when revenue models became part of the video game commentary production and distribution experience.

Video game commentary may be a singular case of media independence, but findings are generalizable. Many of the forces that shape the valuation of UGC on Web 2.0 platforms are present in the popularization of gameplay commentary. Independence is both a promise kept and lost for gameplay commentators. As this chapter argues, eventually some compromises are made by commentators, which bring them into the orbit of the mainstream media production ethos. As a basis for building theory about working in digital spaces, independence is not unlike a boundary object (Bowker and Star 1999; Star and Griesemer 1989). It straddles multiple life worlds and provides multiple ways for making sense out of subject positions related to work life. Within the YouTube platform and business model, independence defines the successful commentator as private contractor or entrepreneur, yet paradoxically success is precariously dependent on not only producing content that will drive views, but also on the continued success of the video game franchise that the "YouTuber" is commentating on as well as on initial investment of free labor, a point I draw out explicitly in the sections that follow. Within the community of commentators, independence is a rhetorical device, an argument for why the work is worthwhile as well as an ideal, one that motivates but that often is not completely within reach. In the introduction to this volume, James Bennett rightly points to the complexity of "independence" in media production: its meaning in theory and in practice is a tapestry of visions, technology and *techne* that orient practitioners toward media institutions old and new, capturing them in their gravity while simultaneously affording the promise of escape velocity. If this metaphor should hold we can envision independence as the tenuous arc of planetary orbit, and those traversing it sometimes losing their place or maintaining it as they gaze at stars and YouTube stardom. Gameplay commentary as an instantiation of independence is seen by the community as convincing enactment of freedom but contested as institutions draw them in.

This chapter's empirical base is taken from eighteen months of participant observation in the YouTube video game commentator community. It follows the life cycles of two of the most popular games ever designed for console: *Call of Duty Modern Warfare 2* (*CoD MW2*) 2009 and *Call of Duty Black Ops (Cod BLOPS)* 2010. The great majority of the videos produced and the community activity studied centered on these games, but it also included content for *CoD Modern Warfare 1 (CoD 4)* and *CoD World at War (CoD WaW)*. These last three games came before *CoD MW2* and *BLOPS*, but remained favorites that commentators played and commentated on on occasion. Being a gamer myself, I feel a deep connection to those whose love of gaming is so strong that they are compelled to share recordings of their joys and frustrations with millions of others. Like other online communities, the YouTube game commentary community can have its unsavory dimensions. They have "trolls" of every stripe: racist, misogynist and homophobic discourses abound, rage is a common emotion and conflict often not neatly resolved. But there are also moments of great empathy, of reaching out and understanding, of teaching and learning. There are moments in some videos when content that paradoxically depicts playing at warfare also provides, in commentary, the most enlightened of human discourse. In those moments the YouTube game commentary community is not so different from others online or offline. The community is a complex collection of individuals in the process of meaning making, engaged in ritual, conflict and alliances. They embrace humanistic values as well as a sort of nihilism that takes the form of trolling and hate. In the case of games with large multiplayer components or online fan communities, the ethos of community becomes part of the game experience. Perhaps, as Lisa Nakamura argues, we should not hate the player but hate the game for its most egregious ugliness (Nakamura 2013). But that would divorce and absolve the platform and its design from its structuring affordances that make community dynamics part of the game experience.

The research for this chapter took three forms: in the participant observation work I watched videos, played the games, commented on videos and made commentary videos of my own. The analytical portion of the project took the form of field notes consisting of memos and notes on videos and commentary, paying particular attention to the discourse and practice of producing content that straddles leisure, hobby and professional aspirations. The design assessment of the project made note of the technical architectures within which "YouTubers" went about their routines and how that architecture afforded video game commentary production independence, but also required a form of production along lines defined by viewer tastes, the video game's popularity/commercial success and resource allocations and maintenance. Thus the gravitational pull of traditional mainstream media production practices are reproduced and inescapable. Niki Strange rightly wondered in the editing of this chapter if that pull is inexorable. I would say some elements of platform and practice cannot be ignored if YouTube stardom is desired. By ignoring their pull a *YouTuber* of any sort risks obscurity, forgoing the roar of applause instantiated as likes and channel subscribers.

MAKING YOUTUBE VIDEO GAME COMMENTARY
AND INDEPENDENCE

Video game commentary is a popular genre of user-generated video content on YouTube. At the time of this writing, collectively the top ten commentators have more than 3 million subscribers.[1] That number grows daily and their videos have been viewed tens of millions of times both on their channels and when reposted on other platforms and channels by other users. The videos themselves, be they from the established commentators or from those with smaller followings, are incredibly rich cultural artifacts. They are not only performances of expertise or gaming prowess, but also serve as performances of identity, community values, conflicts and allegiances, economy and creativity. They are a deep ritual. When the videos come from commentators with large subscriber bases they have the power to set the tone for discourse and shape the videos of other commentators by necessitating "response videos" and more commentary. Moreover, YouTube's commenting and rating system, which allows subscribers and viewers to speak to the commentators and to other community members about videos or other happenings in the gaming community, generate interactions which themselves are rich and meaningful.

Making commentary videos starts as a hobby. I've seldom heard (or read in their comments) any beginning commentator say they are doing it to make money (although perhaps secretly that's their goal long term) or that they are taking it on as a day job. But making a *CoD MW2* or *BLOPS* commentary video is not easy. An aspiring commentator will need at least an Xbox 360 (the majority of *CoD* commentary is from gaming done on this platform), but because most other commentators also have a PS3, then one might need that too. He or she will also need some form of video capture device, either an HD-PVR or a capture card installed onto a high-end PC or Mac that is connected to the console and records gameplay in real time. Last, the commentator will need the game itself (valued at near US$70 dollars) along with any downloadable content (DLC) the game company eventually releases. All summed up it's possible that a burgeoning commentator will need to make a US$5000 dollar investment up front.

Then the commentator will have to practice at the game. The overwhelming majority of commentators with large subscription bases (and even moderate ones) are very good at the game. Gameplay commentary is, if nothing else, an exhibition of great gaming skill. The overwhelming majority of *CoD* gameplay commentary is of online multiplayer team-based matches (players play against each other on teams of six or nine, not against game AI). By their own admission, commentators post only their best gameplay, but they also post their "combat records," which the game software keeps updated and then shares with an online database or leaderboard so that players can see how they stack up against others around the world. The top commentators have win/loss ratios typically above three (most players have match win/loss ratios of 0.5 to 1) and their kill to death ratios are also high (typically between 3 or 4 where most average players are between 0.5 and 1). Together this means that the aspiring commentator has to be able to win three online matches for every one he or she loses and they have to win 80 percent of their virtual gunfights even when they are on a losing team. This is not easy at all. Even if commentators are blessed with natural skill and quick reflexes, the games highlighted here are designed to allow tactical players to win out over the naturally gifted. There are countless places to hide on a map, choke points where mobility is limited and congested and a thousand ways for a player's game character to be shot, stabbed, blown up, bombed, burned, bitten by a pack of attack dogs, shot by helicopters, AC 130s or predator drones and even blown up by a tactical nuclear device. In short, merely staying alive in the multiplayer game is an exercise in skill, luck and tactics. Excelling at the game at the level that most top commentators do is difficult in the extreme and requires lots of practice. The average top commentator will have committed between thirty or forty days of game time in a ten-month period. That's about 2.4 to 3.2 hours of gaming a week on average. Many do more than that.

There are only a few top gameplay commentators that do not regularly post great scores and or gameplay on videos. These are typically trick shot commentators specializing in in-game demonstrations of skill such as jumping off a cliff doing a 360-degree turn while getting a one-shot kill with a sniper rifle or commentators that are more like radio "personalities," deploying humor or making amusing observations about the game. The rest have to be, as the community calls them, "beasts" at the game.

Last, the aspiring commentator will have to be good at commentating. They will have to provide something other than gameplay to keep players engaged. This means they will need to give "tips or tricks" for success, develop commentary that conveys useful strategies or tell interesting stories while their gameplay runs on video. This requires a good speaking voice and style, a quality microphone so that the commentator's voice doesn't sound muffled and good video and sound editing software and skills to combine the captured gameplay with the recorded audio.[2] If the commentator gets more exposure, they might want to design a video introduction to their videos with customized theme music and graphics. Some top commentators do this, although it's not terribly widespread. Ultimately the production quality for many of the videos produced by top commentators is quite high.

Any given video takes about ten to fifteen hours to produce if not more, taking into account time to game, commentate, produce, render and post. Some top commentators post two to three videos a week. This is not a hobby for those who are terribly pressed for time or have extensive family responsibilities, thus a great majority of gameplay commentators are young and still in high school or college. A few have professions outside the game industry and families to support. These commentators are usually recording and producing late at night or early in the morning while their families sleep or before they have to attend to their regular jobs. Independence, the ability for a commentator to choose the content and presentation, is dictated in many ways not only by their personal choice but also by the game they choose to play and the platform's various ways independent promotion of the content can be achieved. YouTube's architecture is designed to translate the video into views. It relies on the technical affordances created by its features (communication and distribution) to create social affordances (buzz around a video and community) to increase views. There comes a moment in a gameplay commentator's engagement with this practice when he or she must make a choice as to the way the content will be produced and their status as amateur, professional or "pro-amateur."

It is important to note that a significant proportion of *CoD* series gameplay commentators are men. There are some women and since this writing, their subscriber base has grown significantly.[3] The *CoD* gaming community is a gendered space and performance of gameplay is defined by the predominantly masculine identifying viewership. Women commentators with large subscriber numbers will perform a sexualized feminine persona; whether the persona is imported from their lives outside the commentary community or ascribed and adopted for the purposes of addressing masculine audiences remains to be determined in my research. To what degree either reason is the origin of those personae is expansive and liberating for women's performance of gender identity in a gendered space remains open for analysis and beyond the scope of this chapter.

A prevailing question among scholars who study hobby culture and its relation to consumer culture and capital has been: When does a hobby become work? The answer is not easy. Some say it is always work if capital can capture its value; others suggest that there is a duality to certain forms of hobbying that makes it both. For many hobbyists it is also a complicated answer. The majority seem to say that once you are paid for it, the hobby no longer is a hobby or at least the "job" aspects of the activity are so prevalent that they cannot be ignored. As the hobbyist becomes dependent on the pay or responsible to an employer, the freedom or independence of production as hobby is lost. Often game commentators who are being paid either by YouTube or machinima.com use this language.[4] They note how they have to produce a video even if they don't want to, or that other work responsibilities prevent them from producing the videos they want to make.

After the video is completed the commentator must release it on his or her channel. The platform does a lot of work once uploaded to YouTube. The video is announced in subscribers' inboxes; it is viewed, commented on, ranked, favorited, linked and so forth. To follow Sut Jhally's notion of the working audience, the video and YouTube architectures capture subscribers' clicks and views, organize them and make them available to others (Jhally and Livant, 1986). The intent is to, first, encourage community activity and, second, to translate it into more views for the video. It is in YouTube's best interests that all videos get as many views as possible, and its technical systems are designed to facilitate that.

But the features alone cannot achieve this. Commentators must market their videos to subscribers, encourage their responses and seek new audiences, all in the hopes of increasing video views. Top commentators are motivated by both the social capital earned in the community when a video garners thousands of views (the well-studied YouTube Star status) and the financial return (Senft 2008). To this end the top commentators use Twitter and Facebook to reach out to their subscriber bases. They tweet about videos, they update their Facebook pages and they engage users. The video's success is closely tied to the personal connection that commentators have with subscribers, so commentators often organize "open game lobbies" where they invite subscribers to play a few matches of the game online, hold "question and answer" sessions via chat, live stream gameplay with subscribers watching and asking questions, and have "giveaways" (an activity that brings with it some controversy, discussed later in this chapter). The top commentators that want to garner the goodwill of the community must do all this without seeming to be trying too hard. For the community, releasing a video on YouTube and then advertising it and raising awareness about it is analogous to going out and seeking friends; if it's done too aggressively or without nuance, then the community (through comments and ratings) will punish the commentator, calling him or her out for fishing for subscribers. Often commentators will end their videos with the tag line, "If you liked this video . . . or even if you didn't, please rate, comment and subscribe . . . it helps the channel grow." Asking for feedback, any feedback, inoculates against accusations from the community that the commentator is fishing for positive ratings or subscriptions.

When this study began, the standard of content quality was not defined. Commentators could simply post gameplay to music, or rants about a particular game style, or even about their personal lives; as the genre gained more views on YouTube, that changed significantly. In many ways, those commentators who were first to market and garner viewers were in the happy position to define not only the standard of gameplay commentary but also the standard of online play. Video game culture, as it is manifested in the *CoD* online gaming community, shaped that standard of play and was shaped by the standards demonstrated by commentators. For, example, because *CoD* online play is often fast paced, players who chose to linger in locations hiding behind corners to catch opponents unawares were labeled "campers," a derogatory term used by gamers to berate players through online communication in game lobby chat and messaging. Thus commentators who exhibited a proficiency in a "run and gun" style of play were typically lauded in the YouTube community as opposed to those who "camped." If camping was a style of play that garnered harassment for any given *CoD* gamer who chose to adopt it, the style became more widely understood and rejected after YouTube commentators used the tensions in the two styles of play as foil for their commentary. Although some top gameplay commentators do camp, they let their commentary create the entertainment value. Those commentators late to arrive to the increasingly fixed milieu of video game culture, who are not as proficient at fast-paced play, had either to find new ways of meeting the existing standard or, through their creative personae, to develop a new "hook" for viewers.

Game designers, for their part, have played close attention to these dynamics in the hardcore gamer community. Subsequent iterations of the *CoD* franchise have patently eschewed design elements that allowed users to camp, making the "run and gun" style the one most likely to bring successes through design affordances. In this way, one can argue, game design interferes with commentator independence in production. Without game design that affords plasticity in play style, commentators are locked into a particular form of content based on a defined play style if they want to garner viewers and a reputation as a gifted *CoD* gamer. One example in the design history of the *CoD* series that illustrates these design changes includes the removal of game features that allowed a player to remain unseen by an opponent team. By removing the ability to remain unseen the designers took away affordances that allowed players to "camp." Without the element of surprise, the "run and gun" strategy became the only viable option for gameplay.

Ultimately for video game commentators, what began as an exercise in leisure and creativity in video gameplay and independent media production was captured in the calculus of mass media audience taste and creation. This form of capture affords commentators an opportunity to create audience taste and production standards but ultimately locks them into a particular gameplay style and video game franchise. Commentators are not ignorant of this dynamic. They express their disappointment:

> once you start doing something for money it loses a lot of the fun it once used to have and that's where video games have gotten at this point in my life. I do them for money. A game like *Fallout New Vegas* comes along I don't want to monetize that. I want that to have the fun that it's always had. I want to just sit back and play the game.
> (*Wings Response to Hutch and Woody 2010*)

Whereas this particular commentator still uploads commentary, others left a potentially lucrative independent entertainment practice on YouTube because they lost that independence and joy, surrendering it to the demands of audience and pecuniary needs. If independence acts as a boundary object, it does so in the sense that it constitutes a subjective experience that straddles life worlds and helps commentators talk about their hobby and work as synergistic sides of the same coin. When that synergy is lost through the inescapability of audience taste, preference and commentator reliance on the social and material capital that YouTube affords, the boundaries between hobby and work become impermeable in commentator discourses about their techno-practice. At times they are even incommensurate.

Intellectual property (IP) concerns have recently impacted commentator independence in the production of video game commentary. As the video game commentary genre has become more popular, game companies have taken note. A key element of copyright law in the United States calls for IP owners to assume an ever-vigilant stance over derivate uses of their valuable IP. Should IP owners not police appropriation of their IP, they risk losing their properties to the public domain. When it became evident that some commentators were developing lucrative businesses made from the public performance of gameplay, some companies used the stringent protections on public performance and use of copyrighted content to argue that YouTube and the commentator community remove some of their content. Nintendo was the first to demand that video using its content not have ads associated with it and some commentators refused to play any Nintendo games. Nintendo eventually reversed its claim and other companies publicly supported the presence of video gameplay commentary on YouTube (Futter n.d.; Gera n.d.; Reed n.d.). At the time of this writing, it remains unclear how that will impact the long-term viability and independence of video game commentators. Much of the success that some commentators have reaped has been tied to the commercial success of the game titles they choose to use for commentary. The *CoD* franchise, because it holds sales records for a number of its titles, has provided a rich content source for commentary. Using *CoD* as a platform, commentators have subsequently ventured into commentating over gameplay in lesser-known games, transforming themselves from hobbyists to independent game reviewers for new releases. Copyright problems notwithstanding, the use of a very successful platform can serve as a vehicle to maintain the viewership that incentivizes and affords the creative latitude/independence to post gameplay of lesser-known titles.

Game companies seek partnerships with the best-known commentators, providing them with early copies of a forthcoming game and inviting them to premier events usually reserved for journalists. If gameplay commentators lose access to posting commentary over the most popular titles, these important elements of their business model will be lost. As has been the case in other instances, restrictive IP law intended to protect creators is also likely also serving as an inhibition to novel and creative business models that afford consumer participation (Cohen 2012; Lessig 2001, 2004; Postigo 2012a; Samuelson 1999).

Not long ago I sat for lunch with corporate legal counsel for a major U.S. telecommunications service provider. He turned to me and asked what should companies like his do with customers using the Web to broadcast content that can be competition to proprietary content delivered by institutional telecommunications companies. I answered, "Let them be and learn from the business models they are developing out of their media-centered hobbies." The notion of a "hobby" is important here. First contemplated by

Thorstein Veblen in 1914, it has come to be understood as a bridging practice between humanistic, community-related endeavors and the industrial
arts and capitalism. As such, the notion of "hobby," the logic of accumulation and the social class strata ordered by a capitalist market system, positions leisure into its calculus (Veblen 2011, 2013). Video game commentary
as hobby is not exactly the practice of a "leisure class," but it's not removed
from values that draw *the work of hands* away from alienation and drudgery. The instantiation of that hobby in infrastructure designed to extract
value for third parties like YouTube, however, slides hobby into work and
so positions it within the orbit of IP laws (meant to create markets in the
expression of ideas) and logics (meant to accumulate wealth by extracting
value from labor).

AFFORDING GAMEPLAY COMMENTARY ON YOUTUBE: THE ARCHITECTURE OF INDEPENDENCE AND ITS SURRENDER TO AUDIENCE TASTE

One ultimately cannot ignore the role of YouTube's search algorithm in
the production paradigm of video game commentary. The algorithm maps
into features that allow for production independence and creativity and also
affords sociality, capturing that dynamic in the calculus of media production within YouTube's business model. Technological features structure how
community is performed on YouTube and how revenue is extracted and
shared.

Channel subscribers, for example, may get e-mails summarizing new content on their channels. YouTube's commenting system provides the tools for
users to post comments on any given video; the comments can be directed
to commentators or other members of the community. Commentators can
address their subscribers directly through the comments system. By affording audience maintenance, YouTube's architecture provides the means of
socially integrating channel subscribers to a "video on-demand" logic in
media consumption.

YouTube's advertising strategy on videos is also important for the commentator's independence. Video creators who are part of the YouTube
Partners Program receive a share of the monies garnered by YouTube from
advertising placed on or near a video. The advertising can take the form of a
banner ad, a pre-video commercial or an in-video box ad. The system moni-
tors unique video views, ad clicks and other metrics that translate the videos'
popularity (gauged primarily in terms of the number of views) into a fee that
can be charged to advertisers and then shared with Partners. The advertising
system and the YouTube Partners Program form the central financial driver
for commentators now that the genre is established on YouTube. The system
makes clear the importance of UGC as a revenue stream. It frames the game
commentary videos so that viewers and commentators are not ignorant

of the value extraction system. Commentators talk about the system; they tell their subscribers about it and often show off the things they have been able to buy or experience because of it. The system gives life to a narrative of entrepreneurial independence among many commentators. In these moments commentators begin to refer to themselves as "directors," effectively admitting both the financial drivers and the staged nature of gameplay that is presented as natural talent. But such narratives of accumulation live in tension with other community norms, such as passion for a craft, hobbying for hobbying's sake, staying in touch with your subscribers and staying true to the values of sharing your passion for video games. This tension is so strong that many find themselves in the most awkward moments of cognitive dissonance. Often the most successful commentators (in terms of ad revenues and subscriber base) are the most vocal in bemoaning what "money has done" to the commentator community. As noted earlier, the discourses regarding productive practices when they become divergent and incommensurable cause independence to lose its bridging power between hobby and work.

Ultimately, the video-ranking algorithm is important in creating the social capital that motivates many commentators and it is important in defining how YouTube extracts maximum value from videos for both its parent company and for directors partnered in the revenue-sharing program. The ways YouTube ranks videos as relevant to a search query or eligible for presentation on its homepage is still unknown. Google, YouTube's parent company, has not made the ranking criteria public in detail. Analysts have noted that community activity around a video is a component of the ranking system (Gabe n.d.). What is known, therefore, is that search return rank is dependent on the social momentum around a video in the form of likes, comments, subscriptions and so forth. Ironically the very features that provide commentators social and monetary capital and provide them independence also lock them into the marketplace of taste and mainstream production standards—causing them to surrender that same independence and elicit the ire of game companies who jealously guard their intellectual property against these new forms of participatory culture.

Over the past decade there has been a considerable amount of work in communication, cultural studies and Internet studies that has addressed the issues raised by the promise of participatory culture for media consumers. A foundational critical work on the topic comes from Tiziana Terranova, whose exploration of "free labor" in 2000 framed much of how many critical scholars have come to theorize participation in digital environments. From Terranova's perspective, networked environments that foster and house social interactions form the framework for harnessing social practice into the capitalist logic (Terranova 2000). The outcome is a "social factory," where our social interactions are captured and monetized. Her work inspired a number of subsequent research articles on topics such as AOL volunteers, video game modifications, media work and other types of activities that add value to online media business and technology companies (Deuze 2007; Kucklich 2010; Postigo 2003, 2009). The overall findings, if they can be summarized briefly, are that in digital networks it becomes easier to harness participation and to capture all manner of activities in the "social factory," or to destabilize work into precarious labor that is transient and contingent.

The manner in which participatory platforms invite independence in media production but simultaneously algorithmically valuates it via search results and search promotion is still in need of exploration (see Ross 2013). The means by which independently produced media (be it video game commentary or independent comedy skits like the popular Jenna Marbles YouTube videos) affords creative and productive license while simultaneously organizing markets suggests a "crowdsourced" programming paradigm that straddles old media primetime models and contemporary on-demand models. In that way, immediately and algorithmically measured consumer tastes (by way of analyzing viewer rating, commentating and subscribing practices) can be translated into positioning a YouTube video in search results as primetime offerings. Earning a place on the YouTube home page, given its daily visit count, is not unlike earning a place on the coveted primetime programming slot in television, a position now courted by game companies and console developers (Gibbs 2014). Having that video available for viewing anytime across platforms (on a computer or cell phone) also gives it on-demand ubiquity.

Prominence, ubiquity and pervasiveness serve to foster more independent productions and, as previously noted, orient producers around creating content that will garner views. In video game commentary this has yielded some patently open machinations and manipulations of the ranking search algorithm. For example, the most reviled way of gaming (pun intended) that ranking system is the "giveaway video." In this type of video, the commentator will offer some small prize (usually a gift card for points on the Xbox Live Gaming Network) to be given to a randomly selected viewer who has rated, commented and/or subscribed. If the channel's viewership is small this can have a limited impact (if any at all); if the channel is large, the giveaway can have a significant impact, all the more so if the prize given away is large.

The case of the young man (XJaws on YouTube) who bought his first car with his YouTube earnings mentioned in the introduction to this chapter is a good example of the impact a giveaway has on a video game commentary channel. Following his car video, the same commentator purchased a large cache of valuable gaming gear, worth about US$3000, and over the subsequent weeks proceeded to give it away in his videos. To be eligible for the prize, viewers had to rate, comment on and favorite a video he produced. As a result of his giveaway and his already larger following, some of his videos appeared on the YouTube home page in the "Most Favorited Video of the Day" category and eventually in the "Most Watched Video of the Day" category. The strategy made economic sense; a relatively modest investment in prizes would return large numbers of video views and then profit from advertisers. In response to this strategy, a very well-known commentator,[5] not in the video game commentary community, posted a video giving away prizes but asked viewers not to do anything that would increase the video rankings. His video was targeted at XJaws, noting that by doing giveaways that required viewers to favorite the video, XJaws was cheating his way into the YouTube home page and maybe even occupying that space instead of some other YouTube UGC producer who would have earned his way to the home page legitimately.

A communitywide controversy followed where gameplay commentators and other genre producers voiced their opinions on the matter of giveaways. Eventually XJaws stopped the practice. He noted that he had gotten "too much hate" and that even though he believed his practice wasn't hurting anyone it just "wasn't worth the trouble." The impact could have been significant for independent production of video game commentary content; if newcomers to the production practice hoped to accumulate views and subscribers quickly, they may have been tempted to follow his lead. But the policing of norms maintained it a less than acceptable practice.

By controlling access to large numbers of subscribers, a successful channel commentator then has a form of monopoly power over the content of others. With a giveaway, an already disproportionate market share of subscribers is leveraged to conquer some valuable space on YouTube's home page. The large subscriber base also allows for the effective deployment of ideology in service of a particular competitor. It's no accident that the YouTuber who accused XJaws of undermining the community participation system was himself an established "YouTube Star" who had in the past occupied some of the categories that XJaws was infringing on. The established YouTuber effectively used the narrative of meritocracy to remove a competitor. Independence in production of this sort, then, is not only a freedom from media industry control over content frames and production aesthetics, but also freedom from a monopoly. But it is a freedom that can be gamed as well.

Participatory culture, then, is not completely isolated from the drivers that motivate capital accumulation and orient creative practices toward production of lucrative content. Henry Jenkins has conceptualized participatory culture as a practice whose inner workings are subject to the rationale of capital accumulation, commodification and profit. Participatory culture's dynamics are also subject to internal moral economies and self-defined systems of recompense and freedom (Jenkins 2006a, 2006b). The participatory cultural view on user-generated content is more optimistic; it sees the social and technological systems that make participation in mass media production in digital environments as having potential for fruitful collaboration, user input into media discourse and independent production in our case. In the context of Starr's notion of boundary objects, it can almost always be a point of contention as much as it is a frame for understanding epistemological validity or meaning across the panoply of social worlds that it may bridge. He or she who controls the dominant frame for the object can hold the keys to the bridge between epistemologies and social worlds. Independence is contested by the structures of hobby, copyright, capital and labor, all orbiting video games and play and media industries.

The best way of seeing video game commentary as an example of independence in video game culture and industry is to view it from both an economic perspective and one that still sees it free of the influence of capital accumulation, social or economic. There are game commentators present on YouTube that eschew *CoD* and the genre standards established by the top commentators. They run the risk of being a whisper in the cacophony of YouTube's "youness." Whispers among a roar of voices screaming, "look at me!" That level of independence remains a risk in so much as the channels may languish and vanish, but it's also a risk that can pay dividends. A few commentators, once having gained prominence while defining or playing within established video game commentary tastes and standards, developed other content. These commentators utilize skilled performances and entertaining personae to serve as the central draw to watch commentary, rather than the popularity of a *CoD* game itself. Seannaners, a video game commentator whose subscriber base is more than 1 million, decided to stop playing *CoD* and play *Minecraft*, an independently (in the sense of outside the mainstream games publishers) produced video game, instead. *Minecraft* gained a large number of players after Seannaners started playing it for his 1 million viewers. The gameplay is nothing like the standards he helped define in *CoD*, but his YouTube persona deploys humor and a great amount of speaking talent. So his channel continues to thrive and his content helped *Minecraft* become a popular sensation (SeaNanners n.d.).

CONCLUSION

YouTube's architecture is founded on a set of communication features that create technical and social affordances. The technical affordance structure allows for the distribution of video, advertising, communication between commentators and subscribers, subscriber recruitment and retention, and community participation. The technical infrastructure also allows for the effective collection of data in the form of a log of the number of views, which, along with the advertising system, can be translated into revenue for YouTube and the video gameplay commentators and allow for independent production and distribution. While on YouTube primarily, videos also find themselves embedded on other platforms. With Twitch.tv, gameplay videos are now a live broadcast enterprise. The social affordances frame practices such as community participation, systems of subscriber recruitment and exchange and valuation, competition, participatory culture and so forth. There is a tension between those sociotechnical affordances that serve independent production and its translation into revenue for commentators and YouTube.

The subscriber is the basic currency in YouTube road to stardom and success. Subscriber recruitment and retention translates into revenue for YouTube and into views for gameplay commentators. Commentators will share subscribers with other commentators by hosting other commentators in dual commentary episodes of gameplay. They will also subscribe to other commentators' channels and make that decision public. Caught in the momentum of reciprocity and social proof, one channel's subscribers will follow a commentator's lead and subscribe to the hosted commentator. Gameplay commentators also serve as "agents" whose work in creating gameplay and fostering gameplay audience community helps YouTube retain viewers for the genre. Once part of the revenue-sharing programs on YouTube, video game commentators are seen by the community as "stars." This moment of ascendance to YouTube stardom enables the top video game commentators to control significant social and material capital but at the cost of the freedoms they enjoyed when they were relatively unknown. Importantly, subscribers and game commentators understand the tension between their independent passionate production of content and the surrender of creativity and independence that YouTube stardom might require. "Selling out" is a common derogatory term used by the community to describe those commentators who have lost sight of the moral economy that fueled their creative appropriation of video gameplay. Despite these tensions, YouTube's revenue-generating machine marches on, and therein lies an important point: even as there is an ideological tension between independence and stardom, the views keep coming. Should a commentator lose subscribers, those subscribers will likely go to someone else who will then be offered a YouTube ad revenue-sharing partnership. Should a channel shrink or a genre go out of fashion, another will take its place and YouTube's architecture will accommodate it and get its share of cash.

From a theoretical perspective, the case of YouTube video game commentators shows some important generalizable characteristics for independence in the social mediascape that might become prevalent in other platforms for user-generated content (e.g., Facebook, Twitter or LinkedIn). First, stars matter. Whether they are seen as important network nodes or YouTube stars, those who rise, hold and grow large follower bases are key players in ensuring revenue generation. But this risks their independence as media producers when those boundaries between stardom and obscurity are crossed. Second, tools that allow for the creation of stars are a basis for rewarding independence and taking it away. Therefore digital media designs that serve dual roles are key tools for digital media industries and should be used with care by producers who seek to retain independence. Using social media distribution platforms, be they YouTube or Facebook, to distribute content that is personal or a creative appropriation of copyrighted goods is an exercise in tightrope walking. It is a balancing act between the loftiness of stardom/creative achievement and the precipice of alienation in producing content for a mass media enterprise. The tools one uses to maintain that balance are not of our making. They are designed to capture, to fix and to capitalize (Postigo 2012b). As much as commentators are invited onto the "youstage," they are only invitees and there is a trade-off.

Game companies have taken note of the potential value that gamers offer to the video game industry. To illustrate this, I point *to CoD BLOPs*, which has a feature called "Theatre Mode" that records, on the game developer's servers, the last 100 online matches played by any online player. These games are viewable to anyone on the gamer's "friend list" and anyone who has recently played a match with that individual. Theater mode allows users to review their gameplay from various perspectives (first person, third person, floating camera) as well as allows them to stop and pause gameplay and view the game from the perspective of any other player who played that game. The theater mode presumes that the average player will at least share their gameplay with friends, and video game commentary commentators have used this mode to give their commentary a dynamic feel. Regardless, given this feature, anyone playing *CoD BLOPS* online is potentially an independent producer of gameplay commentary.

The future of gameplay commentary is still in the making. We are in view of a "future anterior" (Fortun 2008). A present that promises a future for independence, creativity and polyvocality. That promise is rooted in YouTube's history as a risky venture that began by affording anyone with a cell phone and a Web connection a dynamic video distribution platform; even if today the platform is sometimes ossifying into a mass media enterprise not unlike others that have long occupied the mainstream. Independence in production, then, is a promise still being fulfilled, but sometimes abandoned. Freedom from media industry control over content frames and production aesthetics as well as freedom from a monopoly are possible. But to risk a pun on the topic of this volume, freedom can be gamed; it can be afforded in platforms that whisper through their design the old media business logics that extract value, confer it and orient production toward crafted audience tastes and definition.

NOTES

1. The genre described here differs from the genre defined by Pewpiedie, the most popular YouTube vlogger in 2013, and predates his work by nearly two years.
2. Seldom do commentators comment live on gameplay. They may find it too distracting to talk about strategy as they play the game so the commentary is often recorded after the gameplay.
3. See BeatrixKiddo83ps3 or SSSniperWolf on YouTube for examples of women commentators at different stages of their commentator careers.
4. One aspect of game commentating I do not discuss here is commentator relationship with machinima.com, a major outlet for video produced on game

platforms. The connections between directors YouTube and Machinima are complicated and the subject of another forthcoming article.

5. He regularly gets the "Most Watched Video of the Day," one of YouTube's predefined genres.

REFERENCES

Bowker, G. C. and Star, S. L. (1999) *Sorting Things Out: Classification and Its Consequences*. Cambridge, MA: MIT Press.

Cohen, J. E. (2012) *Configuring the Networked Self: Law, Code, and the Play of Everyday Practice*. New Haven and London: Yale University Press.

Deuze, M. (2007) *Mediawork*. Cambridge: Polity Press.

Fortun, M. (2008) *Promising Genomics: Iceland and DeCODE Genetics in a World of Speculation*. Berkeley and Los Angeles: University of California Press.

Futter, M. (n.d.) "Tidal wave of youtube copyright claims underway," www. GameInformer.com. Available http: www.gameinformer.com/b/news/archive/2013/12/11/tidal-wave-of-youtube-copyright-claims-underway.aspx (accessed March 7, 2014).

Gabe, G. (n.d.) "YouTube ranking factors: Youtube SEO beyond views, titles, & tags," *Reelseo*. Available http: www.reelseo.com/youtube-ranking/ (accessed October 5, 2011).

Gera, E. (n.d.) "Nintendo claims ad revenue on user-generated YouTube videos," Polygon. Available http: www.polygon.com/2013/5/16/4336114/nintendo-claims-ad-revenue-on-user-generated-youtube-videos (accessed March 7, 2014).

Gibbs, S. (2014) "Microsoft Xbox One prompts outrage after YouTube stealth-marketing stunt," *The Guardian*, January 21. Available http: www.theguardian.com/technology/2014/jan/21/microsoft-xbox-one-youtube-stealth-marketing-outrage (accessed March 7, 2014).

Jenkins, H. (2006a) *Convergence Culture: Where Old and New Media Collide*. New York: New York University Press.

Jenkins, H. (ed.) (2006b) *Fans, Bloggers, and Gamers: Exploring Participatory Culture*. New York: New York University Press.

Jhally, S. and Livant, B. (1986) "Watching as working: The valorization of audience consciousness," *Journal of Communication* 36, 3: 124–143.

Kucklich, J. (2010) "Precarious playbour: Modders and the digital games industry," *Fibreculture*. Available http: http://journal.fibreculture.org/issue5/kucklich_print.html (accessed February 5, 2014).

Lange, P. G. (2007) "Searching for the 'You' in "YouTube": An analysis of online response ability," *Ethnographic Praxis in Industry Conference Proceedings 2007* 36–50.

Lessig, L. (2001) *The Future of Ideas: The Fate of the Commons in a Connected World* (Vol. 1). New York: Random House.

Lessig, L. (2004) *Free Culture: How Big Media Uses Technology and the Law to Lock Down Culture and Control Creativity*. New York: Penguin Press.

Nakamura, L. (2013) "Don't hate the player, hate the game: The racialization of labor in world of warcraft," In T. Scholz (ed.), *Digital Labor: The Internet as Playground and Factory*, 187–203. New York: Routledge.

Perelman, M. (2000) *Transcending the Economy: On the Potential of Passionate Labor and the Wastes of the Market* (Vol. 1). New York: St. Martin's Press.

Postigo, H. (2003) "Emerging sources of labor on the internet: The case of America Online volunteers," *International Review of Social History* 48, Supplemental: 205–224.

Postigo, H. (2009) "America Online volunteers: Lessons from an early co-production community," *International Journal of Cultural Studies* 12, 5: 451–469.

Postigo, H. (2012a) *The Digital Rights Movement: The Role of Technology in Subverting Digital Copyright.* Cambridge, MA: MIT Press.

Postigo, H. (2012b) "Podcast: Hector Postigo, cultural production and social media as capture platforms: How the matrix has you," *MIT Comparative Media Studies/ Writing.* Available http: http://cmsw.mit.edu/hector-postigo-cultural-production-social-media/ (accessed September 16, 2013).

Reed, B. (n.d.) "YouTube's copyright cops are coming after gamers' 'Let's Play' videos," *BGR.* Available http: http://bgr.com/2013/12/11/youtube-gaming-videos-takedown-controversy/ (accessed March 12, 2014).

Ross, A. (2013) *Real Love: In Pursuit of Cultural Justice.* New York: Routledge.

Samuelson, P. (1999) "Intellectual property and the digital economy: Why the anti-circumvention regulations need to be revised," *Berkeley Technology Law Journal* 14: 519.

SeaNanners. (n.d.) "SeaNanners Gaming Channel," *YouTube.* Available http: www.youtube.com/user/SeaNanners (accessed March 12, 2014).

Senft, T. M. (2008) *Camgirls.* Peter Lang Publishing.

Star, S. L. and Griesemer, J. R. (1989) "Institutional ecology, 'translations' and boundary objects: amateurs and professionals in Berkeley's museum of vertebrate zoology, 1907–39," *Social Studies of Science* 19, 3: 387–420.

Terranova, T. (2000) "Free labor: Producing culture for the digital economy," *Social Text* 18, 2: 33–58.

Veblen, T. (2011) *The Instinct of Workmanship and the State of the Industrial Arts.* New York: Forgotten Books Publishers.

Veblen, T. (2013) *Theory of the Leisure Class.* BoD—Books on Demand.

Wings Response to Hutch and Woody. (2010) Available http: www.youtube.com/watch?v=sBN41wADCv8&feature=youtube_gdata_player (accessed March 7, 2014).

Section III

Independence in a Cold Political Climate

10 From Perestroika to Putin
Journalism in Russia

James Rodgers

Independence—*nezavisimost* in Russian—was, in the dying days of the Soviet Union, a word that helped to describe some of the head-spinning changes that hastened the end of a superpower. It took its place alongside *perestroika* (usually translated as "restructuring") and *glasnost* ("openness"): the key words of the reforms launched by Mikhail Gorbachev after he became the general secretary of the Communist Party of the Soviet Union in March 1985. He was, of course, to be the last to hold that title. It disappeared in the same historical storm that swept away the USSR itself. From the wreckage of the "indestructible Union of Free Republics,"[1] as the Soviet anthem so boldly described it, there arose fifteen new independent states. Ideas of "independence," therefore, began to influence all aspects of late Soviet life, not just the political sphere. Cooperative cafés; joint ventures with companies from the capitalist world; small businesses—all began to appear where once there had only been the state-run economy. For the Russian news media, it was the biggest period of change and opportunity since the advent of Soviet power, and possibly, given the speed with which it happened, since the birth of Russian journalism itself.

The purpose of this chapter is to try to analyze what has followed from the opportunities of that era. Perhaps it did not seem so at the time, but, with hindsight, those hybrid forms of economic activity could almost be seen to anticipate the compromises that Russian journalists would come to make in the world that awaited them. For although this was an era when ideas of political independence took center stage—even Russia itself, despite having been the heart of the Soviet Union, considers that it too became independent at this time[2]—this chapter will seek to show that journalism's independence, in the sociopolitical sense defined by James Bennett in the introduction to this volume, did not last long. I argue that developments in Russian journalism, and therefore ideas of Russian journalism's independence, are inseparable from the political environment in which they occurred. Given that one of Russian journalism's tasks, as in any country, has been to chronicle and reflect on political, economic and social change, any idea of "independence" has that limitation. That being the case, this chapter will try to consider the extent to which Russian journalism has been able to act independently in editorial terms—that is, in "industrial" and "formal" terms. What kind of angles has Russian journalism pursued, what proprietorial or political constraints has it been forced to accept? (Here there are perhaps parallels with the challenges, outlined elsewhere in this volume by Allen and Jukes, facing the British press). I will conclude by raising the possibility of a new kind of "industrial" independence for Russian journalism, which may in turn lead to a renewed "sociopolitical" independence.

The approach will be to consider three broad periods of Russia's post-Soviet history: first the immediate post-Soviet period of the 1990s; then the beginning of Vladimir Putin's time at the summit of Russian politics, during the first decade of this century; and, finally, Russian journalism of more recent years. Has the spread of digital media and social networking given rise to a new kind of independent journalism at the fringes of the news media, if not in the mainstream? My research for this chapter has consisted principally of four semi-structured interviews with journalists who have worked in the Russian news media. The contributors were selected on the basis of the length of their experience in Russian journalism (they began their careers in the 1990s, and continue to work today); the breadth of their experience (they have worked both for Russian and for Western/international news media); and, in order to achieve something of a gender balance, even in such a small sample, the interviewees are two women and two men. My interest in the subject is largely inspired by the long periods I spent working in Russia as a journalist from 1991 to 2009. During that time, I completed three postings to Moscow—one for Reuters Television, and two for BBC News—as well as numerous other, shorter, assignments.

FIRST STEPS: THE END OF THE USSR AND THE EARLY POST-SOVIET PERIOD

"In the unsteady progress towards something that might be called democracy, there is no guarantee that one of its principal supports, a free press and broadcasting system, will remain unconstrained. Neither post-Gorbachev Russia, nor post-Rafsanjani Iran, have managed to sustain what their predecessors were able to achieve," wrote Roger Silverstone in *Media and Morality* (Silverstone 2007: 176). Still, Gorbachev's Russia, if not the Russia that followed it, definitely marked a new departure for journalism. Brian McNair, in 1991, described "the development of new outlets for critical campaigning journalism" (McNair 1991: 59) and argued that "The new approach to coverage of the economy is also evident in photojournalism" (McNair 1991: 60). Newspaper photographers were allowed to cover subjects that portrayed life as it was, not as it was supposed to be: in one example that McNair considers, a "near panic-stricken mob [is pictured] scrambling for the opportunity to buy some scarce commodity or other" (ibid.). "Scarce commodit(ies)" may have been the reality of Soviet shopping, especially in later years when the system began to creak and crack ahead of its collapse. Words or pictures illustrating or discussing such scarcities, however, were absent from the official media—which is why their appearance was rightly noted by McNair as a significant "new approach." This era was also characterized by an unprecedented attempt to come to terms with the bloodier, more brutal periods of the Soviet past. The weekly magazine *Ognoyok*—its name means "little flame" in Russian—was the torch that lit the way. Here, one of its reporters, Ales Adamovich, reflects on the realization that mass graves containing the remains of victims of Stalin's murderous purges in the 1930s could be found near big cities, not just in the frozen wastes of the far north.

> Those of us who live in or around Minsk have only recently discovered that throughout the thirties people weren't only dying on the Arctic Circle, but on our own back doorstep. At first there were the "social aliens," and then the "kulaks," and then whole professions—engineers, teachers, soldiers, veterans and party workers—in the general category of "enemies of the people."
>
> (Adamovich 1990: 9)

Stories such as these made a huge impression—one hard to imagine now—when first they were published. As a student visiting Moscow in the late 1980s, I went to see Tengiz Abuladze's film *Pokayanie* (*Repentance*). It tells the story of the effect a tyrannical mayor had on a small town where his word was law. The story is told in flashbacks at the trial of a woman accused of digging up the tyrant's corpse on the grounds that he did not deserve to rest in peace. The accused woman's parents were among those who had disappeared under his rule. It was not hard to substitute the small town for the world's largest country, the USSR, and substitute the fictional Varlam for twentieth-century dictator Joseph Stalin. Many of the audience obviously did so. What I remember most from the screening was something I have never experienced before or since: members of a cinema audience gasping in disbelief, and possibly shock. Common enough in a cinema perhaps, but common because of an unexpected sudden violent event, or a breath-taking stunt, not, as happened here, because of the political content of a film. Newspaper stories such as Adamovich's or those that McNair refers to, about shortages and other inconvenient truths, were similarly striking. Issues that people would once have hesitated to talk about even at home with members of their own families were now prominently discussed in the press. This, as Zassoursky has suggested, was an important part of the implementation of the reform process that Mikhail Gorbachev had launched. "A freed up (but still controlled) press was in essence the only reliable ally Gorbachev possessed in his struggle with conservative forces in the party apparatus" (Zassoursky 2004: 4). Russian journalists today look back on that era as a time when the excitement and uncertainty of new times was reflected in journalism too. At this stage, as Zassoursky says, the press in Russia was "still controlled"—by a Marxist-Leninist government, which, even if its leader was a reformer, still took decisions over the financing and distribution of news coverage—so it could not be considered independent. Relatively speaking, though, it must have felt at the time like a huge step in that direction. It was a time of new opportunities for reporters, and a time when audiences thirsted for what reporters could uncover and offer. As Leonid Ragozin—a Russian journalist who has worked as a correspondent and editor for the Russian edition of *Newsweek*, and for the BBC—puts it,

> It was a great time—even when censorship still existed in the late 80s it was a great time—for journalists because there were huge, huge areas the audience wanted journalists to explore. People were interested in all sorts of stuff because they were starving for truth essentially, starving for information, after seventy years of communism.
>
> (Interview, November 11, 2013)[3]

What this era of uncertainty did not offer was a clear indication of what was to come: the complete collapse of a system whose leader, Mikhail Gorbachev, had intended only to reform it. With that system gone, a whole new era began—one that some Russian journalists today identify as an era of independent reporting. As Zoya Trunova, editor of the BBC World Service's Global Video Unit, reflects, "The end of the USSR was a massive life-changing moment for the Russian media, for journalists—because in the Soviet Union journalism as we understand it in the West didn't exist" (Interview, November 14, 2013).[4] Of her own training, at Moscow State University in the late 1980s, she says, "we were trained to be ideologists, not journalists." With the sudden collapse of the old system, there was parallel dramatic change in the media landscape. "In the early '90s I believe there was genuinely the environment where in Russia there was independent journalism," Trunova recalls now.

> You would come to a place in Siberia—Krasnoyarsk, or Tomsk, or Novosibirsk—and you would get these people who were working in newly-founded independent television companies, and you would see how much appetite they had to learn how to do it, and how much enthusiasm these people had to actually produce news. And their owners at the time didn't really get involved very much.

Trunova's last observation regarding ownership is perhaps especially useful in understanding the particular time she describes. The television companies she talks of were "independent" in the sociopolitical sense that they were no longer subject to ideological editorial control, as TV journalists were during Soviet times. Journalists were also, perhaps, independent in the industrial sense, although, as will be suggested later in this chapter, that was not to last.

Similarly, Konstantin von Eggert echoes Trunova's sense that the period was "life changing"; seminal; unpredictable—and sometimes dangerous (not least because criminal gangs seeking a slice of Russia's new capitalist riches might settle scores in the street). Von Eggert began his journalistic career in 1990, "from the beginning of independent journalism" (Interview, November 18, 2013),[5] as he puts it now. He has been diplomatic correspondent of *Izvestiya*; editor in chief of the BBC Russian Service's Moscow bureau; and of the Kommersant FM radio station. He says now:

> There was excitement and the feeling that your words count. One felt one was making history every day. We were not very well off moneywise, but still fairly decently paid compared to many others. When one saw the nouveaux riches regularly killed in gangland wars one thought: "Maybe less money but more security." There were elements of community spirit and solidarity among journalists. Although I would not say they do not exist today but there was visibly more corporate solidarity in the 1990s.

If journalists such as von Eggert felt they were "making history every day," it was because Russia itself was undergoing unprecedented and unpredictable change: change that shaped the journalism that chronicled it. The country's first post-Soviet leader was Boris Yeltsin. Coming himself from the Communist political establishment, he had become its critic. He had been elected to the newly created post of Russian president in June 1991 (on the day now remembered as Russia's "Independence Day"). He cemented his position as president of Russia, and already had considerable popularity, built on his open opposition to the coup d'état that hardline Soviet Communists launched against Mikhail Gorbachev's administration in August 1991. Muscovites will long remember Mr. Yeltsin's standing on a tank to make public his refusal to accept the authority of the "State Emergency Committee," as the coup leaders described themselves. His show of defiance was instrumental in the coup's collapse (Service 2003: 500). Mr. Yeltsin's desire to break with the past affected the way that political power interacted with the news media. Von Eggert has a telling story about an incident that would once have landed him in deep trouble. Under Mr. Yeltsin, things had obviously changed and, then at least, the occupants of the Kremlin did not expect to have the final say on what was written about them.

> I remember one particular moment from my *Izvestiya* days. It must have been in 1993. President Yeltsin cancelled a scheduled visit to Japan, and I wrote quite a sarcastic piece about him letting down the Japanese and delaying indefinitely the solution to the territorial dispute between Russia and Japan. Boris Yeltsin called my Editor-in-Chief [who] thought that the president will demand that he fire me. Instead Yeltsin said: "I do not mind criticism. It is just the satirical tone of the piece that I found tasteless and out of place. We know the author. He

is a young journalist and he will, hopefully, learn." With that he said goodbye and hung up.

Von Eggert clearly feels that his personal experience is symbolic of a time without precedent in his country's history:

> The 1990s were the golden age of Russian free speech and free media, not without faults, but still exceptional in Russian history, all things considered. It was a time of boundless enthusiasm and idealism of many journalists who were seen as heroes by the society which was keen on change and transformation. But by the mid-1990s wariness and disillusionment set in due to general tiredness with reforms and instability.

Whilst that "boundless enthusiasm and idealism" was finally going flat—and Rantanen and Vartanova speak of "disillusionment with politics and loss of readers' trust" (Rantanen and Vartanova 2003: 152)—other significant changes were under way: changes that would very much affect the independence of Russian journalism in the industrial and sociopolitical sense. Maria Aslamazyan has worked for Internews, "an international development organisation specialising in supporting independent media, freedom of information and free expression around the globe" (Internews 2013), since the early 1990s. In her role, she has worked with countless Russian journalists over the past two decades. She remembers the early 1990s as a time of huge and rapid expansion for journalism. "After many years of government propaganda, these private channels start to open very fast: every day, every month, new media, new newspaper, new TV station, new radio station—a lot. It was a very interesting time" (Interview, November 13, 2013).[6] However, Aslamazyan suggests that as the decade wore on, the mood began to change; the excitement seemed to be on the wane. She echoes von Eggert's sense that "wariness and disillusionment set in":

> In 93, 94, 95 this *romantizm* [here Aslamazyan uses the Russian word for "romanticism"] that we are independent slowly was going down because people had understood to do the media, you need to get money. And this money, how you can get that? Definitely advertising, but also owner. In the meantime the people who has become richer—we don't have such a big oligarch in 94–95, but we still have rich people—and they start to recognize "ok, this is a very good tool for influence." And they start to pay attention to these small, independent, semi-independent stations, I mean they go to each other. Media are looking for money, and people are looking for influence. And the distance between journalists and big money becomes closer and closer and closer.

This, I would argue, is the beginning of a trend that was to have a profound effect on Russian journalism's idea of its own independence. Journalism's need to be financed, and the recognition by Russia's new rich that the news media could be a "very good tool for influence," were two factors that foreshadowed the way that money, politics and the press would interact during Russia's first post-Soviet presidential election, in 1996. The way that relationship would develop was further influenced by the way Russian journalists would cover the bloodiest episode in Russia's post-Soviet history.

While the sense of anticipation and opportunity carried Russian society, and its newly independent news media, through the immediate post-Soviet period, the massive change and plummeting living standards—not to mention the organized crime referred to by von Eggert—meant that the near euphoria of the end of the Soviet period soon gave way to deep pessimism and cynicism among the electorate. The candidate who had won so convincingly Russia's first presidential poll in the summer of 1991 looked all but unelectable five years later. In addition to the severe economic hardship—unpaid wages, deeply uncertain employment prospects where once the Soviet system had guaranteed lifetime job security—Mr. Yeltsin's administration launched a military campaign in the separatist southern region of Chechnya. Some of the reporting of this campaign may also be considered independent, in that it was characterized by coverage sharply critical of the decisions taken by Mr. Yeltsin's administration, and the actions that followed. As Robert Service writes, "Moscow TV stations and newspapers had reporters in Chechnya who told of the Russian Army's incompetence and the atrocities carried out by its troops" (Service 2003: 533). Zassoursky (2004) offers a summary of subsequent scholarly debate on the nature of this critical reporting, which, he suggests, some saw as an example of a healthy fourth estate, others as an example of the news media being too sympathetic to "terrorists," as Russian officials described the separatists. Among journalists working in what seemed like an exciting new age of media freedom and independence, the war presented a dilemma: many of them, as will be discussed in greater detail later in this chapter, were staunch supporters of Boris Yeltsin's administration. Still, reporting "the Russian Army's incompetence and atrocities" was a journalistic duty—one Mr. Yeltsin's administration did not try to make it difficult to fulfill. Even media under the control of the state contributed to the critical coverage. As von Eggert recalls, "The Kremlin under Yeltsin rarely interfered in media affairs to the extent that one of the most vocal critics of the first war in Chechnya was the government owned Channel Two of Russian TV (RTR)." Yet as citizens, and journalists who enjoyed the new political climate, some were reluctant to be too critical. Aslamazyan's memory of this time is one in which journalistic ideas of balance were actually compromised and clouded by journalists' own feelings toward Mr. Yeltsin and his administration. She seems to suggest that, alongside those covering the "Russian Army's incompetence and atrocities," there were those—she appears to include herself—whose political sympathies put them in a difficult situation as journalists. "We love this new democratic power. We really would like to support them. We really understand they bring democracy in our country," she recalls now. "It was very difficult to really criticize, to really try to be balanced, in this situation." In effect, Russian journalists at this time were beginning to compromise their independence from political authority because they largely sympathized with the ruling administration. As the idealism of the immediate post-Soviet period had ebbed away, the realization had grown that compromise was likely to be the reality of Russia's new journalistic landscape. This trend was to continue. The next milestone in the story of Russian journalism and independence also occurs at this period.

WORKING FOR FREEDOM? JOURNALISM AND THE 1996 RUSSIAN PRESIDENTIAL ELECTION

In parliamentary elections held in December 1995, candidates allied with Mr. Yeltsin had not had anything like the success enjoyed by his Communist opponents, led by Gennady Zyuganov (Service 2003: 530). The "general tiredness with reforms and instability" described by von Eggert had left Mr. Yeltsin in a weak position in the polls—as the strong showing by his political rivals in the December vote had seemed to confirm. Despite this apparently massive disadvantage, Mr. Yeltsin won a second term, thanks, as Service has argued, "to money, patronage and a brilliant media campaign" (ibid.: 531). It is the last of those three points, the "brilliant media campaign," that is of most interest for this chapter. Coming to Russia in the summer of 1996 as part of the BBC News team sent to cover the election, I got the sense that many Russian journalists had taken the decision that, on the basis that their professional and personal lives were better than they had been under the Soviet system, they had no desire to return to it—an impression supported by Aslamazyan's reflections on the period. Journalists therefore took the decision to lend their support to Boris Yeltsin for fear that a victory for Gennady Zyuganov would mean a return to the Soviet system, or at least something close to it. Zassoursky (2004) seems to contend that is too simplistic an interpretation. Having argued, with reference to the parliamentary elections of December 1995, "Mere control over the mass media was clearly not enough to ensure victory" (2004: 65), he goes on to say of the presidential election of the following summer, "Instead of 'supporting' Boris Yeltsin (as can be seen from campaign documents, the mere support by television was considered inadequate) television, and in particular news broadcasts, became a fundamental campaign tool" (ibid.: 70). Based on my experience of covering the election—I remember, for example, TV pictures of Mr. Yeltsin dancing energetically at a campaign rally at a time when his health was not actually good—I take this to mean that Mr. Yeltsin's advisers consciously built their strategy to include television, rather than just expecting it to be supportive. Zassoursky makes his persuasive case with reference to strategy documents prepared for Mr. Yeltsin's campaign. Trunova and Aslamazyan, though, remember something closer to support. In an interview, Trunova uses a Russian phrase "administrativniye resoursy" (literally "administrative resources") to try to describe the way the news media were employed. The phrase generally describes the Russian political establishment's exploitation, during election campaigns, of the means at their disposal—means that they control thanks to their management of the public sector. These might include, for example, providing transport for campaign workers; they extended to using access to the news media in an attempt to persuade the electorate to favor one particular candidate or party. Mr. Yeltsin's campaign team, Trunova recalls,

> Really had to use all *administrativniye resoursy*—administrative resources—to get him to win. That was the first time that Russian media became just one of the resources. They certainly didn't want Zyuganov to win this election because everybody was expecting if the Communists came to power, we would be back to the Soviet Union.

She compares the overall effect to a loss of innocence. "I think they themselves were happy to do that, but it was an orchestrated campaign. It wasn't independent journalism, and Russian independent journalism lost its virginity at that moment." Aslamazyan places the 1996 presidential election alongside Chechnya as a missed opportunity for independent reporting. It is, she suggests, "very easy today to tell that this was big mistake for Russian media, because a few times they lose the opportunity to be really balanced, to really criticize the government, even though they like the government, and criticize the people which they like. Media lose this opportunity." It seems to have been at this time that Russian journalism experienced the harsh reality that working with their newfound freedom also meant taking difficult decisions, and living with what followed. The consequence, Aslamazyan argues, was a loss of journalistic independence. "When you become so close to this government, you start to support it, you lose the opportunity to see the big picture." Von Eggert, who was then working for the respected daily *Izvestiya*, makes a strong case that the way Russian journalists responded to the political climate during the election campaign has to be understood in the context of the time. This is how he describes the role of the news media:

> It was very significant if not decisive in mobilizing support for Yeltsin. It is easy to pontificate today about these events as the moment free media died in Russia. But one has to see the situation as it was then. Ninety-nine percent of journalists were for Yeltsin not because a lot of money was spent on buying them (actually very few top editors benefited from the Kremlin cash flow directly) but because the communists were really using a lot of revanchist rhetoric and threatened the media with reprisals after their win. We had the reds picketing *Izvestiya*, carrying

slogans like "You, dirty Yids, our time is coming soon."[7] We supported Yeltsin because we knew that for him media freedom is essential. I have no regrets and repent nothing.

The 1996 presidential election, then, was pivotal because it ensured that Russia would not try to turn back the clock to an era of Soviet-style communism. The abusive, anti-Semitic demonstrators who picketed the offices of *Izvestiya* did not get their way. It was pivotal too for journalism because the news media had become an integral part of the post-Soviet political process. They were not used simply to exhort people to vote for candidates whose success was all but ensured, as in Soviet times, or as an instrument of communicating the message of reform, as during Gorbachev's *perestroika* period. They were used as a means of broadcasting campaign events of the kind tried and tested in capitalist countries, but then still new in the post-Soviet space. Whether Russia's journalists actively supported Boris Yeltsin, or whether they were used as "a fundamental campaign tool," it can be argued that, just five years after the collapse of the Soviet system, journalistic independence—while it had blossomed and flourished in the years after the end of the USSR—had at best altered, at worst disappeared. As almost unquestioning enthusiasm for the new times had evaporated, idealism had given way to pragmatism. Journalistic independence, especially in Bennett's sociopolitical sense of "journalism acting as a watchdog on the government of the day," had been crucially compromised by the experience of the 1996 election (see introduction to this volume).

THE END OF THE YELTSIN ERA, THE DAWN OF THE PUTIN ERA

It was not only journalists who threw their weight behind Boris Yeltsin's reelection campaign. Powerful business tycoons—the "oligarchs" grown rich on the proceeds of Russia's murky sell-off of Soviet state industries[8]—had also become players on the Russian media scene. The owners who "didn't really get involved very much" were now keen to see what kind of influence their media holdings could have. Journalists encountered the constrained reality of working within the new political "freedom." If this was a loss of, or at least a reduction in, journalistic independence it was nevertheless not a return to what had gone before in Soviet times. That had presumably been avoided with the electoral defeat of Gennady Zyuganov, the Communist candidate in the 1996 election. Yet, as Ragozin says of the period:

> I would be cautious about calling it "independent." It was not as independent as the western press is, and even in the West there are issues

with the independence of the press. So it was much freer than in the Soviet times, and most importantly, instead of being controlled by one party, it was controlled by different financial and political groups. So there was a lot of pluralism in the press . . . but it could not really be described as "independent."

In political life, Mr. Yeltsin's victory in the 1996 election did not translate into anything like the popularity he had once enjoyed. He resigned three and a half years later, going on television on New Year's Eve—the last day of the millennium—to announce his unexpected decision. According to the terms of the Russian constitution, the Russian prime minister, Vladimir Putin, became acting president until elections could be held. When they duly were, in March 2000, Mr. Putin's position at the top of Russian politics was consolidated—and he remains at the top today. If Russian journalism's independence had already started to decline during the first Chechen war, and the 1996 presidential election, Mr. Putin's coming to the presidency marked the beginning of a new era of caution. Mr. Putin's critics have argued that he has presided over a decline in freedom of expression. The country report on Russia compiled by the organization *Reporters Without Borders* summarizes some of that criticism:

> Centralized control of the regions, the creation of something close to a one-party system and draconian excesses in the course of combating terrorism are the main features of a government with little tolerance of criticism. Although most of the Russian population gets its news from TV, there is a glaring lack of diversity in the broadcast media. As for the print media, just a few national newspapers led by *Novaya Gazeta* escape control and ensure a minimum of pluralism. Radio *Ekho Moskvy* and *Radio Svoboda*[9] are other examples of independent news outlets.
>
> (Reporters Without Borders 2011)

Although it does go on to note, "At the local level, the situation is more varied" (ibid.). This "glaring lack of diversity" is a far cry from the world Russian journalists say they remember from the 1990s, but to suggest that some kind of new iron curtain descended with Mr. Putin's taking up office in 2000 would be to misrepresent the situation. Even so, there is no doubt it marked a change. Early in the Putin era, Rantanen wrote of the new president's "attack on Russian media" (Rantanen 2002: 135). Trunova argues that editors' response was to draw on their experience of the time before Russian journalism's era of independence in the early 1990s.

> Russians, they've lived through the Soviet times, we can read between the lines, and we can figure things out relatively quickly. So you wouldn't wait and say, "OK, well, we wonder what he's going to be like." You'd

try to figure out what he's going to be like because your life as say a newspaper editor, or a TV editor, would depend on that. And I think what happened is Putin came with his own background—ex-KGB man, ex-military man, and lots of people would immediately adjust to his expectations. So he might not have expressed it immediately—though actually later on he did, on many occasions—but I think at the beginning it was almost like well, we apply that self-censorship just in case and then we'll see how it goes. Well it never went away, really.

Aslamazyan sees 2000 as a turning point—a time when political authority began to reclaim some of the control it had ceded during the first decade of Russia's post-Soviet history.

> There was some hope in the 1990s. Even people were not so much optimistic—but the words of democracy, words of independence, words of the media was not bad words at that time. But since 2000, I would say the government start to take control.

Not surprisingly, she sees this as a time when journalistic independence was further compromised—although not entirely because of the will of the political authorities. Perhaps in the same way that they decided not to criticize Boris Yeltsin as he ran for reelection, journalists working in the Russia of Mr. Yeltsin's successor joined their compatriots in embracing the easier life that came with an improving economy. If the "words of democracy, words of independence," which Aslamazyan remembers as being "not bad" in the 1990s, had not actually become bad, they were laughable. Maybe the excitement that had come with the early post-Soviet period—and the ideals of freedom and independence that had accompanied it—were also too closely associated with hardship and uncertainty. Times had changed, so had attitudes, and so, argues Aslamazyan, had many journalists' attitudes to their independence.

> People start to get better money, and cynicism becomes the most important mood in Russian society. Journalists were infected with this cynicism and the situation about independence—people started to laugh about independence. What does that mean? Independence means be poor, be not influential.

For many Russians, the Putin era did come to be associated with "better money," especially as the revenues from rising oil and gas prices saw consumer goods and foreign travel become more accessible than ever before. Still, the consequences of the aftermath of the collapse of the Soviet Union were still present—in their bloodiest form. From the autumn of 1999, Russia launched a renewed military campaign in Chechnya. The uneasy truce agreed to in 1996 had not settled the region's long-term status. In the late summer of 1999, there was a series of bombings of apartment buildings in Moscow and elsewhere. The attacks caused hundreds of civilian casualties, and, as Service writes, "were blamed on Chechnya. Lessons had been learned. The government closely controlled news reporting" (2003: 541). "Controlled" is also the word I chose to describe the reporting of this conflict when writing of it elsewhere (Rodgers 2012: 32–35), in comparison to coverage of the First War, which I termed "open" to reflect the almost total lack of constraint (save their own sense of danger) under which reporters then found themselves. Then, journalists were free to arrive in the area without special permission. They were free to travel where they wished, to the extent that some even had the rare experience of encountering combatants from opposing sides in the same day. Traveling into Grozny—the region's main city—reporters would encounter Russian troops. In the city center, they met their enemies. A sense of danger, in fact, was the main restriction. Journalists could go as far as they felt the likely coverage merited the risk. In the Second War, access was limited. Special permission was required to report from inside Chechnya itself. This was rarely granted except where journalists were accompanying officials. Reporters, especially foreign ones, seeking to evade the restrictions were sent back whence they came. There were some journalists, most notably Anna Politkovskaya, who still succeeded in providing unforgettable coverage of the conflict. Politkovskaya, though, was an exception—as was the small circulation newspaper, *Novaya Gazeta*, for which she was working. Her work on Chechnya ended when she was shot dead in October 2006. At the time of writing, April 2014, the trial continues of five men charged with involvement in her death. There have been delays due to appeals and changes to the jury.[10] Whoever is or is not finally held responsible, the killers' bullets meant that one of Russian journalism's truly challenging reporters would write no more (Rodgers 2014).

Whatever Mr. Putin's plans for the news media when he came to power, the Russian journalists interviewed for this chapter seem to agree that his time in office has been a time of declining media freedom. Controls have been tightened, with a corresponding reduction in media independence, certainly in the sociopolitical and industrial senses. In response to a question as to whether the journalistic environment had changed since 2000 (when Mr. Putin was first elected president), von Eggert echoed Trunova's observations on self-censorship, and Aslamazyan's on cynicism.

> Very much so. TV—Russia's most important and effective medium—slipped out of the hands of the oligarchs and came under direct or indirect control of the state. The liveliness of the media scene gave way to uniformity, dreariness, and propaganda. Also the government perfected the economic tools of pressuring the media into submission. The outreach of the state bureaucracy is such that it can block advertising for any publication and thus strangle it without a hint of direct censorship. Most journalists know what is and what is not permissible—self-censorship

really rules and is the most effective tool of the government. I myself felt and practiced it. Government and pro-government media spread cynicism as a way of controlling the society, keeping it atomized, fragmented, devoid of civic responsibility and pride. In these circumstances it is hard to convince anyone that there could be honest journalism and honest debate in the society in general.

Such an atmosphere, like the chaotic freedom of the immediate post-Soviet period, had its equivalent in the political sphere. Voters seemed pleased with the prosperity and relative stability over which Mr. Putin presided—the former due in no small part to rising global prices for the oil and gas that Russia possessed in abundance. That is not to say that there were not those who were concerned with the changes they witnessed in, for example, the electoral process. International observers for the Russian presidential election in 2008 either stayed away[11] or expressed concern[12] at what they did see. As Mr. Putin's time in office continued,[13] some forms of political opposition did start to emerge. It took the form of rallies—poorly attended, and with demonstrators sometimes seemingly outnumbered by riot police—which were advertised by the organizers as "March of the Dissenters" (Russian *Marsh nesoglasnykh*). The marchers were a disparate array of those who were dissatisfied with Mr. Putin's administration: everyone from those, such as the former world chess champion, Garry Kasparov—who wanted to see Russia adopt a political system more similar to those of Western democracies—to extremist groups. Among the latter category, the National Bolsheviks, with their curious mixture of right-wing rhetoric and publicity stunts (not to mention their Nazi-like flag, where the hammer and sickle took the place of the swastika, but was still set on a white background surrounded by red), seemed uncomfortable company for Mr. Kasparov and his liberal supporters. The demonstrations achieved little in concrete terms, but incidents such as the arrest of Mr. Kasparov (BBC 2007) did ensure international media coverage. Perhaps, though, the "Marches of the Dissenters" did pave the way for another, larger wave of protest. It was led by Alexey Navalny. Mr. Navalny started as an anti-corruption blogger, and went on to play a central role in demonstrations against alleged irregularities in the conduct of the Russian parliamentary elections in December 2011, "the biggest anti-government rally in Moscow since the fall of communism" (Rosenberg 2011). The movement has also given rise to a kind of journalistic activity. Noting the large number of followers Mr. Navalny has on Twitter, Ragozin says:

Alexey Navalny, the leader of the opposition, has almost half a million followers.[14] And what he does, his investigations of corrupt officials, it is in many ways genuine journalism. It is what Russian journalists don't do, or can't afford to do. But he does it. He breaks a lot of stories. He produces a lot of information. At the same time, he has a very clear anti-Putin agenda. He's the leader of the opposition. So it's all very muddled.

In other words, this is activism, more than it is journalism. In some respects, the movement's journalistic activity is an example of Fuch's description of citizen journalists as "individuals or groups, that are affected by certain problems, become journalists or at least the positive subject of journalism (concerned citizens). Such journalistic practice is frequently part of protest movement practices" (2010: 178). Nor does Mr. Navalny pretend to be a journalist—it is just that, as Ragozin notes, he fulfills some of the roles of one. The key is the way he does it—by clever use of social media. Even a blog on the Web site of the *New York Times*, recounting the story of Mr. Navalny's arrest in 2011, made extensive use of videos uploaded to YouTube, and photographs posted on Twitter (Mackey 2011). It may be also that these platforms of activism offer opportunities for independent journalism unseen in Russia since the days of the 1990s. As Trunova suggests:

> The internet dramatically changed the way Russians consume news. And the Russian internet is a jungle, really. You have everything there, and generally Russians don't believe there are certain images you shouldn't show, they are certainly interested in new technologies and new ways of storytelling.

This is a continuing trend. Denied a platform in the mainstream news media, Russians have long embraced the Internet as a means of expression.[15] As Lonkila noted of a well-known blogging site, "Russian *Livejournal*, in addition to purely personal journals, contained a huge number of politically active communities" (Lonkila 2008: 1141–1142). Although Lonkila's study focused on antimilitary activism, he also made reference (ibid.: 1135) to Kasparov's running an Internet news site as part of his political campaign. It is hard to see how Mr. Navalny could have drawn so many supporters onto the streets of Moscow in 2011 without social media and other Web sites. For von Eggert, these other sources of information present a challenge to the news provided by state TV—Russia's most dominant news medium:

> At the end of Vladimir Putin's second presidential term if something did not exist on TV, it did not exist in life as far as the majority of the public was concerned. But today Internet penetration is such that it impacts agenda setting even by the behemoths of state-controlled TV.

If one of the factors that compromised Russian journalism in the 1990s was, as Aslamazyan noted, the need to make money (one of the challenges of working with freedom), then the Internet may be starting to offer possibilities of financial, as well as editorial, independence. Not only is it having an influence on agenda setting, it is starting to manage to make money doing so. Ragozin points to the example of TV Rain (*"Telekanal Dozhd"*), described by Shaun Walker on *The Guardian* Web site in 2014 as "the favourite source of news for the so-called 'creative class,' who were at the centre of anti-Putin protests that swept Russia two years ago" (Walker 2014).[16] TV Rain charges viewers to access its content through its site. "Monetization actually seems to work," Ragozin says:

> The question now is if other media outlets can monetize themselves, because if they can, it wouldn't really matter whether they are still based in Russia, or whether their offices are based in a slightly more democratic country, somewhere in Latvia, or in Finland, or in Ukraine, so I think internet eventually, the developing monetization of mass media, will actually help to advance the cause of independent or at least more pluralistic journalism in Russia.

"More pluralistic" may be the best to which Russian journalism can aspire. For if the alternative voices are independent only to the extent that they disagree with the mainstream, and exist outside it, it could be argued that what they offer is in fact another kind of dependence. Trunova sees this as an enduring characteristic of Russian reporting. "Russian journalists don't generally believe they need to be neutral. Russian journalists generally believe that as a journalist you are a campaigner, that you really have to push for a certain idea." There are echoes here of Platon and Deuze's description of Indymedia as "not independent in the strictest sense of the word. Often the code and content of the news are made and regulated by people that are, in one way or another, affiliated with many movements providing their own content" (Platon and Deuze 2003: 338).

More recently, Aslamazyan welcomes the openings that the Internet has brought, seeing a "very good opportunity to create good, independent, information flows around the country." However, she adds:

> two things worry me. First of all, if we are talking about journalism, last ten years when they learned how to be very cautious, how to be careful, how to not touch painful questions—this is not easy to recover. There has to be time for a new generation of journalists to come and change the agenda. This is number one. Number two, journalists these years, especially famous journalists, become really rich people. They get good salaries and they . . . learn how to go to all these expensive Moscow restaurants. I am not sure they are ready to lose all these things and start to work without any money. They would like the independence to be really well paid. And this really worries me.

Contemporary Russian journalism, then, is a product of two main trends: the country's recent history, and changes in technology. The same could perhaps be said of any country, but Russia's case is unique because of the massive social and political change it has undergone in the past quarter century. Journalistic independence flourished in the 1990s as never before. The idealism of those days, however, was compromised by Russian journalists' own political sympathies, and by the need to make money. The news media then suffered a collision with the political and commercial ambitions of their oligarch owners. In turn, the oligarchs' grip was loosened by the more powerful political class of the Putin era. There are now, in the digital age, opportunities for journalistic independence to flourish anew. That does not mean that the future is unquestionably bright. The instability in Ukraine before and after President Viktor Yanukovych's flight from the country in early 2014 has had repercussions in Russia, too—not least for the news media. With the authorities perhaps encouraged by President Putin's spectacularly high approval ratings following Russia's annexation of Crimea—in March, the *Washington Post* cited research by the respected Levada Centre suggesting that these had reached 80 percent—critics of the administration found themselves in trouble. TV Rain, which had already found itself in trouble in January over an opinion poll deemed unpatriotic (see Walker 2014), faced further challenges as the crisis in Ukraine continued to unfold. Its deputy editor, Tikhon Dzyadko, even went so far as to write in April, "In this system, there is no room for independent media groups like Rain, or for me and my colleagues" (Dzyadko 2014). Ragozin, writing in March for the Web site of the New Republic, described "government propaganda, whose main target these days is the 'fifth column': journalists, opposition activists, and anyone else who dares to doubt the wisdom of President Vladimir Putin's decision to send troops into Ukraine" (Ragozin 2014). In February, Alexei Navalny was placed under house arrest, and banned from using the Internet—although, as the BBC reported, his Twitter account continued to be "managed by assistants" (BBC 2014a). Formally, the sanction was the consequence of an earlier case—but in Navalny's view, and doubtless in that of many of his supporters, "the accusations against him are politically motivated" (ibid.). There was an echo, too, of the fate of the more challenging voices of 1990s television noted by von Eggert. The Russian social networking site VKontakte was, according to its founder, Pavel Durov, taken under the "complete control" (BBC 2014b) of allies of Mr. Putin. Durov remained defiant in apparent defeat. "We did a lot. And part of what's been done can't be turned back" (ibid.). How big that part turns out to be will probably, as in Russian journalism's entire post-Soviet history, depend on the political climate. Yet whether independent journalism expands or contracts, is encouraged or suppressed, the fact that it exists at all shows that something fundamental has changed since the end of the USSR.

NOTES

1. This line is often translated, for example on the Marxists.org Web site (www.marxists.org/history/ussr/sounds/lyrics/anthem.htm, accessed March 4, 2014), as "Unbreakable Union of freeborn Republics," but this is presumably in order to make the translation scan with the music. I have preferred "indestructible" for the Russian "nerushimy" and the simple "free" for "svobodny(kh)."
2. June 12 is a public holiday in Russia, officially described as "Russia's Independence Day," which commemorates the adoption in 1991 of the Declaration of

Sovereignty of the Russian Federation (Embassy of the Russian Federation to the United Kingdom 2013).

3. This, and all subsequent citations from Ragozin, come from an interview conducted by Skype between Moscow and London on November 11, 2013.
4. This, and all subsequent citations from Trunova, comes from an interview conducted in London on November 14, 2013.
5. This citation, and all subsequent citations from von Eggert, comes from an e-mail interview dated November 18, 2013.
6. This citation, and all subsequent citations from Aslamazyan, comes from an interview conducted via Skype between London and Yerevan on November 13, 2013.
7. Many Stalinist/Russian Nationalist demonstrators in the 1990s used anti-Semitic insults against those of whom they did not approve. I remember, on at least one occasion, such abuse being directed at Western journalists covering a nationalist march. It did not seem to matter whether the targets of the abuse were themselves Jewish or not.
8. For a comprehensive account of the privatization of former Soviet state assets, see Freeland 2005.
9. Reporters Without Borders' decision to give *Radio Svoboda* as an example of an "independent news outlet" seems questionable. The station is the Russian language service of Radio Free Europe, which is funded by the U.S. Congress (Radio Free Europe/Radio Liberty 2013).
10. See, for example, RIA Novosti, "Five Jurors Dismissed from Politkovskaya Trial," first published January 27, 2014, http://en.ria.ru/crime/20140127/186954003/Five-Jurors-Dismissed-from-Politkovskaya-Trial.html (accessed March 7, 2014).
11. For example, observers from the Organization for Security and Cooperation in Europe (OSCE)'s Office for Democratic Institutions and Human Rights (ODIHR) (Organization for Security and Co-operation in Europe 2008).
12. In the case of the Parliamentary Assembly for the Council of Europe (Parliamentary Assembly for the Council of Europe 2008).
13. Mr. Putin served two terms as president from 2000 to 2008, then, not permitted by the Russian constitution to serve a third consecutive term, became prime minister from 2008 to 2012, when he returned to the presidency—his political protégé Dmitry Medvedev having been president in the meantime.
14. 426,594, according to his Twitter profile on November 27, 2013. The number continued to grow. On March 4, 2014, it was 571,496.
15. Internet access continues to grow. A survey published in spring 2013 by Yandex, a leading Russian Internet portal, suggested that Internet access in the country as a whole had passed 50 percent, with the figure more than 70 percent in both Moscow and St. Petersburg (Yandex 2013).
16. That is, those led by Alexy Navalny. TV Rain fell afoul of the authorities in January 2014 as a result of a poll, which its critics deemed unpatriotic, about Leningrad during the Second World War (Walker 2014).

REFERENCES

Adamovich, A. (1990) "Look about you!," in V. Korotoich and C. Porter (eds.), *The Best of Ogonyok*, 7–14. London: Heinemann.
BBC. (2007) "Kasparov arrested at Moscow rally," *BBC News*. Available http: http://news.bbc.co.uk/1/hi/world/europe/6554989.stm (accessed November 25, 2013).

BBC. (2014a) "Russia opposition leader Alexei Navalny fined for libel," *BBC News* April 22, 2014. Available http: www.bbc.co.uk/news/world-europe-27114436 (accessed April 24, 2014).

BBC. (2014b) "Russian social network founder says he has been fired," *BBC News* April 22, 2014. Available http: www.bbc.co.uk/news/technology-27113292 (accessed April 24, 2014).

Dzyadko, T. (2014) "Triumph of the will: Putin's war against Russia's last independent TV channel," *The Guardian* April 10, 2014. Available http: www.theguardian. com/commentisfree/2014/apr/10/putin-war-dozhd-russias-last-independent-tv-channel#start-of-comments (accessed April 24, 2014).

Embassy of the Russian Federation to the United Kingdom. (2013) *Embassy of the Russian Federation to the United Kingdom.* Available http: www.rusemblon.org/russiaholiday/ (accessed November 7, 2013).

Freeland, C. (2005) *Sale of the Century.* London: Abacus.

Fuchs, C. (2010) "Alternative media as critical media," *European Journal of Social Theory* 13, 2: 173–192.

Internews. (2013) *Internews.* Available http: www.internews.eu/About-Us/ (accessed November 15, 2013).

Lonkila, M. (2008) "The Internet and anti-military activism in Russia," *Europe-Asia Studies* 60, 7: 1125–1149.

Mackey, R. (2011) "Chants of 'Putin's a thief!' ring out in Moscow," *New York Times* May 12, 2011. Available http: http://thelede.blogs.nytimes.com/2011/12/05/chants-of-putins-a-thief-ring-out-in-moscow/ (accessed November 25, 2013).

McNair, Brian. (1991) *Glasnost, Perestroika and the Soviet Media.* London: Routledge.

Organization for Security and Co-operation in Europe. (2008) *OSCE/ODIHR regrets that restrictions force cancellation of election observation mission to Russian Federation.* www.osce.org/odihr/elections/49438 (accessed November 2013, 2013).

Parliamentary Assembly for the Council of Europe. (2008) *PACE pre-election delegation concerned by limited choice in Russian Presidential election.* www.assembly.coe.int/ASP/Press/StopPressView.asp?ID=2008 (accessed November 25, 2013).

Platon, S. and Deuze, M. (2003) "Indymedia journalism: A radical way of making, selecting and sharing news?," *Journalism* 4, 3: 336–355.

Radio Free Europe/Radio Liberty. (2013). *Frequently Asked Questions.* www.rferl.org/info/faq/777.html (accessed November 27, 2013).

Ragozin, L. (2014) "Putin is cracking down on media exactly when we're desperate for answers," *New Republic* March 13, 2014. Available http: www.newrepublic.com/article/117001/russias-putin-cracks-down-media-when-we-need-journalism-most (accessed April 24, 2014).

Rantanen, T. (2002) *The Global and the National: Media and Communications in Post-Communist Russia.* Oxford: Rowman and Littlefield.

Rantanen, T. and Vartanova, E. (2003) "Media in contemporary Russia," in N. Couldry and J. Curran (eds.), *Contesting Media Power: Alternative Media in a Networked World*, 147–160. Maryland: Rowman & Littlefield Publishers.

Reporters Without Borders. (2011) *Reporters Without Borders: Russia.* Available http: http://en.rsf.org/report-russia,131.html (accessed November 20, 2013).

Rodgers, J. (2012) *Reporting Conflict.* Basingstoke: Palgrave MacMillan.

Rodgers, J. (2014) "From Stalingrad to Grozny: Patriotism, political pressure, and literature in the war reporting of Vassily Grossman and Anna Politkovskaya," *Media, War and Conflict* 7, 1: 23–36.

Rosenberg, S. (2011) "Mass protests in Russia put Putin under pressure," *BBC News.* Available http: www.bbc.co.uk/news/world-europe-16135999 (accessed November 25, 2013).

Service, R. (2003) *A History of Modern Russia.* London: Penguin.

Silverstone, R. (2007) *Media and Morality: On the Rise of the Mediapolis.* Cambridge: Polity.

Walker, S. (2014) "Russian cable news channel TV Rain under threat after 'political attack,'" *The Guardian* January 29, 2014. Available http: www.theguardian.com/world/2014/jan/29/russia-news-channel-tv-rain-under-threat (accessed March 7, 2014).

Yandex. (2013) *Development of the Internet in Russia's Regions.* Available http: http://download.yandex.ru/company/ya_russian_regions_report_2013.pdf (accessed March 7, 2014).

Zassoursky, I. (2004) *Media and Power in Post-Soviet Russia.* Armonk, NY: M. E. Sharpe.

11 Independence within the Boundaries

State Control and Strategies of Chinese Television for Freedom

Anthony Fung, Xiaoxiao Zhang and Luzhou Li

The condition for independence varies in different contexts, within which independent media might accordingly be reified differently. In the Chinese politico-economic context, all broadcast media are state owned and heavy-handedly managed by the State Administration of Radio, Film and Television (SARFT). However, this does not mean that Chinese television producers have no autonomy or freedom to produce programs of different genres, with diversity in content and plurality in opinion. Analyzed in this chapter are concrete strategies that China's regional/municipal television stations design to bypass, negotiate or even mildly challenge the state control. Drawing on previous research that explored the state control and the strategic responses of regional television stations in China (Zhang and Fung 2011), our research methods include archival analysis of SARFT documents, textual analysis of programs and analysis of trade press interviews with producers. The first method examines the control from the party-state, while the latter two examine the various independence strategies from Chinese television producers.

This chapter will start with a historical description of the reforms and commercialization of the television industry, which legitimized the endeavor of Chinese producers to pursue certain forms of independence in the nonpolitical region. In return, the gradually increased independence contributed to transforming the once outmoded propaganda machines into profitable cultural industries. We will identify three prominent processes in which China's television industry could produce content that has some degree of independence. First, entertainment-disguised production, especially popular television dramas, is the most common tactic in which social controversies have been incorporated into the themes of contemporary television dramas, where audiences can derive pleasure from reading the mediated or "happy" endings of the drama as if they could solve the unresolved problems in reality. Second, communal production offers mainly variety shows in which participants at their crossroads can raise themselves out of their own personal paradoxes, which meanwhile reveal bigger social contradictions in front of the television audience. Third, some regional television stations could politicize issues by producing programs that highlight their regional social needs, and quite often the latter could be seen as a higher principle to override any political hassles—such as provoking political controversies around sensitive issues, like gender and ethnicity (discussed further later in this chapter).

However, all these struggles for independence do not mean that television stations openly defy state command. In fact, ironically for Chinese television stations, showing submissiveness in rhetorical terms is a way to gain, rather than to undermine, media independence. Thus, while television stations still largely implement media policies of the state, for some programs, they could exercise these three strategies for gaining some momentary media independence. Besides, the pursuit for such independence is uneven across different media. Documentary and films produced by private independent production houses or producers can be more autonomous. For instance, Chinese independent filmmaking emerging in the early 1990s, which at the time was part of the Chinese independent productions that started to produce documentaries in the late 1980s, operated independently of the national system of cultural production and state distribution networks (e.g., being exhibited overseas without official approval and perhaps even with official protests), thereby enjoying higher degrees of autonomy (Zhang 2004). Meanwhile, documentaries might be less independent in terms of industrial formation, as most independent documentary makers are simultaneously producers working for state-owned television stations who moonlight outside their *danwei*—a work unit in state-owned enterprises (Jones 1992)—to make extra money for documentary productions. However, if "independence" here is understood beyond the *industrial* level—that is, at the levels of aesthetic codes, sociopolitical functions or discursive formations as Bennett sets out in the introduction to this volume—documentaries and independent films represent the similar forms of "media independence." Thus, compared with the general television situation, independent documentaries and films are more autonomous in pursuing media independence. But for state-owned television, regional television stations more readily implement these three processes.

The strategies discussed here suggest the possibilities for media outlets to churn out greater content diversity and occasionally push for a wider marketplace of ideas. More importantly, they could also sustain a large pool of passionate and educated media personnel who always look for a greater degree of media freedom. They might not be influential now. But they will be in times to come.

HISTORY OF COMMERCIALIZATION IN THE CHINESE TELEVISION INDUSTRY

The Chinese leadership under Deng Xiaoping announced the "reform and opening up" of the country and built its initial contact with the outside world in 1978. We may never know for sure whether the reform was simply a desperate move of the Communist Party to maintain its political legitimacy or Deng was all along a secret "capitalist roader," as Harvey (2005) commented, but the reform just happened to coincide with the global neoliberal turn. Media reform kicked off in the late 1970s and has been an integral part of the market turn. With the officially encouraged reform project, many state-affiliated media and cultural institutions including state-owned television stations ceased to enjoy governmental subsidies and had to achieve financial self-reliance by the early and mid-1980s. Major sources of financing included advertising, sponsorship and business operations in other areas (Zhao 1998). Catering to popular tastes that did not always follow official prescriptions so as to attract advertisers and sponsors became an important goal for many of these institutions, including television (Baranovitch 2003).

While Chinese media reform was said to begin in the late 1970s, the substantial commercialization in fact took place since the 1990s, especially during the decade since the mid-1990s (Hong, Lu and Zou 2009). Entering the 1990s, commercialization became a convenient option appropriated to fill the ideological vacuum immediately following the crackdown on the Tiananmen democracy movement. The radical commercialization of Chinese society and culture in the 1990s was not only the result of the government's attempt to divert public attention from the political to the economic, but also a local instance of the neoliberal global order in the post–Cold War era (Baranovitch 2003). In broadcasting, as Zhao (2008) documents, provincial television stations began to set up marketed-oriented specialty television channels focusing on entertainment, business, lifestyle, sports and others to lure audiences for an expanding advertising market, and the spread of cable television in the late 1980s and early 1990s created another wave of channel multiplication. By the late 1990s, all provinces in the country had sent their major television channels to a national audience through direct broadcast satellite systems. This move challenged the monopoly of Chinese Central Television (CCTV) in the national television market and also intensified the competition among provincial television stations for programming, audiences and advertising revenues. The increasingly intensified competition has led to the rise of popular entertainment (Wu 2000, as cited in Chan 2003). Thus in the early 2000s, reality television shows captivated Chinese audiences alongside television drama. Often inspired by foreign television formats, reality television provided a cheap alternative to television drama in filling the extended broadcast schedule in the new multichannel environment (Hill 2005; Zhu 2008). The officially sanctioned marketization of television, to a large extent, legitimizes producers' pursuits of certain degrees of autonomy, or so-called independence, in relatively less politically sensitive arenas. Often they pick up the most socially relatable and even debatable topics and transform them into televisual discourses in the hope of attracting the widest possible audience.

The profit-making activities of state television stations have also become the primary mechanisms through which domestic private capital expands its operation in the media and cultural sectors (Zhao 2008). Starting around the mid-1990s, as certain television stations experimented to spin off and corporatize their program productions, some television producers began leaving the state enterprise and started their own businesses in cultural production in the hope of becoming richer and gaining more creativity and autonomy (Lu 2005). There has been a proliferation of private media and cultural production companies since the mid-1990s. Being intricately linked and intertwined with state televisions stations, these companies have innovated various genres of entertainment programming, thereby largely reorienting Chinese television toward mass entertainment. The consequence, then, is that the need for the television stations to turn to the mass market might in fact be oppositional to the state's stringent media policy and political agenda at times. The phenomenon of a sporadic and sudden hype of a Chinese television program, which is not in line with the state agenda, can therefore be understood as a form of independence in Chinese television.

Despite all these market-oriented operations, it is noteworthy that Chinese television is still strictly controlled by the party-state without real privatization. Rather than privatizing existing party-state media outlets or liberalizing entry to transnational and domestic private capital from the outset, the party-state has led and dominated the process of commercialization, incorporating foreign and domestic private capital within the existing structure (Zhao 2008). So, while private capital in media and cultural production is proliferating, the state monopolization of broadcasting outlets determines the reality that almost all private television production companies have different levels of cooperation with the state television stations (Lu 2005). This institutional arrangement constitutes the major control mechanism that ensures the political orientations of private cultural productions. The story of private television production companies tells us that the party's adherence to the socialist legacy of using popular culture and media to serve the politics never wanes. While the party-state allows its affiliated television stations to embrace the market for capital accumulation, it still closely regulates their productions to promote socialist morality so as to maintain political stability. This constant negotiation and compromise between the state and the media results in many hybrid and "co-opted" forms of media programs with the minimum political baseline that it would not undermine the legitimacy of the party-state.

For the party-state, political obligations of the state television station should override its market calculations. This principle is clearly stated by SARFT (2007):

> Cultural products are special commodities with distinct ideological attributes . . . When economic interests contradict social interests, [we] must be subordinated to social interests unconditionally. . . . If we pursue [only] the audience rating and the economic revenue . . . we will make political and directional mistakes [that] jeopardize the state.

Following this, there has been an established control mechanism over television from preproduction (topic approval, etc.) to postproduction censorship. SARFT would also issue ad hoc administrative orders (re-editing, rescheduling, banning etc.) to constantly monitor the screen (Zhao 2008). In line with its political objective, the authority also imposes control mechanisms over provincial and regional commercial television stations so as to protect the financial interests of the national station CCTV. The spread of satellite technology that enables provincial television channels to go national makes such political interventions imperative. In October 2011, SARFT issued a so-called restraining entertainment order to limit the excessive commercial developments of the country's thirty-four satellite channels. Moreover, it reemphasized that each channel must have one program that promotes socialist core values on its current programming, despite that in reality many channels already had such shows (SARFT 2012). Through this order, SARFT prevented provincial television stations from bold economic pursuits based entirely on audience ratings, and simultaneously protected interests of the national CCTV.

Within this political culture, it is worthwhile asking what kind of pragmatic strategies would producers come up with should the political responsibilities of television stations happen to contradict their economic interests? Will they find some loopholes or means to bypass political control? In the following section, we identify and discuss three scenarios in which provincial television stations could strategically pursue autonomy in production as a form of creative and political freedom and independence from state control.

INDEPENDENCE AS ENTERTAINMENT IN DISGUISE

Among the many forms of agency in production practices that can negotiate political control, one is to transform social controversies and popular concerns into entertainment-disguised productions, particularly television dramas. Compared with news and current affairs programming, television dramas as a fictional "producerly text" (Fiske 1987: 95) are endowed with more flexibility in playing with the difference between the representation and the real, thereby giving producers more room to maneuver socially controversial topics. In the past decade, television drama in China has covered a wide range of hot social topics emerging with deepened marketization, from marriage/relationship problems in the private domain to power struggles, layoffs and corruption in the public domain, all of which contribute to the highly dynamic and diverse character of Chinese television discourses (Zhao 2008).

An earlier example of this strategy was costume dramas, particularly those set in the Qing dynasty, or what Zhu (2005) termed "Qing dramas." Qing dramas began appearing on Chinese television in the late 1980s, with a focus on the corruption and cultural decline of the late Qing, and experienced another wave of popularity in the late 1990s and the early 2000s, with a focus shifting to feature emperors and patriots who served the nation afflicted by political corruption, social injustice and external threats (Zhu 2005). These dramas, as exemplified by *Yongzheng Dynasty* (*Yongzheng Wangchao*), broached such sensitive subjects as political corruption, social unrest and moral cynicism, which mirrored contemporary Chinese society and would otherwise have not been approved if set in present-day China (Zhu 2005).

Television dramas about ancient court politics are a more recent attempt to address topics in current politics, whilst packaging themselves in a remote historical setting. Unlike their predecessors such as the Qing dramas that focused on national politics, the recent revisions are structured around interpersonal power struggles at the royal court. Court politics dramas began to receive popularity in Mainland China in 2010 with the production of *Palace* (*Gong*) and climaxed in 2012 with *The Legend of Zhen Huan* (*Hougong Zhen Huan Zhuan*). Produced by Hunan ETV Culture Media Company, a production unit affiliated to the provincial Hunan Economic Television, and aired on Hunan Satellite Television, *Gong* narrates the story of Luo Qingchuan, a modern girl who travels back to Emperor Kangxi's period of the Qing dynasty and is embroiled in the princes' fight over the throne. Beginning with a series of calculated tricks against the innocent crown prince, which eventually lead to his fall, the drama mainly centers on the antagonism between Yin Si, the eighth prince, and Yin Zhen, the fourth prince and the future Emperor Yong Zheng, between whom Luo is torn. Caught in the web of intrigue, conspiracy and political witch-hunting, Luo relies on her wit and knowledge of history to stay alive and play safe. As the producer Yu Zheng reveals,[1] the drama mainly intends to cultivate the process of how modern people survived in ancient times, which is constructed as one replete with deceptions and rivalries in the drama and is seen by Luo as filthier than textbooks. Therefore, it is a story of control and survival in complex social lives in nature. This theme was quickly picked up by audiences as their interpretations of how this drama speaks to modern workplace survival and success began to circulate online. For instance, the audience Mo Ran read five unwritten rules in the workplace out of the drama:[2]

> *Gong* is apparently not a serious production, but it contains fairly useful strategies for workplace survival. There is always politics in human society, and Chinese society is precisely known for its large population and interpersonal politics. *Gong* is about workplace politics. For instance, how did Qingchuan transform from an unsophisticated and often bullied girl to a competent and smooth one at the royal court? In contrary, why did the eighth prince, nicknamed Prince Sage, piss Kangxi, the big boss, off?

Therefore, while court political dramas like *Gong* are set in ancient times, their representations of experiences in rationalizing resources and maximizing profits in complicated power relations seem allusive to contemporary China, where neoliberal subjectivities that constantly make calculative choices about risks and interventions for techno-optimization (Ong 2006) are proliferating with the unfolding market reform in, but not limited to, the workplace. The wide popularity of this television drama genre demonstrates that it indeed arouses sympathy among audiences.[3] To some extent, these implicit neoliberal discourses might create and articulate a new kind of subjectivity that conflicts with the socialist moralities and Confucian virtues the state authority has been diligently promoting, thereby constituting a disruption to current forms of political and cultural control. However, its realistic implications are somehow mediated by its historical setting. In the case of *Gong*, the time-traveling elements further reinforce the fictional nature of the drama and bring a frivolous sense to it. It is evident to the general public that this kind of drama is just entertainment, which, as the audience Mo Ran perceived, is not "serious production." The reduced seriousness or plausibility exempts television stations and producers from potential political and moral charges of showcasing the dark side of human nature. This is the strategy the producer used in striking a balance between rhetorical independence and the performance of subservience. And this strategy was approved to be politically safe, at least temporarily. Although SARFT didn't publicly approve or encourage this kind of production, the subsequent productions of other court politics dramas inspired by the spectacular success of *Gong* and their popularity indeed implied the existence of official acquiescence for a period of time, although later SARFT tightened its control over this kind of production as dramas of the same type ran out of control and caused concerns about the vulgarization from the authority, discussed further in the conclusion.[4]

The operation of this strategy, like the other strategies we discuss, represents an experience of working with constrained freedom for media practitioners in China, which was described by a journalist as "dancing in shackles" (He 2004, as cited in Shirk 2011: 4). This metaphor vividly describes a state of being creative while simultaneously being circumscribed. This process embodies mixed feelings of both enjoyment and helplessness. From a Foucauldian perspective, this is also a process in which individual producers who are informed by neoliberal rationality in their freedom use certain strategies in dealing with political control while at the same time pursuing audiences. In this sense, what is happening within media institutions is part of the neoliberal sociocultural practices that the drama *Gong* is both constituted by and constitutive of.

Likewise, while the medical drama *Xin Shu* (*Angel Heart*)—which builds a plot around two neurosurgeons caught between public duties and private life—tries to speak to the mainstream melody by promoting medical ethics and moral codes in the practice of medicine, it often smuggles in social critiques against the health care system in China by representing the tension between doctors and patients. For instance, the drama begins with an intense scene in which the surgeon decides to operate on a patient who is severely injured in a car accident without the endorsement of the families. While the operation is successful, the patient eventually dies from a heart attack. The son of the dead patient sues the surgeon for compensation. In the drama, this medical incident is played up in mass media (as it would in reality), which eventually leads to the loss of reputation and job for the surgeon. This narrative realistically represents the deteriorating doctor-patient relationship in China, which thus appears to be intriguing to audiences. In this way, television dramas disguised as popular entertainment serve as a relatively safe site to play out ongoing contestations around sensitive social issues.

COMMUNAL PRODUCTION

The second strategy in revealing social controversies so as to pursue audience ratings is realized in communal productions in which ordinary people perform clearly defined roles (contestants, voters etc.) in the program and articulate personal experiences or viewpoints, which often sparks heated public reaction. Audience participation in the mass media has been documented extensively at the level of live broadcasting, notably in talk radio and television talk shows (Giles 2002). The global popularity of the various subgenres (quiz shows, idol show, "docusoaps" etc.) that derived from reality television in the past decade has created another wave of audience participation in television. In China, the participatory nature of such programming is strategically exploited by provincial television stations to mediate popular concerns. For instance, the currently widely popular reality dating show *If You Are the One* (*Feicheng Wurao*), which closely resembles the format of the British television show *Take Me Out*, successfully managed to elicit social debates through controversial speeches of a female contestant in one episode when it was launched at the beginning of 2010.

Produced by and aired on Jiangsu Satellite Television, *If You Are the One* outmaneuvered its traditional counterparts by sophisticated production, innovated devices of voting off and elimination, typical components of beauty pageants, inclusion of "docuvideo," flirt talks and so forth. The show features a single man who attempts to "win" a date with one of the twenty-four single women. In the show, female participants stand behind flashy podiums attached with numbers, facing a parade of eligible bachelors. In each segment, the bachelor presented has to go through three intrusive rounds of questioning from both the host and female participants. In each round, a video clip revealing the personal information of the bachelor such as education, occupation, interests, dating history and friends' opinions is shown, and conversations between the host, psychological analysts and the show participants ensues. Female participants could vote the bachelor off in any one of the three rounds by turning the light off. So, not all bachelors could finish all three rounds. If more than two lights remain on after three rounds of interrogations, the bachelor would reverse the situation to choose from the remaining women, or just give up.

These features are not all that account for its unusual market success. Controversial contestants and speeches from the show further increase its popularity among Chinese people. The episode we discuss here featured a dramatic conflict between a financially insecure bachelor, Zhao Chen, and one of the female contestants, Ma Nuo (henceforth Ma): When Zhao asked female contestants "would you like to go for a bike ride with me in the future?" Ma answered back: "I'd rather weep in a BMW." This sensational and caustic rejection immediately stirred wide debates across various media platforms on relationships and money, including influential discussion forums such as MOP, Tianya Club and Baidu Post. It was also picked up by domestic mainstream media such as CCTV, *West China City News* and *China Youth Daily*, and international media such as the *New York Times* and *Time* magazine. Some people figured that Ma exemplified the typical material girl in a materialistic society who only dated rich people. In the eyes of others, however, Ma was outspoken and brave, voicing what many women think publicly.

This episode apparently touched a raw nerve of a society in which relationship and marriage have become a chance for upward social mobility. Young Chinese women—as disciplined historical subjects who are made aware of their values by force of complicated social and economic relations (single-child policy, unaffordable housing etc.)—are getting increasingly realistic, both by *choice* and under compulsion, expecting their significant other to have at least a house, a car and a stable yet high income. The show intended to dramatize these trenchant social problems (houses, kids, relationships between mothers-in-law and daughters-in-law etc.) that many urban Chinese are grappling with in marriage and relationships. In the words of producer Wang Gang, while it was an entertainment show, it attempted to "serve at the right point."[5] Therefore, sharp dialogues and incisive comments on serious issues by contestants became a feature of the show, as Wang Peijie, the vice director of Jiangsu Satellite Television who participated in the design and production of the show from beginning to end, told the *New York Times*: "We hoped there would be some clashes between different ideas" (Wong 2011).

However, it did so strategically through the program's contestants. As Ma became the target of public opinions, she claimed in an interview with the *New York Times* that the producer asked women contestants not to spare the dignity of the bachelors (Wong 2011). She said: "Because they saw that I was outspoken, they wanted me to say more controversial things" (ibid.). Meanwhile, although constantly denied by Jiangsu Satellite Television, rumors about the show recruiting contestants from entertainment agencies and making up life stories persisted. There is no way to exactly know to what extent the show is artificial. As one commentator put it, "Asking a producer to describe manipulation is like asking a fish to describe an aquarium" (quoted in Gill 2007: 152). The growing appeal of reality programming has raised the question of its authenticity. Thompson has viewed such programming as resembling "the dramaturgical equivalent of jazz: a controlled structure that invites improvisation and unpredictability" (2001: 22). So there are reasons to believe that producers at least set the tone for the show's contestants. Otherwise, as Ma asked in another interview with *Yangcheng Evening Newspaper* when she tried to defend herself against the overwhelming criticism, "why didn't they cut this part before broadcasting if they really thought what I said was challenging to social morality?" (Xiao 2010). While it was the intent of the producer to touch socially controversial topics, he talked about them through Ma's mouth, thereby constructing and delivering a sense of authenticity, which, judging from the development of the event, was well received by the audience.

There have been many studies addressing how audiences perceive reality versus fiction in reality programming. Papacharissi and Mendelson (2007) found that most people watch reality television for habitual pass time and entertainment and those who enjoy reality television for relaxing also tend to perceive the meticulously edited and preplanned content of *reality* interaction as realistic. The overwhelming focus on Ma, instead of the television station, in the case of *If You Are the One*, provided additional empirical evidence to this conclusion. The *realness* of the show perceived by the audience circumscribed the tension between audiences and Ma. In this way, the television station successfully revealed social controversies through Ma without being accused of promoting inappropriate social values such as dating for money. As producer Wang Gang said, "we don't deliberately advocate anything, but the design of the show will *naturally* [emphasis ours] let audiences know what people today are thinking about relationship and marriage."[6]

So the producers mobilized this strategy to rhetorically balance independence and subservience. If we move beyond the rhetorical/discursive level, we can see that the development of this strategy was also a process in which the producer negotiated creativity with political constraints. As Wang Peijie said, "The most important thing in making reality shows is [political] safety. . . . To SARFT, what they try to regulate is not this or that forms or format, but the content. However, a lot of content is attached to the form, so we will have to ensure it is [politically] safe." So, in the Chinese context, working with freedom never means freedom without borders for media practitioners. And, ironically, political subservience can be the premise for more creativity and autonomy.

Similar strategies are found in many other subgenres of reality programming. For instance, in confessional and therapeutic shows that focus on personal problems and dilemmas (destructive relationship, threatened marriage, familial trauma etc.), the morally provoking private and emotional matters narrated by the guest in front of national audiences often reveal the transformation of social relations and social contradictions growing out of this process, and constitute challenges to existing hegemonic values. Prominent examples include *Xing Fu Mo Fang* (*Bliss Cube*) produced by Shanghai Oriental Satellite TV, *Ren Jian* (*The World*) produced by Jiangsu Satellite TV and *Zhen Qing* (*True Hearts*) produced by Hunan Satellite TV. While these shows promise certain sociopolitical functions, the spectacle of personal paradoxes and emotional conflicts mainly involves rhetorical contestations among different social agents, thereby diverting potential political attention away from television stations.

REGIONAL NEEDS

Although the Chinese TV industry has undergone the commercialization and entertainment-ization processes, propaganda agenda and ideological safety are still the main principles that the Chinese broadcasters must stick to, particularly in television journalism. For instance, while private provision of television dramas and entertainment programming is allowed, that of news and current affairs is forbidden (Zhao 2008), which means that the state still retains quite a strong ideological grip over television journalism. In this context, some regional television stations politicize issues by producing programs that highlight their regional social needs, and quite often the latter could be seen as a higher principle to override any political hassles. In so doing, these stations actually proclaim that they care about people's needs first and foremost. As "coming from the masses and going to the masses" (*Cong qunzhong zhong lai, dao qunzhong zhong qu*) is the tenet proposed by the Chinese Communist Party (CCP), emphasizing the regional needs of local people is accordingly quite legitimate. Thus, many local news programs are prosperous in China and popular among audiences, such as *Najing Ling Juli* (*Zero Distance to Nanjing*).

Najing Ling Juli is a live daily news program broadcast since 2002 by the City Channel of Jiangsu Broadcasting Corporation. Focusing on local issues of Nanjing, the capital of Jiangsu Province, the mission of the program is "reporting Nanjing, serving Nanjing, and promoting Nanjing." It achieved the highest rating in Nanjing within nine months after its initial broadcast and produced an advertising revenue of ¥1.008 hundred million RMB (nearly $17 million USD) in 2004 (Baidu 2013). The success was striking given that its broadcaster, City Channel, is not relayed via satellite, which means that it creates a high rating and advertising revenue simply based on local audiences instead of national ones. *Nanjing Ling Juli* gets its fame not only for its close attention to the needs of local people but also from its critical angle, which is the main reason for the program's popularity among its audiences. The critical perspective and subversive potential of the program were noticed and discussed online by audiences. One audience member, with the NetID of mltr, pointed out that "unlike *Xinwen Lianbo*, it is impossible for *Nanjing Ling Juli* to sing the praise everyday and present a false appearance of peace and prosperity. Its presence and reports subvert the traditional (Chinese) model of news reporting."[7] Another audience, with the NetID of tianyawyjiayou, regarded *Nanjing Ling Juli* as "one of the most critical programs in Mainland China."[8] It is noteworthy that Chinese academia remains silent on the program's subversive nature, although there are more than seventy academic articles focusing on *Nanjing Ling Juli*.[9] These papers mainly discuss how *Nanjing Ling Juli* did a good job in reporting civic news and keeping close to audiences (for example, Li and Jing 2003; Qiao 2008). On the other hand, *Nanjing Ling Juli* may not want academics to shed light on its critical spirit either. Being a civic news program mainly attentive to regional social needs is a safe position for the Chinese producers, instead of being famous for critical reports. To step outside this safety could be costly, as the program's host, Meng Fei, found when he was forced to leave the program because of what many speculated was too much criticism of the government when discussing regional social problems.[10]

Nanjing Ling Juli is not unique in the Chinese media system, and there are many other types of media content highlighting regional needs of local the populace. *Huaxi Dushibao* (*West China City News*) is a similar kind of commercial newspaper. Established in Chengdu, Sichuan Province, one of the largest cities in southwest China, *Huaxi Dushibao* is famed for serving urban grassroots audiences with timely local news related to people's daily life (Huang, Davis and Knight 2002). As the editor in chief of the newspaper, Xi Wenju, explained, the target readers of the newspaper are middle-and-lower-level urban residents instead of elites (ibid.). Instead of serving as the Party/state apparatus, the newspaper covers news pertinent to people's everyday life, such as families, education, medical care and so forth. With this orientation, the newspaper has achieved great market success since its launch in 1995 (ibid.).

For innovative local news programs like *Nanjing Ling Juli*, eliciting government support is the key. While emphasizing regional social needs could be used as a pretext to explore media independence, producers still need to rhetorically balance media independence with political subservience. To do so, the former producer of the program and now the director of City Channel, Zhang Jiangeng, said that:

> For the topics of news, we can make a distinction between "positive topics" and "negative topics." For instance, car accidents, fire accidents, and fighting incidents are all "negative topics." . . . For negative topics, as long as we frame it in a socially positive way, it can create positive social impacts.[11]

This is the rhetorical strategy the producer uses in experimenting with innovations within state media. Similarly to the other strategies discussed in this chapter, the priority placed on regional needs by some producers creates a working experience of greater autonomy and freedom for those producers working inside the Chinese media than first appears possible.

In a country well known for stifling media independence despite its increasing economic liberalization (Hassid 2008; Nhan 2008), the Chinese media system has witnessed a move from totalitarianism to market authoritarianism, which still has to follow the party line and cannot cross the bottom line (Winfield and Peng 2005). Programs like *Nanjing Ling Juli* are cases in point of falling in the "outer circles" (Winfield and Peng 2005: 261) of the Chinese media system, which includes regional news from media units traditionally affiliated with local government institutions but not considered as official. Local media sectors are able to prefer regional needs to the central state's political agenda because of the legitimacy of people's needs, as we have discussed. This media independence is nevertheless dependent on the local governments' acquiescence. Esarey (2005) found that commercialization of the Chinese media demonstrates two liberalizing effects: the first liberalizing effect is the shifting of the media's loyalty from the party to audiences for the sake of profits; second, and in turn, the local state is willing to support its media ventures because of access to tax revenue. In the early 1990s, Chan (1993) thought that the Chinese media system was commercialized without independence. In general it is still the truth nowadays as the party/state still retains its ideological grip over Chinese media, especially over key areas such as news and editorials, but Chinese producers are making more to gain greater agency in, what might prove after all, a less strictly controlled country. Emphasizing regional needs, communal production and entertainment are all efficient and euphemistic ways to gain some rhetorical/discursive independence in China. The emphasis on regional needs is particularly important in the context of understanding the extent and limits of media independence in China because this takes place in news programs, the most heavily supervised genre in the authoritarian country. Here we can understand why such bids for media independence might matter.

CONCLUSION

While provincial television stations come up with these strategies to gain rhetorical independence, it does not mean that they can perform bold political transgression. In fact, this rhetorical independence is strategic, as we have discussed, with a lot of political considerations and constraints underpinning its development and operation, which leads to calculated exclusions of some aspects that otherwise could be included in the pursuit of media independence. Rhetorical independence is simultaneously accompanied by rhetorical submissiveness. But such struggles for rhetorical/discursive independence are never accomplished forever. In fact, their attempts are constantly regulated by state authority. In late 2011, for instance, SARFT issued a special administrative order to tighten regulation over court politics dramas by removing the genre—along with time-traveling dramas, shows involving law and crimes and copycat shows—from primetime satellite TV schedules. It also tightened the approval of new productions on these topics. As for the case of communal production, its *authenticity* also appeared to be disturbing to the censor. Immediately following the wide popularity of the show among audiences, these shows were forbidden to "hype up marginal issues" and "show the ugly side of things, or overly depressing, dark or decadent topics" (Yang 2010). Following the sweeping policies that asked for a promotion of core socialist values, *If You Are the One* made changes by approaching social topics in a more subtle way so as to avoid a mandatory cancellation. Besides, the show also added a professor from the local Communist Party school as its guest host, which is widely believed to be a move with political considerations. Therefore, while provincial television stations' struggles can bring temporary independence, it is noteworthy that this independence is usually immediately followed by control. Rhetorical independence is only made possible by the official acquiescence. It "expires" when the state decides to intervene. But this does not mean that the energy for independence dissipates with state intervention. When ad hoc political control happens, television stations perform rhetorical submissiveness as a tactic to seek more living space and brew, perhaps, the next resistance. Thus, the struggle for independence within the political boundaries in China has always been, and will continue to be, a dynamic and unfinished process.

Viewed from this perspective, we should then abandon the notion that political control over Chinese media has succeeded in anticipating and annihilating any challenges. Instead, we have highlighted the agency within the structure by pointing out the liberating potential of local television stations' struggles for autonomy. While the resulting independence often appears to be temporary, we should never ignore its political implications. As we have seen, what is mediated through televisual discourses is often a series of trenchant social issues and immediate popular concerns that the authority attempts to tone down instead of hyping up in order to maintain social harmony and stability. Televisual mediation of these topics brings about a ferment and multiplication of public discourses in society, which tend to articulate new subject positions imposing threats to the established social order. In this way, it pushes the limits of what could be discussed both on Chinese television and in Chinese society. We see this as the main politics of the struggles taking place within the structure.

However, we don't intend to exaggerate the political potential of these efforts. It has to be realistically pointed out that the provincial television stations come up with these pragmatic tactics mainly to pursue audience ratings and advertising revenues. Here we need to be suspicious about the sincere nature of capital in liberalizing political control. Garnham (2011) has argued that the relatively stable capitalist operation does not necessarily require a dominant ideology. Rather, within the capitalist mode of production, increasingly media and cultural enterprises would produce anything that could make profits. Therefore, within certain parameters, capital can ally with any social forces that can help to achieve its goal. Perhaps because of this, Garnham (1990) argued that, even within the capitalist mode of production, the market has acted as a liberating force at *crucial* historical junctures. Here he refers to the industrialization of cultural production and circulation in the eighteenth century, which broke down the ideological control of the feudal and religious opponents of modernity and capitalism. In our case, the state-owned but market-driven media that *capitalize on* social controversies constitute a liberating force against political control in authoritarian China. So media independence in China is quite different from that in the Western context. While media criticism in the Western context is mainly performed against the capitalist mode of media production and cultural provision, the role of the market is more nuanced than imaged in the Chinese context. Therefore, the meaning of media independence varies in different context, which is always contingent and local. Such independence might not be as "radical" as that found in the Western context, but it doesn't make it any less important or powerful in the context we have explored.

Last, market-driven Chinese television, with productions concerning social concerns and controversies, provides a discursive space for individual audiences, formed primarily in the private realm including the family, to articulate the needs of the society as a public. In this way, it not only satisfies its economic needs but also social needs.

The three strategies implemented by regional and provincial television stations for gaining some temporary independence not only suggest some political implications discussed herein but also sustain a large pool of passionate cultural producers, as exemplified by Wang Gang, who, while caught between the state and the market, have kept finding ways to circumvent political restrictions. This aspiration to more autonomy and freedom often leads to a mutation and expansion of political boundaries. We should believe in the ability of this process to keep the ambitions and aspirations of cultural producers alive and bring in more resources and talents.

NOTES

1. "Yu Zheng talked about the five 'must see' in *Gong 2*," *NetEase Entertainment* January 20, 2012. Available http: http://ent.163.com/12/0120/07/7O6PD72800031GVS.html (accessed August 1, 2013).
2. Mo Ran, "Reading 'unspoken rules' in workplace from *Gong*," *Renren Blog*. Available http: http://blog.renren.com/share/232378958/5459677598 (accessed August 1, 2013). Renren is one of the most influential social networking sites in China, which is particularly popular amongst college students.
3. The popularity of *Gong* can be demonstrated through its high ratings. The premier rating of the show reached 1.99, which meant that it occupied 8.24 percent of the television drama market. And for two weeks after its premier, it was the most watched television program among all shows shown at the same time nationwide

for sixteen consecutive days, with a rating rocketing to 3.08 during grand finale episodes.

"What is behind *Gong*'s high rating?" *Xinmin News*, February 23, 2011. Available http: http://ent.xinmin.cn/2011/02/23/9448862.html (accessed August 2, 2013).

4. "SARFT tightens control over prime-time programming," *Sina Entertainment*, December 2, 2011. Available http: http://ent.sina.com.cn/v/m/2011–12–02/12403497524.shtml (accessed August 20, 2013).

5. "The rise of domestic entertainment shows as exemplified through *If You Are the One*," *SouthCN.com* February 11, 2010. Available http: http://ent.southcn.com/8/2010–02/11/content_9200322.htm (accessed August 10, 2013).

6. Ibid.

7. mltr, "*Nanjing Ling Juli* and the ugly Nanjing?," *Tianya BBS* November 14, 2003. Available http: http://bbs.tianya.cn/post-free-122352–1.shtml (accessed October 25, 2013). Tianya BBS is one of the most influential online discussion forum in China. *Xinwen Lianbo* is the official news program of CCTV Channel One, which is scheduled at 19:00 p.m. every day. The program is famous for singing the praise of the CCP and the Chinese government.

8. tianyawyjiayou, "*Nanjing Ling Juli* should be one of the most critical programs in Mainland China," *Tianya BBS* March 24, 2011. Available http: http://bbs.tianya.cn/post-333–88295–1.shtml (accessed October 25, 2013).

9. There are more than seventy articles focusing on *Nanjing Ling Juli* according to the searching result of CNKI. CNKI is the most popular and comprehensive database of journal papers, theses and dissertations in Mainland China. The academia's silence is understandable, as any harsh criticism is not permitted to be published in the academic journals that are owned and run by official organizations or universities.

10. Mengfei was the host of *Nanjing Ling Juli* between 2002 and 2010. He has been the host of the popular dating program *Feicheng Wurao* (*If You Are the One*) of Jiangsu Satellite Television since 2010.

11. "The producer of *Nanjing Ling Juli* spoke at the 2004 China International Radio Film and Television Exhibition Special Forum," *Sina Entertainment* July 26, 2004. Available http: http://ent.sina.com.cn/v/2004–07–26/2103455311.html (accessed February 10, 2014).

REFERENCES

Baidu (2013) "Nanjing Ling Juli," *Baike Baidu*. Available http: http://baike.baidu.com/link?url=zZmlqNHP4KPaMK09tEEaVK7v4SOitq1bm4oOlU34mAKwNpVAIsqdclugu7wl2e2aD0NscayMJsX4oHhoI9LFzVpLfTORCyV3JJm9pvtOFp3 (accessed October 25, 2013).

Baranovitch, N. (2003) *China's New Voices: Popular Music, Ethnicity, Gender, and Politics, 1978–1997*. Berkeley: University of California Press.

Can, S. (2010) "Do any Tianya users like Meng Fei the host of *Feicheng Wurao?*" Available http: http://bbs.tianya.cn/post-funinfo-2140953–1.shtml (accessed October 25, 2013).

Chan, J. (2003) "Administrative boundaries and media marketization: A comparative analysis of the newspaper, TV and internet markets in China," in Chin-Chuan Lee (ed.), *Chinese Media, Global Contexts*, 159–176. London: Routledge.

Chan, M. (1993) "Commercialization without independence: Trends and tensions of media development in China," *The China Review: An Interdisciplinary Journal on Greater China*, 25.

Esarey, A. (2005) "Cornering the market: State strategies for controlling China's commercial media," *Asian Perspective-Seoul* 29, 4: 37.

Fiske, J. (1987) *Television Culture*. London: Routledge.

Garnham, N. (1990) *Capitalism and Communication: Global Culture and the Economics of Information*. London: Sage Publications.

Garnham, N. (2011) "The political economy of communication revisited," in J. Wasko, G. Murdock and H. Sousa (eds.), *The Handbook of Political Economy of Communications*, 41–61. Chichester: Wiley-Blackwell.

Giles, D. C. (2002) "Keeping the public in their place: Audience participation in lifestyle television programming," *Discourse & Society* 13, 5: 603–628.

Gill, R. (2007) *Gender and the Media*. Cambridge: Polity.

Harvey, D. (2005) *A Brief History of Neoliberalism*. Oxford: Oxford University Press.

Hassid, J. (2008) "Controlling the Chinese media: An uncertain business," *Asian Survey* 48, 3: 414–430.

Hill, A. (2005) *Reality TV: Audiences and Popular Factual Television*. Oxon: Routledge.

Hong, J. H., Lu, Y. M. and Zou, W. (2009) "CCTV in the reform years: A new model for China's television?," in Y. Zhu and C. Berry (eds.), *TV China*, 41–55. Bloomington: Indiana University Press.

Huang, C., Davis, C. L. and Knight, A. (2002) "Beyond party propaganda: A case study of China's rising commercialised press," *eJournalist*. Available http: http://ejournalist.com.au/v2n1/propaganda.pdf (accessed October 28, 2013).

Jones, A. F. (c1992) *Like a knife: Ideology and Genre in Contemporary Chinese Popular Music*. Ithaca, NY: East Asia Program, Cornell University.

Li, X. and Jing, Z. (2003) "Constructing a new model of Chinese TV news: A talk on *Nanjing Ling Juli*," *Modern Communication* 121, 2: 60–62.

Lu, D. (2005) *Decoding Private Television (Jiexi zhongguo minying dianshi)*. Shanghai: Fudan University Press.

Nhan, V. L. (2008) "Media in China: Methods of state control," *The Orator*, 3: 36–50.

Ong, A. (2006) *Neoliberalism as Exception: Mutations in Citizenship and Sovereignty*. Durham, NC: Duke University Press.

Papacharissi, Z. and Mendelson, A. L. (2007) "An exploratory study of reality appeal: Uses and gratifications of reality TV shows," *Journal of Broadcasting & Electronic Media* 51, 2: 355–370.

Qiao, Q. (2008) "*Nanjing Ling Juli*: Dancing with audiences," *Journalism Fans*, 3: 56.

"SARFT tightens regulation over satellite television programming," *Xinhua News*, October 25, 2011. Available http: http://news.xinhuanet.com/newmedia/2011-10/25/c_122197336.htm (Accessed September 15, 2014).

SARFT (2007) "Do the work to resist the trend of vulgarity fast and well with the high sense of political mission and responsibility," *SARFT News* June 14, 2007. Available http: www.sarft.gov.cn/articles/2007/06/14/20070908161234410265.html (accessed October 25, 2013).

Shirk, S. (Eds.) (2011) *Changing Media, Changing China*. Oxford: Oxford University Press.

Thompson, R. (2001) "Reality and the future of television," *Television Quarterly* 31, 4: 20–25.

Winfield, B. H. and Peng, Z. (2005) "Market or party controls? Chinese media in transition," *Gazette: The International Journal for Communication Studies* 67, 3: 255–270.

Wong, E. (2011) "Censors pull reins as China TV, chasing profit, gets racy," *New York Times* December 31, 2011. Available http: www.nytimes.com/2012/01/01/world/asia/censors-pull-reins-as-china-tv-chasing-profit-gets-racy.html?pagewanted=1&_r=0 (accessed October 29, 2013).

Xiao, Z. Y. (2010) "The Real Ma Nuo?" *Yangcheng Evening Newspaper* June 29, 2010. Available http: www.ycwb.com/ePaper/ycwb/html/2010–06/29/content_864040.htm (accessed October 29, 2010).

Yang, X. Y. (2010) "China curbs 'vulgar' reality TV show," *New York Times* July 18, 2010. Available http: www.nytimes.com/2010/07/19/world/asia/19chinatv.html?pagewanted=all (accessed October 29, 2013).

Zhang, X. and Fung, A. (2011) "Market, Politics and Media Competition in China: Competing Media Discourses in TV Industries," *The Journal of Oriental Society of Australia* 42: 133–154.

Zhao, Y. (1998) *Media, Market, and Democracy in China: Between The Party Line and the Bottom Line.* Urbana: University of Illinois Press.

Zhao, Y. (2008) *Communication in China: Political Economy, Power, and Conflict.* Lanham, Md.: Rowman & Littlefield.

Zhu, Y. (2005) "Yongzheng dynasty and Chinese primetime television drama," *Cinema Journal* 44, 4: 3–17.

Zhu, Y. (2008) *Television in Post-reform China: Serial Dramas, Confucian Leadership and the Global Television Market.* London; New York: Routledge.

12 Uneven and Combined Independence of Social Media in the Middle East

Technology, Symbolic Production and Unproductive Labor

Gholam Khiabany

A year and a half after the Iranian uprising in 2009, the unprecedented popular revolts in several Arab countries at the beginning of 2011 provided some of the most evocative moments when power met its opposite, in decisive and surprising ways. In a matter of weeks, some of the most powerful hereditary/republican regimes in the region, such as those in Tunisia and Egypt, crumbled under relentless pressure and opposition from highly mediated "street politics" that shook the foundations of authoritarian and repressive rule, undermining hegemonic structures and configurations of power within nation-states and between nations. Technology, as in the case of the Iranian uprising, emerged as one of the main explanations on offer to make sense of this new wave of revolts against tyranny. Outside of the region, the big media players, faced with political and financial obstacles, relied on vast amounts of "raw material" (images, sounds, texts) to construct stories and theories of revolutions and of technologies. If sophisticated monitoring of the Internet in Iran and the Arab World, alongside "filtering," remained major obstacles for symbolic producers/activists in the region, the filter of credibility and journalistic validation of Western Big Media proved to be another site of struggle over the legitimacy of the monopoly of meaning. In addition, according to some commentators, social media users are exploited to enrich big media companies in the West.

James Bennett's introduction in this collection provides an overview of various definitions of and approaches to media independence. As he demonstrates, the label of independent (and we might add the practice and applications of it) remains problematic and contradictory. In the first place the issue of independence always begs the question of independent from and in relation to what? The answer, depending on whether the term is defined on the basis of structure (horizontal/vertical; participatory/hierarchical); funding (commercial/public); political (left/right, state/commercial) and so forth varies. To this we add the problems of precise definition of public and private; political and commercial; alternative and mainstream and so on. Again as Bennett suggests, the criteria listed under the label of independent and dependent can be, and indeed are, contradictory. Conflations of independence with the alternative also raise the question—alternative to what? Linked to this, and rather crucial to any discussion about independent media and their perceived role in societal change, is the idea of praxis. On this issue it is worth remembering the distinction that Raymond Williams made between alternative and oppositional. "There is a simple theoretical distinction between alternative and oppositional, that is to say between someone who simply finds a different way to live and wishes to be left alone with it, and someone who finds a different way to live and wants to change society in its light" (2005: 41–42).

This chapter examines these issues further by assessing the contradictions of production and distribution of information in the Middle East. I focus on Iran, where cyberspace came to be seen as an independent, unified and unsegmented site of resistance. The first part of this chapter reviews the recent discussion about user-generated content and digital labor that posits that user-generated content is a form of exploited free labor. However, it will be argued that while the focus on "labor" is crucial for any meaningful assessment of the cultural industries, seeing the producers of user-generated content as "free labor" and as exploited workers simply ignores the varying composition of work, production and control in social media environments. This chapter then examines the case of the Middle East and argues that the power of bloggers as "independent producers" is enhanced and constrained by a variety of factors. This chapter takes a broader comparative frame, beyond technology, to explore the issues of dependency and unequal division of labor in our neoliberal time.

THE PRODUCTION OF UNPRODUCTIVE LABOR

The whole world appears to be on the move. Indeed, the recent period has seen an explosion of participatory politics around the globe, from the uprising in Iran, to the so-called Arab Spring movements of 2011, to Occupy activities, to events in Greece, Spain, Turkey and Brazil. The whole world, also, appears to be watching the very same events. Much of the hype about the "movement" and its audiovisual manifestation has been about the power of new and social media. These movements and uprisings have had in common the objection to the uneven distribution of political and material resources. They have been, in one way or another, a response to the theft of "abundance" during the era that has been characterized supposedly by the "logic of abundance" (Vercellone 2007). What has abounded, however, have been images and texts—photos of demonstrations and short video clips often taken from mobile phones and uploaded to YouTube and mashups of photographs made into video, accompanied by music. The pictures and films of fallen heroes, police brutality and the bravery of activists have appeared on YouTube, Facebook and blogs in a number of different forms, and accompanied by different musical scores. The wide range of media and communicative platforms, the innovative use of image, sound and music to mobilize, have at times, been the sole focus in some media and academic circles. Some journalists and scholars celebrate this abundance of text/image as heralding a new form of social and political activism that is more participatory than the past. However, some cautionary and critical assessments of user-generated content have reminded us of the contradictory nature of online activities and have suggested that user-generated content is also a source of value in capitalist societies (Andrejevic 2008; Arvidsson 2005; Terranova 2000). For instance, Terranova argues:

> The digital economy is an important area of experimentation with value and free cultural and affective labor. It is about specific forms of production (web-design, multimedia production, digital services, and so on), but is also about forms of labor we do not immediately recognize as such: chat, real-life stories, mailing lists, amateur newsletter, and so on. These types of cultural and technical labor are not produced by capitalism in any direct, cause-and-effect fashion; that is, they have not developed simply as an answer to the economic needs of capital. However, they have developed in relation to the expansion of the cultural industries and are part of a process of economic experimentation with the creation of monetary value out of knowledge/culture/affect.
>
> (2000: 38)

For Terranova, such digital activities are at the same time "voluntarily given and unwaged, enjoyed and exploited" (ibid.: 33). However, the critique of free labor is not the only critical analysis on offer when it comes to "creative labor," the relationship between production and consumption and the nature of digital work and play (for an overview, see Hesmondhalgh 2010). However, because digital activities of citizens across the globe, the Middle East included, are increasingly seen as "free labor" (see, for example, Palmer's [2012] account of the reliance of CNN on citizen journalists in Iran), it makes sense to engage with the origins of this concept. Terranova's work is firmly located in the tendency that argues that information has become the main productive force. If information is the central commodity of the current phases of capitalism, it then follows that "immaterial" forms of labor (cognitive work and services) have become the dominant forms (if not the only one) of labor. Hardt and Negri, in particular, have argued that these new forms of labor necessitate a significant revision of Marx's theory. As Hesmondhalgh points out:

> Autonomist concepts of immaterial labor, affective labor and "precarity" have been of increasing interest to critical commentators on contemporary work, including labor in the cultural and creative industries. The concept of immaterial labor has its origins in a series of papers in the journal *Futur Antérieur* by Michael Hardt, Maurizio Lazzarato,

Antonio Negri and Paolo Virno in the early 1990s. The concept was there defined as "the labor that produces the information and cultural content of the commodity."

(2010: 272)

The concept has been modified and expanded to include not only those that produce information and cultural content but any "that produces an immaterial good, such as a service, a cultural product, knowledge, or communication" (Negri cited in ibid.).

Immaterial labor, however, has a much longer history. The concept was used first in the early nineteenth century by Henry Storch. As Haug states, Storch was one of the economists who "were concerned with defusing Adam Smith's notion that 'the labour of some of the most respectable order in the society is . . . unproductive'" (2009: 177). Marx devotes an entire chapter to this question in *Theories of Surplus Value Part 1*. Marx himself doesn't actually use the term, but makes a distinction between productive and unproductive labor. Productive labor, as it means in capitalist production, is defined as "wage-labour which, exchanged against the variable part of capital (the part of capital that is spent on wages), reproduces not only this part of the capital (or the value of its own labor-power), but in addition produces surplus-value for the capitalist" (Marx 1963: 152). That is, productive labor refers to labor that produces surplus value over and above the wages paid to the workforce. The worker exchanges her labor for a wage from capital, but that labor produces more value than what she is paid, and is hence the source of the capitalist's profit. This is why capitalists try to push wages down (in order to increase their rate of profit) and why workers' collective organizations resist this downward pressure. In contrast *unproductive labor* is defined as one that is not "exchanged with capital, but *directly* with revenue" (ibid.: 157). This means that in the exchange between labor and payment, unproductive labor does not directly produce surplus value, but instead is labor exchanged for income. The distinction, as Marx further elaborates, is not to do with the nature of the product that is produced or the specific features of the labor, but rather "the social relations of production, within which the labor is realised" (ibid.). Marx illustrates this distinction by giving an actor or a clown as an example. They are a productive laborer if they are in the service of a capitalist who takes away from their labor a lot more than he gives the actor or the clown as a wage. In contrast a tailor who goes to the house of the same capitalist to patch his trousers for him is an unproductive laborer, for what he produces is a use-value. That labor does not produce profit for that capitalist. "The former's labour is exchanged with capital, the latter's with revenue. The former's labour produces a surplus-value; in the latter's, revenue is consumed" (ibid.).

The form of labor and its product, Marx asserts, is not determined by the specific character of the labor but rather by the social relations of production. A seamstress, a cook, a cleaner and so on, who work as the wage-laborers for a capitalist (and in doing so create surplus value) inevitably must also perform the same tasks for themselves, however, they can only do so once they have labored "productively" and earned enough to have a home to clean, food to cook and clothes to mend. Their "unproductive labor" is dependent on them laboring "productively." On this basis Marx offers an expansive definition of labor, which not only includes an engineer or a factory worker, but also includes writer, actors and musicians. They are productive laborers because they produce ideas, contents, performance, emotions and so forth that enrich entrepreneurs. That is, they create surplus value. Marx famously argued that the

> historical conditions of its [capitalism's] existence are by no means given with the mere circulation of money and commodities. It can spring into life, only when the owner of the means of production and subsistence meets in the market with the free laborer selling his labor-power. And this one historical condition comprises a world's history. Capital, therefore, announces from its first appearance a new epoch in the process of social production.
>
> (Marx 1976: 274)

Such a distinct approach is precisely why labor has occupied the most significant space in Marxism. This and the organization of labor is precisely why it was natural for Marx to place labor in the very center stage of human productive activity. Human history is not defined only by technologies or by the division of labor, but also by different forms of "social relations of production" that exist in each epoch. Because capitalism is an economic system driven by profit, the social relations of production determine when and where labor is productive or unproductive, on the basis of whether it directly contributes to the creation of surplus value—whether the capitalist exchanges a wage for labor that not only reproduces the value of that wage, but produces surplus value over and above it.

Marx was concerned with the specific forms of material and symbolic production, the material as well as symbolic products and services. In his endeavor to understand and explain social relations he dismissed the idea of "immaterial labor." The revival of the concept in the past two decades and its use even by those who insist that "labor is always material" (Negri cited in Haug 2009: 177) can be understood not by reference to the origin of the concept but within the context of neoliberalism. There is a rather disturbing overlap between the buzzwords of the business magazines and some leftist publications: new economy, digital economy, knowledge economy, prosumer, cognitive capitalism and so forth. The main thrusts of the arguments are well rehearsed and well known (Negri, 1996; Vercellone 2007). Novel forms of productive subjectivities are considered to be a key feature of the recent transformation of capitalism; cognitive aspects of living labor have seemingly become the main force of production and the major source of value creation (Lazzarato 1996); and the separation between manual and mental labor is vanishing. Such perspectives then proceed to argue that the very same process, by producing or creating the new form or species of laborer that embodies the capacity to organize production independently from capital, threatens the command of capital or even renders it superfluous (Lazzarato 1996; Sayers 2007; Vercellone 2007). A significant element of this approach has been about the particular and peculiar features of the commodities that this new form of labor produces. Cognitive commodities, we are informed, are products for which the knowledge necessary for their production overshadows the manufacturing labor required for production. This in itself has major consequences for the cost structure of such peculiar products, namely the massive cost of production of the first copy and the marginal or zero cost of reproduction.

This argument is not unfamiliar to the students of the political economy of media. Cultural commodities, argued Collins, Garnham and Locksley, share certain economic features that stem

> first from the fact that their essential quality from which their use-value derives is immaterial—it is in one form or another symbolic meaning which is merely carried by a material carrier such as celluloid, vinyl, or the waves of radio spectrum and a cathode ray tube. It is the message not the medium that provides value to the user and the message is immaterial or intangible.
>
> (1988: 7)

This immateriality also makes the cultural commodity non-rival; that is to say, it will not perish by the act of consumption. Another feature of cultural commodities is the marginal to zero cost of reproduction. The cost of providing the same commodity to additional readers, listeners or viewers (that is, broadcasting to another home, making an extra copy of the same record or paper or book) is very low indeed.

Autonomous Marxists expand these characteristics to the whole economy in general and suggest that the introduction of the computer and the informationalization of production (and large sections of the economy) has transformed laboring activities and processes (for a critique of this position, see Sayers 2007 and Camfield 2007). In this transformed knowledge-intensive economy, what is produced is immaterial products of labor that are costless to duplicate, non-rival, non-excludable and so forth. This economy is seen to be marked by the logic of abundance and the end of scarcity (Vercellone 2007). However, the value form is undermined by the imposition of artificial scarcity such as copyright and integrated distribution. The reality is that the proponents of this approach share many mainstream claims about the new/digital/knowledge economy. Their saving grace seems to be their optimism for the potential of knowledge workers to make capital redundant and the radical transformation of society. They reframe the mainstream account of the role of knowledge and ITC in the economy and at the same time over-state the emancipatory potential of the current phase of capitalism. They underestimate the significance of "knowledge" under industrial capitalism and overestimate the impact of the computer on social relations and the con-ditions of production. This is, more or less, the framework that Terranova borrows and modifies to explain the main features of free labor. This labor is unpaid and exploited and creates surplus value for capitalists, and yet has an unparalleled mobilization potential (Terranova 2000).

The "cognitive capitalism" thesis, expounded by Autonomous Marxists and others, not only exaggerates the transformation in the process of production—that is, fails to realize that symbolic commodities can't insti-gate, regulate and manage the exchange in the market on their own—but they also, contrary to their promise, fail to be specific and substantiate their arguments. The issue of the exploitation of free digital labor is equally prob-lematic. As Hesmondhalgh has pointed out, it is not really clear how the use of someone else's effort for one's own benefit is the same as exploita-tion, which is based very specifically in the creation of surplus value that is extracted from labor. That many areas of public life are reified and every surface, every minute, every garment, every roof and other use-values are also potentially commodities is beyond doubt. But for the idea of exploita-tion to have any analytical meaning, it has to be seen as an historical concept that is intended "to explain how capitalism was able to generate such mas-sive surplus values and at the same time such immiseration" (Hesmondhalgh 2010: 274). In addition, new and seasoned political activists in Iran, Egypt, Tunisia, Turkey and elsewhere, young and old, might be surprised to learn that indeed, even in their effort to challenge capitalism and dictatorship, they were being controlled and exploited further. We might ask: Isn't the mainstream media coverage of the Occupy movements, or its coverage of the gathering and protests of people in the now celebrated squares across the world, also exploitation? Doesn't such coverage fill the pages, schedules and pockets of mainstream media? Is it not true that activists giving inter-views to the papers or appearing on radio and television to put forward their arguments provide capitalist media with free ideas and content? How about the thousands who have marched in the streets? Indeed if any use (or abuse) of other people's work, ideas, emotions and protests by capitalists can be labeled as exploitation, is there any space outside of this immaterial "cage" of cognitive capitalism?

Let us explore these two dimensions, economic and political, of social media activities further. Can blogging be regarded as an exploited intellectual labor? Is the notion applicable to all online activities? To what extent is the immaterial turn global and, as Toscano asks, is "such a turn . . . truly world-wide? If so, in what ways is it subject to uneven and combined geographical development" (Toscano 2007: 9–10)? Blanket terms such as "immaterial turn" and "information society" fail to recognize societal multiplicity and the consequent variations of "development." Societies indeed do develop, but not with the same pace or depth, or even in the same direction. Much like the term "culture" (which always should prompt one to ask whose culture?), the idea of immaterial labor should also be followed by where and when. The experience of the Middle East itself, and, indeed, even the diversity of outcomes of the Arab revolts, is a clear indication of the importance of concrete analysis of concert situations. This is not to succumb to the beloved "plurality" and "multiplicity" of variants of postmodernism, but an urge to recognize the contradictions, unevenness and independence as well as the interdependency of social developments in relation to the external and internal dynamics. To say that Saudi Arabia and Sweden are both capitalist countries is certainly true and that fact should not be overlooked. Yet that statement of fact for social scientific analysis is as useful as the statement that "mouse and elephant are mammal" for a biologist. Before considering some of the contradictions in the development and uses of social media in the Middle East let us examine the issue of exploitation of social media users and their level of independence from the state and the market from a different source and angle.

SOCIAL MEDIA AND FREE LABOR

In their contribution to this debate Christian Fuchs and Sebastian Sevignani draw on Marx's writings on labor and alienation in the *Economic and Philosophical Manuscripts* to make a distinction between labor and work. They suggest that labor "is based on a fourfold alienation of the human being: the alienation from oneself, the alienation from the objects of labor (instruments and objects of labor) and the alienation from the created product" (2013: 257). It is important to note that they fail to mention the fourth type of alienation, the alienation of man from man, workers from workers, which Marx suggests is an "immediate consequence of man's alienation from the product of his work, his vital activities, and his species-being" (1976: 83). In their attempt to apply this distinction to social media, Fuchs and Sevignani also argue that the users of social media platforms are indeed coerced to use them. This coercion, they insist, is not the same as what other workers face, which is to die of hunger if they don't "voluntarily" sell their labor to capitalists. But "rather a social form of coercion that threatens the users with isolation and social disadvantages" (ibid.). This makes Facebook users unpaid workers. In this digital field the instruments of labor "are the platform and the brains of its human users." The users not only don't own or control the platform, but also by entering into "voluntary" contract with Facebook give those who control the means of production of human experiences (in this instance) to use ideas/experiences/generated data for their own commercial benefit. Fuchs and Sevignani dismiss many of the well-rehearsed myths around Facebook and point out that in a usually one-sided emphasis on the use-value of Facebook (and its benefit for its users) there is no or little mention of the exchange-value that is extracted by the owners and shareholders. "Facebook labour creates commodities and profits. It is therefore productive work. It is however unpaid work and in this respect shares characteristics of other irregular work forces, especially houseworkers and slaves, who are also unpaid." The working condition for this unpaid labor is rather different, but "100% of their labour time is surplus labour time, which allows capitalists to generate extra-surplus value and extra-profits" (ibid.: 262).

But how is this surplus value generated? Fuchs and Sevignani start from the well-known argument (again) that cultural commodities have dual character and operate in two markets and write:

> We can therefore speak of the double character of Facebook's use-value: on the one hand, users produce use-values for themselves and others, they create a social relation between users and public visibility. On the other hand, users produce use-values for capital, i.e. targeted advertising space for the advertising industry. For Facebook, both use-values are instrumental for achieving exchange value, i.e. selling to the advertising industry what it wants (ad space) and what is produced by the users. The dual character of use-value stems from the circumstance that the Facebook product/use-value is informational: it can be exchanged with money and at the same time stay under the control of the users.
>
> (ibid.: 260)

This analysis seems rather straightforward. However, such framing of the activities on digital labor, values, control and the condition of production in social media (leaving aside the authors' confusion over use-value and exchange-value) raises some interesting questions. The main focus of Fuchs and Sevignani, as the title of their article clearly indicates, is *digital* labor and work. Yet in their contribution the very idea of *digital* is used interchangeably with *informational*. Not all immaterial goods are digital and not all kinds of "immaterial labor" are "digital labor" or "digital work." The conflation of all "informational," intangible, immaterial and symbolic goods with "digital" will only add to the confusion over the nature of labor, digital or otherwise. The production of immaterial goods has a much longer history than digital manipulation of the same intangible products and more.

Fuchs and Sevignani's analysis of the audience as a commodity—and that all users' time on Facebook is "productive" labor—is based on Dallas Smythe's notion of the media commodity form. Smythe had argued that the crucial function of the media was to sell audiences to advertisers, and that the act of consuming media was a form of unpaid labor and what this unpaid labor of audiences consisted of was to "learn to buy particular 'brands' of consumer goods, and to spend their income accordingly. In short, they work to create the demand for advertised goods which is the purpose of the monopoly capitalist advertisers" (1977: 6). It is not just that Smythes' approach loses all connection to political struggle (Hesmondhalgh 2010) but also, as Garnham argues it:

> misunderstands the function of commodity form as an abstraction within Marxist economic theory, and thus neglects the relationship between specific forms of the commodity, in this case the audience and the commodity form in general. As a result his theory lacks any sense of contradiction, failing to account for the function of those cultural commodities directly exchanged, failing to account for the role of the State, failing sufficiently to elaborate the function for capital of advertising itself and, perhaps most crucially of all, failing to relate the process of audience production by the mass media to determinants of class and to class struggle.
>
> (Garnham 1990: 29)

Furthermore, in their critique of the "cognitive capitalism" approach, Fuchs and Sevignani highlight that immaterial labor is hardly outside the sphere of existing capitalist social relations. But by labeling all social media users (or to be precise Facebook users) as unwaged, exploited and alienated workers, the degree of inequality and unevenness in "exchange" is simply brushed aside. The law of the market is of course based on the very idea of inequality of exchange between labor and capital. Indeed, if exchange was equal or one of equivalents, there would be no surplus. However, this concern is simply not limited to the inequality between Facbook shareholders and users, but also between productive laborers (Facebook employees) and unproductive laborers (those who can only be on Facebook after having worked productively to pay for their accommodation, food, bills and computer and Internet access). A general statement that there exists "a class relationship between users and non-owners and stockowners at the heart of Facebook" (ibid.: 258) is not sufficient for any meaningful class analysis.

In addition, the general terming of users as "non-owners" disguises the variations and diversities among the so-called unwaged workers of Facebook. All Facebook users are equal in as much as they can be labeled as "non-owners." But some of the Facebook users are more equal than others. There are commercial users (and not owners) who exploit the platform for their own benefit/gain/profits. There are users (celebrities) who are nationally and internationally recognized. Their fame is there to extract "rent" and to promote the very product that they have turned into. There are users (again not owners) who have pages that cannot be friended but can only be "liked." Not all of these users can be said to be subject to the same "class relations." The cleaners of Facebook offices in Dubai, Sao Paolo, Mexico City, Seoul, Hyderabad, Buenos Aires, as well as in Paris and New York, cannot be said to be subject to the same class relations, and exploited as "non-owners" like Justin Bieber, Rihanna, Lady Gaga, Coca

Cola and YouTube (just some of the top pages on Facebook). Indeed we have to recognize not only the varying composition of intangible products (digital or otherwise), and varying composition of capital (cognitive and material), but also varying composition of "users." If the theory of "immaterial labor" offers very little insight about the different kinds of paid work that the cognitive capitalism approach tries to lump together, the labeling of all user-generated content as free labor and all users as unwaged, exploited and alienated labor suffers from a rather stylized image of users as a singular worker. This homogenization of users is as problematic as attempts to brush aside the heterogeneity of working-class formations and experiences.

The problem that surrounds the idea of "unwaged" or "free labor" will not go away even if we narrow down the definition of symbolic products and users. Let us assume for a moment that we only address the question of user-generated content in relation to ordinary, noncommercial, nonfamous individuals on Facebook. Hesmondhalgh points out "there has been a tendency to bandy about the phrase 'free labor' as if it describes one huge, interconnected aspect of inequality and injustice" (2010: 277). He rightly points out that only very limited numbers of cultural producers have produced simply to gain financially from their "labor." Take, for example, the large number of people who practice music or football or basketball. Such practices contribute to training the future workforce and as such are crucial in making available a reserve army of workers in these fields. Should people get paid for such practices on the basis that these talents are/will be exploited by businesses (ibid.)? And how should we feel about shopping and our time and energy that is spent on walking to the shops, searching for goods, testing, selecting and purchasing them? Closer to "home," we might reflect on how we should feel about academic publishing. Those who write journal articles, book chapters and monographs are usually generating content for commercial publishers. Can we label academics as unwaged laborers in this very instance? What should we call the journal editor, then: "foreman of capitalist publishing?"

To consider wage as the only meaningful reward in such cases, as Hesmondhalgh warns, "would run the danger of internalising capitalism's own emphasis on commodification" (ibid.: 278). If the general idea of immaterial labor is connected and inspired by the neoliberal fantasy of dematerialization of the economy, the unintentional consequences of the discussion of user-generated-content as unwaged and exploited labor is that everything of (potential use) value should have a price and a financial reward in wage form.

Instead of seeing independent production of content generated by users as exploitation, it is possible to frame these forms of activities in the context of the narratives of intellectuals. This perspective allows us to recognize and pay attention to the division of labor in symbolic production without falling into the trap of internalizing and legitimizing capitalist "morality."

At the same time it also allows agency for media producers while providing us with ground to critically assess the performance and content of media. This is how Nicholas Garnham has tried to address the problem of the relationship between knowledge producers and knowledge. He defines the specialists in symbolic production as intellectuals and divides them into three groups: those whose "symbolic power derives from monopoly control over the production of knowledge and cultural legitimation"; those who "may be defined functionally as information workers; those whose specialized position within the division of labor is the manipulation of symbolic form"; and finally the group that "may be defined normatively as a vocation, as representatives of a critical, emancipatory tradition appealing to universal values" (2000: 84–85).

The question of intellectuals was also central to Gramsci's argument about intellectual work, in which he stressed that everyone has an intellect and uses it but not all are intellectuals by their social function. Gramsci offered a very expansive definition of intellectual labor: "there is no human activity from which every form of intellectual participation can be excluded" so that everyone "carries on some form of intellectual activity . . . , participates in a particular conception of the world, has a conscious line of moral conduct, and therefore contributes to sustain a conception of the world or to modify it, that is, to bring into being new modes of thought" (1971: 5). He classically identified two types of intellectuals—traditional and organic. Traditional intellectuals are those who think of themselves as autonomous and independent of the dominant social group and are so regarded by the general population. Organic intellectuals develop together with the dominant social group, the ruling class, and constitute its thinking and organizing element. Such people are produced by the educational system to perform a function for the dominant social group and it is through this group that the ruling class maintains its hegemony over the rest of society. Gramsci further suggested that in order for any kind of counter-hegemonic position to grow and challenge the taken-for-granted common sense that prevailed, both traditional and organic intellectuals needed to "change sides" while the working-class movement had to produce its own "organic intellectuals." Any ideological struggle for social change required not only consciousness raising but consciousness transformation while the creation of a socialist consciousness would develop out of actual working lives (Gramsci 1971: 5–23).

Following Sartre's distinction between "intellectuals" and "technicians of practical knowledge," Edward Said also famously divided intellectuals into two broad camps, amateur and professional. Said himself identified with the former, one of whose tasks, as he put it, is to "raise embarrassing questions, to confront orthodoxy and dogma (rather than produce them), to be someone who cannot easily be co-opted by governments or corporations, and whose *raison d'etre* is to represent all those people, and issues that are routinely swept under the rug" (cited in Garnham 2000: 87). If the intellectual sphere is thus not confined to a small elite but rather is something that is grounded in everyday life, and indeed should "speak" to and about that life in language that all could understand, then Gramsci is right to suggest that "the mode of being of the new intellectual can no longer consist in eloquence . . . but in active participation in practical life, as constructor, organizer, 'permanent persuader' and not just a simple orator" (1971: 10). Social media equally contain not only a wide range of "users" (consumers) but producers of ideas and contents. However, as has been suggested elsewhere (Sreberny and Khiabany 2007), the online environment is not exclusively the stomping ground of traditional intellectuals who position themselves as independent. These producers (productive or unproductive, in the Marxist sense) are representative of their class and of knowledge. Their level of "independence" (as producers) is varied, historically shifting and "dependent" on not only the material resources but also on their location in geography and in politics.

Critiques of uncritical accounts of the role of information technologies also need to take into consideration what Williams has called "uncontrollable effect." Williams always insisted on finding ways to democratize culture and cultural production. At the heart of this attempt—and long before anyone started playing around with the words producer/consumer—he argued for access to cultural resources that allowed everyone to be both producer and consumer. Williams also pointed at alternative uses (and regulation) of technologies. In the case of television in particular, he suggested while it is possible to discuss the social history of broadcasting on its own, "it is unrealistic to extract from it another and perhaps more decisive process, through which, in particular economic situations, a set of scattered technical devices became an applied technology and then a social technology" (1974: 18). In other words, the level of one's independence as a producer is shaped by the broader material realities that structure, regulate and circulate symbolic production. However, it is also in the same book that we read the memorable sentence: "For there was no way to teach a man to read the Bible which did not also enable him to read the radical press. A controlled intention became an uncontrolled effect" (ibid.: 134–135). In the case of social media it is not just the paradox of the collapse of productive and unproductive labor into one (i.e., the unproductive labor of users contributing to the commercial success of media companies), the contradiction between the original design (controlled intention) and the use of technology (uncontrollable effect), and the obvious and stark interplay between public and private and so forth that are confronting us. The recent events in the Middle East and the much celebrated alternative uses of social media provide a clear example of the "uncontrolled effect" of new technologies. Yet a closer look at the case of production and "regulation" of user-generated content in the Middle East provides us with more evidence of contradictory processes of independent production.

TECHNOLOGIES OF LIBERATION AND/OR OTHERWISE

The uprising and revolts that shook Iran in the aftermath of the electoral coup in 2009, and the revolts in Tunisia and Egypt that toppled the governments in those countries in twenty-eight and eighteen days respectively, had three significant similarities. First, the Arab revolutions like the uprising in Iran in 2009 were, in the first place, revolts against dictatorships and in direct opposition to the ruling regimes. These uprisings, like many such movements against despotism, were also marked with demonstrations and the visible participation of young people in the uprisings. Second, all three happened at the time during which, unlike 1979 (the time of the Iranian Revolution), the world is not divided into two camps, but is confronted with a U.S. hegemony and globalization of financial capital. And finally, they all happened at the time during which advances in communication technologies, in particular the Internet, have allowed for a much faster circulation and dissemination of information. Hence the constant association of these revolts with Twitter, Facebook, YouTube and so forth.

Indeed one of the main explanations emerging immediately after the Iranian uprising of 2009 and the Arab revolutions revolves around new technologies. Terms such as Twitter Revolution, WikiLeaks Revolution, Facebook Revolution and so forth, by associating these revolts with new technologies, not only pointed out the potentials of new technologies but more significantly claimed that such tools were the main engine and agents of social change in the region. This is certainly not an entirely false explanation. Imaginative use of new technologies to disseminate information, to focus the collective minds of a population, to break down the barrier of censorship and to pave the way for the emergence of a "public" was real and not simply a figment of Western journalists' imagination. Many activists in Iran and the Arab world articulated and forwarded such interpretations of events in the region.

However, if a single incident, or a technology, or a revelation about the glamorous lifestyle of the ruling elites can spark a revolution, then we have to demonstrate that in every context and location the same phenomena should produce identical results. In that case we are confronted with the question of why the desperate act of Mohamed Bouazizi ignited the Tunisian revolution but the repeat of the same act in Algeria could not? Similarly an explanation that puts new technologies at the heart of the debate about the why and how of the Arab revolutions not only has to demonstrate that the Arab revolutions would not have happened if there was no Twitter, Facebook, YouTube or WikiLeaks, but also has to explain why the imaginative use of the very same technologies failed to produce the same result in Iran. These terms of course vanished as soon as the big media corporations left the squares of major cities in the Arab world. The buzzwords had served their purpose, at least for the mainstream media. No one has used these terms to describe the ongoing struggle in these countries since the fall of Mubarak and Ben Ali (see Poell and van Dijck's contribution in this volume on the use of social media in relation to journalistic independence).

As Ahmed Saleh and Nadine Wahab, administrators of the "I Am Khaled Said" page on Facebook, have argued, "all of the administrators of the Facebook pages and even the political activists were surprised that the demonstrators continued protesting all over Egypt on January 26th and beyond, without any Facebook page calling for it or organizing it." "The administrators," they point out, "were now on the receiving end of the news" (2012: 243). It might have been exciting for many journalists (and academics) to offer an inflated assessment of all things "virtual," however, the "material" element, thousands of people who gathered, who occupied, who fought the police and the army, and who died, was not an online profile or a hashtag. The fact is technological determinist perspectives are also apolitical and ahistorical, failing to consider the wealth of activities by various players in various locations and over the course of decades that paved the ground for the eruptions and uprising. These perspectives, also despite claiming to fluidity, liquidity, flow and so forth, are too rigid in recognizing concrete political and social circumstances. However, such terms at the same time had another role to play. The Western focus on social media, Saleh and Wahab speculate, was "probably motivated by the desire to take credit for the Arab Revolution, given that the West is credited for the invention." Hence the focus on social media "rather than the more important, stronger and more direct effect of the injustice perpetuated by the dictators sponsored by Western regimes" (ibid.).

It was famously reported that during the Iranian uprising in 2009 the U.S. government had asked Twitter to postpone its scheduled maintenance service because of the alleged significance of the role of Twitter for the Iranian activists. Such attempts at taking credit for the uprisings and promoting the myths of "technologies of freedom" (de Sola Pool 1983) were being made at the time that not only the very same technologies (or alternative uses of them) were being suppressed by the U.S. government, but also that the U.S. policy was contributing to the censorship of the Internet in Iran. It was not until Obama delivered his famous YouTube message for Iranian New Year on March 20, 2012, and when he asked Iranian leaders to bring down the "electronic curtain" of censorship, that he promised to lift sanctions that disconnect Iranians from the Internet. The tragedy is not just that the U.S. government was/is contributing to that "electronic curtain," but rather hypocritically trying to "help" Iranians to break free from government at the time that the U.S. economic sanctions were making the Iranian people more dependent on the Iranian regime (as was also the case in Iraq). U.S. sanctions threaten the livelihood and the health of the Iranian people, but at least, thanks to U.S. government generosity, they could access Google+!

The U.S. government's endorsement of the perceived role of the technologies in the Iranian uprising and Obama's promise to help bring down the "electronic curtain" (a play on a Cold War term) further promote the myth that under dictatorship the online is the very opposite of "hardline" (conservative factions in the Islamic Republic of Iran). As far as Iran is concerned, and in the context of the war on terror, the "visibility of bloggers in mainstream international media cannot be solely attributed to technological developments. Nor can this hypervisibility be reduced to the usual narrative of lack of freedom of speech in Iran" (Shakhsari 2011: 7). For Shakhsari the rise and proliferation of Iranian bloggers outside Iran is a result of the fact that "the knowledge production about Iran has become a lucrative business for those who provide expertise in different capacities, from testimonials in media, books and human rights reports, to research and collection of information in think tanks, state and private intelligence firms and universities." As such the figure of an Iranian blogger outside of Iran, therefore, is a neoliberal subject "that acts as an entrepreneur, who is responsible for his/her own economic well-being and markets him/herself as the source of valuable information" (ibid.: 11).

The pressure to provide information about stories and situations that Western media have been unable to report firsthand has also "allowed" for a far greater reliance on user-generated content by big media companies. In her analysis of the CNN coverage of the Iranian uprising Palmer suggests that the company "simultaneously denigrates and depends" on its iReporters, "especially when covering a political uprising." She suggests that the professional journalists' denigration of their amateur counterparts is a sign of "anxious effort at maintaining the professional monopoly on meaning itself in an era where traditional journalism is indeed in crisis" (2012: 369).

Further contradiction can be seen in the operation of the U.S.-based Internet companies in the global south. These companies are rapidly expanding their operation in the global south. The figures provided by Schiller are illuminating. The number of users of these services in 2010 were as follows: Skype, 560 million; Facebook, 500 million; Microsoft, 789 million; Yahoo, 633 million; and Google had registered more than a billion searches each day by 2009. The share of the global south in some respects is also fascinating. As Schiller argues, "Facebook is visited by 92% of the Internet population in Turkey, 87% in Indonesia, and (merely) 67% in the United States" (2011: 932). By September 2013 Facebook claimed more than 1 billion users. The uprisings in the Middle East and the hype about the role of social media have certainly been good for the likes of Facebook and Twitter. Yet, as many have recorded (Ghonim 2012; Saleh and Wahab 2012), Facebook had shut some pages, including "I am Khaled Said," for violating Facebook terms and conditions. In some cases the activists in the region, Egypt included, not only had to break the firewall of the state but also of Facebook (for other examples of dependencies of activists on mainstream structures, see Kreiss in this volume). For obvious reasons it is impossible for activists to use their real identities to administer political pages on Facebook, which is yet another violation of terms and conditions. Activists who fight against tyranny have to bypass the laws of the very same company that would like to take credit for the struggle against dictatorship.

These contradictions are to some extent "external," that is, mostly (not entirely) related to how the role of social media was perceived, framed, explained and "influenced" by/in the West. The sanctions, the filters, the commercial interests, terms and conditions of the U.S.-based digital companies and so forth have in fact contributed to the containment of the potential of those technologies, but more importantly, of people. These all acted as significant barriers to truly independent activism. The "internal" contradictions are also as interesting and as complex, with specific consequences for the level of independent activities and voices. One significant outcome of the myth of the role of social media in the Iranian uprising was to confuse, or perhaps even substitute, media for the movement. "You are the media," was one of the claims of the so-called Green Movement. Yet at the same time that activists were being confined to the realm of small media, many of the well-known figures appeared on mainstream media as the voice of the movement. What was brushed aside was the historical fact that how individuals are organized as intellectuals is by definition a social process. Who gets noticed, who gets to speak and who is allowed to "represent" the public is never a given. The same people also controlled the organized networks, including the Facebook pages of the Green Movement. The Iranian uprising in 2009 grew out of the division "above," when the Iranian state tried to entice people to the polls and give the electoral game in Iran a democratic gloss. The revolt against the "electoral coup" certainly went further. However, radicalization of the slogans and demands was not matched with the expansion of the revolt. The leadership of the movement (the two other presidential candidates) had no interest in challenging the Islamic state that they had contributed to building. Once they retreated they took their resources and networks with them.

The myth of "you are the media," however, wasn't the only myth around. This was a movement that, its leaders claimed, had no leadership. "You are all leaders," was the famous claim. The Egyptian and Tunisian uprisings did breathe new life to such myths. This, as Gerbaudo (2012) has argued, encourages accepting no responsibility among those who are playing a leading role. The experience of Iran, Tunisia and Egypt in the aftermath of the uprisings in these countries clearly indicates what can happen in the absence of real networks and political organizations. Public spaces such as Tahrir Square (as was the case in Wall Street in New York, Puerta del Sol in Madrid, Syntagma Square in Athens and St Paul Cathedral in London) were the most significant instrument of resistance when other means of struggle had been denied to the public. As Harvey has suggested, "what Tahrir Square showed to the world was an obvious truth: that it is bodies on the street and in the squares, not the babble of sentiment on Twitter or Facebook, that really matter" (2012: 162). Furthermore, the myths of leaderless social media revolutions should not obscure the most significant lessons of the uprisings in the region: that is, how different social groups and actors behaved and operated in these movements. The freedom that the leaders of the Green Movement were demanding, the reforms that the Islamists in Tunisia and Egypt were asking for, were not exactly what other groups demanded. This is not to deny their relevance or contributions to the struggles, but rather to point out, again, the existence of variations of aspirations, ideas, users and producers.

CONCLUSION

In discussions of media independence it is always crucial to ask independence from what? The aim of this chapter was to point at diverse layers of dependencies and interdependencies in social media, and what has been viewed as the latest examples of independent production. The literature that I have examined, in particular the cognitive capitalism thesis, the issue of free labor and the reductionist approach that lumps all users of social media into one and confuses exploitation with alienation, fail to substantiate their central arguments. At issue is not just that those who claim to continue Marx's revolutionary legacy and methods are relying heavily on neoliberal myths. Equally problematic is the idea of free labor, or rather, posing the idea of free labor as the main problem or the main way to explain and understand significant aspects of symbolic production on new media platforms. Rejection of such approaches neither means rejection of the role of "knowledge" in the economy, nor the dismissal of particular sets of social relations and division of labor in the realm of social media. It is possible to discuss and to examine intellectual life, practice and production in a different way. This chapter certainly doesn't claim that every online voice constitutes intellectual activity. Not everyone is an intellectual nor does everyone need to perform intellectual tasks. Yet those who are benefiting from the existing intellectual activities are massively constrained by a combination of commercial, political and social interests/institutions.

REFERENCES

Andrejevic, M. (2008) "Watching television without pity," *Television & New Media* 9, 1: 24–46.

Arvidsson, A. (2005) "Brands," *Journal of Consumer Culture*, 5, 2: 235–258.

Camfield, D. (2007) "The multitude and the Kangaroo: A critique of Hardt and Negri's theory of immaterial labor," *Historical Materialism* 15, 2: 21–52.

Collins, R., Garnham, N. and Locksley, G. (1988) *The Economics of Television: The UK Case*. London: Sage.

Fuchs, C. and Sevignani, S. (2013) "What is digital labor? What is digital work? What's their difference? And why do these questions matter for understanding social media?," *TripleC* 11, 2: 237–293.

Garnham, N. (1990) *Capitalism and Communication: Global Culture and the Economics of Information*. London: Sage.

Garnham, N. (2000) *Emancipation, the Media and Modernity*. Oxford: Oxford University Press.

Gerbaudo, P. (2012) *Tweets and the Streets: Social Media and Contemporary Activism*. London: Pluto Press.

Ghonim, W. (2012). *Revolution 2.0: The Power of the People Is Greater than the People in Power*. Boston, MA: Houghton Mifflin Harcourt.

Gramsci, A. (1971) *Selections from the Prison Notebooks of Antonio Gramsci*, ed. and trans. Q. Hoare and G. Nowell-Smith. London: Lawrence and Wishart.

Haug, W. F. (2009) "Immaterial labor," *Historical Materialism* 17, 4: 177–185.

Harvey, D. (2012) *Rebel Cities: From the Right to the City to the Urban Revolution*. London: Verso.

Hesmondhalgh, D. (2010) "User-generated content, free labor and the cultural industries," *ephemera* 10, 3/4: 267–284.

Lazzarato, M. (1996) "Immaterial labor," in P. Virno and M. Hardt (eds.), *Radical Thought in Italy*, 133–147. Minneapolis: University of Minnesota Press.

Marx, K. (1963) *Theories of Surplus Value: Part 1*. London: Lawrence & Wishart.

Marx,K. (1971) *Selected Writing*. Oxford: Oxford University Press.

Marx, K. (1976) *Capital: Volume 1*. Hermondsworth, Middlesex. Penguin.

Negri, A. (1999) *Insurgencies: Constituent Power and the Modern State*. Minneapolis: University of Minnesota Press.

Palmer, L. (2012) "'iReporting' an Uprising: CNN and Citizen Journalism in Network Culture," *Television & New Media* 14, 5: 367–385.

Saleh, A. and Wahab, N. (2012) "Interview with administrators of Facebook's 'I Am Khaled Said' page," *Middle East Law and Governance* 3, 1–2: 238–243.

Sayers, S. (2007) "The Concept of labor: Marx and his critics," *Science & Society* 71, 4: 431–454.

Schiller, D. (2011) "Power under pressure: Digital capitalism in crisis," *International Journal of Communication* 5: 924–941.

Shakhsari, S. (2011) "Weblogistan goes to war: Representational practices, gendered soldiers and neoliberal entrepreneurship in diaspora," Feminist Review 99: 6–24.

Smythe, D. (1977) "Communications: Blindspot of Western Marxism," *Canadian Journal of Political and Social Theory* 1, 3: 1–27.

de Sola Pool, I. (1983) *Technologies of Freedom*. Cambridge, MA: Belknap Press.

Sreberny, A. and Khiabany, G. (2007) "Becoming intellectual: The blogestan and public political space in the Islamic Republic," *British Journal of Middle Eastern Studies* 34, 3: 267–286.

Terranova, T. (2000) "Free labor: Producing culture for the digital economy," *Social Text* 18, 2: 33–58.

Toscano, A. (2007) "From pin factories to gold farmers: Editorial introduction to a research stream on cognitive capitalism, immaterial labor, and the general intellect," *Historical Materialism* 15, 1: 3–11.

Vercellone, C. (2007) "From formal subsumption to general intellect: Elements for a Marxist reading of the thesis of cognitive capitalism," *Historical Materialism* 15, 1: 13–36.

Williams, R. (1974) *Television: Technology and Cultural Form*. London: Fontana.

Williams, R. (2005) *Culture and Materialism*. London: Verso.

Contributors

Stuart Allan is a professor of journalism and communication in the School of Journalism, Media and Cultural Studies at Cardiff University, UK. Much of his research focuses on journalism and democracy, with particular interests in civic engagement—not least where citizen reporting of war, conflict and crisis is concerned. His books include *Citizen Witnessing: Revisioning Journalism in Times of Crisis* (Polity Press, 2013) and the edited *Routledge Companion to News and Journalism* (Routledge, 2012 revised edition) and *Citizen Journalism: Global Perspectives, Volume Two* (coedited with Einar Thorsen; Peter Lang, 2014).

James Bennett is the head of the Media Arts Department and a reader in television and digital culture at Royal Holloway, University of London, UK. His work focuses on the relationship amongst television, digital culture and celebrity. He is one of the founding editors of *Celebrity Studies Journal* and his publications include *Television as Digital Media* (Duke University Press, 2011) and *Television Personalities & the Small Screen* (Routledge, 2010).

Aymar Jean Christian is an assistant professor of communication at Northwestern University, USA. He has written about television and digital production in the journals *Continuum, Cinema Journal, Journal of Communication Inquiry, Transformative Works and Cultures* and *First Monday* and in industry publications *indieWIRE* and *Tubefilter*, among others. His manuscript *Open TV: Indie Innovation and the Transformation of Creative Economy* explores how independent producers and entrepreneurs are creating a dynamic television market via Internet distribution. He has curated and consulted on indie TV for the Tribeca Film Festival, International Press Academy, Streamy Awards and IAWTV Awards, among others. He received his PhD from the University of Pennsylvania.

José van Dijck is a professor of comparative media studies at the University of Amsterdam, The Netherlands. Her research areas include media technologies, digital culture, popularization of science and medicine and television and culture. Her latest book, *The Culture of Connectivity: A Critical History of Social Media*, was published by Oxford University Press (2013). http://home.medewerker.uva.nl/j.f.t.m.vandijck

Anthony Y.H. Fung is Director and Professor in the School of Journalism and Communication at the Chinese University of Hong Kong. He is also a Pearl River Chair Professor at Jinan University at Guangzhou, China. His research interests and teaching focus on popular culture and cultural studies, popular music, gender and youth identity, cultural industries and policy, and new media studies.

David Hesmondhalgh is a professor of media, music and culture in the School of Media and Communication at the University of Leeds, UK. He is the author of *Why Music Matters* (Blackwell, 2013), *Creative Labour: Media Work in Three Cultural Industries* (Routledge, 2011, co-written with Sarah Baker), and *The Cultural Industries*, now in its third edition (Sage, 2013). He is also editor or coeditor of seven books and journal special issues, including *The Media and Social Theory* (with Jason Toynbee, Routledge, 2008) and (with Anamik Saha) a special issue of the journal *Popular Communication* on "Race, Ethnicity and Cultural Production" (2013). His PhD thesis (Goldsmiths University of London, 1996, supervised by Georgina Born) was on independent record companies and democratization.

Stephen Jukes is the dean of Bournemouth University's Media School and a former foreign correspondent and editor at the international news agency Reuters. During a series of overseas postings he covered, or oversaw coverage of, stories ranging from the ousting of Margaret Thatcher to the fall of the Berlin Wall, two Gulf wars and September 11. In his final position at Reuters, he was global head of news and executive editor for a series of books focusing on the Middle East conflict. He chairs the Dart Center for Journalism & Trauma in Europe and is a trustee of the Institute for War & Peace Reporting.

Gholam Khiabany teaches in the Department of Media and Communications, Goldsmiths, University of London. He is the author of *Iranian Media: The Paradox of Modernity* (Routledge, 2010) and coauthor of *Blogistan*, with Annabelle Sreberny (I. B. Tauris, 2010). He is an editor of the *Middle East Journal of Culture and Communication*, and is a member of the council of management of the Institute of Race Relations.

Geoff King is a professor of film studies at Brunel University, London, and the author of multiple books, including *American Independent Cinema* (2005), *Indiewood, USA: Where Hollywood Meets Independent Film* (2009),

Indie 2.0: Change and Continuity in Contemporary American Indie Film (2013) and *Quality Hollywood: Markers of Distinction in Contemporary Studio Production* (forthcoming, 2015). He is also coeditor of *American Independent Cinema: Indie, Indiewood and Beyond* (2013) and editor of the Blackwell *Companion to American Indie Film* (forthcoming, 2016).

Daniel Kreiss is an assistant professor in the School of Journalism and Mass Communication at the University of North Carolina at Chapel Hill, USA. Kreiss's research explores the impact of technological change on the public sphere and political practice. In *Taking Our Country Back: The Crafting of Networked Politics from Howard Dean to Barack Obama* (Oxford University Press, 2012), Kreiss presents the history of new media and Democratic Party political campaigning over the past decade. Kreiss is currently working on a second book project, provisionally titled *Networked Ward Politics: Parties, Databases, and Campaigning in the Information Age* (under contract with Oxford University Press and due for publication in 2016). Kreiss is an affiliated fellow of the Information Society Project at Yale Law School and received a PhD in communication from Stanford University. Kreiss's work has appeared in *New Media and Society*, *Qualitative Sociology*, *Critical Studies in Media Communication*, *Research in Social Movements, Conflict, and Change*, *The Journal of Information Technology and Politics* and *The International Journal of Communication*, in addition to other academic journals.

Luzhou Li is a doctoral candidate in communications and media in the Institute of Communications Research at the University of Illinois at Urbana-Champaign, USA. She received her M.Phil. in communication from the Chinese University of Hong Kong and her B.A. in journalism from Fudan University, Shanghai, China. Her research interests broadly include popular culture, television studies, state and political ideologies, digital technologies and political economy of communications. She has published articles in journals such as *Media, Culture & Society*, *Communication, Culture & Critique* and *Chinese Journal of Communication*.

Andrea Medrado is a lecturer in communications at Federal Fluminense University in Brazil. She has also worked as a lecturer for various British universities (Bournemouth, Royal Holloway, London Metropolitan and Westminster). She completed a postdoctoral fellowship at Royal Holloway, received a PhD from the University of Westminster and was a Fulbright Scholar during her master's degree studies at the University of Oregon. Andrea specializes in ethnographic research, having spent more than forty weeks conducting participant observations in a range of television and digital production companies. In addition to her academic background, she has worked as an advertising copywriter in various election campaigns across Brazil over the past ten years.

Leslie M. Meier is a lecturer in media and communication at the University of Leeds, UK. Her work has appeared in the *Journal of Popular Music Studies*, *Popular Music and Society*, the *Canadian Journal of Communication*, and in the edited volume *The Routledge Companion to the Cultural Industries* (edited by Kate Oakley and Justin O'Connor, Routledge, 2015). Her PhD thesis (University of Western Ontario, 2013, supervised by Jonathan Burston and Alison Hearn) examined the intensifying relationship between the music industries and consumer brands in the digital era.

Thomas Poell is an assistant professor of new media and digital culture at the University of Amsterdam, The Netherlands. His research is focused on social media and the transformation of public communication in different parts of the world. He has published, among others, on social media as platforms of alternative journalism (*Journalism*), Twitter as a multilingual space (*Necsus*), Weibo and Chinese online contention (*Chinese Journal of Communication*), social media and activist communication (*Information, Communication & Society*) and social media logic (*Media and Communication*). http://home.medewerker.uva.nl/t.poell/

Hector Postigo is an associate professor of media studies and production at Temple University, USA. He is the author of *The Digital Rights Movement: The Role of Technology in Subverting Digital Copyright* (2012), and the cofounder of the blog *Culture Digitally*. In his work on cultural production, he studies notions of value, participation and "free" labor on the Internet, as well as technologically mediated activism.

James Rodgers is a lecturer in journalism at City University London, UK, where he teaches modules on the history of journalism; reporting conflict; and TV journalism. He spent twenty years as a journalist, most of them covering international events for BBC News. He lived and worked in Moscow for long periods during the 1990s, and again, as BBC correspondent, from 2006 to 2009. He studied modern languages at the University of Oxford, and completed his PhD "Reflective Journalistic Practice in an Environment of Uncertainty and Change" by prior output at London Metropolitan University. He is the author of *Reporting Conflict* (Palgrave, 2012) and *No Road Home: Fighting for Land and Faith in Gaza* (Abramis, 2013).

Niki Strange is a research fellow at the University of Sussex and runs her own digital media consultancy, Strange Digital (www.strangedigital.co.uk), where she provides research, business development and strategy consulting for creative businesses and organizations. Her research focuses on production and broadcasting in the digital age, including *Television as Digital Media* (Duke University Press, 2011) and *Multiplatforming Public Service Broadcasting* (2013).

Xiaoxiao Zhang is an assistant professor in the School of Journalism and Communication at Jinan University, Guangzhou, China. She received her PhD degree from the School of Journalism and Communication at the Chinese University of Hong Kong. Her research interests focus on television studies, cultural studies, global communication and popular culture. She teaches commutation theory, communication methods, international communication, and TV entertainment programs.

Index